SACRAMENTO PUBLIC LIBRARY
3 3029 06194 8584

D0953231

A MORE PERFECT CONSTITUTION

BY THE SAME AUTHOR

Feeding Frenzy: Attack Journalism & American Politics

The Rise of Political Consultants: New Ways of Winning Elections

*Divided States of America:
The Slash and Burn Politics of the 2004 Presidential Election*

Get in the Booth: 2006 Edition

The Sixth Year Itch: The Rise and Fall of the George W. Bush Presidency

A More Perfect Constitution

23 PROPOSALS
TO REVITALIZE OUR CONSTITUTION
AND MAKE AMERICA A FAIRER COUNTRY

Larry J. Sabato

WALKER & COMPANY
New York

Published by Walker Publishing Company, Inc., New York
Distributed to the trade by Holtzbrinck Publishers

An excerpt of chapter 4 appeared as an essay by Larry J. Sabato in the *Virginia Quarterly Review* 82:3 (Summer 2006): 149–61. Some of the section "The Founding of a College" in chapter 4 is adapted from *The Report of the National Symposium on Presidential Selection* (Charlottesville, VA: University of Virginia Center for Governmental Studies, 2001), pp. 39–51.

Figure credits—1.1: http://www.pollingreport.com/CongJob1.htm. 4.1: data from 1968–96, Rhodes Cook, *United States Presidential Primary Elections, 1968–1996: A Handbook of Election Statistics* (Washington, DC: CQ Press, 2000), p. 10; data from 2000 and 2004, Richard E. Berg-Andersson, *The Green Papers,* http://www.thegreenpapers.com; data from 2008 compiled by Larry J. Sabato.

All papers used by Walker & Company are natural, recyclable products made from wood grown in well-managed forests. The manufacturing processes conform to the environmental regulations of the country of origin.

Library of Congress Cataloging-in-Publication Data has been applied for.

ISBN-10: 0-8027-1621-0
ISBN-13: 978-0-8027-1621-7

Visit Walker & Company's Web site at www.walkerbooks.com

First U.S. edition 2007

1 3 5 7 9 10 8 6 4 2

Designed by Sara Stemen
Typeset by Westchester Book Group
Printed in the United States of America by Quebecor World Fairfield

To the memory of Thomas Jefferson,
who wrote to James Madison on January 30, 1787:
"I hold it that a little rebellion now and then is a good thing,
and as necessary in the political world as storms in the physical."

CONTENTS

PREAMBLE

> We the People of the United States, in Order to form a more perfect Union, establish Justice, insure domestic Tranquility, provide for the common defense, promote the general Welfare, and secure the Blessings of Liberty to ourselves and our Posterity, do ordain and establish this Constitution for the United States of America.
>
> —*Preamble to the United States Constitution*

MOST OF US grew up memorizing and venerating these words. Their historic import is obvious. A great nation came into being once they were ratified. Each phrase is clear, the meaning eternal. These great American goals of Union, Justice, Tranquility, Defense, Welfare, and Liberty have also been revised and extended in law and practice by each succeeding generation. Yet this is not true for critical parts of the Constitution itself, whose basic structures and systems have largely remained untouched. We need to apply the ageless values contained in the Preamble to the new demands of a very different country than the one that existed in the founders' world. I have written this book to begin a discussion with you about why and how we must do so, and about the potent possibilities of such action.

Americans care deeply about fairness and equity, for themselves and for others, and we have made impressive strides since the founding of the Republic. Yet that historic progress, which has affected our daily lives for the better, is being eroded and impeded by archaic parts of the original United States Constitution, and the situation is getting worse with each passing year. The Constitution is failing America in some vital ways. The time is now to begin a generational process of moderate, well-considered change to remedy these inequalities. The time is now to form a more perfect Union by creating a more perfect Constitution. Beginning with local, state, and national mock conventions, and Internet-assisted debate, we can start the dialogue of reform.

I want to begin by asking you some important questions.

Do you believe that Congress is often inadequate as a representative body, that your views on the pressing issues of our time—from health care to the environment to tax fairness—find insufficient voice in the legislature while well-connected lobbyists and moneyed groups grab all the goodies they want, year after year? Most Americans do. There are various causes, but one important one is the Constitution, which does little to prevent core abuses such as partisan redistricting and the stacked deck of incumbency—the ills that can lead Congress, whichever party is in control, to ignore your interests while serving special interests. The permanent, dominant elites—the congressmen-for-life, the senators who are never seriously challenged for reelection, the lifetime judges who are often out of touch with changing popular sentiments, and the well-heeled lobbyists who frequently protect the "haves" at the expense of the "have-nots"—have skillfully used constitutional shortfall and silence to build a system that delivers for themselves, not average citizens. They have been aided by the Constitution's dictates for the Senate (two senators per state, regardless of size), a body now so unrepresentative of America's population that a mere 17 percent of the voters install a majority of senators. No one wants a "tyranny of the majority," where 51 percent of the voters run roughshod over the rights of the other 49 percent, but we have now achieved the opposite, equally distasteful extreme, a tyranny of a small minority. Unquestionably, this structural reality impedes progress.

Are you among the millions of Americans concerned about how the Iraq War has been waged? Probably many of you were equally unhappy with the Vietnam War. Some unpopular wars are begun by Republican presidents, and others by Democratic presidents, but the personalities and parties may be less revealing than one major contradiction embedded in the Constitution itself: the confused muddle of war-making powers uneasily divided between president and Congress. The president is the commander in chief, but the Congress declares war, a jumble that has been exploited by a series of executives to expand their supremacy at the expense of legislative accountability (too often with the acquiescence of Congress). Some constitutional sorting-out is long overdue.

Are you pleased with the Electoral College and the way it chooses your presidents, or do you hold your breath every four years on election eve, wondering if the popular majority will actually get the chief executive of its choice?

Even before November, are you pleased that two highly unrepresentative, presumptive small states, Iowa and New Hampshire, have the lion's share of power in picking the party nominees, one of whom will control the White House and likely owe them to a greater degree than the other 98.6 percent of America's population?[1] No doubt you are, if you are from the Hawkeye State or the Granite State, but if you reside in one of the other forty-eight, you probably realize the unfairness of this tilted system—an imbalance that has its roots in the Constitution's total absence of guidance on political parties and presidential selection. How about the permanent campaign—are you content that the battles for high office go on forever, elevate political necessity over sound public policy for a ridiculously large portion of the terms of presidents and members of Congress, and cost a king's ransom to conduct, discouraging those without access to huge sums from running for office? We may well be able to do something about all these deficiencies by means of a constitutional reevaluation of term lengths for top officials, the structure of the campaign season, and the rules for campaign finance. It is time to stop consenting to the consequences of predictable electoral flaws and turn instead to creative reforms that can restore trust and encourage the honest efforts of many legislators.

Do you believe it is just and evenhanded that 14.4 million American citizens are automatically and irrevocably barred from holding the presidency simply because they had the "misfortune" to be born outside the United States—because they are immigrants or their mothers simply were outside U.S. territory at the moment of their birth?[2] This may appear to be a small matter, but it is not. As Americans, we take pride in saying that here, any mother's son or daughter can grow up to be president, but it's not true. Immigrants built the country, and except for the descendants of Native Americans, we are all the offspring of immigrants. The constitutional ban on non-native-born presidents is a potent, disturbing symbol of change too long delayed—one of the best examples of outmoded design that must be abolished in order for the nation to fully realize its promise.

Are you a parent or grandparent who watches the mounting national debt—now on track toward $10 trillion—and realizes that your children and grandchildren will have to pay the piper? The government's fiscal recklessness can be traced to another constitutional flaw of omission, a requirement for a balanced federal budget.

How about the distribution of citizenship's greatest demands? Does it bother you that the burdens of service—especially in the military—fall on a relative handful of citizens, disproportionately poor and lower middle class, while many Americans contribute little beyond taxes to the nation's welfare? Look to the Constitution—at what is in its text and at what is absent from it. Maybe at long last we should add a constitutional Bill of Responsibilities to match the Bill of Rights. We could stress the obligations and duties of citizenship as much as the rights and liberties conferred upon all our people. We could make sure that everyone, regardless of status and wealth, contributes his or her fair share of service and sacrifice. One naturally wonders whether the Iraq War would have been as eagerly prosecuted had the children of congressmen and presidents been among the ones designated to fight it.

It is not that the founders botched the original Constitution, except for the tragic enshrinement of slavery as a fundamental element of American political life.[3] To the contrary, the Constitution's brilliance and originality have inspired millions around the globe to seek a better society where they live. Much of the Constitution's superstructure needs no fundamental fix, including the separation of powers into three branches, the system of checks and balances (with a few exceptions), and the Bill of Rights. The fault is not with these basics, and it is important to stress one fundamental truth from the outset: The framers of the Constitution did not fail us. Our forefathers designed the best possible system that could be achieved at that moment in time. The wiser heads in Philadelphia understood that some of the necessary compromises in the Constitution were flawed, and that some aspects of the new nation—especially the evil institution of slavery—contradicted the very notion of human equality expressed in the text. Yet the Constitution of 1787 reached the pinnacle of equity in the world's history to that time. The framers left it to us, and expected of us, that we would continue at regular intervals to perfect their work. As you will see throughout this book, some of the most beloved framers said so repeatedly in their lives, yet we have overlooked their wisdom. Instead, we have preferred to assume perfection in the original Constitution, sometimes viewing it as a sacred text. Especially in the modern day, the excuse used by those opposed is that that reform is too dangerous, and they have elected to avoid the hard, necessary work of creating a more perfect Constitution.

In fits and starts earlier generations were more inclined to rise to the challenge, mainly through a handful of decisive constitutional amendments passed in the wake of the Civil War, during the Progressive era of the early 1900s, and during the tumult of the 1960s. But over time, these admirable efforts have proven to be inadequate to the demands of twenty-first-century America. The inequities in our system have grown grotesque in some cases, and the vital structures of government have developed rust and creaks. Our response has been the opposite of the founders'. When the Articles of Confederation proved insufficient in the mid-1780s, they were bold and embraced change in the form of the Constitution. We avoid change—even a robust discussion of it—and prefer insufficient tinkering to the substantial reframing that is required. This book is an attempt to alter America's political ossification.

MY PERSONAL JOURNEY

I come to this subject as an admirer of the magnificent achievements of the nation's founders and the Constitution's framers. I live and write among the purplish shadows cast by Thomas Jefferson's Pavilion IV, on the East Lawn at Jefferson's beloved University of Virginia, near his own home at Monticello. For thirty-seven years I have been a student and faculty member at UVA's "academical village," and I consider myself a Jeffersonian in many respects. How could anyone not be inspired by these surroundings, with every step drenched in history?

Like almost all Americans, I also grew up believing in the Constitution—every bit of it. But having chosen American politics as my primary passion in life, over decades of daily thinking about the issues that confronted the nation, I gradually began to see that parts of the system were no longer working very well, that the day-to-day, incremental political process was inadequate to fix the root causes of the system's dysfunction. In this, I was encouraged by the bright young people in my classrooms, who asked good questions, pointed out wrongs that needed righting, and were unwilling to accept "that's how we've always done it" as the final, correct answer. Students wondered, as did I, why the Congress couldn't assert itself more when presidents waged unsuccessful wars. They pointed to the accumulated evidence of corruption in Congress, year after year, and argued it suggested something beyond the imperfectability of man. They were repulsed by the way the nation conducted elections for the White House, the House of Representatives, and the Senate. Students listened respectfully to a sitting Supreme Court justice tell them in class that the courts were designed to be baldly "undemocratic,"[4] but they wondered whether the tenured-for-life judiciary had become too insulated.

Bit by bit, in response to superb student critiques as well as my own—and the public's—growing doubts, I began to construct an alternate universe for parts of the American system. The ideas comprising this universe are at the heart of this book.

By no means are my proposed reforms a repudiation of the founders' principles. The heart of their Constitution (individual liberty, the separation of powers, and federalism) is untouched in these pages. Yet it's worth remembering that the Philadelphia framers were operating in something of a pressure-packed vacuum. They were attempting to build a system that had never existed in this form before, and to do it with dispatch. Much of what they built was pure jerry-rigged experimentation. Moreover, they recognized this and fully expected that future generations of Americans would rework their designs to fit both actual practice and the needs of new times.

Instead, I believe that Washington, Madison, and Jefferson would be the first to insist that the words that ended up in the Constitution are not the final word, and they would encourage us to start thinking about constructive changes in the constitutional framework. (Indeed, as the reader will see, several of the reforms proposed in this book are derived from Madison's initial ideas that were rejected at the original Constitutional Convention. Others have been inspired by Jefferson's warnings about topics omitted from the Constitution.) At the very least, we'll be better off for having thought carefully about the Constitution. More people may even read it! Chief Justice John Roberts recently commented, "Nobody reads [the Constitution]. We talk about it a lot. We have cases about it. But to actually sit down and read it doesn't happen that often—and that is a very rewarding exercise."[5] (To assist the reader as the text is discussed throughout this book, the Constitution and its twenty-seven amendments are printed in full in an appendix at the back.)

Jefferson was especially and justifiably proud of his authorship of the Declaration of Independence, the first of three accomplishments he designated for his tombstone.[6] He also enormously admired the constitutional handiwork of his friend and political ally James Madison, who lived just down the road in Orange County, Virginia, and who became his favored successor as president of the United States. With all due honor to the many other founders who contributed to the fundamental documents of state, it is crystal clear that Jefferson's Declaration and Madison's Constitution essentially created the governmental philosophy and system we recognize and revere today.

Many today resist any substantial change in structure for the United States. They say the inspired founding design must remain unaltered, save for the occasional tweak to accommodate a national desire to strengthen the presidential line of succession (the Twenty-fifth Amendment) or extend the vote to eighteen- to twenty-year-olds (the Twenty-sixth Amendment). After all, the nation has survived and prospered for 220 years under a Constitution that has been amended only twenty-seven times. Even that is an exaggeration, since the first ten amendments (the Bill of Rights) were attached to the ratified Constitution; the Twenty-first Amendment simply repealed the ill-advised Eighteenth (Prohibition); and several other amendments are relatively minor in impact.

These arguments should not be casually dismissed, yet they can be convincingly refuted. Few will deny that a country that ceases to have an ongoing discussion about change will not adapt successfully over time to ever-changing conditions. Also, a society that stops trying to invent the better mousetrap will cede the spark of innovation—a key to political and economic prosperity—to other nations. A people who permit their government to become rigid and inflexible will suffer, sooner or later. A governing class that grows too comfortable with the status quo that often benefits it will be the ruination of the common good. And the foremost exponent of these beliefs was none other than Thomas Jefferson.

In a letter to Madison from his Paris post as ambassador to France, two years after the Constitutional Convention first met, Jefferson wrote these memorable words on September 6, 1789.

> On similar ground it may be proved that no society can make a perpetual constitution, or even a perpetual law. The earth belongs always to the living generation. They may manage it then, and what proceeds from it, as they please, during their usufruct. They are masters too of their own persons, and consequently may govern them as they please. But persons and property make the sum of the objects of government. The constitution and the laws of their predecessors extinguished them, in their natural course, with those whose will gave them being. This could preserve that being till it ceased to be itself, and no longer. *Every constitution, then, and every law, naturally expires at the end of 19 years. If it be enforced longer, it is an act of force and not of right.*[7] (Emphasis added.)

Through these powerful sentiments, which Madison himself—"a Constitution-maker but not a Constitution-idolater"[8]—supported, Jefferson lives and speaks to us today. No doubt he did not literally mean that a Constitution or a statute must vanish automatically every nineteen years (then, the length of a generation). Rather, he challenged posterity to take nothing he and his brethren had created as sacrosanct. Later in life, after retirement to Monticello, he penned a more considered version of his advice in a letter to a friend,

Samuel Kercheval, on July 12, 1816: "I know, also, that laws and institutions must go hand in hand with the progress of the human mind. As that becomes more developed, more enlightened, as new discoveries are made, new truths disclosed, and manners and opinions change with the change of circumstances, institutions must advance also, and keep pace with the times."

At our considerable peril, the American institutions of government have not "advanced and kept pace with the times," and in the nation's interests, we must take a serious, energetic look at reforming them.[9] In each chapter to come, on the presidency, the Congress, the courts, the political process, and a Bill of Responsibilities, I will suggest some ideas that fit today's country. I will also suggest how these changes should be enacted and made effective by arguing the case that we should employ the one major constitutional provision never before used: a national Constitutional Convention.[10]

Only Americans who are well versed in the law know that the framers gave us two separate methods to change the Constitution. By the first method, outlined in Article V, two thirds of both houses of Congress must approve a constitutional amendment, forwarding it to the states for ratification. Only when three quarters of the state legislatures (currently, thirty-eight of the fifty) assent to the amendment does it become part of the Constitution. This process depends first and foremost on the Congress, obviously, and some framers wanted to ensure that states and citizens would have recourse if Congress proved obstinate on, say, a proposed amendment affecting its own organization, behavior, or pay. Therefore, a second method was included in Article V. Two thirds of the state legislatures (currently thirty-four) can petition Congress to call a convention for the purpose of proposing amendments, and Congress is obliged to do so. Three quarters of the states would still have to ratify any amendments resulting from the convention. It seems clear that the second, untried method would suit our purposes better today.

First, Congress has proven to be a dependable graveyard for constitutional reform. More than three thousand amendments have been proposed in Congress over the last forty years, with a grand total of six sent to the states for their consideration—and none at all since 1978.[11] While many of the amendments may have been bad ideas or poorly conceived, surely more than six were worthy of deliberation in the states. By comparison to Congress, state legislatures are probably more responsive to grassroots movements of citizens, being closer to the people and insulated from many of the paralyzing forces that make progress difficult in Washington, D.C. (For example, no state capital can rival, or would want to rival, Washington in the number of influential lobbyists maneuvering in the corridors of power.) Moreover, some of the reforms proposed in this book affect Congress in particular. Few powerful and hidebound institutions like Congress willingly reform themselves. Finally, Congress would likely be loath to propose multiple amendments for simultaneous submission to the states, while a convention is designed to do just that. This is a crucial distinction, since the American system is an interdependent whole, and effective reform must come as a package that concurrently reframes each of the three branches of the federal government. Constitutional change via Congress will almost certainly be incremental at best, while reform via convention has a much better chance of being comprehensive.

Many of our nation's most prominent elites will resist such an approach. These beneficiaries of the current system in government—officeholders, bureaucrats, and supplicants of all sorts—are concentrated in the District of Columbia "Beltway," where the status quo has delivered a comfortable life of privilege and power. Some sincerely and others conveniently believe that a Constitutional Convention would become "runaway" and enact destructive changes from the far right or left. I believe these dangers are greatly exaggerated, and a convention may be precisely the device needed to open up a closed system, to seize back for the people the ability to define their destiny.

Critics may already have sensed a whiff of one of their most scorned movements. Populism has had a decidedly mixed history in American life, having sometimes promoted the evil of racism; yet on other occasions, it has encouraged progressive citizen involvement and good goals, from a clean environment to consumer protectionism.[12] Enlightened populism, by energizing the citizenry, can overcome inertia that has lasted for generations. Today, we require creative adaptation of our system to the needs of a continental country now exceeding 300 million people in an age of advanced technology that was undreamed of by the founders. The Internet provides the welcome mechanism needed for widespread citizen participation, both to stimulate creative discussions about constitutional change and then to help organize mock constitutional conventions throughout the country, which can eventually lead to the real thing. The ideas in this book must first take root among community leaders, opinion shapers, and ordinary citizens in every part of America in a deliberative process.

Whatever the origin of reform, change will not come easily. Some of the reforms proposed in this book will be highly controversial. Others will be merely obvious—almost consensual and commonsensical. No one will agree with all of them, and a vigorous debate is guaranteed. That debate has raged in my own mind over the many years that I have spent formulating these ideas.

A NEW CONVERSATION ABOUT TIMELESS AMERICAN VALUES

My purpose in writing this book is to start a creative conversation—the kind of discussion Jefferson thought would happen naturally every couple of decades. Thoughtful people of every persuasion, political party, and place today can be enlisted for the task of improving the system.

It is not just "a system," of course, but the basis of our daily civic life. You and I are directly affected by whether Congress is well run, and whether our representatives and senators look out more for our interests or moneyed interests. The kind of health care we receive, the quality of the air and water we breathe and drink, the excellence of the education we get, the types of taxes levied on us, and the choice of wars in which we engage are all products, in part, of the rules for government and politics to which we assent. I will demonstrate throughout the book that we all have a vital stake and an essential role to play in the subject of constitutional reform; this is not an airy debate to be left to legislators, journalists, and intellectuals.

As the saying goes, now is the time for all good men and women to come to the aid of their country. It's time for a little rebellion, precisely as Jefferson advocated in this book's dedication to him. At the very least, our minds will be stretched by new ideas, and we may appreciate our unique system all the more.

The founders' values when they wrote the Constitution should remain our guiding stars, refined by the experiences we have acquired as a nation over the centuries. These principles and standards are idealism, pragmatism, fairness, and a focus on the needs of the present and future, rather than overly relying on the past.

*

Idealism. Some statesmen in other established nations probably saw this as naïve, but Jefferson insisted that "every human mind feels pleasure in doing good to another,"[13] and therefore in the United States, "the care of human life and happiness, and not their destruction, is the first and only object of good government."[14] Abraham Lincoln defined more than his hopes for a post–Civil War nation when he urged "malice for none, charity for all." John F. Kennedy will always be remembered for his stirring inaugural address in which he told his fellow Americans, "Ask not what your country can do for you, but what you can do for your country." Ronald Reagan referred often to America as "that shining city on a hill." From its beginnings, America has responded to the clarion call of idealism, and has defined itself, almost apart from other nations, as a land of true democracy and liberty, of equality and opportunity for all, of relatively unfettered pursuit of happiness. Of course, these ideals began as the province of a few, but over time, they have become far more inclusive. And it is our intense belief in their reality that drives us to participate in so many good works—and yes, some questionable adventures—both foreign and domestic, whether it is to respond to the needs of tsunami victims or to volunteer time and money at home for community needs or to "spread democracy" to the world. Constitution-revising without the motivation of idealism would be an empty endeavor, sure to disappoint and, even more, to fail. From our deep well of idealism must come the inspiration for the task at hand.

*

Pragmatism. For all our rhetorical emphasis on ideals, we have more often been directed—and our ideals reasonably tempered—by practicality. Pragmatism is the true genius of the American people. Unlike the citizens of some societies that have had less successful experiments with democracy, we Americans have always been able to separate clearly our eventual goals from our immediate ability to get to them. In other words, except for the small, extremist elements on right and left, we are generally willing to settle for incremental progress toward our goals. Occasionally, as in the crisis of the Great Depression in the 1930s or the civil rights movement of the 1960s, we will insist on massive change and improvement in a short time. In most other situations, from environmental policy to feminism to economic opportunity, Americans are content with gradualism, whatever the hypercharged rhetoric of the day's politics.

There are two consequences of this view that affect constitutional change. First, Americans are overwhelmingly centrists, gathered around the middle of the ideological spectrum, from moderate-conservative to moderate-liberal. Any fair reading of academic survey research or the news media's opinion polling would lead one to conclude that at least two thirds, and arguably three quarters, of the American people are pragmatic, practical centrists—willing to split the difference on most issues and eager for rational compromise, lest this massively diverse society come apart at the seams. We must always remember that the United States, alone among the world's nations, contains sizable communities of almost every other country's ethnic, racial, and religious populations. No longer a "melting pot"—if it ever were that—the United States today is a cauldron of competing tensions, agendas, and interests, and this will become ever more so as the twenty-first century unfolds. Americans understand this, and the desire to "get along" and hold together overrides many human fears. How else can we survive?

The second consequence of pragmatism is the American dedication to the idea of progress. Our hopes for an ever-improving standard of living and greater equality of opportunity, and the belief that by means of education, enlightenment, and new inventions, tomorrow will be better than today, all stem from our embrace of the idea of progress. As a result, one could view politics through the prism of two slogans, the old standby "It's Time for a Change" and another influential but less familiar and articulated one, "Not Left, Not Right, Forward." Change is hard, but throughout our history, the country has voted for it whenever the needs of the people demanded it. Think FDR in 1932, Nixon in 1968, Reagan in 1980, Clinton in 1992, Republicans for Congress in 1994, and Democrats in 2006. In retrospect, not all these changes produced the desired results, but the electorate felt compelled to reject the status quo ante in all six cases. Contrary to the "instant analysis" of the pundits in each of those elections, Americans were not choosing to move left or right. Those determined centrists in the electorate were selecting change over stagnation, adhering to the idea of progress as they sought to move around the current administration's failed policies, its stalemate, its deadlock, in order to push society forward. This kind of pragmatism also prevents most Americans from voting for third-party and independent candidates. Most of these candidates are simply too ideological for our pragmatic electorate; the others are viewed as spoilers who cannot win and may divide the nation.

*

Fairness. The American rebellion against Great Britain in the 1770s began almost wholly because of perceived unfairness in taxation and treatment of colonists as second-class citizens. As a people, we have always embraced fairness as a central goal of government and society, even if our actions belied it. The original Constitution brought aspects of representative democracy to life, but it also sanctioned the evil institution of slavery and complete disenfranchisement of women, among other severe defects. Over time, just as some of the wiser founders had quietly hoped, these defects were corrected. Yet other significant flaws persist, and, in fact, some have grown over time. So vital is fairness to the American sense of identity that it must be a guiding light as we reconsider the Constitution. Unfairness breeds disrespect for the system itself, and as unfairness grows, it threatens citizens' willingness to follow and abide by the decisions rendered under the system.

*

The needs of the present and future, not the past. When reading modern history books about the Constitutional Convention of 1787, one would think that the founders were imagining a system for the ages. To the contrary, they were attempting to design a structure that could get passed at the convention and ratified by the required number of states. If they thought about the future at all, it was the near-term, for they had an armload of critical problems that needed immediate attention: the economy, the currency, trade, food supplies, insurrection, defense against foreign powers with possible designs on the new nation, and much more. The founders would be amazed that we have held on with so few changes to a governmental superstructure built for the end of the eighteenth century.

It is true that we may be no more capable than the founders of peering into the future and perceiving the needs of the nation a century or two from now. But we are in a much better position to evaluate how well the American system has worked, after two-plus centuries' experience, and then to adapt the structure to a vastly changed continental country. The founders were magnificent innovators, yet they had to rely mainly upon speculation and theory as they constructed a government for which there were no compelling precedents. Most inventions are dramatically improved upon in succeeding centuries.

*

These four standards (idealism, pragmatism, fairness, and the needs of the present and future) should be supplemented by age-old principles that undergird our present Constitution—none of which should be altered in any significant way. These include the maintenance of the written basis for the Constitution, in 1787 a significant departure from the British preference for an unwritten constitution that "grew" informally over time in the accumulation of statutes and precedents; the establishment of a republic to the exclusion of a monarchy; the separation of powers into legislative, executive, and judicial branches, with a rich system of checks and balances among the branches; further limitation upon any potential for overweening power by any individual officeholder, branch of government, or level of government through the maintenance of the federal division of governmental authority between the nation and the various states; the preservation of individual liberties (via the Bill of Rights), thereby preventing government from depriving citizens of the fundamental freedoms and rights they enjoy inalienably; and the rule of law itself, the ground upon which constitutionalism stands to prevent the arbitrariness of would-be dictators.[15]

Few seriously question any of these time-tested principles, though unwise proposals that encroach upon the principles are sometimes made. For example, over the decades, well-intentioned reformers have argued that the separation of powers should be abandoned for a parliamentary form of government in the United States.[16] Such a radical change in the American system would have no chance of adoption; nor would the parliamentary system satisfy the deeply held desire in this nation for generously checked power. Anytime a prime minister has a healthy parliamentary majority, he or she has wide-ranging, barely limited authority despite the theoretical existence of "cabinet government." In the modern era, the prime minister is everything and the cabinet is nothing, to judge by recent experience in Great Britain. For instance, the prime minister's power to set the next election date, taken alone, is a stunningly heady authority, completely contrary to the U.S. precedent of preset, unchangeable, fixed election dates. American presidents and Congresses are stuck with the conditions that prevail at the moment of the long-scheduled election, but prime ministers can pick the moment, thus potentially stacking the results. In this and many other ways, a parliamentary makeover is unlikely ever to find public acceptance in America.

Another instance of unwelcome proposed reform is a purely domestic product. Following the practice of twenty-four states that permit voters to "initiate" laws by putting proposals on the ballot, various suggestions for nationwide initiative or referendum (in the latter case, allowing Congress to "refer" possible laws to a vote of the people, as many state legislatures now do) have been put forward.[17] This form of pure democracy is clumsy enough when used to excess in various states, California being the most visible example, but if it were to be used nationally, all sorts of gridlock and mischief would likely result. As Madison wrote in *Federalist No. 10*, "[Pure] democracies have ever been spectacles of turbulence and contention; have ever been found incompatible with personal security or the rights of property; and have in general been as short in their lives as they have been violent in their deaths." And Madison could have scarcely imagined the cost of such ventures. In the Golden State alone, some initiatives can attract campaign spending of tens of millions of dollars. In the whole of the United States, just the network television advertising for important ballot issues would surely cost $100 million or more.

Besides avoiding pitfalls such as parliamentary government or a national initiative process, the new Constitutional Convention would have to steer the ship of state around the shoals of hot-button social and cultural issues. The Civil War had to be fought to resolve the social issue of slavery and add the needed correctives to the Constitution. The stormy modern subjects of abortion, gay rights, the death penalty, gun control, and the like, often threaten to generate their own form of civil war between the Democratic Blue states and the Republican Red states. Opinion is intensely divided on all of them, and they are best fought out on the political landscape, in the legislatures and election campaigns, until such time (if ever) that there is a national near-consensus on them. For now, these issues almost always generate more heat than light, and their introduction into the new Constitutional Convention would be poison, bitterly dividing delegates, soaking up disproportionate debate time, and making compromise on other critical topics, such as the systemic proposals of this book, much more difficult to achieve. Any attempt to place constitutional provisions on either side of these cultural grenades would probably explode the process. Thus, for pragmatic reasons, these subjects simply must be excluded, and explicitly, in any call to convention for the purpose of revising the U.S. Constitution.

So also must any attempt to alter the current Bill of Rights, whether to "strengthen" or "weaken" elements of it. The addition or deletion of a single phrase in the first ten amendments could be deadly to ratification. Just as with the social issues, the intense contemporary disputes about First Amendment matters (such as the perceived excesses of the press or the church-state relationship) or the rights of crime victims versus the rights of the accused arising from the Fifth and Sixth amendments would undermine the overriding goal of the next constitutional revision: to fix the decrepit machinery of American government. In these categories of controversy, the practical must dominate the ideological. The core imperative to reform the structure of U.S. government and politics is more than enough on the plate for this new Constitutional Convention.

Before we have any chance of securing a twenty-first-century Constitutional Convention, of course, we must demonstrate both the need for such a conclave and what might be gained despite the risks such a gathering would entail. After all, what would be the point of a massive countrywide mobilization necessary to bring about a convention if the effort were more or less automatically doomed to defeat?

Cynicism has been in vogue since the horrors of the 1960s, a natural byproduct of multiple assassinations, the Vietnam debacle, and the Watergate scandal that brought down President Nixon. However, competing with this cynical impulse is another American value I have stressed, idealism and hope for a better future. This side of the American people prefers the ennobling, energizing words of an early constitutionalist, George Mason, one of the fathers of the Bill of Rights to the U.S. Constitution. Mason had earlier expressed these powerful sentiments in the constitution of his native Virginia. In Article One of the Old Dominion's original constitution—maintained word-for-word through many constitutional revisions from 1776 to the present day—Mason wrote "that all power is vested in, and consequently derived from, the people, that magistrates [elected officials] are their trustees and servants, and at all times amenable to them."[18] This section reminds us that if the U.S. Constitution is ever to be updated, the people have the power and must show the initiative to do it. Mason continued:

> That government is, or ought to be, instituted for the common benefit, protection, and security of the people, nation, or community; of all the various modes and forms of government, that is best which is capable of producing the greatest degree of happiness and safety . . . ; and, whenever any government shall be found inadequate or contrary to these purposes, a majority of the community hath an indubitable, inalienable, and indefeasible right to reform, alter, or abolish it, in such manner as shall be judged most conducive to the public weal.[19]

This eye-popping paragraph, along with the Declaration of Independence, establishes the right of revolution, just as the colonists were exercising that right. It also ascertains the right to reform and alter the government, as required by the times. While the people have been hesitant to avail themselves of this opportunity at the national level, the American states have set the pace for the country. Of the thirteen original states, all but Massachusetts have conducted extensive constitutional revisions of their fundamental documents. Virginia has had six such rewritings, for instance, and the total number of "new constitutions" for the first thirteen states is forty. Expanding this examination to all fifty states, many of which were not admitted to the Union until the mid-nineteenth century right up to 1959, we find that a total of ninety-two very thorough, top-to-bottom constitutional revisions have been conducted.[20] Unquestionably, national constitutional revision is more far-reaching and challenging than the state variety. Nonetheless, if most of the fifty states have found it necessary to engineer major overhauls of their basic documents of state on ninety-two occasions, can it really be true that all the inadequacies discovered in the U.S. Constitution over two centuries have been corrected by a handful of amendments, some of them trifling?

A wide-ranging revision of the Constitution is a radical idea that will be tricky to achieve, and most sensible citizens are right to be skeptical at the outset. As that great America-watcher Alexis de Tocqueville observed in the 1830s: "I think it is an arduous undertaking to excite the enthusiasm of a democratic nation for any theory which does not have a visible, direct, and immediate bearing on the occupations of their daily lives. Such a people does not easily give up its ancient beliefs. For it is enthusiasm which makes men's minds leap off the beaten track and brings about great intellectual, as well as political, revolutions."[21]

I fully understand that I need to persuade you that this is the right course, and that it is worth your participation even if the results are a generation or more away. The suggested constitutional revisions that follow strive to be bold, but also realistic, mixing idealism and pragmatism. It will ultimately be up to you and all the other citizens of the United States to decide whether these ideas deserve to become reality.

If you like these proposals, or other constitutional reforms not discussed in this book, you can make them happen. Many people, probably a solid majority, are wrongly convinced they can have no effect on the life of the nation, and that their views don't matter and their preferences are insignificant. The reverse is closer to the truth. We Americans are privileged to live in one of the freest and most responsive countries on earth. Individual initiative is arguably more prized in the United States than anywhere else. There are few senators or representatives or state legislators who cannot be moved by a roused, determined group of high-minded voters possessing a good cause. To one degree or another, this has always been the case in the American Republic, but the new methods of communication and organization centering on the Internet make it far easier than ever to provoke thought, spark debate, and mobilize fellow citizens.

The cynics are wrong: Shadowy, überpowerful conspiratorial forces do not run this country. We do. If we choose to act, change will be the result. Just in recent decades, the civil rights pioneers, the grassroots peace activists during Vietnam, consumer advocates, and the tax reduction supporters at all levels have proven the point. And these Americans did not have the dominant tool of communication and organization available to us today, the Internet. More than at any other time in our history, progress can be generated from the bottom up, not just the top down. We the people can use the World Wide Web to move the discussion about constitutional revision forward, and to bring together like-minded citizens to participate in a movement to reform our own government and make it work better for our families, communities, and country.

CHAPTER ONE

✶

CREATING A CAPITAL CONGRESS

IT'S NOT HARD to discern how most Americans look at Congress. Whether in public opinion polls or person-in-the-street interviews, citizens regard the national legislators the way they would disliked relatives: They know they have to live with them, but they hope to have as little contact as possible. Can Congress blame us for feeling this way? Year after year, the Congress seems hopelessly deadlocked on issues of immediate concern to the country. Global warming? It needs more evidence, maybe deep water in the streets of coastal cities. How about reform of our complicated, special interest–driven tax system that remains a national disgrace—arguably the worst in the industrialized world? This is never a priority. Health care for the millions of uninsured Americans? It always appears to be on the agenda for the next decade or the one after that. A balanced budget so that the nation could begin whittling down trillions of dollars of debt before it completely consumes our ability to meet the growing needs of an expanding population? But that would cost special interests their pet programs, corporate subsidies, and tax breaks—and they fund the congressional members' campaigns. It would also mean disappointing the legions of well-paid lobbyists who have developed close relationships with long-serving members of Congress. The lobbyists deliver lots of campaign cash, and whatever the ethics laws of the moment, they find ways to richly reward their legislative friends.

Instead of seeing positive action, Americans witness headline after headline of congressional corruption. Some is old-style sleaze—bribery, influence-peddling, and personal scandals reflecting ancient vices—that reeks of a sense of entitlement. Other congressional fraud reflects modern forms of dishonesty. The congressmen, in cahoots with their allies in the state legislatures, have cooked the redistricting books, using sophisticated computer programs to draw the district boundaries in such a way that they can almost never lose reelection. The campaign finance laws are deliberately tilted heavily in the incumbents' direction, too.

It's wrong and cynical to dismiss all of this as the inevitable consequence of the corrupting power of, well, power. What we have not focused on enough is the effect that the rules and structures of the American constitutional system have in encouraging the corruption. Some fraud is likely under any regime, and as I will explain, any legislature will probably be out of public favor most of the time. But the degree and depth of the corrupt practices can be reduced over time with sensible reforms. To the degree that Congress's unpopularity is due to unfairness and ineffectiveness, the proposals herein can make a difference.

In some ways, we can pity the poor Congress. It is not popular now, and it has never been popular save for brief periods during national crises. Right from the very beginning, Americans instinctively distrusted the legislative branch and made fun of it. One of the earliest ditties summed up the people's view well.

These hardy knaves and stupid fools,
Some apish and pragmatic mules,
Some servile acquiescing tools,
These, these compose the Congress!

When Jove resolved to send a curse,
And all the woes of life rehearse,
Not plague, not famine, but much worse—
He cursed us with a Congress.

These verses were directed against the Continental Congress of 1776![1] But nothing much has changed, save the colloquialisms, and modern Americans could easily be at home reciting similar lines.

The reasons for the public's semipermanent disaffection with Congress are all too clear. No committee of 535 can act with dispatch or appear especially organized; even with strong legislative leadership, Congress is composed of independently elected members, each of whom has a sizable ego. The division of the legislature into two separate bodies, House and Senate, creates more disunity and contributes to the chaotic image Congress frequently projects. The legislative branch is also elected from districts and states, not the nation as a whole, so its concerns often seem parochial, with

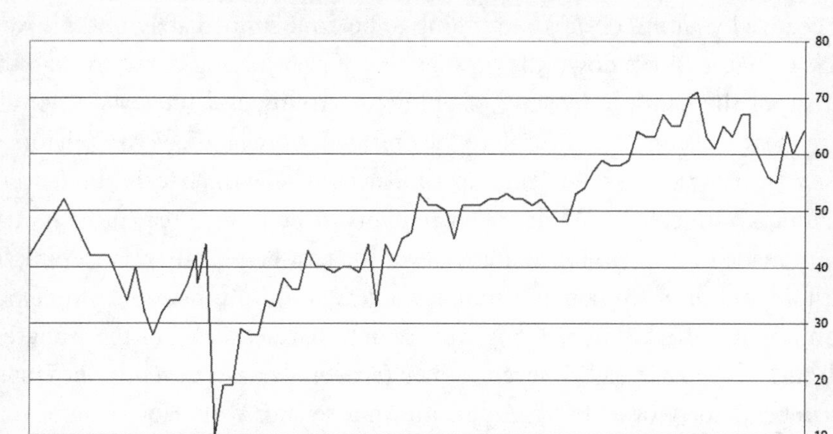

FIGURE 1.1. CONGRESSIONAL DISAPPROVAL RATINGS (USA TODAY/GALLUP POLL)

the national interest lost in the welter of special interests clamoring to be heard. Moreover, with so many members of Congress, at least a couple dozen, at any given time, are bound to be involved in legal or ethical scrapes. Bad news being news, these delinquent legislators soak up much of the media coverage devoted to Congress, giving the public a distorted view of the branch's composition. And let's not forget that the best metaphor for any legislature is the sausage factory. People may like to eat the savory product, but only if they haven't watched it being made. Reporters don't cover sausage factories, but they follow every jot and tittle of the legislative process—and it's rarely a pretty sight. Add all these factors together, and it is easy to understand why Americans hate the Congress. The only brief exceptions are at times of national crisis, such as Watergate or 9/11, when the instinct to "rally 'round the flag" includes support for virtually all U.S. governing institutions, or moments of special optimism, such as the opening days of a new presidency or victory in war.

While acknowledging the justification for much of the criticism, we also ought to note that Congress works much as the founders intended. The legislative branch was and is designed to be the "inefficient" element of the federal government, slowing the "efficient" branch, the presidency. The chief executive by nature desires everything to be done immediately, and his way. The Congress slows down the president's policies, forcing them through the prism of the nation's diversity of opinions, groups, and interests. After all, Congress comes much closer than the president or the judiciary to mirroring the country's richness of talent—by gender, race, religion, background, occupation, and ideology. While much remains to be done, great progress has been made in diversifying Congress over the past half century. For example, just a handful of women and minorities served in both houses in the 1960s (an average of fifteen per Congress through that decade), but the Congress elected in 2006 had eighty-seven women (sixteen senators, seventy-one House members), forty-one African Americans (one senator, forty House members), six Asian Americans and Pacific Islanders (two senators, four House members), and one House member each for American Indians and Asian Indians.[2] The cacophony of congressional voices is not harmonious and will never be smoothly orchestrated by anyone, yet how could it be otherwise in a nation that is so exceptionally decentralized and so decidedly diverse?

No one should ever tamper with these aspects of legislative representation, except to strengthen them. Toward this end, I propose to build upon the founders' congressional model in several ways. First, we need a larger, more representative U.S. Senate that better fits the massively increased population of twenty-first-century America, with a new category of senator whose job is to advocate for the national interest *first*, rather than the needs of individual states. Second, the House needs reforming, because extreme partisan redistricting has virtually drained the lifeblood of vigorous competition in elections. It is time for a new era of real choice in House campaigns, so that the House can resume its position as the federal body closest to the current thinking of the American people. Further, the founders' idea of expanding the House along with population growth should be renewed, so that each member of Congress can represent a smaller constituency and have personal ties to more citizens. Finally, the election schedules and term lengths for both the U.S. House of Representatives and the Senate need to be realigned, so that there is a better chance the diversity of Congress can be harnessed for constructive cooperation with the executive—in the interests of sound public policy to serve the people. (This last topic is explored in chapter 2.) Taken as a whole, this reform agenda can reinvigorate not just the Congress but American government and politics overall.

In addition, a couple of additional constitutional amendments can make Congress more responsible in fiscal matters (via a balanced budget mandate) and more secure in a dangerous era. The latter is an unnerving but necessary addition to the new Constitution: a Continuity of Government provision in case Congress should be the victim of a terrorist attack or other calamity. While the current Constitution includes a detailed plan for presidential succession, there is no such plan for the legislative branch. There ought to be; the frightening age in which we live demands it.

REFORMING THE SENATE

Toward a More Representative Senate

In a special Saturday session on February 17, 2007, the U.S. Senate took up a Democratic-sponsored resolution disapproving of President George W. Bush's so-called troop surge in Iraq—his controversial and unpopular decision to send 21,500 more U.S. troops to that war-torn country. The 2006 election was decided in the Democrats' favor essentially because of this issue, and the Democrats in the U.S. House of Representatives had earlier been able to secure a large (246 to 182) majority for the same resolution. At the end of the day, the Senate voted 56 to 34 to end debate and take up the resolution—the fifty-six senators comprising the majority that would have supported the resolution itself. But the Senate is not run simply by means of majority. This measure required 60 votes under Senate rules, and so the Senate took no position at all on the biggest issue on the national agenda. And the fifty-six senators represented 62 percent of the country's population—a large majority of the American people.[3] Keep this day, and this vote, in mind as we think through the structure of the Senate.

Two principles embraced by the founders about the Senate are worth preserving. Fundamentally, the Senate represents semi-sovereign states, and despite all the changes wrought by time and technology over the centuries, most Americans still identify with and have great devotion to their individual state. Yes, we are all Americans, but we are also New Yorkers, Floridians, Iowans, Utahns, Oregonians, and all the rest. We're proud of our state, learn about its heritage throughout life, and even if we live in many states over the course of our lifetimes, we adopt each one as part of us—and hope they adopt us. Woe to the researcher or journalist who believes that all states are basically the same, or that a homogenization of state cultures has occurred as the world has shrunk. True enough, Holiday Inns and McDonald's restaurants are everywhere, but the cultures of Louisiana and Minnesota, or Kentucky and New Mexico, could not be more divergent. Cartographers often decry the crazy-quilt pattern of state boundaries and logically assert that they could draw the lines far more rationally if given the chance. They won't have the opportunity, because the land is spoken for in Americans' hearts and heads; change is out of the question. North and South Dakota, both lightly populated and essentially rural, could easily be combined into one mega–prairie state—but try telling that to the residents of those states. The Dakotas are less alike than outlanders think, and the people in each state, while outwardly pleasant to one another, regard each other a bit reservedly. The same is true with the Carolinas and the Virginias, the Pacific Coast states, and the Southwest states that may have similar topography on a map. The United States is still a federation of semi-independent entities, and the public is reasonably happy with the status quo.

The second principle was equally dear to the founders. They insisted that the structure of the Senate should protect minority rights from the "tyranny of the majority," or "mob-ocracy." The United States was to be a republic, a representative democracy, not a pure democracy run by 50 percent plus one of its residents. Among the institutions protecting the Republic is the Senate, originally appointed by the state legislatures rather than elected by the populace. The House of Representatives would be responsive to ever-shifting popular majorities, yet nothing would become law without the acquiescence of the Senate, meaning at least a majority of those representing the various states had to agree. (In some cases, such as treaties with foreign governments, an extraordinary majority of two thirds of the senators was required to concur.) Even after the passage of the Seventeenth Amendment to the Constitution in 1913, providing for popular election of senators, the Senate remained a bulwark against majority tyranny by virtue of the six-year term, the equal representation of states rather than proportional representation by population, and the upper house's internal rules (such as the filibuster) that gave extraordinary influence to a small minority of senators.

All of this is salutary to a degree. But a powerful case can be made that today's Senate has taken the founders' desires to an extreme. In the early years of the Republic, the population ratio of the most populated state, Virginia, and the least populated state, Delaware, was 12 to 1. In 2004 that ratio was an incredible 70 to 1 between California and tiny Wyoming.[4] Therefore, the current Senate is absurdly skewed in the direction of the small states. Theoretically, if the twenty-six smallest states held together on all votes, they would control the U.S. Senate, with a total of just under 17 percent of the country's population![5]

And from time to time, something similar does indeed happen in a contemporary Senate vote, especially when government spending and benefits (such as transportation projects, homeland security monies, or agricultural price supports) are at stake. Some researchers have even convincingly claimed that the structure of the Senate has resulted in a fairly consistent, and dramatic, redistribution of wealth from the large states to the small states.[6] Some redistribution is inevitable in order to meet the states' varying needs, but it is impossible to justify the massive inequity of the actual redeployment of billions of dollars away from some states with the greatest needs toward many lightly populated states.

The situation is actually worse than I am depicting here. On most crucial policy votes, such as the Iraq resolution example that opened this section, the arcane rules of the Senate permit 41 of the 100 senators to prevent a final vote on the floor by means of a filibuster—that is, continuous debate. Put another way, even if 59 of the 100 senators favor a particular bill, it will fail if the filibuster is employed, since 60 votes are needed to invoke *cloture*—the shutting off of the filibuster to permit a floor vote to proceed. Therefore, just 21 states can provide the 41 senators necessary to block action. The 21 most lightly populated states comprise a mere 11.2 percent of the nation's population as the Senate is currently constituted.[7]

The key to keep in mind is that under the Constitution's bicameral system for the legislature, nothing passes without Senate assent. Therefore, the Congress has a one-house veto on legislation, and to control the Senate is to control the legislative outcome, and indeed much of what the federal government actually does. The small-state stranglehold on the Senate is not merely a bump in the road; it is a massive roadblock to fairness that can and often does stop all progressive traffic. James Madison foresaw this dilemma, and he vigorously argued, during the Constitutional Convention, for proportional representation by population in the Senate, not just the House.[8] When his proposal was defeated by a coalition of the small states, the large states seriously considered withdrawing from the conclave. In desperation, Madison gave in, but he openly admitted he despised the compromise. Madison's fears have been validated as the gap between small and large states has grown to the point that California and Texas, with fifty-one times the population of Vermont and Wyoming, have the same representation.[9] It is the height of absurdity for our gargantuan states to have the same representation as the lightly populated ones.

So how can the animating principles of the Senate be preserved while making the institution fairer to all the people, whether they live in big, medium, or small states? The Senate needs an adjustment that is both simple and potentially acceptable to most small states—in part, because some of them are growing by leaps and bounds, and they will one day benefit from the change. We should give the ten largest states two more Senate seats each, with the next fifteen largest states gaining one additional seat. The twenty-five states with the smallest populations would not forfeit any representation and keep their current two Senate seats. As with seats in the House of Representatives, the Senate seats would be reapportioned among the states, according to this formula, every ten years after the census assesses population changes. From decade to decade, for example, a state might move into the list of the ten largest states and thus be awarded an extra senator; the state dropped from that exclusive list would lose a senator.

The new Senate, then, would consist of 135 members. This change has an additional advantage. With the population of the United States having expanded dramatically (by almost two thirds, in fact) since the current 100-member Senate was established in 1960,[10] the 35 additional senators can assist in meeting the needs of millions of new Americans in their large states. And the cost to the Treasury is relatively little.[11] Some might argue that this novel scheme creates three tiers of states—first-, second-, and third-class states, in a sense. Yet this has not turned out to be the case in the U.S. House of Representatives, which allots seats strictly on the basis of population, because even single-seat states in the House can end up with great power. Seniority can make a sole House member someone to be reckoned with. Alaska's Don Young, in his eighteenth term as of 2007, is a superb example. As past chairman of the House Transportation and Infrastructure Committee, he steered hundreds of millions of dollars in highway spending to the Frontier State (whether truly needed or not).[12] Or a representative can be elected to a key leadership position in his or her party's House caucus. Wyoming's Dick Cheney served as Republican House whip before being selected as defense secretary in President George H. W. Bush's cabinet in 1989. Other small states have the good sense to elect experienced, widely respected individuals to their sole House seat. Delaware's Michael Castle is a former governor of the First State, and his moderate sensibilities give him clout on both sides of the party aisle. The cases cited here are not atypical, and Alaska, Delaware, and Wyoming have a total of just three seats in the 435-seat House. The smaller states in the new Senate would, individually and collectively, retain plenty of clout. The difference is that the distorted, decidedly unfair world where the Lilliputians rule the giants would be dissolved.

Overall, the new Senate arrangement would be a far more equitable one, preventing a small minority from frustrating the will of a large majority of the population. For example, in the Iraq War "surge" resolution cited at the beginning of this section, it is highly probable that a sufficient number of senators would have voted in the affirmative for it to pass in a large, reformed Senate.[13] Furthermore, the appropriations of monies for transportation, education, and homeland security could also be expected to flow more lavishly to the larger states that have gained representation in the Senate; that is how politics works, after all. At the same time, because the more lightly populated states would still have two senators each, they would remain a larger proportion of the Senate than the House. This fact permits smaller states to continue to have considerably greater influence in the Senate than they would in the House.[14] Also importantly, there is an added, hidden bonus in this new arrangement. Should the country choose to keep the Electoral College (to be discussed in chapter 4), the new Senate would give the Electoral College less of a tilt to the least populous states. Since every senator produces one electoral vote under the Constitution, thirty-five new electoral votes would be added, all in the more heavily populated states. There would be less of a chance for a candidate to win the Electoral College while losing the popular vote. On the four occasions when presidents have been elected under such circumstances, they found their terms circumscribed to some degree by the popular-vote tabulation. Only George W. Bush, of the four, managed to get reelected, and this was due in part to the lingering effects of the extraordinary events of September 11, 2001.

Finally, the deplorable situation concerning the District of Columbia could more easily be addressed under the proposed Senate regime. This Republic was founded on the principle of "no taxation without representation," yet District residents, numbering about 550,000—more than the population of Wyoming—currently have no representation in the U.S. Senate (and only a nonvoting delegate in the U.S. House).[15] While the residents have no voting representation in the federal legislature, Congress unilaterally sets many of the city's policies and manages its affairs, which is certainly not the ideal situation in a democracy.[16] The District is clearly not a state, and the arguments about whether it should be made one are now decades old.[17] At the moment, there is little chance D.C. will be given voting representation in the Senate, in part because the population of the District, which is more than 80 percent

Democratic, would almost automatically elect two Democratic senators.[18] A constitutional amendment would be required, and few Republican members of Congress would vote to reduce their chances of controlling the Senate; nor would many states agree to water down their clout in the Senate with the addition of two more senators; nor would GOP-led states ratify any amendment that adds two Democrats. This almost irreconcilable deadlock might be broken in a new Constitutional Convention that focused on the disgraceful refusal to extend the full rights of democracy to the District—a prominent circumstance involving the capital city of the United States that makes our claims to be the world's leading democracy ring hollow abroad. Perhaps this proposal would also have a better chance of passage in a 135-member Senate, rather than in the current 100-member one. The addition of one or two senators to join 135 others would not be nearly as likely to upset the party applecart in the Senate as the addition of two senators in a 100-member body. Notice that we said *one or two* senators; the D.C. city council and electorate (assuming the matter is put to a District-wide referendum, as is probable) might be willing to accept a compromise of one senator in order to finally achieve some voting representation. Whether in a Constitutional Convention or the new Senate itself, this is a possible way out of a dilemma that is deeply troubling to many people: the unfair lack of voting representation for over a half-million Americans who must pay taxes, often serve in the armed forces, and sometimes die for their country. That the District's population is heavily minority (about 60 percent African American and 10 percent other minorities)[19] adds to the discomfort in the existing disenfranchisement.

Forging the National Interest in the New Senate

With a larger Senate, a further addition to its membership becomes more possible: Former presidents and vice presidents, with their individual consent, should be given Senate seats.[20] These new members of the upper house of Congress would be given the title of *national senator*.

The arguments for such a change are powerful. As the only officials elected by the nation as a whole, former presidents and vice presidents have a perspective sorely lacking in a legislative body that is state-based. We the taxpayers have a major investment in these individuals, and while they are all active after their service at the White House, some are rarely heard from in critical national debates and others pursue mainly their library-based endeavors or private concerns. From time to time, they are called upon to head up a commission or to endorse candidates or White House policies, but these events are incidental and intermittent. The country would benefit enormously from their individual and collective counsel as senators. One can easily imagine the former executives leading major debates on the floor of the Senate, shaping public opinion, and nudging their fellow senators away from parochial concerns and toward some conception of the national interest on the major issues of the time. This would be especially true in the arena of war and peace, treaties, and foreign relations, where their rich base of knowledge and contacts would exceed even that of the chairman of the Foreign Relations Committee. Former presidents and vice presidents are in a unique position to call for national sacrifice in domestic matters as well. The policy areas of Social Security, Medicare, energy independence, and the national debt come immediately to mind—topics that cry out for bipartisan reform.

Former elected officials are more likely to break ranks with their party when the nation's needs demand it. Yes, a one-term president might, like Grover Cleveland, have another White House candidacy in mind, and certainly former vice presidents might still harbor presidential ambitions. Even two-term former presidents have political interests; Bill Clinton's obvious concern for his senator-spouse is one example. Still, the reward system in the news media and the public is tilted toward statesmen, not politicians. Former presidents and vice presidents would understand this and act accordingly. It would be especially influential when the former officeholders agreed across party lines—and this would happen more often than cynics think. Once out of office, Presidents Gerald Ford (R) and Jimmy Carter (D) worked together on many issues for decades. President George H. W. Bush (R) and Bill Clinton (D) have taken to doing the same thing. Certainly, each regular senator would continue to weigh his or her constituents' concerns in deciding a stand on any issue. However, the ex-presidents and vice presidents could potentially shape public opinion, making it a bit easier for senators to cast an unpopular vote in the national interest.

Some might prefer that these new national senators be purely honorific, that is, they should have only the power to speak and roam the Senate floor and cloakrooms; however, an actual floor vote would be critical to their influence. In close votes, the national senators, no longer attached to their respective states, would make the difference. These special Senate seats would not be subject to election. The occupants of the vice presidency, of course, would already have had experience presiding over the Senate, so these senior statesmen would have a special affinity for their new position. While the seats would be of indefinite term, potentially lifelong, the former executives could resign their seats for any reason, such as ill health or the desire to take a public- or private-sector job outside the Senate. Recognizing that ex-presidents maintain a grueling pace and that even former vice presidents stay quite busy, the national senators would not be expected to participate in committee hearings, for the most part, or to cast votes on many procedural and minor substantive issues before the Senate. Rather, these special senators would probably choose to husband their influence for those major occasions when their opinions could make a sizable difference.

What of the case of a corrupt vice president such as Spiro Agnew, who served from 1969 to 1973 before resigning in a plea bargain on tax evasion to avoid jail time? Just as Agnew was forced to leave the vice presidency to pay for his crime, he also could have been forced to resign from the Senate seat simultaneously. Richard Nixon and Bill Clinton also are special cases, since both presidents were subject to impeachment. Nixon resigned in August 1974 before the House could vote on the articles of impeachment, but he certainly would have been impeached and convicted by the Senate. Clinton was impeached by the House in late 1998, but he won acquittal in the Senate in early 1999. An impeached *and convicted* president (or vice president) should certainly be deprived of the privilege of sitting in the Senate, and the articles of impeachment could legally specify that prohibition. But neither Nixon nor Clinton was fully condemned by the constitutional process. I would argue that, for all his felonious faults and exceptional errors as president, Nixon's rich knowledge of foreign affairs and his influence abroad would have proven very useful to the Senate over time. Similarly, despite his detestable lies and multitudinous peccadilloes, Clinton's extensive experience in foreign and domestic affairs could prove equally useful in the Senate today. When we look at the current membership of the Senate, it is manifestly obvious that sainthood is not a criterion for service there.

Part of my argument for national senators is dollars and sense. The taxpayers already richly reward former presidents; each is paid an annual pension of at least $180,000 and, in the case of former president Clinton, our most recent presidential retiree, given staff and travel allowances totaling more than $900,000. While no one denies that presidents have served the nation in the most demanding of jobs, and therefore deserve financial security and rewards, I would also contend that Americans should get more for their money than they currently do.[21] In the Senate, former presidents and vice presidents would still be able to write the million-dollar books and memoirs for which they have become known, but they ought to be limited in their acceptance of speaking fees and other goodies from private interests, just as are other senators.[22] That might be a loss to the ex-executives, but surely it would not be a debit for the country, and none of the former presidents and their families would starve. The new arrangement might save the ex-presidents from themselves. From time to time, former presidents have embarrassed themselves by accepting large sums and gifts from foreign and domestic entities. This practice would be prohibited under the proposed regime.[23]

These good arguments aside, every postpresidency is different. Each ex-president and ex–vice president should be free to accept or decline the position of national senator. No doubt, the party leaders on both sides of the aisle would encourage them to accept, in order to bolster the party's numbers and influence in the Senate. In order to maximize the usefulness of their experience with current world leaders, they should be compelled to decide whether to take up the post within four years of leaving office. Those four years could permit some decompression after an intense time in high office. (If the person so chose, however, he or she could take up the Senate seat immediately, or anytime within the four-year maximum period.) Once the position is accepted, the former president or vice president would be a national senator for life, or until his or her resignation. Once having resigned, he or she could not take up the post again, though theoretically, the former officeholder could decide to seek a regular Senate seat in his or her state of residence. More often, I suspect, the former presidents and vice presidents would decide to call it a day at some reasonable retirement age in their seventies. The Senate's hectic lifestyle is not likely to encourage many in their eighties and nineties to hang on, though there is the possibility of an occasional presidential Strom Thurmond (R-SC) or Robert Byrd (D-WV), two senators who chose to run again in their late eighties, and in Thurmond's case, nineties.[24]

In sum, then, the addition of all former presidents and vice presidents to the U.S. Senate would be a potentially healthful tonic for a legislative body that sometimes appears bogged down in selfish parochialism with little devotion to the national interest. Not many seats would be added to the new 135-member Senate. At the present time (2007), a total of only six (Jimmy Carter, Walter Mondale, George H. W. Bush, Dan Quayle, Bill Clinton, and Al Gore) could be seated—four Democrats and two Republicans. As of early 2009, presumably, the potential partisan total would shift to an even split, four Republicans and four Democrats, with the addition of George W. Bush and Dick Cheney. It is doubtful that there would be many time periods with more than ten national senators, and normally they would come from both parties, given the American tendency to alternate power between Democrats and Republicans. Nor would these national senators affect the calculations for the Electoral College; only state-specific senators would count in the college's allocation of votes for the presidential contest.

The American people have an enormous investment in each of the persons they have placed in our highest executive offices. The citizenry has paid literally hundreds of millions of dollars to train and support them over the decades, in and out of office. Not incidentally, by gift of the electorate, the executives have been granted unparalleled opportunities and, to a man, have become very wealthy—not just materially[25] but as people guaranteed to be remembered by history. It is time the country saw to it that these unique investments pay off long after the end of the executives' terms of office. The creation of national senators would achieve the goal by helping both the Senate and the United States as a whole, while enabling former presidents and vice presidents to continue formal, senior service to America.

REFORMING THE HOUSE

A More Competitively Elected House

As the hotly contested 2006 midterm elections for Congress unfolded, Americans across the nation looked forward to going to their polling places to register their views on Iraq, the economy, and other pressing matters. Imagine the disappointment, perhaps even disgust, that millions of voters felt when they arrived at the polls on election day. In fifty-five House districts across the country, there was no realistic choice. The opposition party had not even bothered to nominate a candidate and give people a choice. In a whopping 263 other districts, the competition was minimal, with an unknown, underfunded challenger listed on the ballot in opposition to the incumbent, who received more than 60 percent of the vote in the end.[26] To some degree, this was the fault of the political parties. Yet the real culprit—the true cause of the parties' inability to recruit and fund good challengers to the incumbent members of Congress—was the corrupt system of redistricting, the redrawing of district boundaries that occurs after each decennial census. This political surgery, which concentrates partisans from just one party in a district in order to guarantee the election of the party's nominee, has nearly snuffed out the competition in dozens and dozens of districts across the nation.

The founders had great affection for the U.S. House of Representatives and wanted it to be a reliable barometer of popular sentiment, produced by open and competitive elections, with all its members elected every two years. (The number of members was far smaller in their day, but in our time the House has 435 voting members.) How sad the founders would be to see the ultra-stable, uncompetitive House of professional politicians that exists today. The House of Representatives has become a House of Lords, with fewer than sixty truly competitive contests being waged out of 435 in most election years. Note that this enormous proportion of uncompetitive seats is an average that includes "open contests," without an incumbent, where the first victory is normally less impressive than subsequent reelections. Moreover, the vast majority of congressmen win in landslides (considered to be a victory margin of 10 percent or greater). In 2004 just twenty-two races for U.S. representative in the country were decided by fewer than ten percentage points, and in 2006—supposedly a highly competitive year—only sixty-one contests fell into that category.[27]

House members would have you believe that this is because of their popularity and competence compared to days of yore. More neutral observers understand well the real reasons. The incumbents have used their power of appropriations to provide for "permanent campaigns," thinly disguised as constituency service operations, within their taxpayer-paid offices and personnel retinues. Large staffs (at least nineteen per House member, more with important committee assignments), fixed and mobile offices within the home district, and free and extensive mailings to constituents (called the *frank*)[28] amount to millions of dollars spent to strengthen each incumbent during every two-year term.[29] Easy access to the electronic and print media by virtue of their position is supplemented by satellite TV offices in Washington provided by their political parties for direct communication with home television stations.[30] The money chase, a key component of reelection, is more like a stroll in the park for incumbents. Interest groups and wealthy individuals with legislative desires line up to pay homage by paying cash to the House members' campaign treasuries. The growing power of incumbency to raise obscene piles of cash in order to deter opposition entirely or gain a daunting advantage over daring challengers has become a staple of the House landscape. In 2004, just to cite one recent election year, incumbent U.S. representatives spent a total of $428 million, compared to just $23 million for all challengers combined—a crushing ratio of 19 to 1.[31]

Yet most devastating of all to nonincumbents is the incumbent-friendly pattern of redistricting, usually conducted after the census every ten years and now supplemented in a few states (such as Texas and Georgia) by re-redistricting in mid-decade when power shifts and one political party gains the upper hand in the governorship and the state legislature. It all boils down to this: Geography is destiny in politics. Incumbent representatives, the political parties, and their state legislative supporters have embraced that elementary principle with both arms, and in so doing they have squeezed the life out of political competition in most states.[32] Both parties are guilty, of course. Just to cite one example from the last midterm election in 2006: All the Democratic House candidates combined won the popular vote for the U.S. House in Michigan by a sizable margin of 54 to 46 percent. But the Republican state legislature had been in charge during Michigan's 2001 redistricting. The result? The GOP lost no seat in Congress and maintained a nine-to-six House majority in Michigan even in a year when Democrats won landslides for governor and U.S. senator in the Wolverine State. This is not a new phenomenon, of course. The founders themselves were aware of redistricting's power, and Madison himself was nearly redistricted out of the House by unfriendly forces in Richmond.[33] In their day, it was called *gerrymandering*, after Massachusetts governor Elbridge Gerry, who designed a salamander-like district for a political ally in 1812.[34]

But the founders could not in their wildest nightmares have imagined today's redistricted House, where elaborate, exquisite computer programs permit the politicians to carve up the map precisely to protect virtually every incumbent, while draining the competition out of House elections.[35] Competition is the lifeblood of any representative democracy, permitting the people to choose not just personnel but policies. When the electorate has the ability to "refresh" the House in a dramatic way at each election, the voters can send clear signals about their intentions *and* they can empower the House to accomplish the people's preferred objectives. Yet in the twenty-first century, there is not enough competition to permit the electorate to send decisive, eye-popping signals in any ideological direction. Instead of the people choosing their House members, the House members now use redistricting to choose their voters.

More is at work than merely redistricting in the high reelection rate for incumbents. As Professor Alan Abramowitz has argued, "Americans are increasingly living in communities whose residents share their values."[36] However, even Abramowitz's statistics show some difference in competition between states with nonpartisan redistricting and those with partisan line-drawing. Unfortunately, the majority of states are redistricted in a partisan fashion, with the largest party in each state legislature holding sway in the process. When the two houses of the legislature are controlled by different parties, or when the governor is of the opposite party to the legislature, a less partisan outcome is possible. Alas, even in these circumstances, what results is usually an "incumbent protection act," where the House members of both parties get "safe," uncompetitive districts. Just six states now leave redistricting entirely to balanced or nonpartisan commissions (where judges or other less partisanly interested individuals draw the district lines), and all six are small to medium-size states. Two other states, Iowa and Arizona, have chosen a similar route: relatively nonpartisan forms of redistricting that build in competition rather than smother it.[37] Beyond these eight, California, Florida, Massachusetts, Ohio, and Tennessee have seriously considered major redistricting reform in recent years, with the proposals calling variously for the line-drawing to be performed by retired state judges (balanced by party) or a team of nonaligned demographic professionals or a carefully constructed group of appointees designated by statewide officials and the legislature.[38] Sadly, intense partisan politics and entrenched interests have stalled or beaten all these efforts, leaving forty-two states with fundamentally, unrelievedly partisan redistricting.

This state of affairs should not be surprising. Incumbent politicians and the dominant political party in most states will never permit their system to go in the Iowa or Arizona direction. They can mobilize the forces and the resources to defeat even a referendum that is manifestly in the public's interests. (It is easy to portray redistricting reform as an attempt by "them"—the other party—to take power away from "us.") And voters in many states that lack the initiative process have no real recourse at all—even as legislators gear up for the next round of redistricting's bloodletting.[39]

That is why the Constitution itself must call for universal nonpartisan redistricting. The states should be given a choice of methods, including redistricting by a panel of retired judges or an independent citizens commission—carefully balanced to prevent control by any party. With the necessary allowances for drawing required racial and ethnic minority districts,[40] the guiding principles of the new regime of constitutional redistricting would be compactness in the districts, increased partisan competition, and the needs of voters rather than politicians.

Compactness means that a district will not meander around a state for partisan purposes, as was the case in the original "Gerry" gerrymander as well as hundreds of districts today. The point of modern redistricters is nothing more than the creation of absolutely predictable elections for members of a certain party, even if the boundaries of the districts are confusing to voters, a given district has no unified interests for the congressman to represent, and it includes a large body of water, mountain, or other harsh terrain that makes continuous travel to all parts of the district challenging (except by air). Citizens surely prefer that their cities and counties not be carved up into more pieces than absolutely necessary, and where possible, localities should be included whole in a congressional district. There is obviously great value in compactness for both the representative and the represented, with the necessary exception for minority representation. (Judicial interpretations of the Voting Rights Act require that the push for added minority representation take precedence over virtually all other objectives in the redistricting process.) The representative would have a better conception of the interests contained in the district for which he or she must advocate in Congress. Citizens would see how they fit into the district more clearly since they are used to describing territory in terms of neighboring cities, towns, and counties. In other words, congressional districts might actually make sense for a change, instead of resembling the paintings of Jackson Pollock, the abstract expressionist artist.

Many observers over the decades have argued that increased compactness will often directly conflict with augmented minority representation.[41] But to the contrary, path-breaking research by a young scholar suggests we can have our cake (minority representation) and eat it too (compactness)—that compactness can actually have a major positive effect on the process of redistricting *without* costing minority representation. David Wasserman advocates *minimum-split districting* (*MSD*) as a key standard, requiring that locality lines be honored and preserved wherever possible. He shows statistically that MSD produces districts that conform more closely to media markets, thus aiding citizen education about their representatives and the opposing candidates. A mandate to avoid splitting cities and counties unnecessarily also reduces the opportunities for partisan redistricting, and therefore increases political competition in many districts. Moreover, representation by African Americans and other disadvantaged groups is not reduced through application of MSD.[42] Computer geographic software—the source of some of the present problem with redistricting—may be advanced enough by the 2010 census to aid significantly the compactness standard without doing any harm to minority representation.[43]

The goal of increased partisan competition ought to require that, within the demands of compactness, we should create as many two-party competitive districts as possible. This is what Iowa tries to do, quite successfully. Why is this so important? If there is a national swing of just two or three percentage points in the overall House vote from one party to the other in successive elections, then many dozens of seats might switch hands to the more politically successful party, empowering the people to send their electoral messages. At present, a swing of 2 or 3 percent would produce only a handful of party turnovers, in all probability, so that the voters are cheated of their opportunity to affect the governmental policies that affect them. Finally, the needs of voters instead of politicians are almost guaranteed to be better met if districts are compact, rationally drawn, and politically competitive. "Putting People First" has been the slogan of many a candidate for high office. Redistricting reform is a major way to achieve it permanently, without depending on individual politicians.

Mandatory term limits (the proposed constitutional limitation on the number of consecutive terms that a House or Senate member may serve,[44] to be discussed later in this chapter) could be troublesome because they would deprive Congress of the institutional memory of senior members. But term limits would not be needed as much if a new nonpartisan system of redistricting is adopted. Instead, turnover of the membership would increase for the right reasons—the decisions of voters about candidates and issues—and not just because members have reached an arbitrary, artificial limit on the number of years they can serve. Rather than being tenured into office by the advantages of incumbency and corrupt district line-drawing, House members would have to win each new term on their own merits, by means of their accomplishments and their accurate representation of the views of a diverse partisan constituency.

Building a Bigger House

Most of the reforms advocated in this book are primarily structural, without a clear leaning to left or right. Others might be considered liberal or progressive, with a few falling squarely in the middle of the road. Yet constructive constitutional change can and must come in all ideological hues. No one philosophy has a monopoly on good ideas, and if a package of amendments is to be ratified—given the extraordinary majorities required for adoption in Congress and the states—there must be backing across the mainstream political continuum. The following proposals, supported mainly by conservatives, ought to be given serious consideration for inclusion in the new Constitution: expanding the size of the U.S. House, term limits for national legislators, and a balanced budget amendment. (In chapter 3, on the Supreme

Court, I will also suggest some novel arrangements that will find favor in the conservative community.)

The first of these ideas will surprise many. Why would an increase in the size of the U.S. House of Representatives be considered conservative—or be regarded a good thing? As is frequently the case, we need to go back to the Constitutional Convention of 1787. The number of representatives to be elected to the House was of such importance that the presiding officer, George Washington, made a rare intervention. As James Madison recounted it in his convention notes, Washington spoke to urge that House members should have smaller rather than larger districts: "When the President rose, for the purpose of putting the question, he said that though his situation had hitherto restrained him from offering his sentiments on questions depending in the House, and it might be thought, ought now impose silence on him . . . he thought this of so much consequence that it would give him much satisfaction to see it adopted."[45]

Washington wanted the size of each congressional district to be reduced from a projected 40,000 Americans to 30,000; thus, there would be a larger House as a result. Many delegates were concerned that the projected House of just 65 members would be too small to represent the will of the people accurately.[46]

About calls for a much bigger House, Madison made this observation in *The Federalist Papers.*

> Within three years a census is to be taken, when the number may be augmented to one for every thirty thousand inhabitants; and within every successive period of ten years the census is to be renewed, and augmentations may continue to be made under the above limitation. It will not be thought an extravagant conjecture that the first census will, at the rate of one for every thirty thousand, raise the number of representatives to at least one hundred . . . At the expiration of twenty-five years, according to the computed rate of increase, the number of representatives will amount to two hundred, and of fifty years, to four hundred. This is a number which, I presume, will put an end to all fears arising from the smallness of the body.[47]

There is every indication that the founders believed the House would grow with the population. At the same time, they no doubt understood that there was some undefined limit to that growth in the House, and Madison so cautioned: "Sixty or seventy men may be more properly trusted with a given degree of power than six or seven. But it does not follow that six or seven hundred would be proportionably a better depositary. And if we carry on the supposition to six or seven thousand, the whole reasoning ought to be reversed."[48]

Had the founders realized that the United States of America would persevere and grow to more than 300 million people, would they have held to this view? Or would they have been willing to consider another arrangement for the House? We cannot know, but we must ask the same question of ourselves.

Let's return to the first House of 65 members. With a U.S. population of about 3.9 million, each House member represented approximately 60,000 individuals.[49] By 1860 a larger House of 183 members represented on average about 100,000 people each. After the 1910 census, the size of the House peaked at 435, with each member representing 213,000.[50] Today, each member of the lower house of Congress represents *690,000*![51]

That number is staggering, and it precludes personal contact between a representative and the vast majority of his or her constituents. Could this be yet one more reason for the general alienation of many citizens from their federal government? Surely it fosters the widespread belief that "no one cares about us, no one is listening to me and my family." It is worth noting that some other industrial democracies have much better representation ratios. For example, the average member of Parliament in the 646-member British House of Commons represents 91,000 people. And in France, the average member of the 577-member French National Assembly represents 102,000 people.[52]

If the new Constitutional Convention were to tackle this issue, it would be vital not to go from one extreme to the other. Based on the original constitutional minimum district size of 30,000 people per House member, we would have a House of 10,000! Some conservatives have argued for a House of 2,000 up to more than 9,000, but more reasonable is the conservative commentator George Will's suggestion of a 1,000-member House.[53] It may seem counterintuitive that conservative pundits would want to expand this part of government, but the key is in the follow-through. By increasing the size of the House, the influence of most members is thus severely limited. Resources per member, such as personal staff and office space, should also be proportionately reduced. The essential codicil to this reform is that the House would have no larger a staff than it has now, but divided by 1,000 instead of 435.[54]

A larger House would produce much smaller constituencies of 300,000 people or so, permitting representatives to stay in touch with a larger proportion of their districts and also allowing for the election of a more diverse group of representatives. More ethnic, social, racial, and religious groups might well have majorities in these new, smaller districts, and they could elect a House member to carry their banner in Congress. The need for money in order to mount a campaign would be reduced as well. A compact district of fewer people gives the opportunity for more personal campaigning and potentially lower costs of communication in many districts. Granted, wealthy candidates would still probably spend fortunes on TV ads, wasting much of it in large media markets just to reach the sliver of people in their district. But the less well-funded opponents would have cheaper ways to counteract the TV ads, through door-to-door campaigning, leafleting, radio ads, and the Internet. Voters place the greatest value on one-to-one contact anyway, and personal connections can outweigh media presence in campaigns.[55]

A larger, more representative, less "politically professional" House may be just the tonic needed to restore popular energy and backing to the federal legislature. Should this constitutional amendment be ratified, it could be put into effect after the decennial census following its adoption. That way, the new system of less partisan redistricting could be combined with the creation of the House's expansion to 1,000 members. These dual reforms would reinforce one another to transform representation in "the people's House," and very likely for the good.

By the way, the larger House would also have a salutary effect on the Electoral College. While we have already proposed a Senate-based expansion of the college, and in chapter 4, we will advocate still greater reform, an expanded House of Representatives would nicely complement those changes. Since each House member produces one electoral vote for a state, the additional 565 electors created by the 1,000-member House would put added emphasis on the popular vote for president, reducing the chances of an Electoral College "misfire"—the election of a chief executive who has lost the popular vote.

CONGRESSIONAL TERM LIMITS: EXTREME OR MAINSTREAM?

> Politicians in government should be changed regularly, like diapers, and for the same reason.
>
> —*term limits advocate Richard Davies*[56]

Let's think again about how the average American views Congress. The voter watches the campaign, studies the issues, and comes to the polls prepared to vote for the candidate closest to his or her views. From time to time, a new House member or senator is elected, promising to take the local perspective of "the best district or state in the nation" to Washington. Years pass, the incumbent is reelected over and over, often with little or no opposition, and the legislator is seen less and less at home. Good old Senator Mary Smith or Representative John Doe has "gone Washington," and it shows. The lobbyists and political action committee directors receive more face time with the member of Congress than the citizen at home does, and the voter becomes alienated. Practically, there is little that the poor voter can do, given the advantages of incumbency, to change the situation. Is there any way to short-circuit this age-old dilemma and restore the average person's faith in the representative system?

One of the oldest debates in American politics centers on the question of *term limits* for federal and state legislators. Should U.S. senators, House members, and state legislators have the right to run for an unlimited number of terms (as is the case now at the federal level), or should they be restricted to a set number of terms, consecutively or in their lifetimes (as some states now designate for their legislatures)?

The rationale for term limits is obvious to their advocates. The founders fully expected that there would be frequent "rotation in office."[57] They could not have imagined the professionalization of public service we see today, with some legislators serving for many decades and accumulating enormous seniority and power—elements that distort the federal budget and produce great unfairness in appropriations of the money we all pay into the federal Treasury. The overwhelming advantages conferred by incumbency and partisan redistricting can only be counteracted by a mandated maximum on office-holding, say term limit supporters. In addition, new ideas and fresh blood, perhaps even greater representation for historically underrepresented women and minorities, are guaranteed with term limits. Lord Acton's warning that "power corrupts and absolute power corrupts absolutely"[58] is heeded, for term limitation promises that the lengthy concentration of power, and attendant abuses, including arrogance and corruption, might be constrained. One could also insist that legislatures might see more profiles in courage, more votes cast in the national or state interest instead of decisions made out of a desire to get reelected. After all, legislators may be defeated for votes of conscience—for acting as trustees of the people's best interests instead of pure delegates of the public's transient desires—but with a fixed number of years that could be served in office, these elected officials would have less to lose.

Opponents of term limits have powerful rebuttals to at least some of these arguments. Fundamental to their case is that term limits are undemocratic: They limit the ability of the people to elect the individuals they prefer. If those individuals are longtime incumbents, who produce for their constituents and keep them happy, what of it? Increasingly, public policy issues are complicated and need a sophisticated approach, produced in part by long experience in office. Should all this experience, and the accompanying institutional memory of a Congress or state legislature, be sacrificed on the altar of term limits? That experience and memory also help to balance the great power of other high officials and branches in the political system, not least the executives (presidents and governors) who have natural advantages over a slow-moving legislature. And what about lobbyists, administrative bureaucrats, and legislative staffers? Do not experienced legislators also counterbalance these groups' institutional memories? There are no term limits on these wily governmental players who can twist unwary legislators into pretzels, say term limit opponents. Finally, some contend that we already have informal term limits. Very few legislators at the federal and state levels actually serve much longer than a decade or so; there is already rotation in office, for the most part.

Acknowledging the strength of some arguments on both sides of the debate, we can still make an assessment of which side is more convincing.

The Absence of Term Limits in the Current Constitution

Despite its prominent emergence in state and national politics during the late 1980s and 1990s, the term limits concept is hardly novel in the history of the Republic. Following their break with Britain in 1776, five states—Delaware, Maryland, New York, South Carolina, and Massachusetts—ratified constitutions that imposed some sort of limitation on the number of years that the state's chief executive could serve. Following abuses among the colonial governors and of the British Crown, the impulse to limit the power of the executive was an underlying cause of the American Revolution itself. The logic of rebellion focused on the elimination of perceived tyranny and the distribution of power to ensure the sovereignty of the people as a whole. Revolutionary lawmakers drafted new state constitutions in all the former colonies to ensure that foreign tyrants would not be replaced with new, homegrown demagogues.[59]

The impulse to limit power among some of the newly independent former colonists extended beyond the executive to the legislature. The 1776 Pennsylvania Constitution barred lawmakers from serving as state representatives for more than four years within a seven-year period. The Virginia Constitution of 1776, in section 5 of its bill of rights, enshrined legislative and executive term limits as fundamental to republican government itself.

> That the legislative and executive powers of the State should be separate and distinct from the judiciary; and that the members of the two first may be restrained from oppression, by feeling and participating [in] the burdens of the people, they should, at fixed periods, be reduced to a private station, return into that body from which they were originally taken, and the vacancies be supplied by frequent, certain, and regular elections, in which all, or any part of the former members, to be again eligible, or ineligible, as the laws shall direct.[60]

Here, then, was the Roman ideal of the *citizen-legislator* serving his country when necessary and then happily returning to private life. Benjamin Franklin put it succinctly: "In free governments, the rulers are the servants, and the people their superiors and sovereigns. For the former, therefore, to return to the latter [is] not to degrade but to promote them."[61] This ideal remains powerful in American political culture and predictably resurfaces in contemporary debates over term limits.[62] Naturally, the sentiment is more widespread among those not ensconced in public office.

The impetus to decentralize power reached its apex with the Articles of Confederation (1781), which included a specific provision barring any individual from serving as a congressional delegate for more than three years within a six-year period. Given the crushing difficulties of governing the new Republic, though, term limits proved to be a low priority—problematic and unenforceable. In 1784, the Congress created the Committee on Qualifications, which attempted to apply the term limits rule. The committee challenged long-serving delegates from Massachusetts, Delaware, and Rhode Island. William Ellery and David Howell of Rhode Island disputed the committee's findings, and rather than enforce the rule and expel Ellery and Howell, Congress dropped the matter altogether so that it could tend to more pressing business.[63]

Due to episodes such as this, the enthusiasm for term limits had waned by the time of the Philadelphia Convention of 1787, where the notion of legislative and executive term limits simply fell off the delegates' radar screen in the absence of vocal backers. Both the competing Virginia Plan and the New Jersey Plan contained legislative term limits, yet the limits were dropped from consideration because they went "too much into detail for general propositions."[64] In the hurried days that followed, term limits never rematerialized in the final draft. In the debate over ratification, supporters of the new Constitution—most notably James Madison—argued that frequent elections in the House of Representatives, without term limits, would guarantee that the federal government accurately reflected the will of the people.[65]

Against the backdrop of colonial political culture, this was a rather sensible argument. The initial impulse for term limits was not to prevent the emergence of "career politicians" so much as to avoid a dangerous concentration of power in the hands of an unaccountable few. Indeed, the idea of a "career politician" would have made very little sense to the founding generation. George Washington solidified the principle of voluntary rotation of office as a central facet of American federal politics with his decision not to seek a third term. The District of Columbia was difficult for most legislators to travel to, and few wanted to remain in the swampy city any longer than needed. Early legislators also were poorly compensated for their troubles, and public service was considered an act of civic volunteerism far more than an opportunity for personal gain.[66]

Legislative norms and times have dramatically changed since the founding generation, and the ideal of the citizen-legislator has in large measure given way to a more professionalized and careerist style of politics. Consider the fact that only six out of seventy-three freshman members of Congress elected in a recent, typical year received lower pay as congressmen and -women than in their previous jobs.[67]

Federal and state legislators may have been content with the status quo of unlimited terms, but in at least some states, the electorate began to signal a desire for change by the early 1990s. Political activists around the country began to agitate for a return to the citizen-legislator ideal, generating new enthusiasm for term limits and changing the American political landscape.

Throwing the Bums Out, Wholesale: The Modern Push for Term Limits

The term limits movement gained its first victory when Oklahoma imposed a twelve-year limit on legislative service in 1990. California soon followed suit, instituting a six-year lifetime limit on service in its assembly and an eight-year lifetime limit for service in the state senate. Currently thirteen states have

TABLE 1.1. STATE LEGISLATIVE TERM LIMITS

		HOUSE		SENATE		
State	Year Enacted	Limit (in years)	Year of Impact	Limit (in years)	Year of Impact	% of Public Voting Yes
Arizona	1992	8	2000	8	2000	74.2
Arkansas	1992	6	1998	8	2000	59.9
California	1990	6	1996	8	1998	52.2
Colorado	1990	8	1998	8	1998	71.0
Florida	1992	8	2000	8	2000	76.8
Louisiana	1995	12	2007	12	2007	76.0
Maine	1993	8	1996	8	1996	67.6
Michigan	1992	6	1998	8	2002	58.8
Missouri[a]	1992	8	2002	8	2002	75.0
Montana	1992	8	2000	8	2000	67.0
Nebraska[b]	2000	n/a	n/a	8	2006	56.0
Nevada[c]	1996	12	2010	12	2010	70.4
Ohio	1992	8	2000	8	2000	68.4
Oklahoma	1990	12	2004	12	2004	67.3
South Dakota	1992	8	2000	8	2000	63.5

Source: National Conference of State Legislatures (http://www.ncsl.org/programs/legismgt/about/states.htm). Current as of December 2006.

[a] Because of special elections, term limits were effective in 2000 for eight current members of the House and one senator in 1998.

[b] Nebraska has a unicameral state legislature.

[c] The Nevada Legislative Council and attorney general have ruled that Nevada's term limits cannot be applied to those legislators elected in the same year term limits were passed (1996). They first apply to persons elected in 1998.

"termed" legislatures of one variation or another, with the fourteenth and fifteenth—Louisiana and Nevada—slated for term limits to take effect in 2007 and 2010, respectively. (See table 1.1.) Term limits have been passed but then rescinded, either by state courts or state legislatures, in six states: Idaho, Massachusetts, Oregon, Utah, Washington, and Wyoming. (In the case of the courts' reversals, unhappy legislators or interest groups generally brought the judicial challenges.) This pattern of "yes, then no" states suggests anew that term limits are controversial and are by no means universally welcomed or hailed.

Accompanying this movement for term limits applied to state legislatures was a simultaneous national effort to impose term limits on U.S. congressional representatives and senators by means of state law. Twenty-three states had passed such laws in the five years before the Supreme Court struck them down as unconstitutional in 1995 in *U.S. Term Limits, Inc. v. Thornton*, which arose out of Arkansas's federal term limits provision.[68] Following this decision, many term limits advocates pushed for an amendment to the U.S. Constitution, though that impulse—predictably—never gathered much steam in Congress, even though term limits had been one element in the GOP's famous "Contract with America" during the 1994 midterm election. That contract promised only to bring the matter to a House floor vote, not to actually enact the limits. Thus, the pledge was fulfilled when several term limits proposals came to a floor vote in the House in 1995; none earned the necessary votes to move on to the states for ratification. The last time Congress dealt with the issue of term limits was in 1997, when a proposed amendment creating a twelve-year cap in both the U.S. House and the Senate failed to garner the necessary two-thirds majority by a vote of 217 yea to 211 nay.[69]

Despite the failure of the congressional term limits effort, due to an insurmountable judicial roadblock, term limits as a concept clearly has strong backing from the public. In just a handful of years, more than twenty states imposed term limits on either their state legislators or their congressmen, sometimes with as much as 70 to 77 percent of the electorate voting in favor. Unquestionably, Americans believe in the citizen-legislator ideal, and their belief in it has been reinforced by the dozens of major scandals involving senior members of Congress and state legislators in modern times. Nonetheless, there is a contradiction in the public's behavior, since the electorates almost everywhere have reelected their own state legislators about 90 percent of the time and their federal members of Congress as much as 98 percent of the time,[70] a bewildering inconsistency.

In the midst of the term limits debate, political scientists and commentators offered up any number of explanations to make sense of this. For example, Jeffrey Karp, writing in *Public Opinion Quarterly*, cited four popular rationales that result in the backing of term limits: (1) dissatisfaction with legislative performance, (2) cynicism with government more generally, (3) perceived self-interest (for example, from a minority party attempting to break up the majority), and (4) ideological predispositions against career politics.[71] Relying on data from the National Election Studies and analogous surveys in Florida and Wyoming, Karp concluded that voter cynicism has the strongest correlation to voter preference for term limits, partially debunking the notion that term limits are a direct result of voter frustration with legislative performance. Karp argued that "term limits support stems not from legislatures' inability to produce outputs in accordance with individual expectations, but, rather, from a frustration with the political process, manifested in an increasingly cynical electorate."[72]

Additionally, Einer Elhauge borrowed from public choice theory to explain how putative rational voters might continually reelect their own incumbents while simultaneously supporting term limits for the state legislature as a whole. On the one hand, "barriers to entry" resulting from the perks of incumbency (that is, the difficulty of defeating an incumbent in the vast majority of cases) might limit the voter's choice so that the incumbent appears to be the best option. At the same time, Elhauge argued that rational voters face a serious "collective action" problem. In a system that rewards seniority, voters have an interest in reelecting an incumbent even when that incumbent might not best reflect voter preferences, since the incumbent will more likely be successful in steering pork projects and money into his or her home district. Under these circumstances, a voter might (a) rationally desire that all districts stop reelecting incumbents by imposing term limits, and (b) realize that, since this is unlikely to happen, it is in his own best interests to keep his personal incumbent in office.[73] This sounds complicated, and you may legitimately question whether most voters actually engage in such a sophisticated analysis before casting their ballots. Yet at some level of the conscious or unconscious, this is a perfectly sensible, logical way of approaching legislative elections. As the great political scientist V. O. Key put it in his seminal book, *The Responsible Electorate*, "Voters are not fools."[74]

Term Limits in Theory: Promoting or Restricting Democracy?

Given the contradiction of term limits advocates reelecting their incumbents, a much more fundamental question needs to be asked: Are term limits compatible with the basic principles of representative democracy? Many critics of the term limits movement have asserted that term limits are not, expressing a concern dating back to the colonial period—that by arbitrarily preventing a legislator from seeking the same office again, regardless of performance, term limits indefensibly eat away at the sovereign right of the people to choose whichever candidate they most prefer. Following Madison's arguments in *The Federalist*, these critics insist that the only term limits compatible with democratic principles are free and fair elections. Otherwise, infringing on the people's right to choose their leaders is inherently undemocratic.

Elhauge challenged such critics to identify what, precisely, is meant by *undemocratic*, suggesting two possibilities.[75] First, *undemocratic* might mean that term limits unfairly allow the current electorate to restrict the choices of future electorates, which seems antithetical to the notion of popular sovereignty. However, if one accepts that barriers to candidate entry and the collective action problem are real—and both are—then voters already experience a great deal of electoral filtering. According to this view, voters do not face a clear choice between reelecting an incumbent and installing an alternative. Instead, they have the choice of returning to office an incumbent who has used his superior financial resources and political connections to spread his message and tout his achievements among voters, or rolling the dice on a relatively unknown, underfunded challenger. At the same time, voters face a vital strategic choice: In a world in which most incumbents return to office, should they elect a challenger who will be at a clear disadvantage without seniority, or should they sacrifice their possible preference for the challenger in order to obtain certain material benefits? Thus, the structure of any un-term-limited legislature already reduces the choices of present and future electorates as long as the collective action problem and barriers to candidate entry distort the political landscape.

Second, *undemocratic* might imply that term limits unfairly infringe on the voters of districts that wish to return their incumbents to office because of genuinely good incumbent performance, rather than because of the collective action problem. Undeniably, this may in fact be one result of term limits, but it hardly means that term limits should be rejected. The majority of the public in a state may see greater democratic good resulting from across-the-board term limits than from the preservation of some outstanding individuals in office. Majorities always frustrate minority preferences, but so long as the "tyranny of the majority" is not denying the minority its basic rights and liberties, it is difficult to argue that a great wrong is being done. The restriction of legislator choice on the basis of incumbency (which is what term limits are) simply does not qualify as an irreparable evil. Majority rule on term limits—especially when 60 to 80 percent of voters in a state cast ballots in favor of term limits—seems like a reasonable application of majoritarian democracy.

In the end, term limits can only be called inherently undemocratic if elections serve as perfect opportunities for voters, possessing equal information about all potential candidates, to evaluate each candidate on the merits and elect the contender they deem most deserving. Yet it is obvious these conditions do not exist in today's incumbent-protected American politics. As long as seniority matters, voters have a strong incentive to return incumbents to office. Moreover, the entire thrust of this book is that governmental structures, ossified by constitutional neglect, have become fundamentally unfair and tilted to those already in power. The insulation provided to incumbents by partisan redistricting, the mass media, and campaign fundraising are just several examples of how the democratic process is distorted by our current system. Under such circumstances, term limits certainly do not appear to be objectionable on their face.

Term Limits in Practice: Silver Bullet or Blank Cartridge?

If term limits can be justified as a reasonable remedy to growing pro-incumbent distortions in American democracy, are they still wise public policy? Do they have positive effects that give good reason to restrict some popular choices at the ballot box?

As it turns out, now is the first time we can begin to evaluate fairly the effects state legislative term limits have had on the democratic process, because any empirical analysis of term limits has a necessarily lengthy time horizon as legislators elected in different years reach the statutory or constitutional maximum number of terms. The first legislative body to start "terming-out" legislators was the California house in 1996, followed by a smattering of other statehouses in 1998 and a slew of them in 2000, providing evidence of what happens when large numbers of legislators reach the term limit. Case studies from two key states, California and Michigan, are especially revealing. Both of these states have large, diverse electorates and highly professionalized legislatures that more accurately reflect the congressional experience than the part-time "citizen legislatures" in many other states.

California enacted state legislative limits in 1990 after a series of legislative delays in passing the state budget, coupled with a number of FBI probes which called into question the integrity of some Golden State officeholders.[76] California also makes a useful case study because it has experienced an entire term limits cycle, with the house retiring its first incumbents in 1996 and the senate doing so in 1998.

Overall, the analysis of California's experiment with term limits has mixed results. On the one hand, term limits do seem to be offering voters greater choice at the polls. In many elections, there are more open seats and more closely contested races than in the past, indicating a higher degree of competitiveness. (Nonetheless, in 2006 not a single California legislative seat on the ballot changed parties in a tumultuous midterm year.)[77] Moreover, women and Latinos have made significant gains in the percentage of seats they hold in the legislature—though it is difficult to disaggregate this result from other cultural changes.[78] On the other hand, the relative lack of legislative "old hands" has resulted in a period of great instability within the legislature itself. Committee chairs and party leaders have less experience than before, while in some years California has experienced even longer delays than in the past in passing its state budget.

Perhaps most interesting, California has in no way seen a return to the ideal of the citizen-legislator posited by so many term limits proponents. In a phenomenon that appears to hold true in many other states, termed-out legislators are simply moving into other offices. That is, more assemblymen are running for the senate than before, more state senators are running for Congress, and more legislators overall are running for local elected offices. Many observers have referred to this as a game of "legislative musical chairs." In any case, the percentage of legislators who identify their primary occupation as "legislator" in California has *increased,* from 39 percent in the assembly and 35 percent in the senate in 1989, before term limits were enacted, to 47 percent in the assembly and 37 percent of the senate in 1999. Term limits, therefore, have arguably resulted in an even *greater* degree of legislative careerism than before.[79]

Michigan, like California, has stringent term limits—a six-year lifetime limit in the house and an eight-year lifetime limit in the senate. Moreover, Michigan's highly professionalized legislature has endured a very high degree of turnover—64 out of 110 legislators elected in 1996 were rendered ineligible for reelection in 1998 alone.[80] As in the Golden State, the record in the Wolverine State is mixed. Michigan has definitely experienced a "musical chairs" effect, with even more career politicians serving in the legislature. Unlike California, however, Michigan has seen no change in the racial or gender makeup of its legislature in the wake of term limits. James Penning's study of Michigan's experience also concludes that term limits have not in any way diminished the amount of lobbying in state legislatures. However, shrewd lobbyists have adapted their tactics. In some instances they have substituted for political parties by recruiting young candidates to run for lower-level positions, such as school boards and city commissions, establishing trusting relationships with these elected officials before helping to run them for state legislative office. Penning also explores the impact of term limits on legislative collegiality, finding that the shortened time-horizon for legislators to shape an impressive record has produced intensified competition and conflict among some lawmakers. No doubt, this can have both good and bad effects, depending on the circumstances. The point is that term limits create different legislative norms and atmospherics, as one would expect when the rules of the game are altered. Many Michigan politicians have expressed concern and exasperation over these effects on the legislative process. For example, former state senator Glenn Steil, who headed the term limits campaign in 1992, now wants to elongate the tough limits (six years in the house, eight years in the senate) currently in place. Commented Steil about the current limits: "It's not long enough. You're just getting on your feet and you're saying bye-bye."[81]

Additional studies compare the experience of legislators across term-limited states, and once again, the results are a mixed bag of positives and negatives.[82]

- *Diversity.* While some variation in the characteristics of legislators is recorded here and there, term limits have not fundamentally changed the composition of legislatures. One survey concludes, "[There is] virtually no effect of term limits on the demographics of those elected to state legislatures [including] professional backgrounds, education levels, income levels, age, or ideology." Term limits might have increased minority representation in some places, though generally the limits simply accelerated demographic changes already occurring. Similarly, there have been slight gains by women in a couple of term-limited states—perhaps due to term limits, perhaps not—while in some other states, the number of women legislators has actually dropped.[83]

- *Broader perspective versus parochial governing.* Some evidence has emerged that termed legislators tend to focus more on statewide issues of broad concern than on the purely parochial concerns of their own districts. But this is consonant with the "musical chairs" phenomenon since these legislators may be planning to run for higher office with larger constituencies.[84]

- *Legislator productivity and effectiveness.* In general, legislatures have passed about as many bills after term limits as they did before. Importantly, however, *who* passes those bills changes. In most states, term limits have increased the power of the majority party's leaders while substantially eroding the effectiveness of the rank-and-file members of the minority party. This is not surprising since inexperienced legislators are more likely to seek instruction from their leaders than to step out on a limb. In turn, the more often rank-and-file members "get in line," the more partisan the legislature becomes and the more power accrues to the majority party.[85] The legislators left out most frequently are less senior minority-party members—a result that is consequential to the constituencies of those legislators.

- *Institutional power*. Many political scientists predicted that term limits would shift power in favor of the executive and legislative staff and lobbyists, and away from the legislature itself. Initially, states do seem to experience this kind of shift, though the institutional effects erode as newly termed legislatures reorient themselves to the new political realities. For example, many term-limited legislatures have now instituted intensive training programs for new legislators so they can hit the ground running, while others are strengthening their budgeting and appropriating capabilities to help balance gubernatorial advantages.

- *Politics and voter experience.* Term limits seem to result in a marginally greater degree of electoral competition (a good thing) and substantially higher campaign costs (a bad thing). Also on the debit side of the term limits ledger is that voters in states with termed legislatures are less likely than before to know who their legislator is or what his or her positions are. After all, incumbency breeds familiarity, not just contempt.[86]

Term Limits, for Here the People Rule

Surely, no seasoned political observer would be startled to learn that a dramatic reform such as term limits has both superior and negative consequences. Is there any reasonable, overall conclusion that could help us evaluate the usefulness of a constitutional amendment providing for congressional term limits?

First, voter support for term limits serves less as an endorsement of this particular institutional change and more as a barometer of disgust with the system as a whole. When voters are fed up, term limits appear to be an attractive way to "throw the bums out" in one fell swoop. I defend this release valve for a democratic people, though I also understand that it can be seen as superfluous, given our frequent elections and extensive natural legislative turnover.

Second, clearly neither the proponents nor the opponents of term limits have a corner on wisdom. The prophecies of doom and gloom by term limit skeptics have not come to pass in the states—and this is exceptionally significant evidence that bears on my recommendation here. Neither have many of the term limiters' promises of political and governmental salvation materialized, judging by the preliminary research discussed in this section.

For me, though, the third reasonable conclusion about term limits is the real determinant. If democracy means anything, we need to take into account the public's strong predisposition for term limits. Both the actual voting results across the states and the findings in poll after poll demonstrate that the electorate wants this reform. (In chapter 6, a public opinion survey taken specifically for this book will show anew Americans' intense backing of term limits.) That is not to say that every reform favored by the public ought to be adopted in the new Constitution. Alas, if given the chance, and without proper reflection, Americans might unfairly limit the rights of some unpopular minorities (Muslims right after 9/11, for example) or even cut back on specific liberties contained in the Bill of Rights (a few of the guarantees for those accused of crimes, for instance, since they undoubtedly result in some guilty parties going free). But term limits have no such distasteful cost for minorities or basic liberties. As such, the twenty-first-century Constitutional Convention should defer to superior popular wisdom in this matter. The states have ably served their role as laboratories of American democracy on the topic of term limits, and they have paved the way for the adoption of this reform. Generous limits, following the recent pattern of Louisiana and Nevada (twelve years in each house), might be preferable to the more stringent limits of California and Michigan (six years in the lower house and eight years in the upper). But these specifics would be matters for the convention to ponder and decide.

BALANCING THE BUDGET: SETTING THE STAGE FOR A GREAT CONVENTION DEBATE

> I sincerely believe . . . that the principle of spending money to be paid by posterity under the name of funding is but swindling futurity on a large scale.
>
> —*Thomas Jefferson to John Tyler, 1816*[87]

> [A] constitution is not meant to embody a particular economic theory.
>
> —*Oliver Wendell Holmes, 1905*[88]

Talk of national debt and balanced budgets brings a MEGO response from most Americans: "My Eyes Glaze Over." Yet these numbers matter greatly for the future of the nation and especially to our children and grandchildren. We all need to take seriously Jefferson's wise warning of nearly two centuries' ago, which was a reiteration of George Washington's admonition in his farewell address of 1796. Completing his two terms as president, Washington urged us to avert "ungenerously throwing upon posterity the burden which we ourselves ought to bear."[89] Despite our avowed devotion to the teachings of Washington and Jefferson, we have permitted a giant fiscal problem to build. The new Constitution can start us on the road to solving it.

It's important to define our terms for what can be a confusing subject. For all but a handful of years since 1970, the U.S. government has spent more on its operation and programs than it has taken in from taxes and other sources of income, thus producing a series of *annual deficits*. The annual deficits, when not repaid (as they have not been in large part), create a long-term national debt—the simple addition of the deficits *plus* the interest that must be paid annually on the debt. The government has to borrow money to make up the difference between revenues and expenditures each year; that money is lent by individuals and banking institutions at home and abroad. Naturally, the lenders expect to be paid their principal as well as a handsome profit (interest) over time. Already, the annual interest payments on the debt constitute the third largest expenditure in the federal budget (after entitlements such as Social Security, and national defense). As the years have rolled by, the annual deficits have continued to mount up, the interest payments have climbed, and the nation's debt has grown mountainous—as a glance at figure 1.2 will show you.

When President Bush took office in 2001, the accumulated debt of the United States stood at a sobering $5.6 trillion. This is despite the fact that the high-tech bubble of the late 1990s had produced one of the most prosperous

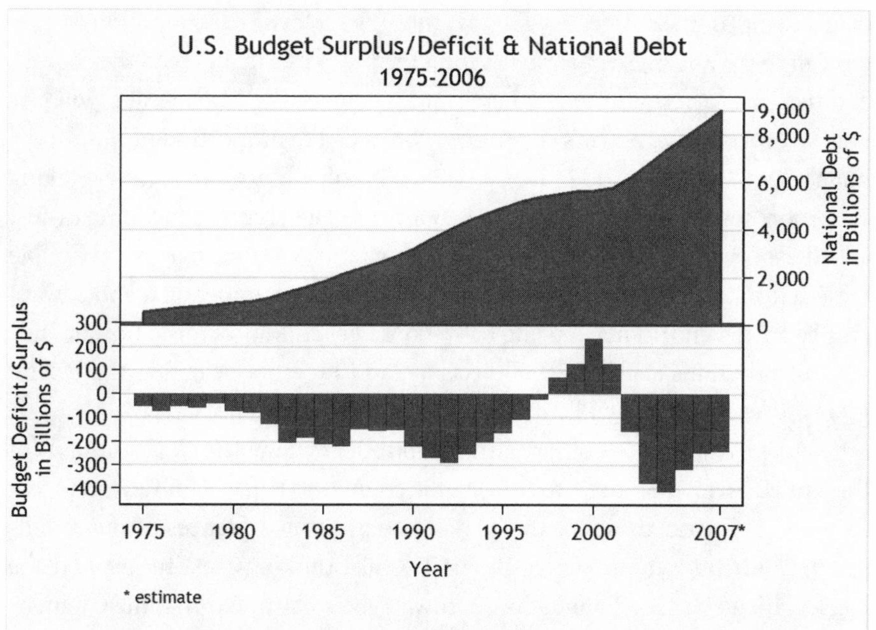

FIGURE 1.2. U.S. ANNUAL BUDGET DEFICIT/SURPLUS AND GROSS NATIONAL DEBT

moments in American history, pouring tax revenues into the Treasury as businesses and individuals grew richer. In fact, from 1998 to 2001, the annual deficits were eliminated—but the surplus of more than a half a trillion dollars was mainly spent on government programs rather than used to retire a substantial portion of the national debt. The good times faded, as they always do. The high-tech bubble burst in 2001, triggering a mild recession, and the shock of 9/11 produced more economic gloom. President Bush's deep tax cuts, enacted in 2001, may well have been the right short-term medicine for a weak economy, but long-term, they helped to push the deficits upward again. By 2007 the national debt had mushroomed to a staggering $8.8 trillion, which is equivalent to more than $29,000 of debt for every American citizen, adult and child.[90] The debt has been growing at a rate of more than $2 billion *per day*.[91] Indeed, since 2000, we have added almost half as much to our national debt as we had accumulated in all the previous years of the American republic.

Even after we account for inflation, government expenditures since 1960 have expanded fivefold while the population has only grown by a factor of 1.6.[92] Payment of the interest on the debt is consuming hundreds of billions of dollars of the federal budget every year, meaning that less is available for national defense and domestic needs. This is only tolerable while the nation is rich enough to pay the interest as well as fund the programs that defend the country and meet basic human needs. There is no guarantee that such wealth will forever be a staple of America's economy; moreover, the proportion of the annual budget spent on interest to retire the debt will probably grow over time—taking even more resources from other needs. Sooner or later, future generations—just as Jefferson warned—will have to pay the bill and sacrifice massively. Couple these statistics and generational inevitabilities with the impending shock wave created by the enormous, retiring baby-boom generation's expectation of entitlement programs such as Social Security, and it seems clear that the federal government is veering wildly in the direction of potential fiscal ruin.

David Walker, the nonpartisan comptroller general (head accountant) of the United States, has taken to touring the country as a new Paul Revere, trying to caution Americans about the dire impending consequences of our profligacy.[93] With budget experts from the liberal Brookings Institution and the conservative Heritage Foundation in tow, Walker has noted that the frightening budget deficit and debt numbers are not really in dispute by the political left or the right. Over the past forty years, the proportion of the federal budget devoted to so-called mandatory spending (Social Security, Medicare, and the like) has more than doubled, from 26 to 53 percent of the federal budget. The interest on the national debt, which also must be paid on schedule, now consumes about 9 percent of the annual federal budget. The money available in the federal budget for everything else—all other national needs—has declined from 67 percent in 1966 to 38 percent in 2006. Given the huge commitments already made for Social Security, Medicare, and other health care programs such as the prescription drug subsidies for the elderly, Walker can see a point near the middle of the twenty-first century when there may be nothing at all left for discretionary expenditures; mandatory spending on entitlements and debt service would consume the whole federal budget. As Walker noted, in just six years between 2000 and 2006, America's "total liabilities and unfunded commitments . . . have soared from about $20 trillion to about $50 trillion. Fifty trillion dollars translates to about $440,000 per American household." With the median household income in America a bit below $50,000 a year, "the typical American family now owes more than nine times their annual income."[94]

In the face of all these troubling fiscal realities, dedicated citizens and some elected officials have been pushing for a Balanced Budget Amendment (BBA) to the Constitution for several decades. Essentially, with most versions of a balanced budget provision, federal expenditures in any given fiscal year could not exceed federal revenues in that same year, unless three fifths of both the House and the Senate waived the balanced budget requirement. In years when the United States was experiencing a recession or a war (declared or undeclared), a simple majority of both the House and the Senate could suspend the balanced budget requirement.[95]

Indeed, the activism for a BBA nearly led to the calling of a second Constitutional Convention during the early 1990s, when as many as thirty-two states—just two short of the required thirty-four—had submitted applications for a second convention.[96] Several states ultimately rescinded their applications for a BBA, though.[97] Nonetheless, the effort for a BBA was revived in 1995 after the GOP takeover of Congress, when a BBA proposal passed the House with over 300 votes and fell only one vote shy in the Senate of the necessary two thirds for promulgation to the states for ratification.[98] A recent reincarnation of a BBA came in 2003, when Congressman Ernest Istook (R-OK) introduced a new draft amendment in the House.[99] The amendment died rather quietly, however, after only a single day of hearings before the House Subcommittee on the Constitution, featuring a mere four witnesses.

Continuing support for a BBA among the electorate, coupled with a lack of support for it in recent Congresses, is a curious anomaly of the balanced budget debate. One survey shows citizen support for a national BBA at more than 80 percent, though it should be noted that the proportion of adherents declines precipitously, to around 30 percent, if respondents believe a BBA will reduce Social Security benefits.[100]

The chilling numbers and the generational imperatives cited earlier should prod the new Constitutional Convention to put a BBA on its agenda for action. Few subjects merit more attention or will spark a fiercer debate. The solution is not as obvious or simple as BBA advocates or opponents contend, however.

Mixed Political Metaphors: Balancing a Checkbook Versus Balancing the Federal Budget

Two inaccurate, pejorative comparisons are often made concerning the federal budgeting process, one to the family checkbook and the other to the budgets of the fifty states—all of which are required to balance their books. Supporters of a BBA often ask why it is so hard for the federal government to keep its books in the black when American families and most states seem to be able to do so as a matter of course.

As critics of a BBA are quick to point out, the comparison to family budgeting is largely misplaced. Most BBA drafts require all the expenses for a given fiscal year to be paid for with receipts from that same year, essentially barring the use of government surpluses to finance year-to-year deficit spending. Instead, such surpluses would be used either to pay down the debt or to be returned to taxpayers as a tax refund or credit. As Robert Greenstein of the liberal Center on Budget and Policy Priorities argues, this may be economically unwise, and furthermore, it is nothing like the way in which families (or even businesses) operate.[101] A good chunk of federal outlays goes toward public sector investment in education, infrastructure, and research and development. While these expenditures might lead to short-term deficits, they would result in long-term economic gain as well as more revenue for the U.S. Treasury. In a related fashion for individual households, families do not pay large expenses, such as mortgages and college tuition, out of the same year's income. Rather, they rely on investments, saving accounts, and short-term loans to make ends meet. Most businesses follow exactly the same practice, by borrowing to invest in new equipment and modernizing technologies in order to remain competitive. The "family" metaphor about the "balanced checkbook," then, tends to confuse more than clarify the balanced budget debate.

What about the comparison between state governments and federal governments? Currently, every state but Vermont has a legal requirement in its constitution, laws, or judicial decisions that the governor and the legislature should produce a balanced budget.[102] If states are able to balance their budgets consistently—and even in Vermont, the leaders do so by tradition—why should we not require the same from the federal government?

First, there are some commonsense differences between the federal budget and state budgets, both in terms of policy (states do not fight wars, for example) and in magnitude. More pertinent to the debate is the question of whether state requirements for balanced budgets are actually analogous to a similar federal requirement, and here it seems clear that there are major differences. First, most states with balanced budget rules require that the state operating budget (programs and salaries) and not the total budget be balanced. Major capital investments are thus not included in the relevant math. Similarly, many states allow for certain forms of borrowing, including bond proceeds, to count toward the revenue for a single year's budget, thereby relaxing the balanced budget rule. A fifty-state study found that "state budget requirements rarely if ever require that all current expenditures be paid for out of current revenues without borrowing."[103] Since the federal budget currently makes no such distinctions between operational expenses and long-term investments, it would necessarily be more difficult to balance. A federal BBA should create this distinction in some form in order to ward off damaging economic effects, using the state systems as a model. Balancing the budget would be senseless if the method of balancing it resulted in serious injury to American prosperity.

Moreover, a significant body of research calls into question exactly how "balanced" state budgets actually are. First, most states now manage a wide array of "off-budget funds" which help round out their annual budgets, such as Ohio's Unemployment Trust Fund and New York's Medical Malpractice Reserve Fund. One investigation found that across the country, monies from a state's general fund (which are subject to balanced budget rules) only comprise, on average, 48 percent of states' annual spending. In Hawaii, for example, as much as 74 percent of the state's budget comes from outside the general fund and hence is not subject to balanced budget rules.[104] This is in addition to a myriad of strategies states will use to keep their books in the black, including "optimistic economic forecasts, manipulation of fiscal periods, delayed payment to creditors, under-funding public employee pension funds, backdoor financing such as sale and leaseback schemes, refunding outstanding bonds, and inter-fund transfers."[105] It is probably safe to assume that the federal government would be at least as creative under any BBA regimen. Politics is politics, at any level, and politicians want to spread good cheer (pork and benefits) and minimize fiscal pain to get reelected.

An additional fact is worth mentioning when comparing state budgets to the federal budget. BBA supporters often highlight that states are able to stay afloat even under the duress of recession, making the dramatic cutbacks necessary to keep the government operational. The federal government, so the argument goes, ought to be able to make the same kinds of difficult choices. However, it is critical to understand that in an economic downturn, federal assistance payments to states necessarily increase in the form of entitlement programs, unemployment insurance, food stamps, Medicare payments, et cetera. On average, states receive anywhere between one fourth to one third of their total revenues in the form of payments from the federal government. In California, for example, federal payments as a percentage of state revenues increased from 29.5 percent in 1990–91 to 38 percent in 1993–94, largely as a result of the economic downturn.[106] Therein we find the rub: Under a strict BBA regime, the federal government would have to balance its budget in times of recession (when revenues inevitably decrease) either by increasing taxes or cutting spending. The former would severely hamper a recovery effort, since it would remove purchasing power from the economy precisely when it was most needed. The latter could be equally catastrophic, since spending cuts would drastically reduce revenue inflows to all fifty states precisely when state budgets were most bare.

For this reason, some critics claim that a BBA tends to favor the wealthy over the disadvantaged. After all, the wealthy—who generally favor spending cuts over many forms of tax increases—tend to be politically active and influential. By contrast, those at the lower end of the socioeconomic spectrum, the very people most likely to be hurt by spending cuts and relatively untouched by income-based tax increases, face greater hurdles in political organizing and issue advocacy. Most past versions of a BBA have been tilted to the "spending cut" deficit solution, requiring supermajorities to raise taxes but only simple majorities to cut spending. Conservative advocates of a BBA, including the Heritage Foundation,[107] insist that otherwise the federal government will never cut bloated but popular entitlement programs. The counterargument, of course, is that making it easier to cut spending programs that benefit the poor disproportionately rather than to raise taxes violates fundamental principles of equity and fairness.[108] In any BBA regime, policymakers will have to take care not to ignore those with the greatest needs and quietest voices.

A Balanced Budget Amendment as Economic Policy and Political Principle

Does a BBA make sense from the perspective of sound economic policy? The economic debate has raged for decades without consensus, though a few salient conclusions have been reached.

The BBA discussion is often framed as a liberal-versus-conservative argument, though in the real world of politics, this black-and-white distinction has turned very gray. Since the mid-1990s some liberal Democrats have been as ardent as many conservative Republicans in calling for a balanced budget, and the fiscal profligacy of the Bush administration and the GOP Congress since 2001 is not defended by most conservatives. Nonetheless, most supporters of a BBA are properly categorized as economic conservatives since the main goal here is to force the "wasteful and inefficient" federal government to limit its own growth and let the private sector flourish.[109] Conservatives hope to duplicate at the federal level a state finding they believe is politically and economically encouraging: States that include supermajority provisions for raising revenue have lower spending. In such states, spending per capita increased at a rate of about 95 percent between 1980 and 1990, as opposed to a marginally higher rate of 102 percent in states without supermajority requirements.[110]

Many conservatives also reject Keynesian economic theory, which holds that federal deficit spending can help lift an economy out of recession. With interest payments on the federal debt alone already consuming $240 billion of the federal budget annually (more than the combined budgets of the Departments of Commerce, Agriculture, Education, Justice, Energy, Labor, Interior, Housing and Urban Development, State, and Transportation), commentators on the right argue that the ballooning debt presages an entitlement-generated budget crisis which must be addressed now.[111]

On the other hand, some traditional liberals are ready to defend deficit spending as both safe and necessary under certain conditions. The massive economic boom after World War II, which saw considerable deficit spending, serves as a vital reminder that there is no proven "iron law" correlation between economic strength and the size of the federal deficit. Karen M. Paget, writing for the *American Prospect*, asserted that the soundest fiscal policy for the federal government is simply to keep the annual increment added to the national debt below the rate of real economic growth.

> If the economy grows at 3 percent a year, and the deficit is 2 percent of GDP [gross domestic product], then the all-important debt-to-GDP ratio declines by one point every year. The difference between absolute budget balance and a deficit of 2 percent of GDP is about $160 billion a year of public outlay. It is the difference between massive cuts in public spending and the capacity to address national problems with public dollars. It is the difference between a liberal and a conservative view of fiscal policy.[112]

Obviously, there is not much room for agreement between, say, a liberal like Paget and the conservative Heritage Foundation. The key observation here is that a BBA clearly institutionalizes the classical conservative view over the modern liberal position in the field of fiscal policy.

An additional criticism of BBA proposals is connected to ideology. A BBA can prevent the federal government from exercising its role as a force for economic stability in times of recession. As mentioned earlier, should we adopt a strict BBA that does not permit exceptions for recession or wartime, the federal government would have to either cut spending, thereby reducing the purchasing power of citizens and undermining the recovery effort, or raise taxes, which would similarly take money out of the economy and stymie a recovery effort. Robert Reischauer, a former director of the Congressional

Budget Office, invoked the memory of the early 1930s, when the government's response to the Depression—cutting spending and raising taxes—only worsened the economic crisis.

> If it worked, [a balanced budget amendment] would undermine the stabilizing role of the federal government. [A depression or recession] temporarily lowers revenues and increases spending on unemployment insurance and welfare programs. This automatic stabilizing occurs quickly and is self-limiting—it goes away as the economy revives—but it temporarily increases the deficit. It is an important factor that dampens the amplitude of our economic cycles.[113]

Any welcome BBA, then, ought to include reasonable exceptions in the case of economic downturn and wartime, when the nation's survival and triumph must take precedence over fiscal responsibility, at least temporarily.

A Balanced Budget Amendment as Constitutional Policy

So much for the balanced budget in political and economic terms—and a mixed assessment it is. The most relevant question for us is this: Does a BBA make sense as a constitutional insertion?

In his testimony before the California legislature on the question of whether or not California should apply for a BBA-stimulated Constitutional Convention, the liberal constitutional scholar Laurence Tribe expressed intense opposition to the inclusion of budgetary policy within the text of the Constitution itself.[114] Tribe argued that constitutions ought to serve as embodiments of fundamental law, and hence should focus on the structure of the government and the relationship between its parts. Including *any* specific policy questions in the document is antithetical to this principle. As Tribe reminds us, the only economic arrangement the Constitution has ever explicitly endorsed is slavery, and the only social policy the Constitution ever enshrined was Prohibition. The precedents of slavery and Prohibition do not provide sound precedents for a BBA. Tribe argued:

> It demeaned our Constitution to embrace slavery and Prohibition not only because neither arrangement expressed the sorts of broad and enduring ideals to which the Constitution and the country can be committed—not just over a decade or two, but over centuries. The goal of fiscal austerity expresses no such ideals—notwithstanding its immediate popular appeal or the long-term soundness of at least some of its premises.[115]

Tribe's contentions underline that balanced budgets, tax limitations, and a fixed federal debt ceiling all flow from a particular economic theory and hence represent an ideologically based policy judgment.[116] These judgments have found their way into constitutional interpretation before. The most famous historical example of an economic policy being "read" into the Constitution occurred during the so-called Lochner era, which lasted from the late nineteenth century through most of the New Deal.[117] During this period, the Supreme Court essentially read a "liberty of contract" into the Constitution, holding that any economic regulation that interfered with the freedom of employer and employee to reach an agreement violated constitutional guarantees. This, in turn, led the Supreme Court to overturn all manner of workplace regulation statutes, such as child labor laws, maximum work hours per week, and other facets of New Deal legislation that we now consider vital elements of federal oversight in the workplace. It was in response to the original Lochner decision that Justice Oliver Wendell Holmes famously commented that the Constitution does not—and, by implication, should not—endorse any single economic theory.[118]

To counteract this reasoning, proponents of a BBA attempt to demonstrate that a balanced budget requirement actually solves key structural problems impeding sound fiscal policy, rather than sanctifying a particular economic policy. Several able proponents of BBAs, including the Yale law professor E. Donald Elliott in an article titled "Constitutional Conventions and the Deficit,"[119] have developed sophisticated arguments on this score.

Central to Elliott's argument is the claim that the founding fathers were simply wrong when they argued that their constitutional machinery could withstand pressure from special interest groups ("factions") in order to work toward the public good. Elliott cites James Madison on this point from *Federalist No. 10*: "If a faction consists of less than a majority, relief is supplied by the republican principle, which enables the majority to defeat its sinister views by regular vote. It [a minority faction] may clog the administration; it may convulse the society; but it will be unable to execute and mask its violence under the forms of the Constitution."[120]

Elliott argued that Madison failed to understand those structural features of the Constitution that would allow minority groups to wield dominant power over government policy, suggesting two explanations for this phenomenon. The first is central to so-called public choice literature,[121] which simply stipulates that politicians are inherently rational and therefore seek to do things that help their election or reelection. In this model, politicians will not pay attention to the interests of all of their constituents equally but will instead focus most on the concerns of those citizens who are better able to organize and influence the electoral process.

Elliott couples this to Mancur Olson's famous work on the "logic of collective action," embodied in a 1965 article (and later book) of the same name.[122] Olson attempted to show that individuals are always more likely to form political associations when the costs of a particular policy weigh more heavily on a discrete group, since doing so is overwhelmingly in their interests and not doing so will cost them dearly. In the alternative scenario, where the benefits of a particular policy are clear but very diffuse among a large section of the population, Olson maintains that it is very difficult for an advocacy group to organize. In this circumstance, the broad affected group may assume that reason will naturally prevail or that other members of the group will take the lead. This is the legendary logic of "let George do it," and when juxtaposed with the notion of politicians as rational election-seekers, it has major consequences for the government's fiscal policies—and it comprises one of the best arguments for a mandatory constitutional balanced budget mechanism.

In our system, day-to-day politics simply does not compel a legislator to bring the budget into balance. The benefits of a balanced budget are so diffuse that there is no powerful and aggressive constituency behind it, while running a deficit allows for greater government spending which will benefit smaller but more politically active and influential interest groups. As Elliott summarizes, "[By] creating a deficit and borrowing to finance it, politicians are able to confer benefits on current voters while imposing a portion of the costs on future generations who have to pay the bill. To put the point a different way, the interest group that is the weakest politically is the one that is even more difficult to organize than taxpayers—the unborn."[123]

Therefore, unhealthy budget deficits are a direct consequence of institutional mechanisms that make it not only easy but rational for politicians to acquiesce to special interest groups—at the expense of creating enormous costs for future generations. Viewed in this light, a BBA appears to solve a structural problem rather than a policy problem and hence is far more amenable to those who insist that the Constitution should only concern itself with fundamental law. Consider the experience of David Stockman, President Reagan's onetime budget-cutter-in-chief who told his story in a 1981 *Atlantic Monthly* article titled "The Education of David Stockman."[124] Stockman confessed that while he and his compatriots came to power determined to cut spending on the merits of particular programs, in practice they found this to be impossible. Stockman ultimately learned that "the power of [certain] client groups turned out to be stronger than [he] had realized. The client groups know how to make themselves heard. The problem is unorganized groups can't play in this game."

Of course, BBA opponents have a counterargument. There are other ways of remedying these institutional deficiencies, they say, without wrapping them in a clear policy prescription. These include more stringent rules for lobbying and campaign contributions, more explicit disclosure of the costs and benefits of federal tax legislation, et cetera.[125] Their counterargument would be more convincing had the numerous campaign and lobbying reforms adopted into law since Watergate been more effective. Yet every few years, reformers return with additional prescriptions because of new scandals that were supposed to be prevented by the earlier reforms.

Two additional BBA-related questions that have constitutional import need to be mentioned here. The first one concerns the supermajority requirement for waiving BBA strictures, usually three fifths of the membership of both houses of Congress. The problem is this: There may be situations beyond the noted exemptions for recessions and wars in which the only responsible course of action for Congress to take would be to waive the BBA in order to enter a necessary period of deficit spending. Natural disaster may be one. A series of Katrina-level hurricanes in one year, a major tsunami, or a large meteor impact could devastate large portions of the United States. Depending on the underlying state of the economy, a recession may well occur. Katrina did not cause a recession, for instance, since the economy was experiencing a strong rebound from several years of difficulty. Yet that did not make Katrina any less of a cause for massive, essential new spending. Faced with such a scenario, Congress would be constitutionally paralyzed unless it could garner the necessary supermajority in both houses. Thus, a minority party that commanded a mere two fifths of the Congress in just one house could wield enough power to block supermajority passage of a relief bill. Former representatives Dan Schaefer (R-CO) and Charles Stenholm (D-TX), who cosponsored a BBA in the mid-1990s, freely admitted that it would have the effect of "lowering the blackmail threshold from 50% plus one in either [house] to 40% plus one."[126] It may be that three fifths is too high a supermajority to suspend the BBA. Perhaps 55 percent in both houses is a more reasonable requirement for BBA waiving. Given the modern tendency of Congress to be fairly evenly divided between the parties, at least some members of the chief opposition party would be needed to suspend the

BBA. Yet it would still not be easy to bypass the balanced budget requirement. As always, we have to seek the golden mean. Too high a majority for BBA suspension can lead to unfortunate consequences, but so can too low a majority. If a mere simple majority of each house were all that was necessary for suspension, Congress might well get in the habit of annual BBA suspensions. At this point, the BBA would be meaningless.

The final constitutional point we should consider when evaluating a BBA as sound constitutional policy is an extreme case, but conceivable in these hyper-partisan times. Suppose the Congress is unable to muster the required supermajority necessary to allow for deficit spending while simultaneously it fails to pass a balanced budget. The question of what would happen was explored at some length in a *Columbia Law Review* article by Gay Aynesworth Crosthwait,[127] who made clear that there are no ideal scenarios under which such a budget crisis could be resolved. Leaving it up to the president to propagate a balanced budget in the face of congressional deadlock would constitute a huge shift in power toward the executive. Leaving enforcement to the Supreme Court is just as problematic. On the one hand, the Court might decide that such questions are nonjusticiable (inappropriate for the Court to decide, given the prerogatives of the other two federal branches)—rendering a BBA something of a nullity. Alternatively, the Court could determine (or be required by the text of a BBA itself) to sort out the constitutional mess created by congressional gridlock. There are essentially three possibilities.[128]

1. The Court could order Congress and the president to enact tax increases or program cuts necessary to achieve a balanced budget, and if either Congress or the president failed to do so, the Court could find the relevant actor(s) in contempt. This would of course be unprecedented.

2. The Court could order tax increases or budget cuts, and if Congress and the president failed to comply, the Court could design and enact such measures itself. This would signal a massive, unwelcome power transfer to the judiciary and place the courts in a more activist policy-making role than is consonant with American political tradition or the desire of the public.

3. The Court could strike down as unconstitutional all spending bills that led the government into deficit spending. Here, too, the Court would

exercise a commanding policy role. Which bills could be struck down? In what order? Which groups would suffer most at the hands of this "arbitrary" budget cutting?

As critics of BBA proposals are quick to point out, none of these solutions is attractive or likely to extricate the country happily from the constitutional crisis created by an intractable Congress unable to adopt a balanced budget. Is it too much to expect this scenario would never occur? One hopes for the best but fears the worst. Thus, this also argues for the 55 percent supermajority discussed above, rather than the three-fifths rule. There may also have to be a constitutional codicil that, in the instance of total congressional deadlock, as the end of the fiscal year approaches, a simple majority of each house may waive the balanced budget requirement. BBA proponents can only pray such a provision does not become an annual cop-out by Congress. If this becomes regular practice, it will be up to the voters to insist that the BBA be enforced, and that assumes a lot.

Budget in the Balance: The Tough Choice Facing the Convention

The question of a BBA is one of the thornier constitutional reform issues raised in this book, and for all the reasons discussed in this section, such an amendment is not a clear-cut choice for inclusion in a revised Constitution. The mixed analysis I have offered here is an indication that the BBA will make for a great debate at the convention.

Three points are worth reiterating and stressing.

1. Much of the political rhetoric surrounding the BBA debate is fundamentally misleading. Analogies to the family or private businesses obfuscate more than they clarify about federal budgetary policy. Just as important, state budgetary requirements are not appropriate analogues to the kinds of restrictions that would be created by a BBA. States rely on the federal government for much of their revenue; the states have a far more limited impact on the federal economy; and the states have developed a complicated regime of budgetary rules that work against their own balanced budget requirements.

2. It is wrong to assert that balanced budgets or constitutionally limited federal spending are absolute political pluses. Many intelligent policy analysts argue that some deficit spending, particularly deficit spending

that is indexed in accord with the rate of economic growth, is both desirable from a policy perspective and a necessary insurance policy against recession and economic downturn. Proponents of a BBA have not yet definitively proven these critics wrong, meaning that endorsing a BBA is necessarily to back a controversial set of policy claims about the economy and the desired size of government.

3. A BBA is not the only mechanism that would limit the institutional forces leading to deficit spending. Members of Congress could enforce a balanced budget regime any time they chose, simply by insisting on it, and refusing to approve any budget that did not provide for one. The voters could create a balanced budget imperative by ousting any member of Congress who would not vote for it when the budget came up for a vote in the House or the Senate.

Rhetoric aside, legislators are unlikely to cause more pain and suffering among their constituents than absolutely necessary, and voters are even more unlikely to request the same. It is true that in 1992, Ross Perot received 19 percent of the national presidential vote by running on a deficit-elimination platform, and that his success caused President Clinton and the Congress to move toward a balanced budget in the 1990s. It is also true that (1) a billionaire, self-financing, deficit-determined candidate such as Ross Perot does not come around very often; (2) a magnificent, technology-driven, maybe once-in-a-century golden economy filled the federal Treasury to overflowing and actually enabled the federal officeholders to fulfill their balanced budget promise for a few years in the late 1990s;[129] and (3) once a new recession and 9/11 rolled in during 2001, the balanced budget was an immediate casualty, with deficits soaring in the hundreds of billions of dollars annually ever since.[130]

No, political behavior among both officeholders and voters seems relatively fixed with respect to spending and taxes and deficits. The bad, special-interest spending takes place in other states and districts, not one's own, where spending is good and in the national interest. Taxes must be kept low—always considerably lower than the level of spending, so that free lunches abound. And deficits are just big numbers that mean nothing to the average American.

Except that the deficits matter a great deal for fiscal solvency in the future. Those of us who have let this situation continue for decades are selfishly living at the expense of today's children or tomorrow's grandchildren. Sooner or later, the deficits have to be curtailed or stopped, at least in prosperous years when the Treasury overflows, and the debt drawn down, lest interest payments consume an increasing share of annual tax revenues—a dreadful situation that would limit the federal government's ability to meet the urgent needs of forthcoming American generations. Already, almost a tenth of the annual federal budget is eaten up by interest payments—$229 billion just in one year, 2007![131] Imagine how much good could be done in education or health care or national security with this additional $229 billion—almost $763 per person, available to be spent on the legitimate requirements of every man, woman, and child in America. And this spending is annual; over a decade, more than $7,500 per person could be devoted to programs that help Americans.

For many decades, under Republican and Democratic presidents alike, the country has thrown an expensive party, but the sad thing is, future Americans are bequeathed the hangover. Despite all the difficulties, misrepresentations, and questionable argumentation that some have offered for a Balanced Budget Amendment, Thomas Jefferson's warning with which this section began still resonates. We are indeed "swindling futurity," and for that reason the new Constitutional Convention should design and adopt a balanced budget requirement. The particulars are important—and the traditional, strict BBA will have to be watered down to make it workable (55 percent supermajority, end-of-fiscal-year escape clause, etc.). But whatever the details, a Balanced Budget Amendment in the Constitution will be a powerful symbol that the nation values fiscal responsibility. The principle is vital—a principle about which all parents should think when they ponders their children's senior years, and which all teachers should consider when they look at their students. These children and students may judge us harshly, and justifiably so, if we fail in this basic test of character, discipline, and foresight on their behalf.

CONTINUITY OF GOVERNMENT: PREPARING FOR THE UNTHINKABLE

The events of September 11, 2001, made all Americans think about the unthinkable. One of the hijacked planes—the aircraft courageously commandeered by passengers who died in the Pennsylvania crash—was probably headed for the U.S. Capitol. Had the terrorists completed their mission on Constitution Avenue and drove the jetliner into the Capitol dome, hundreds of members of Congress conceivably could have been killed simultaneously.

At a moment of maximum crisis, the United States might have been left without a functioning federal legislature, with no quick way to restore Congress to full capacity. The stakes are too high to allow this potential tragedy to occur. Violent terrorist acts are not always preventable, but at least the continuity of government can be assured with a well-constructed provision in the new Constitution.

Concern over doomsday scenarios involving the death or incapacitation of legislators and government officials is not new. Continuity of Government (COG) plans have existed in earnest ever since the early 1950s, when the threat of a U.S.-Soviet nuclear war prompted President Harry S. Truman to begin developing an elaborate and secretive infrastructure for continuing government operations even under the most apocalyptic conditions. Truman's successors advanced his efforts, but some of these programs lapsed following the fall of the Soviet Union. However, the terrorist attacks on foreign soil that occurred in the mid-1990s led President Bill Clinton to sign an executive order requiring all departments and agencies to draw up contingency plans for resuming critical functions in the hours following a warning of impending disaster.[132] On 9/11, many of these COG programs were put to the test—and it is now clear that they failed outright.[133]

President George W. Bush's administration has since tried to reinvigorate COG programs. For example, in June 2006, four thousand government workers participated in a massive COG exercise involving dozens of classified facilities along the mid-Atlantic. The evaluations have been mixed, but no doubt progress has been made in some areas.

However, the progress does not include Congress in the event of a massive calamity. The Continuity of Government Commission, launched as a joint project by the D.C.-based Brookings Institution and the American Enterprise Institute in the fall of 2002, described an all-too-imaginable nightmare in the first pages of its official report on COG and the Congress.[134] The commission envisioned a debilitating terrorist attack on a presidential inauguration ceremony, killing the president-elect, the vice president–elect, the Speaker of the House, the president pro tempore of the Senate, and many dozens of other senators and congressmen. As frightening as such a scenario is for presidential succession, it is even more troubling for a decimated Congress. Thanks to the Twentieth, Twenty-second, and Twenty-fifth amendments and supplementary legislation, the succession to the presidency and its likely operation under almost any scenario is guaranteed. The same cannot be said for Congress. While the Seventeenth Amendment to the Constitution allows state governors (if their legislatures assent) to fill Senate vacancies by executive appointment, no such provision exists for House vacancies. Article I, Section 2 of the Constitution explicitly states that the only remedy for a House vacancy is a special election. The COG Commission then responsibly asked: What would happen if only a handful of House members survived the attack? Could Congress, and hence the federal government, still function?

It's possible, but barely. The Constitution makes clear that a "Majority of each [house of Congress] shall constitute a Quorum to do Business."[135] The individual houses of Congress, however, are permitted to set their own rules of procedure so long as they do not explicitly violate the Constitution, and on a number of occasions (beginning with the challenge posed by the absence of southern congressmen during the Civil War) the House of Representatives has clarified its interpretation of what, exactly, constitutes a quorum. Ever since a decision made by Speaker Joseph Cannon in 1906, a *quorum* has been understood to be a "majority of those members chosen, sworn, and living, whose membership has not been terminated by resignation or by the action of the House."[136] Under this interpretation, the handful of surviving House members could conduct the House's business following a terrorist attack. Still, while the House could continue to function with only a few members, there is grave doubt about whether or not the actions of such a pale shadow of the full House would be seen as legitimate or would go unchallenged by a future Congress.

More vexing, however, is the problem of incapacitation. There is no constitutional procedure for replacing, be it by appointment or by special election, those congressmen who are unable to fulfill their duties. In the past this has led to some highly unfortunate situations, when House or Senate members were too infirm or ill to take up their duties but sometimes refused to resign for years.[137] However, these instances are minor compared to what might happen if terrorists unleashed radiological, biological, or chemical weapons on Congress, possibly leaving a majority of members in one or both houses alive but totally incapacitated. In such a scenario, neither house would be able to conduct business in the absence of a quorum, yet the incapacitated members would remain irrevocably in office until they resigned or died—neither of which, according to the terms of this hypothetical, they would necessarily be able to do. What then?

In the case of incapacitation, a constitutional amendment is essential for both houses. Governors should be able to appoint temporary members of both the Senate and the House. There is relatively little controversy about governors filling Senate seats where the senators have become incapacitated, since in almost all states, governors already perform this function when senators die or resign.[138] As discussed later in this section, it is essential to require that the substitute appointees be of the same political party as the incapacitated members, so as to prevent an inadvertent shift in party control of the House or the Senate.[139]

For the House, though, gubernatorial appointment is more controversial. From a philosophical perspective, there is a strong argument to be made for the filling of the House of Representatives by election only, regardless of the circumstances. The "people's house" is, by design, the institution of national government meant to be closest to the electorate. In the nation's history, every single member of the House has been elected, even during the Civil War and Reconstruction, as well as other crises. The appointment of representatives, even under the horrific contingency of a terrorist attack, strikes some as contrary to a fundamental principle of American government. The AEI/Brookings report led to the formation of an organized group dedicated to defeating proposals for a constitutional amendment allowing for the appointment of House members: the Committee to Preserve an Elected Congress (CPEC).[140] These critics[141] often cite the founders, such as James Madison in his *Federalist No. 52*: "As it is essential to liberty that the government in general should have a common interest with the people, so it is particularly essential that the branch of it under consideration should have an immediate dependence on, and an intimate sympathy with, the people. Frequent elections are unquestionably the only policy by which this dependence and sympathy can be effectually secured."[142]

Certainly an elected House of Representatives is the ideal, but a catastrophic terrorist attack leaves only two possibilities: Either Congress is unable to function at all until after special elections are held, or Congress continues to act, but with a far-reduced membership that calls into question the legitimacy of the legislature. Some insist that Congress should simply pass legislation dictating that, in the instance of a national disaster in which a large number of representatives are killed, the states hold expedited special elections to fill the vacancies as soon as possible. Yet from a practical standpoint, it is unclear in the aftermath of a terrorist attack whether the country would be capable of organizing impromptu elections in hundreds of districts. Elections are complex logistical affairs. Even if party primaries were eliminated and candidates were nominated directly by political party committees, the challenge of assembling these enterprises quickly would still be immense. It is virtually impossible for even expedited elections to be held across the country in less than several months; meanwhile, Congress could well be paralyzed.

It is undeniably true that the country survives—quite nicely—during the long breaks Congress typically takes in the summer and other holiday periods, but following a terrorist attack, the nation would almost certainly require a fully functioning legislature, both for symbolic reassurance and specific recovery legislation, including fiscal appropriations and a possible declaration of war. Also, suppose the terrorist strike disproportionately killed members of one political party or representatives from one region (perhaps due to a caucus meeting near the site of a bomb)? Is the remaining, far less diverse House, though elected, more representative than a partially appointed House would be?

It is also worth considering the disturbing scenario in which an attack kills lawmakers in the presidential line of succession. A dysfunctional House would not be able to consent to the appointment of a new vice president or select a new Speaker. The presidency might then have to pass to a member of the presidential cabinet, a possibly little-known, unelected individual who could have less legitimacy in the public's eyes.

The critics are right about one basic argument. The principle of elected representative government is a precious cornerstone of American democracy, and it should not be altered except in the most dire of circumstances, and then only temporarily and cautiously. A constitutional provision that provides for continuity of government must be carefully drawn. It should be a concise clause that permits Congress to provide for the details of the temporary appointment procedure in legislation, such as the following: "Congress shall have the power to regulate by law the filling of vacancies that may occur in the House of Representatives and Senate in the event that a substantial number of members are killed or incapacitated. Congress shall have the power to determine when this Amendment shall be operative, and how it shall be operative, through appropriate legislation."[143]

The particulars of such a plan are worth detailing, since they would constitute the essence of the American democratic government in the instance of a disaster.[144] When a large number of members are killed or incapacitated, temporary replacements will be made immediately to fill vacant seats and to stand in for incapacitated members. What would constitute a "large number"?

One approach would classify as an emergency enough vacancies to constitute a substantial proportion of the House (perhaps a minimum of 25 percent), while another option would designate a number of vacancies equal to a majority of members in at least half of the state delegations—anywhere from 55 (12 percent of the House membership—if, somehow, all the vacancies occurred in the states with the fewest representatives) to 199 (46 percent of House membership—if all vacancies occurred in states with the most representatives).

Temporary appointments, in cases of both vacancies and death, should be made by governors, selected from a succession list of three qualified residents of the state or district, drawn up in advance by the member who holds the seat. The succession list, which should be filed by every representative and senator with the governor upon the member of Congress's election, is a clever way to avoid an unintended switch of party control that would happen if a governor were to appoint a congressman from a party other than the incumbent's. It would also prevent political games, barring a governor from picking a pliable member of the other party who might not vote as the deceased or incapacitated member would have done. Members of Congress would undoubtedly choose their successors with care, knowing their legacy and pet programs could hang in the balance. Ideally, one provision of the law would strictly prohibit relatives (blood or by marriage) from the members' lists; there is too much nepotism in congressional seats as it is.[145]

In the case of incapacitated members, replacements should stand in for their congressman or senator until the member recovers, the member dies and the vacancy is filled, or until the end of the term. In the case of deceased House members, the appointment would last only until the end of the term or until the state could arrange a full-fledged special election (depending on how early it is in the term). In the case of deceased senators, the appointment would last until a special election or until the next regularly scheduled federal election—thus, a maximum of two years, just as it is now for appointed senators chosen by governors to replace members who die or resign.

All Americans hope that we will never need to use the COG provision in the Constitution, but in these perilous times, we had better be prepared. Some members of Congress from both parties have tried to move forward on the idea,[146] but as usual the inertia and resistance to change within Congress has proven impossible to surmount.[147] As with so many other items advocated in this volume, it may take a new Constitutional Convention to bring this necessary reform proposal into being.

*

There can be no doubt that the changes outlined in this chapter would substantially reshape Congress. The Senate would be a larger, more representative body, with heavily populated states adding seats. The upper legislative chamber would also be a place to harness the experience and talents of former presidents and vice presidents. The House would be renewed as well, mainly by redistricting reform to build in more electoral competition. Following the founders' original intent, the size of the House would be expanded considerably to draw congressman and constituent closer together. To reduce the number of "professional politicians" and increase public confidence in Congress, generous term limits would be applied to both House and Senate. For the sake of the country's future generations, a reasonable Balanced Budget Amendment would be added to the Constitution's text. And both the Senate and the House would be protected by a Continuity of Government provision.

The essence of the legislative branch will be a constant, of course. It will continue to check the executive, persist in representing the magnificent diversity of a continental country, and maintain its place as the undisputed source of democratic law in the Republic. But the reforms proposed here can scrub the sclerosis from the legislative arteries, thus assisting the Congress in carrying out its mandate and renewing its treasured place in the American federal system.

CHAPTER TWO

★

PERFECTING THE PRESIDENCY

FOR ALL OF Congress's problems, the public complains more loudly about the presidency most of the time. It's not hard to see why. First, the presidency has become the premier branch of government, even though it is listed second in the Constitution (and therefore, appropriately, in this book). All television cables lead to the White House, and when disaster strikes, the American people turn first to their chief executive. The framers would be surprised to see just how dominant the president is in the modern era—but then our forefathers could not have imagined our hardwired world, brimming with hair-trigger weapons and dangerous threats. This reality requires split-second decisions in wartime and peacetime, the kind of decisiveness only a unitary executive can provide. Second, citizens' dissatisfaction with the contemporary presidency goes beyond the many controversial individuals who have held the post since the 1960s. The flaws of, say, Lyndon Johnson, Richard Nixon, Jimmy Carter, Bill Clinton, and George W. Bush were real enough and character-based, but their personal faults have been magnified by the constitutional imperfections in their office.

Let's mention just two examples. We Americans have become all too familiar with wars and "police actions" initiated mainly or solely by presidents, such as Johnson's Vietnam War, Nixon's invasions of Laos and Cambodia, Ronald Reagan's moves into Grenada and Lebanon, George H. W. Bush's incursions into Panama and then the Persian Gulf, Clinton's entry into Haiti and Bosnia, and George W. Bush's wars in Afghanistan and Iraq. Observers differ drastically about the merits of each of these conflicts, but the point here is that one man made the decision in every case, sometimes after little or no real consultation with Congress. Even when Congress was formally consulted and cast a vote (as with the Persian Gulf, Afghanistan, and Iraq), presidents made clear that in their view they had full authority to make war whether Congress agreed or not, and that they reserved the right to move forward in the case of a contrary decision by the legislative branch.[1] It's a rare American who hasn't worried about the president's unfettered war-making powers. Granted, Republicans mainly balked about Bill Clinton's actions while Democrats were the ones who targeted George W. Bush, but partisanship does not necessarily make the concerns less valid. The Constitution equitably divides war-making powers between the president and Congress, but that sharing has become theoretical rather than actual. Wouldn't a restoration of some reasonable balance between the branches give us greater protection from ill-fated and poorly thought out foreign adventures that take many young lives and drain our national Treasury?

Second, in the realm of politics, Americans now openly complain about the permanent campaign that consumes far too much of a president's time in office. Half or more of the first term is spent seeking a second. We no longer evaluate what a chief executive says or does without interpreting it substantially through the prism of the next campaign. Opponents from the other major political party are openly jockeying and electioneering to the president's detriment just months into his term. This reduces the opportunities for presidents to accomplish things in the national interest, and it encourages a cynical overemphasis on politics as the complete motivation and explanation for everything. Is there a way to restructure the presidency to maximize the prospects for achievement and minimize the tendency of White Houses to focus too soon and too heavily on reelection?

Any reform of the presidency has to be flexible enough to accommodate chief executives of widely varying talents and backgrounds, and sufficiently elastic to enable its occupants to deal effectively with crises of all types, from war to depression to insurrection, and more. Most of all, the top executive post must remain able to combine, in one person, the often contradictory roles of chief of state, head of government, and boss of party faction.

The office did not emerge easily from the Constitutional Convention. The founders were naturally suspicious of a strong executive, having just endured the excesses of the British Crown's royal governors in colonial times. Inevitably, proposals to limit the executive were plentiful, including one to create a "committee of three" to represent the administrative branch of government,[2] and another to encumber the president with a limiting "council,"[3] while placing the legislature on a constitutional pedestal. Fortunately for the United States, no three-headed hydras or committee camels were approved in the end. The founders agreed with Jefferson when he wrote, "173 despots would surely be as oppressive as one."[4] The sad experience with a powerless executive and an inefficient, and relatively toothless, Congress under the Articles of Confederation in the 1780s caused many to wonder whether the young Republic could survive. The president was merely the figurehead chairman of the unicameral Congress; he had a one-year term and no special powers separate from the legislature. (Technically, George Washington was not the first president of the United States, he was the ninth. Eight men served one-year terms as "President of the United States of America in Congress assembled" under the Articles of Confederation, beginning with John Hanson of Maryland.[5]) As for the Congress, it derived its authority not from the people but from the state legislatures, which chose and paid its delegates to Congress. Every state, regardless of size, had a single vote in Congress, and a two-thirds vote was required to approve many vital measures. Even worse, the Congress had no power to levy taxes, merely the ability to ask states politely for needed finances. This "league of friendship" among the states, which left no one actually in charge, failed miserably, and the outcome stiffened the founders' spines for what was needed.

What was needed, of course, was a presidency filled by a unifying figure for the nation—already obvious in George Washington—and an office commensurate with Washington's substantial skills and containing sufficient powers to counter the threats, domestic and foreign, that were clearly on the horizon. So the new country gained an "elective kingship,"[6] large enough to rise above "faction," deal with Congress as an equal, and command respect at home and abroad. At the same time, the founders believed they had created enough checks and balances to keep the president from becoming a dictator or completely overriding the will of Congress and the states. This was a delicate balance, all derived from Article II's simple statement that "the executive Power shall be vested in a President of the United States of America," plus nine specific grants of power such as receiving ambassadors, vetoing laws, and making key appointments.[7]

The balance held, more or less, into the twentieth century. Some presidents had a greater impact than others, through sheer force of will, vision, talent, and the circumstances of history. Thomas Jefferson, Andrew Jackson, Abraham Lincoln, and Theodore Roosevelt were extraordinary presidents for their eras, but over time—and after their terms, during which the presidency became exceptionally dominant—a reasonable balance between the executive and the legislative branches was restored almost naturally. Weaker presidents usually succeeded the stronger chief executives, and the power of personality vanished from the White House.[8]

The events of the twentieth century altered the balance between the branches for good. National and international emergencies—World War I, the Great Depression and a series of intermittent but serious recessions (one or two per decade), World War II, Korea, the Cold War, Vietnam, 9/11, and the War on Terrorism—made the presidency front and center for most Americans. Only the president was in a position to make the quick decisions needed to handle all these übercrises, and gradually he gathered up emergency powers to deal with them. The advent of television greatly augmented presidential authority; with the president able to command center stage on TV, a kind of "electronic throne" was created.[9]

Briefly in the 1970s, the "imperial presidency," as the historian and former Kennedy aide Arthur Schlesinger Jr. called it,[10] came crashing down, a result of the excesses of Johnson, Nixon, Vietnam, Watergate, a presidential resignation, and the Democratic congressional landslide of 1974. Presidents Gerald Ford (R) and Jimmy Carter (D) bore the brunt of the backlash to imperial trappings, and they were forced to share more power with Congress than their immediate predecessors. The War Powers Resolution of 1973, congressional revocation of some presidential emergency authority, and a serious attempt by Congress to regain the upper hand in budget making were all part of this development.[11]

But the change was temporary and transient. The enfeebled presidency was a very brief phenomenon, affecting only Presidents Nixon, Ford, and Carter, and ended by a voter revolt against Carter in November 1980. Responding to America's international humiliation during the Iranian hostage crisis of 1979–81, plus a persistently weak economy, the electorate gave Ronald Reagan and the Republicans a landslide victory in 1980.[12] Reagan and many nonpartisan observers interpreted the vote as support for a tougher, more robust presidency at home and abroad—a renewed energy in the White House that continued to be seen in the administrations of Reagan's successors. Presidential freedom of action was expanded further by the terrorist threat visible after September 11, 2001.

Given America's status as the world's only remaining superpower and the president's omnipresent status at the top of the nation's power pyramid, it is both inevitable and unalterable today that the chief executive will win the contest for dominance within the United States' governmental system. Any effort to change the executive-legislative-judicial balance of power in an overall sense will be wasted and fruitless, perhaps with the sole exceptions of war-making powers and the budgetary item veto. However, the appropriate question to ask is: Have we structured the presidency properly so that the occupant of the highest office can accomplish the greatest good in the least time? Or is the modern presidency too hampered by political machinations and a lack of support in the Congress and the courts to work as well as it should? There are various ways of considering these fundamental queries, beginning with an examination of the president's term of office.

THE PRESIDENTIAL TERM OF CHOICE

The four-year term of office for president is deeply ingrained in our national schedule and psyche. It seemed reasonable enough in 1787, a good compromise between the short, two-year U.S. House term, which forced members of the lower house of Congress to stay close to their constituencies, and the six-year U.S. Senate term that gave its members a lengthy hold on office and the luxury, in theory, to consider the national interest. For the first thirty-five years of the Republic, just the House was popularly elected. Senators were chosen by the state legislatures and presidents by the elite, state-based Electoral College. Gradually, however, states began offering qualified voters an opportunity to register their preferences about presidential candidates at the ballot box. For the first presidential election in 1789, just four states (Delaware, Maryland, Pennsylvania, and Virginia) held direct popular elections to choose members of the Electoral College; other states used a combination of methods to pick electors, mainly selection by the state legislature. By 1824, citizens in eighteen states had been granted the right to vote for electors, with only six retaining state legislative selection. However, the popular votes had no real influence on the outcome, since the vote winner, Andrew Jackson, was denied his victory first in the Electoral College and then in the U.S. House of Representatives, with runner-up John Quincy Adams emerging with the presidency.[13] Much of the public was outraged by this denial of nascent "popular democracy," and between 1824 and 1828, more states yielded to the public election method. With citizens in twenty-two states voting at the ballot box in 1828 (and only two states, Delaware and South Carolina, denying their electorates the choice of electors), Jackson took his revenge, ousting Adams from the White House in a landslide.[14] Now, the precedent was clearly set, and so-called Jacksonian democracy—the right of Americans to choose electors and many other public officials by themselves at the polling places—became dominant almost everywhere in the young country.[15] No longer could presidents govern for the vast majority of the four-year term, turning only occasionally to plotting and scheming for the next Electoral

College selection. Instead, slowly but with inexorable motion, the process of politics, of seeking votes, consumed a greater and greater portion of the term.

For the first century or so, political maneuverings came to dominate only one half to two thirds of the fourth year of the term. As winter gave way to spring in the election year, and easy travel could resume, politicians gathered in Washington and state capitals to talk and act in preparation for the parties' presidential nominating conventions and the general election to follow in early November. While significant, the devouring of this portion of time was tolerable and necessary for the health of the democratic process. Early in the twentieth century, though, the next step in the politicization of the presidential term took place: the advent of popular primaries.

A product of the Progressive movement, the idea of the primary as a method to eliminate "boss control" of the political parties was inspired by U.S. senator Robert La Follette of Wisconsin. Beginning with his state in 1902, fully forty-seven states adopted statutes in just six years that required primary elections for many offices.[16] Mostly, these laws affected elections for statewide posts and some district and local positions.[17] But immediately in a few states, decades later in most others, popular primaries were added to select delegates to the national nominating conventions.[18] By 1968, sixteen states and the District of Columbia held presidential primaries from late March until early June, with New Hampshire taking the lead-off role as it had done for decades.[19]

The period from 1968 to the present can fairly be called the "age of the primary." Normally now, at least forty of the fifty states conduct presidential primaries, beginning in January with New Hampshire and ending in early June.[20] The starting date for primaries has crept back almost three months as other states have jockeyed for influence by establishing their own primaries—and increasingly, "front-loading" them as early in the process as possible, when the nominees are usually (but not always) effectively chosen.[21] Furthermore, other states, especially Iowa, have chosen the *caucus* method of nomination. The caucus is a gathering of party activists who spend several hours discussing, and then voting among, the candidates. While the caucus is more "elite" than a larger-turnout primary election (that is, it draws many fewer participants consisting mainly of the most dedicated party workers), this method of delegate selection has begun to attract just as much media attention. This is especially true of Iowa, which traditionally precedes the New Hampshire primary by eight days, guaranteeing an even earlier start to the presidential nominating season.[22] Therefore, the entire fourth year of the president's term (assuming the chief executive is running for reelection) is devoted to reelection politics.

As you well know, of course, reelection is far more consuming than that. The real presidential season begins at least a full year earlier, right after the conclusion of the midterm congressional elections. Most presidential candidates now announce their White House bids in the weeks following that November election. This is essential, since they need at least a year to campaign for the nomination contests. Thus, the next presidential contest begins in earnest before the president has even reached the halfway mark in his first term! The average incumbent president certainly has politics on his mind a fair amount even in the first two years, but it will not consume him unless he is facing a serious intraparty rival for the nomination. However, if that happens, politics becomes Job One at the White House for years prior to the election; the bipartisan examples of President Ford, who knew rather quickly after his succession to the Oval Office that former California governor Ronald Reagan would likely be challenging him for renomination in 1976, and President Carter, who faced as of 1979 a devastating renomination assault from Senator Ted Kennedy, prove the point. Of survivalist necessity, reelection politics ruled the roost in both White Houses. Ford and Carter managed to fend off their intraparty rivals, but the challenges unquestionably contributed to their November defeats.

Therefore, the structure of the system today guarantees full-fledged campaigning for at least half of the president's four-year term. There is nothing inherently wrong with doses of politics at key moments during the term; nor is a focus on political choices in the final months of the term anything but good for the public. Yet constant, unremitting political battle with potential foes is a serious drain on a president's time and energies, and it almost certainly causes presidents to make policy choices less for their governmental wisdom than for their political salability. Is this productive for the country? Or should the system be restructured to permit presidents to focus like a laser on their programmatic responsibilities for most of the term, with the political season telescoped into a shorter span of time? And does the current constitutional arrangement for presidents of two, four-year terms add to the problem?

Because of the precedent set by George Washington in refusing to seek a third term that he would certainly have won, presidents—with the exception only of Franklin Roosevelt—have maintained the two-term limit. At times, some attempted or actively hoped to go beyond two terms. The Republican U. S. Grant may have been willing to accept a third term had it been offered by his party in 1876,[23] and the Democrat Woodrow Wilson wanted a third term in 1920, despite his physical incapacity.[24] The Republican Theodore Roosevelt served almost all of assassinated William McKinley's second term from 1901 to 1905, followed by his own elected term from 1905 to 1909. The young president perhaps unwisely declared on election night 1904 that he would not seek election to a third term in 1908, which would have been Roosevelt's for the asking.[25] Dissatisfied with his handpicked successor, William Howard Taft, Roosevelt challenged Taft's renomination in 1912, and despite impressive primary victories, the GOP bosses stuck to the incumbent. So Roosevelt marched off and formed the Bull Moose third party, and outpolled Taft by a wide margin in both the popular vote in November and the Electoral College vote—while losing the general election to Woodrow Wilson, thanks to the split in the GOP.[26] Within a half-dozen years, Roosevelt had made amends, and amazingly, he appeared to be the likely Republican nominee for president in 1920, and thus the next president, given the GOP landslide that was coming for the party that year.[27] Sadly, Roosevelt died unexpectedly at the age of sixty in 1919. TR would have been the first president to secure a third term and serve almost twelve years (or more, if he had sought a fourth term) as president. Instead, that honor would go to another Roosevelt, distant cousin Franklin.

FDR set a record—four election victories and 12.1 years as president—that, under the current Constitution, will never be surpassed. That is because of the backlash to Roosevelt's revocation of George Washington's two-term precedent. The Twenty-second Amendment to the Constitution, adopted in 1951, was pushed hard by Republicans who had opposed Roosevelt's third and fourth terms. It took effect in time to stop the popular two-term Republican president Dwight Eisenhower from seeking the third term he wanted, and would probably have won, in 1960. The only other president who has been a sure bet to win a third term since Ike, Ronald Reagan, was also a Republican, of course. Despite his advanced age of seventy-seven, and his status as the oldest president in American history, Reagan stated repeatedly that if the Constitution had not prevented him, he would have run again in 1988. Both Eisenhower and Reagan called for the abolition of the Twenty-second Amendment, without success.[28] With a better crystal ball, the GOP might not have insisted on the Twenty-second Amendment, a good example of the unintended consequences of reform.

The long and short of the Twenty-second Amendment is that it limits all presidents to two elected terms, whether they are consecutive or, like President

Grover Cleveland's terms (1885–89, 1893–97), nonconsecutive.* It is true that the very occasional president who succeeds to the Oval Office and serves less than half of his predecessor's term can serve up to ten full years in the White House. Only Lyndon Johnson qualified under this provision, and as it happened, he did not exercise his right to run for a second full term in 1968.[29]

Therefore, under current conditions in most circumstances, a president has less than two years in office during his first term before reelection politics begins intensively. Should he be fortunate enough to be reelected to a second and final term, the president is an instant lame duck. If he is very lucky, he may get a short honeymoon of influence with Congress and the American people, but under the best of circumstances, that will last a year or so before his influence begins to ebb considerably. His potential successors, running for an attractive open shot at the presidency (no incumbent in the contest), line up early and are numerous in both parties. In most cases, presidential politics begins even earlier and is even more dominant in the second term than in the first. One could persuasively argue, then, that under our prevailing Twenty-second Amendment regime, an eight-year president has perhaps three years (two years in term one, one year in term two) of undivided attention from the press and public to accomplish his agenda—before the circus begins coming to town for the next election go-round. Is there a better alternative?

THE SIX-YEAR TERM

The most frequently suggested option is the one six-year term for the presidency, which would not be renewable (that is, one term to a person in a lifetime).[30] Over many decades, scholars and practitioners have constructed a good case for the six-year term. First, as noted above, a four-year term is increasingly eaten up by the political schedule; nothing wastes time, resources, and capital for a president and his chief advisers like planning for a reelection campaign, say advocates of the six-year term. In addition, more than a few presidential scandals can be traced, in whole or in part, to reelection pressures—from bad appointments and sold ambassadorships to a little episode called "Watergate."[31] Elections are not the only time wasters in a presidency. A new president, especially one who has not been vice president or served at the highest levels of a previous administration, will take the first year to a year and a half just to get

* Cleveland, Democrat, was defeated for reelection in 1888 by the Republican Benjamin Harrison, who in turn lost reelection to Cleveland in 1892.

adjusted in this unique office. Also, Congress often takes many months to confirm a president's senior officials, and some studies conclude that, because of all the lengthy background checks required of modern nominees, this interregnum period is growing.[32] The longer a president is "home alone," the lengthier the transition for him. Much of the federal budget is also preset for a year or longer, limiting the influence a new chief executive can have.

Beyond these advantages, argue the six-year-term reformers, the lack of worry about reelection would free up a president to focus on the true national interest rather than his personal election interests. Long ago, in the 1830s, Alexis de Tocqueville made precisely this point in his seminal *Democracy in America.*

> It is impossible to consider the ordinary course of affairs in the United States without perceiving that the desire to be re-elected is the chief aim of the President; that the whole policy of his administration, and even his most indifferent measures, tend to this object . . . If ineligible a second time, the President would not be independent of the people, for his responsibility would not cease; but the favor of the people would not be so necessary to him as to induce him to submit in every respect to its desires.[33]

Without the possibility of reelection, presidents would have no motive to postpone controversial decisions, and their critics would be deprived of the frequently heard plaint that the occupant of the White House took specific actions just to ensure his reelection. Might public cynicism decline as a consequence?[34]

Finally, some of the best debating points in favor of six years can be awarded for the perceived advantages to the presidency of two additional years to the normal term. Congress and the bureaucracy, lacking any statutory term limits, are often inclined to "wait out" a president they do not like; six guaranteed years for the president would make this less likely (though still possible). The extra couple of years would also give presidents a chance to follow up on their most important policies, reducing bureaucratic foot-dragging and guaranteeing greater implementation. And the most persuasive argument of all for the six-year term may be in the foreign policy arena, where personal relationships with other nations' leaders—nurtured over time—can assist America's global efforts in this dangerous post-9/11 world. Once again, the absence of reelection impulses might well permit presidents to act more often and more decisively in the country's best interests, whether those actions were popular or not.[35]

And yet the case for the six-year term is far from airtight. Most of the advocates seem to prefer an antiseptic, apolitical presidency that is neither possible nor wise. The check of reelection is a vital one on the powerful chief executive, every bit the equal of the Constitution's many official checks and balances. To insist that responsiveness to public opinion is somehow antithetical to a successful administration borders on the antidemocratic. To mix our metaphors with purpose, politics is the oil that greases the creaky machinery of government, and it is the glue that holds together the most ethnically and racially diverse democracy on the face of the earth.* And even if these arguments could be overcome, how exactly does an individual who has practiced politics all during adult life, and reached the pinnacle of politics, go cold turkey? All the usual sins of political pandering might well appear just as visible in a six-year term as under the current reelection scheme. Was there less politics in the second Reagan or Clinton terms compared to their first? That would be a difficult case to make. Wouldn't the greater threat in a six-year system be the one identified by the late U.S. senator J. William Fulbright in his famous book about presidential misdeeds in Vietnam, *The Arrogance of Power*? "Power tends to confuse itself with virtue," Fulbright observed, "and a great nation is peculiarly susceptible to the idea that its power is a sign of God's favor, conferring upon it a special responsibility for other nations—to make them richer and happier and wiser, to remake them, that is, in its own shining image."[36] Power is intoxicating for all leaders, and a president without the threat of humiliation by defeat would be potentially dangerous.

The best argument against the six-year term is the most widely accepted. Six years may simply be too long for bad presidents, and it is certainly too short for good ones. Concerning the former, we Americans don't like to admit we make mistakes in choosing presidents, having been told by politicians for eons how much wisdom we collectively have. But the results of American elections prove the point. Of the thirty-five presidents who have actively sought reelection, fifteen have been denied it (five for party renomination and ten in the general election)—fully 43 percent.[37] By comparison, since World War II, only about 8 percent of U.S. House members seeking another term have been denied it. Would Democrats have wanted President Herbert Hoover (R) to have continued his failed presidency for another two years during the depths

* It's not India; it's the United States. Literally every significant ethnic, social, racial, religious, and national group from around the globe is concentrated in one or more parts of the United States. No other country on earth can make that boast.

of the Great Depression? Would Republicans have wanted President Jimmy Carter (D) to maintain his unsuccessful domestic and foreign policies for an additional two years in the 1980s? The answers are obvious. On the other side of the equation, Americans have been fortunate that the man has met the moment so often in our history. Think of your favorite eight-year president. Would you have liked it if his time in office had been cut to six years?

By the way, some reformers take the opposite tack to the one, nonrenewable six-year term, and believe that the Twenty-second Amendment should simply be abolished. In so doing, they would permit, potentially, a series of FDRs, serving three, four, or more four-year terms, for as long as the people would reelect them. But Roosevelt is not a good model for their reform. By breaking with George Washington's wise precedent, he opened the door to an incumbency so lengthy and overweening that, with the wrong person in office, basic freedoms might be abridged. Yes, America benefited from Roosevelt's strong hand as we semi-secretly prepared to enter war, but it is very possible that the impressive, internationalist Republican nominee Wendell Willkie or an able Democrat of Roosevelt's stripe could have led the country well, had either been elected in 1940.[38] And if we can credibly suggest that a presidential giant like FDR was replaceable, then *any* president is. Remember, too, that while Roosevelt's third term was highly successful, the lack of a prohibition on a fourth term led our thirty-second president to seek it, despite the fact that he was on the verge of death—and FDR and many of those around him either knew it or strongly suspected it.[39] In any event, after passage of the Twenty-second Amendment, it is highly unlikely that most citizens, already concerned that too much power is concentrated in the Oval Office, would be eager to repeal the eight-year limit. Nor are many attracted to another idea that is sometimes floated by politicians and scholars: that the Twenty-second Amendment should apply only to consecutive years in office. Merely requiring that a president stay out of the White House for a term after eight years in office would only encourage more presidential dynasties—and one could contend we have had enough of those somewhat undemocratic pairings already.[40]

THE ALTERNATIVE: A PRESIDENTIAL CONFIRMATION ELECTION

I respectfully submit a new proposal in this stale, stagnant debate between four-year- and six-year-term advocates, an adaptation of the judicial confirmation election (to be explained shortly) for the presidency—a compromise

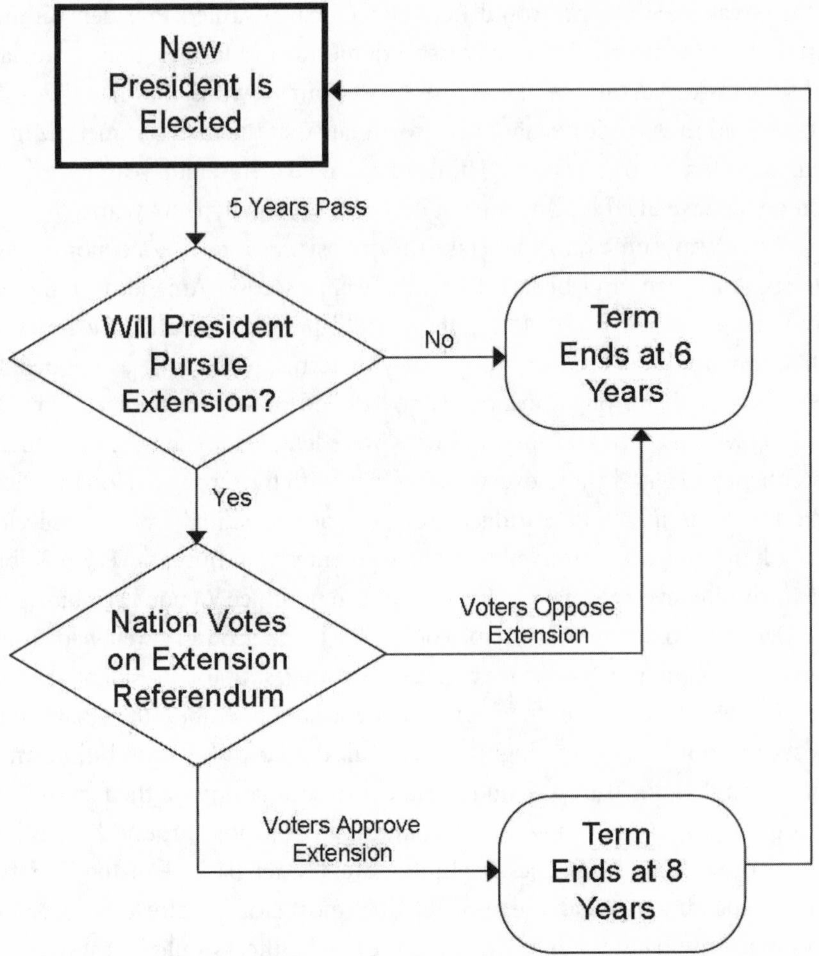

FIGURE 2.1. NEW ELECTION SCHEDULE FOR PRESIDENT

that takes the best aspects of the present arrangement (two four-year terms), and the concept of one six-year term. Under it, a president would be elected to a six-year term but would have the option to request a two-year extension, so that he would potentially serve the same eight-year tenure as currently. A president would not have to exercise his right to request an extension (illness or unpopularity might lead to that choice), but most chief executives would surely do so. (See figure 2.1.[41])

The extension election, which would occur in November of the president's fifth year in office, would not be a competitive choice between opposing party candidates, but rather a yes-or-no referendum from the American people on the president—similar to the "confirmation elections" of judges in some states. In other words, he would run with or against his own record, as ideally should be the case in a democracy that emphasizes accountability to the people for elected officials. If the president were to lose that straight up-or-down vote, a popular election would be held to fill the presidency in November of the sixth year in office (with the swearing in, as usual, the following January). If the president were to win the "confirmation election," he would go on to serve out an eight-year limit. Any vice president succeeding to the presidency would be locked into the same timetable as the replaced president. Presumably, his agenda would be largely the same, and as a member of the same administration, he would be judged by the achievements, or lack thereof, of that administration. Also, a president would be free to change vice presidents for the sixth-year election, as he is presently able to do at the fourth-year election. Moreover, the fifth-year confirmation election would focus solely on the president; as I will explain in the next section, congressional elections would be held on a different schedule, when a challenger to the president appears on the ballot.

The advantages of this new arrangement are clear.

- A new president is given an added year to produce achievements before the voters will render a decision in the fifth-year confirmation (or referendum) vote. This comports with a primary goal of the six-year-term advocates. One assumes, too, that real governing without daily campaign politics would also be extended by at least a year. Opposition party candidates would not be organizing as openly or as early, nor constantly seeking their own aggrandizement at the expense of the incumbent president, since there would be no two-party choice on the ballot in the fifth-year referendum. Depending on the outcome of the referendum election, a two-party election would not be held until a minimum of six years, and quite possibly a full eight years.

- Since a president has no opponent but himself in the fifth-year referendum, he will focus almost exclusively on creating a positive agenda to sell, rather than basing a victory for a second term on the political destruction of an opponent. The fifth-year referendum has the potential to transform our presidential reelections from increasingly negative affairs, highlighting little more than the politics of personal destruction, to vigorous, issue-oriented contests that would throw the spotlight squarely on what the president had achieved and where he had fallen short. Campaigns could become, at least in part, tightly focused and educational events, rather than dreaded quadrennial spectacles that leave the electorate deeply cynical and in need of a figurative shower. This vision is not as Pollyannaish as it may seem. Unquestionably, negative campaigning would be directed at the president. The opposition party and some interest groups would employ television ads and all the technologies of campaigns to try to convince voters that the president had failed and could not improve his performance in the future. On the other side, the president's party and his interest group backers would respond with an affirmative case. In the end, on election day, voters would have been able to sum up the administration's pluses and minuses in their minds, and they would cast a thumbs-up or thumbs-down ballot on the incumbent. No longer would presidential reelections be simply a vote for the lesser of evils. Either the president had produced sufficiently to deserve more time, or he had not. The campaign might not always be clean, but the electorate's decision would be.

- To judge from recent elections, the citizenry would send a president packing every three or four confirmation elections. Rejection would allow the president a year to wind up the affairs of his administration, and the American people would then have a fresh choice. Citing the difficult November-to-March transition between Presidents Herbert Hoover and Franklin D. Roosevelt in 1932–33, critics will say that this is too long a time to wait for a change of administration after a no vote—and it is undeniably a long time when there are critical circumstances such as the Great Depression awaiting presidential action.[42] In a parliamentary system, the delay would indeed be intolerable. But America's separation of the branches could make this interregnum quite useful. Members of Congress, who would be running for reelection shortly (under a schedule to be outlined in the next section), would pay close attention to the vote and act accordingly in the legislature, adapting to the expressed will of the people and changing national policy. And the president, who has had his wings clipped by the voters, would certainly have less influence and might sulk through his final year; but if smart, he would try to make amends and burnish his record for history in that year. Moreover, there would be plenty of time to organize an orderly handover of power. Is this one year of transition any more dangerous than the automatic four years of lame-duck status imposed on the current second-term president? Technically, a president who would not face the voters again could take any actions without regard for public opinion. Yet all presidents want to be popular or regain popularity. All presidents want to play to history, which usually keeps their movements constructive. And all presidents, under normal conditions, would surely prefer to see the election of their own party's candidate in the next election. In order to preserve at least some of the president's legacy, his party's nominee must be elected next time out. The opposition party's candidate for the White House is far more likely to eliminate all traces of the incumbent's programs.

- In the event of a confirmation rejection, the campaign to succeed the president would necessarily be limited to a single year—quite a reduction in wasted time from the full-fledged, all-out, four-year campaigns currently. (In chapter 4, we will suggest constitutional ways for this one-year election season to be productively scheduled and organized, unlike the crazy-quilt pattern of primaries and caucuses today.) Once again, a good argument can be made that this new scheme would permit more precious presidential time to be devoted to governing rather than campaigning.

- Importantly, a president would not need renomination from his party for the fifth-year "confirmation" vote—another critical change. Instead of spending his first five years catering to the ideological activists in his party base (the left for a Democrat and the right for a Republican), a president from Day One can govern closer to the moderate center of the entire American electorate—the best place to be, in order to ensure that the eventual confirmation vote is won. How often have we lamented that presidents pander far too much to the relatively small party base of ideologues rather than the broad body of centrist Americans! The party activists will nominate the presidential candidates the first time around, it is true, but smart politicians, even the relatively ideological ones, will gradually adjust to the more moderate needs of the confirmation vote. If Supreme Court justices can "evolve" without even the impulse of reelection (or reconfirmation), so much more so can the practical politicians who are elected president, and who want to win the extra two years. And the country will be the better for it, with policies closer to the real ideological midpoint of the whole body of modern Americans.

Lastly, a provision should be included about the so-called constitutional standby equipment, the vice presidency. A vice president who succeeds to the presidency before the fifth-year confirmation election (and, thus, becomes the focus of the confirmation vote) would not be able to seek the presidency on his own for what might become another eight-year stint; after all, potentially this single individual could serve as long as fifteen-plus years consecutively in the Oval Office—much too long a term in an office of such concentrated power.[43] But in the rare instance of a vice president who succeeded after the confirmation vote, in the latter stages of a presidency, the new president could seek nomination and election for a full term. He would serve for no more than three years before the next election, and even if successfully elected and then confirmed in the fifth year, about ten to eleven years total. This regime would be a logical application of the provisions of the current Twenty-second Amendment, which limits a vice president who succeeds to the presidency to a maximum of ten years in office.[44]

As noted earlier, this set of proposals concerning presidential elections would also affect midterm congressional elections. Every piece of the American system connects to every other piece, and part of the challenge of redesigning the constitutional apparatus is in discovering all the connections—and trying to make the wheels and gears work together for the common good. Readers of this volume will come to appreciate this more as we move from chapter to chapter.

At the moment, having redesigned the presidential term, we need to revisit Congress. There's no getting around it: The current two-year House terms and six-year Senate terms do not neatly coincide with a White House confirmation election in the fifth year, and a possible new presidential contest in the sixth year of the executive's term. We do not want a system where legislative and executive elections are unaligned. First, there would be more frequent national elections of one sort or another, and there is little question the public would not appreciate that change. Second, since there would be a reduced chance of the president and Congress being elected simultaneously, the executive and legislative branches would rarely be on the same page, having run campaigns on different issues—the issues dominating the national discourse in the year when they faced the voters. We need for the leaders in both branches to want to tackle an analogous agenda for the American people. In order to produce this result, how should the terms for U.S. House and Senate members be realigned to fit the new presidential regimen?

A LENGTHENED HOUSE TERM (AND CHANGES IN THE SENATE TERM)

The perfect complement for a transformed term for the presidency and a competitively redistricted House that produces elections with real meaning would be a longer term after those meaning-filled elections. The length of the House term should be increased from two to three years. At the 1787 Constitutional Convention, the two-year term for House members was a simple compromise between Roger Sherman's one-year-term proposal and James Madison's three-year-term argument. Two years once made sense, with governing consuming three quarters of the time and the reelection campaign one quarter. Those estimates are now reversed, at least for the minority of House members who have competitive contests. And for congressmen in "safe" districts, their natural insecurity about reelection has encouraged them to spend enormous time away from legislating on the all-consuming task of building large war chests, in order to ward off future challengers.

Madison's original term length now appears far more attractive and wise. An extra year would provide additional insulation for House members, both to focus on the substance of governing and to cast more votes in the national interest, even if the votes temporarily inflame some folks in their home states. Perhaps this "national interest effect" would only last for the first half of their term, but the first half of any Congress can be quite productive. Plus, the expanded second half of their term would give enough time for some early vote controversies to fade from constituents' memories. In today's House, there are few "profiles in courage." Perhaps with an extra year, more would emerge—more members of Congress willing to serve as true trustees rather than just pure delegates who vote for the popular prejudices of the moment.

Moreover, a three-year term would fit nicely into the just-proposed regimen for presidential elections. Any time a president were to lose a confirmation vote, and a new presidential election be scheduled for November of the sixth year, House members—in their newly competitive districts—would be more likely to ride the coattails of their party's presidential nominee to another term, or go down to defeat with their party's candidate. In any event, the electoral mandate for the new president, whether it be for continuity or change, would be stronger with more members from the new president's party elected alongside him, and perhaps beholden to him for their victories. Importantly, when combined with competitive redistricting, the new president would more likely have a House majority of his own party with which to work, so that the platform on which the president ran could be passed. Under our current system, five modern presidents—Eisenhower, Nixon, Reagan, Bush Sr., and Clinton—have been elected and/or reelected only to be immediately stymied in Congress, due to hostile majorities from the other party. George W. Bush might be added to this list since his party lost control of the Senate only four months after he first took the oath of office.[45] No doubt, these presidents' opponents in the other party and the electorate were delighted at their impotence in this circumstance, but a divided federal government right after a president is elected with a fresh mandate is simply not good for the nation. Both parties have suffered from this result, and both ought to realize it is time to reform this aspect of the system.

Critics will claim that this tendency of the new electoral structure—resulting in more "unified governments" (with the president and Congress of the same party)—would upset the system of checks and balances that preserves American liberty. But the many other checks would still be in place, from a bicameral Congress to the real possibility, even under this system, that some presidential elections would still produce a divided president and Congress. The proposed change would merely reduce somewhat the chances for paralyzing gridlock in the federal government. That gridlock—with a president and Congress completely at loggerheads and unable to move forward with the country's pressing business—ought to be broken, or at least weakened, and this one reform would make a difference.

One other adjustment would be necessary whenever a president wins the confirmation vote in the fifth year. During the next year's regularly scheduled House election, candidates would run for a special two-year term; that is, for that one election only, the House term would be cut from three years to two. This must be done in the interest of keeping the presidential and House elections on the same schedule, and to make certain that every new president has the possibility of a mandate with added congressional support for his programs. The last two years of any lengthy presidency are usually the least productive legislatively, so breaking the president-Congress electoral tie in this one case will not have a severe impact. In addition, while it is important to have fixed terms for all public offices, it is not essential for each election to give the elected official the same length of term. For example, at the state level, when an election schedule has been changed in modern times—say for governor and statewide posts—the terms have been shortened or lengthened as needed to fit the new schedule.[46]

Not surprisingly, Senate terms (one third elected every two years) would also need to change. In order to maximize the potential for presidential coattails and to consolidate the elections schedule, staggered Senate terms would be abolished. The entire Senate would be elected every time the presidency was on the ballot in a competitive election. (Note that this excludes the fifth-year confirmation vote, which is not a competition between candidates.) Practically, this would mean that Senate terms would vary, from six years on many occasions to an eight-year term, whenever a president were to successfully achieve a term extension in the confirmation election. Again, the principle here is clear. Presidents should be given reasonable opportunities to enjoy supportive congressional majorities in order to break gridlock and implement their platforms. There would still be midterm elections for the House, three years after a president's first election and also in the president's sixth year, if he has won the fifth-year confirmation vote, and the voters could, if they so chose, either strengthen the chief executive's mandate by electing more of his fellow party members, or put the brake on presidential programs by electing more from the opposite party. In our bicameral, one-house-veto Congress, the shift in the House alone at this three-year interval would be enough to affect the president's legislative output considerably. Midcourse corrections would occur, then, but absolute gridlock—a function of simultaneous anti-presidential change in both houses of Congress—would not happen. This is a nod to a parliamentary system without actually going there. America would keep its presidential system but simply increase the odds that a president would have working majorities, at least at first, in the legislature. And the Senate would be more closely tied to the president throughout his term since the entire upper chamber of Congress would always, and only, be elected at the same time as the chief executive.

This latter point deserves elaboration. Unquestionably, both the Senate and the House as institutions would be altered substantially by the shift in term lengths, and this new scheme would add a needed element of the parliamentary system into our own. After a reasonably decisive election, a prime minister in Great Britain is guaranteed a substantial legislative majority and near-certain passage of his major election planks since the executive and legislative branches are fused into the House of Commons; the prime minister and his cabinet, all members of Parliament, determine the legislative agenda. By contrast, as noted earlier, all of our full two-term presidents since Eisenhower

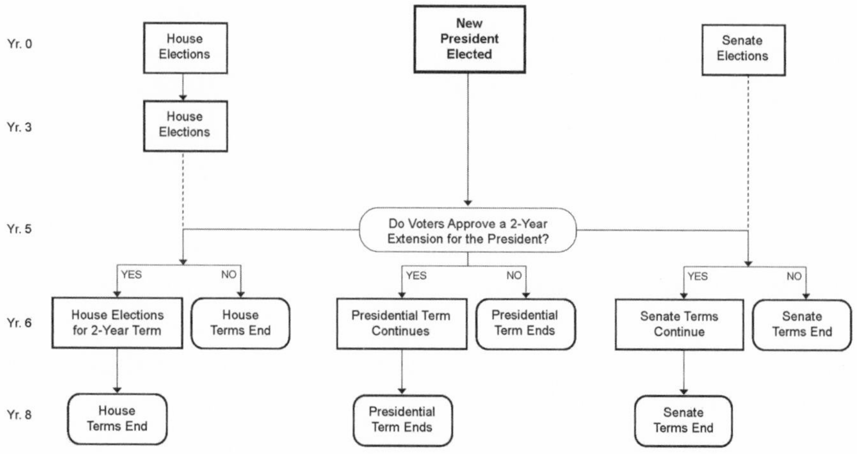

FIGURE 2.2. NEW ELECTION SCHEDULE FOR PRESIDENT, HOUSE, AND SENATE

(save George W. Bush) won healthy electoral majorities at least once without winning full control of Congress. An independently elected Congress will never be a mere rubber stamp, but presidents need more help in enacting their program, so that they (and their party) can be judged on their collective degree of success at the next election, just as prime ministers and their parties are.

The American system is currently so fragmented that every elected official is something of a free agent and always has an excuse, sometimes many excuses, to explain away failure to a confused electorate. The United States will never have a system as orderly as a full parliamentary government, in part because a British-style system would not be able to accommodate many of our cherished traditions, such as separation of powers, checks and balances, and federalism. But the United States now has too much separation, too many checks, and excessive inefficiency in its constitutional arrangement. We need a political and governmental system that works better and produces more coherence at election time. The structure outlined in this chapter (see figure 2.2) and throughout this volume would provide a golden mean between the extremes of the current frequently gridlocked reality and a parliamentary arrangement. These proposals are also consistent with a long tradition in political science of advocacy for a more responsible "party government," so that the voters can actually know who and what to hold responsible for good times and bad.[47]

WAR-MAKING LIMITS: PRESIDENTIAL DOWNSIZING

A new Constitutional Convention should also focus on the increasingly difficult question of war-making authority, and it ought to consider ways to reduce overweening presidential power in the awesome arena of war and peace. Even though congressional consideration of foreign military adventures can be awkward and dilatory, the legislative branch should be given constitutional opportunities to reclaim its greatly diminished role, in search of a better balance of war powers between the president and Congress.

Few American political observers deny that the presidency has now absorbed the lion's share of war powers, and fewer still argue that the founders intended our system to work this way. The great divide is over the inevitability—or not—that the chief executive must be the one to wage war. Even after highly controversial, bloody conflicts in Korea, Vietnam, and Iraq, as well as many shorter-term "police actions" directed primarily by presidents, most scholars and practitioners who have focused on the topic are unsure what, if anything, can be done to alter the power equation. At the heart of this uncertainty is an inescapable fact: The current Constitution has left us with an ambiguous framework since the president is commander in chief "of the Army and the Navy of the United States" but the Congress possesses the power to declare war.

Many scholars convincingly argue that the framers of the original Constitution wanted the Congress, not the president, to be the prime mover in initiating military action.[48] As John Hart Ely notes, "Only one delegate to either the Philadelphia convention or any of the state ratifying conventions, Pierce Butler, is recorded as suggesting that authority to make war be vested in the president."[49] There was no naïveté in the preference shown for Congress, but rather a belief that if the executive's call for war were subjected to greater scrutiny by hundreds of legislators, there would be fewer wars—events that Madison called "among the greatest of national calamities."[50] The delegates to the Constitutional Convention did change one key phrase in the draft: Instead of empowering Congress "to make War," the legislature was given authority "to declare War." Yet there is little evidence that the delegates intended this word substitution to shift more authority to the president,[51] as shown by Madison's shrewd evaluation of an executive's bias toward war making: "The constitution supposes, what the History of all Govts demonstrates, that the Ex[ecutive] is the branch of power most interested in war, & most prone to it. It has accordingly with studied care, vested the question of war in the Legisl[ature]."[52] In a folksier manner, Congressman Abraham Lincoln made much the same observation in 1848.

> Allow the President to invade a neighboring nation whenever he shall deem it necessary to repel an invasion, and you allow him to do so whenever he may choose to say he deems it necessary for such purpose, and you allow him to make war at pleasure. Study to see if you can fix any limit to his power in this respect, after having given him so much as you propose . . .
>
> [K]ings had always been involving and impoverishing their people in wars, pretending generally, if not always, that the good of the people was the object. This our convention understood to be the most oppressive of all kingly oppressions, and they resolved to so frame the Constitution that no one man should hold the power of bringing this oppression upon us.[53]

Madison and Lincoln's view has not prevailed in modern times. During the twentieth century, America's emergence as a superpower, and the swiftness of decisions required for waging war in the nuclear age, put the president on the front burner and relegated Congress to the back, if indeed Congress is even on the stove at all in some conflicts. Resourceful presidents gradually assumed more power in the war-making arena, mainly with the assent of Congress. With each new foreign crisis in the twentieth century, beginning with World War I, Congress gave the executive additional emergency authority so that the United States could prevail in its conflicts. After World War II, Congress appropriated vast sums of money for the prosecution of hostilities abroad in the shadowy era of the Cold War, when the United States and the Soviet Union fought many proxy battles for influence and control in other nations. Congress finally took a step back—and reclaimed some of its authority—as the Vietnam War wound down. The public's unhappiness with this long, savage, undeclared war led to the War Powers Resolution of 1973, passed over President Nixon's veto.[54] In essence, the act mandates that a president during peacetime should secure the assent of both houses of Congress before sending U.S. military forces into combat; notify Congress of any deployment of troops to combat on foreign soil within forty-eight hours of the event; and limit the deployment of troops to sixty days (with an additional thirty days for withdrawal, if needed) unless Congress gives its official sanction for a longer deployment.

While its intent was to divide war-making authority more equitably between the executive and legislative branches, the effect of the act has been less clear. Some presidents, beginning with Nixon, have insisted that the act is an unconstitutional infringement upon the executive's war-making authority, and thus have been inclined to observe the law in the breach. Citing the need for speed and secrecy, presidents of both parties (Ford, Carter, Reagan, and Clinton) have taken "emergency actions" as they saw fit, as President Clinton did in dispatching troops to Haiti in 1993 in order to restore overthrown president Jean-Bertrand Aristide to power. When President George Herbert Walker Bush sought the support of Congress for the Persian Gulf War in 1991, he made clear that he believed he had the constitutional authority to launch the war even if Congress eventually turned him down.[55] Bush won the vote in both Democratic-controlled houses, though there was substantial opposition.[56] More recently, after the terrorist attacks on September 11, 2001, Congress simply ceded its powers to the presidency without a fight. President George W. Bush was granted a joint congressional resolution permitting all necessary military action against "those responsible" for 9/11 and waiving the sixty-day limit—a more sweeping resolution than his father had received in 1991.[57] Similarly, both the House and the Senate voted by wide margins in October 2002 to let Bush use military force in Iraq "as he determines to be necessary and appropriate," in other words, carte blanche authority.[58]

In the unsettled aftermath of the Iraq War, the president's basic justification for the war (destroying the apparently nonexistent weapons of mass destruction) was highly questionable, and not thoroughly examined by Congress in advance. Perhaps that will always be the case even if Congress were less inclined to give up its rights under the War Powers Resolution. The natural tendency in a frightening era, when the nation is under threat, is to defer to a tough-talking president who can take swift action—even if the action is unwise or poorly thought out. And yet, as the war-powers scholar Louis Fisher has argued, "The Framers also lived in a dangerous time, possibly more hazardous than today," as they faced the superpowers of their era (England, France, and Spain) with few military advantages.[59] "Contemporary Presidential judgments need more, not less, scrutiny," wrote Fisher, and Iraq surely proves the point. While the press can supply some of that scrutiny, there is no substitute for Congress. Its powers of the purse, subpoena, and Article II's Senate approval of ambassadors and treaties entitle it to a full share of authority in this most important sphere.[60]

An enduring lack of will in Congress may be at the heart of this dilemma, and there is no constitutional fix for that. Remarkably, the leaders of Congress often appear less interested in protecting the powers of their branch than presidents seem determined to do in their sphere.[61] But since presidents have often insisted that the provisions of the War Powers Resolution are unconstitutional or should be waived—a claim that is a pretext for ignoring them when they are inconvenient—the major provisions of the act should be made a part of the Constitution. In a hair-trigger world, presidents need to be able to take decisive action quickly. But real consultation with congressional leaders of both parties ought to be an unavoidable part of the process. The "advice and consent" mandate that refers to federal court nominations ought also to apply in reasonable fashion to the most awesome power of the presidency.[62]

Most important of all, there should be a time limit on unilateral presidential war making—ninety days appears reasonable—at which time Congress would need to either give its assent or, through a resolution of disapproval, cause the orderly withdrawal of American forces. Given that Congress, especially the Senate with its unlimited debate rule, can be dilatory, this new constitutional provision should mandate a congressional vote on military action in both houses, up or down, by the end of the ninety-day period. The legislative resolution of approval ought also to set a time limit on the grant of war-making power for any conflict—six months, or a year at most. By the end of that time period, Congress should vote either for a continuation of the conflict, or by its disapproval, direct that our military forces be withdrawn on a reasonable timetable. Such a resolution would not be subject to the presidential veto. This resolves the problem of congressional approval, once given, being interpreted by presidents as an endless blank check for years of war—precisely what Lyndon Johnson did after the 1964 Gulf of Tonkin Resolution[63] with respect to Vietnam, and George W. Bush did after the 2002 congressional vote on the Iraq War. New information comes to light, and new conditions develop—and Congress should regularly review the situation, checking the president in this life-or-death realm of constitutional power.

The era of open-ended, unilateral war making by presidents should be brought to an end, and it will not happen without a remedy such as the one discussed here. If this be "hamstringing a president," as critics might charge, it is time to use a little string—and the Vietnam and Iraq wars show why. Should combat be in the American national interest, it ought to find favor in both elective branches, not just one, for we will surely fail to win the battle eventually if the nation is not substantially behind the war effort. Thomas Jefferson wrote, "In questions of power, let no more be heard of confidence in man, but bind him down from mischief by the chains of the Constitution."[64] There is no greater presidential power than to wage war, and if ever our preference to avoid great specificity in a constitution should be suspended, it is within this breathtaking arena of power. The particular reforms I have proposed will "bind the president down from mischief" in war, without unwisely eliminating executive flexibility.

All Americans understand that this is not an arcane debate about a few phrases in the Constitution. The most awesome authority contained in the text of our basic document of state is the war-making power. How it is described and allocated determines the fate of millions of our sons and daughters—those who wear the American military uniform. Just as vital, America's decisions to wage war affect our ability to survive and succeed in a dangerous world. It is long past time to rethink the inadequate constitutional arrangement that was well suited to the eighteenth century but is out of step in the twenty-first.

ITEM VETO

In the war-making arena, presidential power should be downsized. In the appropriations sphere, presidential power should be expanded. The reason is the same in both cases: It serves the interests of the people of the United States.

The new Constitution should add the line-item appropriations veto to the arsenal of presidential power. The *item veto* has been much discussed and thoroughly analyzed over the years—and it actually existed for more than twenty-six months between April 1996 and June 1998.[65] The Supreme Court ruled the congressionally granted item veto to be unconstitutional after a challenge, but one of the advantages of constitutional revision is that prior Court decisions can be overridden with appropriate language in the new Constitution's text.

Essentially, the line-item veto would permit the president to do what forty-three of the fifty state governors can already accomplish: cutting specific appropriation line-items out of an appropriations bill sent to him by Congress, without vetoing the entire appropriations bill. The latter option is cumbersome, and often impossible because of urgent needs that must be funded immediately. It also risks months of arduous negotiations by both elected branches for an uncertain future.

The addition of an item veto is a significant augmentation of presidential power, though not necessarily in the ways one might think. The type of item veto most prized by executives is called *enhanced rescission*.[66] Under this scheme, the president can item-veto any appropriations provision, and the item veto automatically takes effect unless it is overridden by a two-thirds vote of both the U.S. House and the Senate within thirty days. This was the basis of the item-veto legislation that finally passed the Republican-dominated Congress in 1996, after it had been requested by every president since Franklin D. Roosevelt.[67] With the dramatic expansion of the federal budget during the New Deal, Roosevelt saw the need for an executive "second look" at many of the appropriations being inserted into the budget by members of Congress. In retrospect, FDR's budgets were small compared with the trillion-dollar ones passed today. The issue of waste and unnecessary pork projects loomed larger with each passing decade, until the Republicans made it a part of their proposed new agenda for the watershed congressional election of 1994, when the GOP took over both houses of Congress for the first time in forty years. As passed, the item veto was not unlimited. In addition to the possibility of congressional override of the veto, the president was not able to reduce funding for a line item, only eliminate it, and he was not permitted to delete any substantive language in the bill. (By contrast, some state governors are permitted to do both. For example, in Wisconsin for a time, governors were actually allowed to remove words or letters from an appropriations act, and in at least one case, Governor Tommy Thompson [R] actually struck the key modifier *not*, reversing the meaning of the legislative language!)[68] Additionally, the congressional Line Item Veto Act of 1996 required that all savings from the line-item veto should be applied to the reduction of the national deficit or debt, so that the moneys could not be used for more congressional spending or tax reductions.

President Clinton was able to utilize the item veto on seventy-eight occasions in eleven appropriation acts, before the Court struck the veto down.[69] The total saved for the Treasury during the brief time that the item veto was in effect was $483.6 million. To put this in perspective, the annual national deficit since 2001 has averaged over $200 billion, and the total national debt now exceeds $8 trillion.[70]

However, it is important to acknowledge that there are considerable advantages gained for the country by means of a line-item veto—advantages that, considered together, make the veto a worthwhile addition to the new Constitution. First, as we have already noted, some pork projects are eliminated and some money, however modest, is saved. Actually, only in the United States could half a billion dollars be considered "modest." Perhaps another president might item-veto far more than the amount targeted by President Clinton between 1996 and 1998, and all of it would go toward paying down the national debt. If the discussion about the skyrocketing debt in chapter 1 has left any impression, it is that we ought to encourage any effort, small or large, to reduce the burden on future generations.

Second, the very fact that a Republican Congress passed the Line Item Veto Act for the use of a Democratic president is an open admission that the legislature will probably never be able to curb its appetite for more spending and unnecessary local pork. The Congress basically said, "Only a president can exert the discipline to control expenditures." It is possible that a permanent item veto would actually remove what little spending self-restraint exists in Congress by promoting the attitude that "the president will save us from ourselves," yet if we look back at the enormous deficits in most years and the massive amounts of pork served up by Congresses over the past four decades, it is difficult to argue credibly that there is much legislative restraint to lose.

Third, the presidency gains in other useful, productive ways from an item veto. This sword of Damocles can be a welcome inducement for members of Congress, both from the opposition party and the president's own party, to cooperate and negotiate with the executive branch on specific provisions of the appropriations bills. Indeed, President Clinton used the item veto not just to eliminate waste but also to enhance his programmatic objectives overall.[71] The analysis of Clinton's vetoes did not reveal a pattern of partisan motivation, by the way, though this new power would be an especially vital tool for any president facing a Congress controlled by the other party. If we want an effective presidency, we must structure it to be effective even, or especially, in difficult situations such as split party control of the White House and the legislature. A president's power to reward or punish members of Congress in the appropriations process can be subject to abuse, but so is any presidential authority. Most vetoed local projects, even if they are cut for the wrong reasons by a president, will not adversely affect the national interest. Yet constituency-based pork is so highly prized by legislators that, in order to get it, they might be willing to give the executive their favorable vote on a bill that truly serves the national interest. Pork spending generates jobs and benefits for the lucky states and localities that receive it, but most of all, it produces votes at election time for members of Congress. They will give up a great deal to keep some of their projects in the budget.

When the Supreme Court declared the Line Item Veto Act unconstitutional in *Clinton v. City of New York*,[72] the justices found that the act violated the "presentment clause" of Article I, Section 7, of the Constitution.[73] According to that provision of the Constitution, after both houses of Congress pass a bill, "[it] shall, before it become a Law, be presented to the President of the United States; if he approve he shall sign it, but if not he shall return it, with his Objections to that House in which it shall have originated." The Court ruled that the language of the Constitution only gives the president two options: to sign a bill or return it. Since the Line Item Veto Act allowed the president to change the bill and *then* sign it, it violated that procedure and was therefore unconstitutional. Some senior members of Congress, such as West Virginia senator Robert Byrd, joined in the effort to strike down the bill in Court, believing that it infringed upon congressional prerogatives.[74] The Court did not insist that all versions of the item veto would automatically be unconstitutional, but clearly this would be a treacherous subject for another Congress to tackle. The far easier route is the adoption of an item-veto clause in a revised Constitution. The president would gain some powerful leverage at the federal level, but the real beneficiary would be us—the American public. Unneeded pork would be slaughtered, and over time, the national debt would be reduced.

FAIRNESS FOR ALL: MAKING THE PRESIDENCY POSSIBLE FOR AMERICANS WHO ARE NOT "NATURAL-BORN"

The archaic constitutional requirement that the president must be a natural-born citizen should be replaced with a condition that a candidate should be a U.S. citizen for at least twenty years before election to the presidency (or vice presidency).

The "natural-born" provision made sense in the Republic's early years, when the nation was seeking its own distinct identity and worried appropriately about undue foreign influence from the Great Powers of the day: Great Britain, France, and Spain. Like the current century, the late 1700s were perilous, but *peril* was defined differently. Skulduggery and corruption in the governing elites of most countries were a part of daily life. At the time of the Constitutional Convention, there were already rumors that some delegates hoped to attract a European of royal blood to serve as America's constitutional monarch. Thus, even though seven of the thirty-nine signers of the Constitution were foreign-born, the delegates wisely sought to allay fears that such a plot was afoot.[75] The founders were also right to be concerned that a future Electoral College might be importuned by agents from abroad, bearing gifts, in order to produce a president or vice president of the United States with strong ties to one of the continental countries.[76]

However, the original intent of the framers regarding the "natural-born citizen" clause is murky since the records of the Constitutional Convention provide no conclusive evidence as to what the writers intended the phrase to mean. On June 18, 1787, Alexander Hamilton's sketch for the executive simply included wording to require the president to be born a citizen. A letter from John Jay to George Washington also mentioned the clause but without helpful background. The convention's Committee on Detail did not include any reference to citizenship in its proposed wording of Article II, and the "natural-born" phrase did not appear in official drafts until the Committee of Eleven produced its proposal on September 4, 1787. The records of the convention reveal no debate on the floor; nor have the federal courts ever entertained a case in the centuries since that might have refined the exact meaning of *natural-born citizen*.[77] It appears fair to say that these critical words received scant attention, and their future impact on generations yet unborn was almost certainly not understood.

In today's America, illegal immigration is one of the most controversial and emotional issues in our politics, and some Americans are inclined to question the enduring loyalty of new arrivals. The presidency is the nation's highest office, and without a doubt, there should still be a requirement for lengthy citizenship before one assumes the highest office in the land. Yet, except for Native Americans (Indians, Eskimos, and so on), all Americans are either immigrants or the descendants of immigrants. Some of the most prominent of our citizens throughout U.S. history have been first-generation immigrants, amazingly accomplished and yet sadly ineligible for the presidency. In modern times, the list includes former secretaries of state Henry Kissinger and Madeleine Albright, and two members of George W. Bush's cabinet, Elaine Chao and Mel Martinez.[78]

Recently, the issue has arisen anew because of Austrian-born California governor Arnold Schwarzenegger (R) and Canadian-born Michigan governor Jennifer Granholm (D), whose party leaders have sometimes expressed interest in nominating them on a national ticket if they were eligible. The current constitutional insistence on natural-born citizens rules out far more people than Schwarzenegger and Granholm. An astonishing 14.4 million foreign-born U.S. citizens are automatically excluded from consideration for the presidency.[79] There are also thirty thousand foreign-born Americans serving in the armed forces of the United States, many risking life and limb in trouble spots around the world. Add to this the impressive fact that more than seven hundred foreign-born Americans have won the Medal of Honor for their valor. Are these brave people less worthy of the Oval Office than the millions of native countrymen who have never put their life on the line for U.S. interests?[80]

Moreover, under a prevailing interpretation of the "natural-born" test, many thousands of American citizens who were born abroad while their parents were visiting or doing church missionary work in foreign lands are excluded from the presidency. So, too, are those born while their parents were stationed abroad while serving in the U.S. military or civilian government jobs, such as diplomatic or intelligence agencies. All of the people discussed in this paragraph have been American citizens from the moment of their birth, yet because of an outdated constitutional phrase, they are probably barred from the presidency. I say *probably* because, again, the full scope of the term *natural-born citizen* is unclear. Unless the language is stricken from the Constitution, it will take a Supreme Court ruling at some point to determine the presidential eligibility of a candidate who falls into one of these last two categories.[81]

All of this actual and potential exclusion from the presidency must end. Surely, we are now at the point where we can reasonably consider non-native-born citizens for the White House, as long as they have enjoyed full citizenship for at least twenty years. It is worth remembering that, in the end, Americans will have a wide choice both in the presidential nomination process and at the general election for president. Should there be any reasonable question of a candidate's loyalty to the nation, the voters will sort it out at the polls. After all, 99.9 percent of the population is eliminated from consideration for the presidency for one reason or another: They have no interest in running, they lack the money or office experience, they have criminal records, and so on.

On this critical question of fairness, though, it is essential to trust the people of the United States at the ballot box. The little-discussed constitutional provision barring non-native-born citizens from the White House is a stain upon our democracy. Fundamental to our national self-image is a belief that here in the United States, however humble one's origins, anyone can rise to the highest office in the land. Striking the prohibition on non-native-born citizens will be a powerful symbol of America's rising inclusiveness and equality in the twenty-first century. And for 14.4 million Americans—a number that grows daily—the dream of one day becoming president will complete their citizenship, making them whole in the eyes of the Constitution at long last.

✶

I have just referred to the presidency as the nation's "highest office," but that is not entirely correct. As coequal branches, the Congress and the courts have leaders that can balance executive authority in many ways. Nonetheless, Americans look to the occupant of the White House as the central figure in American government, and so anything a new Constitutional Convention can do to improve the office will help the nation.

In this chapter I have made the arguments for some major changes in the presidency. The proposed term configuration and the new confirmation election for the president are probably the most significant structural alterations. Complementing the executive term shift, I have also proposed realigning the terms of members of the U.S. House of Representatives and the Senate. There is good reason to believe that this novel, synergistic arrangement of executive and legislative terms could encourage more cooperation between the branches—and that would serve the national interest. Of greatest concern to the public, though, may be the reforms in executive war-making power. In modern times we have all been witness to the weaknesses inherent in the current, muddy constitutional divide of war authority between president and Congress. In the most practical and specific proposal yet made to rebalance war-making powers, I have tilted the scale back somewhat to Congress. In another arena, budget making, the president would gain, with the suggested addition of line-item appropriations power. Finally, I have made the case for all Americans to have the opportunity to serve as president, whether they are native-born citizens or not.

Having now looked at both Congress and the presidency, I am fascinated by the eternal tug-of-war that goes on between these mighty branches. They are required to work together in order to accomplish anything, yet they appear constitutionally destined to fight each other constantly for supremacy. It is in the public's interest that neither succeeds in this struggle, since our lives are best safeguarded by equilibrium of power. The reforms proposed in these first two chapters, taken together, reinforce the system of checks and balances while improving the operation of both institutions so that they can more ably and equitably serve us.

CHAPTER THREE

★

THE NEW COURTS: SUPREME BUT NOT ETERNAL

A TELLING INCIDENT about the aloofness of the Supreme Court occurred in early 2007. For many years, advocates of open government have been trying in vain to get the justices to allow television cameras into their courtroom—which is common practice in many states[1] and is allowed in some federal appeals courts.[2] The motive is obvious: to help Americans understand their system of justice via the most universal and powerful means of modern communications: electronic broadcasting and also webcasting. U.S. senator Arlen Specter (R-PA) introduced a bill to push the Court in this direction,[3] and a Senate hearing attracted Justice Anthony Kennedy as a witness. An obviously agitated Kennedy took Senator Specter to task, saying, "Please, senator, don't introduce into the dynamics that I have with my colleagues the temptation, the insidious temptation, to think that one of my colleagues is trying to get a sound bite for the television . . . We don't want that!"[4] Another Justice, David Souter, had made it clear on an earlier occasion that cameras would be allowed at the Supreme Court over his "dead body."[5]

Keep in mind that we taxpayers support the Court's operations to the tune of $63.4 million in 2007 alone,[6] and that its members have life-and-death power over some citizens, while dramatically influencing the lives of the rest of us with their decisions. Justices already compete with one another for journalistic ink bites (the featured newspaper quotes from Court hearings) and the favorable judgments of editorialists, the legal community, and historians. Most every public event involving the president, the Congress, state governors and legislatures, many courts, and even local city councils is televised so that citizens can directly see what they are getting for their money and can judge—yes, judge—the contributions of their leaders. Yet the Supreme Court insists that it is special, and above the scrutiny that comes with its awesome authority. It is not enough that its members have lifetime tenure; they insist on the need to be comfortable and removed from broadcast monitoring, even at the cost of the public's full understanding of their work. As I will mention in this chapter, the Court's brethren have on occasion protected members who became senile, incompetent, or too ill to serve. Not only is this behavior unacceptable for top jurists, but cameras might have exposed the problem and nudged off the Court those justices who had overstayed their useful service.

There is extraordinary arrogance and privilege embedded in the justices' preferences on this topic—a revealing glimpse of the often-unapproachable people who are accorded demigod status in this most undemocratic institution embedded in America's democracy. Can anything be done to encourage justices to remember that they are our servants and not our masters?

Alexander Hamilton termed the judiciary the *least dangerous* branch to the political rights granted by the Constitution since he believed that the executive and the legislature, not the courts, had been given the real power in the American system.[7] Hamilton's phrase may have fit the Supreme Court of his day, but many would adamantly disagree that the moniker still applies today. What is most significant is that both liberals and conservatives are now very unhappy with the Supreme Court, and the federal courts generally.[8] Liberals see the courts as dominated by right-wing activist judges who are on the verge of overturning *Roe v. Wade* and other key progressive rulings. Conservatives insist that decades of liberal judicial decisions have created a court system that acts as an unelected super-legislature, arrogantly inventing rights such as "privacy" not found in the Constitution.

If the ideological extremes are displeased, moderates are no less so. Middle-of-the-road citizens just shake their heads at Supreme Court rulings such as *Kelo v. City of New London* in 2005, where local governments were given the right to seize private property for nonpublic purposes.[9] (Even Justice John Paul Stevens, who provided a key vote in the ruling, later said he personally disagreed with it![10]) Not surprisingly, public confidence in the Supreme Court has fallen to low levels. A recent CBS News Poll showed that only 22 percent of the public had "a great deal of confidence" in the Court, well down from the support voiced in some recent years.[11] The American people, by and large, sense that a warning issued by a great jurist has come to pass. "It would be most irksome to be ruled by a bevy of Platonic Guardians," wrote Learned Hand in 1958.[12]

The confirmation process for justices and judges has become a humbling experience for judicial nominees in many cases, and one of its effects may be to counteract at first the sense that one has become a Platonic guardian. But lifetime tenure for the federal judiciary—a remarkable privilege granted by the Constitution—is the unwelcome antidote, affecting liberal and conservative judges alike. (Ideology is irrelevant to human frailty and vanity.) As the years pass and their isolation grows, the exercise of great power without consequence leads some judges to a state of arrogance and permanent judicial activism. Without the need for reappointment or review, they are free to "evolve," changing philosophies to some degree and discarding the suit of clothes they wore to gain appointment. Without any effective checks, they can "discover" interpretations not found in the Constitution's text in order to validate their own personal political and moral choices. In mandating their own opinions in sweeping judgments that sometimes lack convincing legal foundations, they write themselves into the history books and curry favor with the media and academic elites—all the while ignoring original intent and casting off the wise restraints of prudence and caution. Without a retirement age, they serve well into their seventies, eighties, or beyond, ignoring the aging process and even serious illness.

It is past time to level the mountain, with several commonsense reforms to limit the tenure of federal judges and bring some balance back to a judiciary that has become far more powerful than the founders could ever have imagined or wanted. It is true that "vanity of vanities, all is vanity"[13] in almost any system. But my suggested changes may encourage the humility of narrow interpretations of law—judicial incrementalism—by keeping judges anchored to reality. Service on the Court would become a phase in a career, rather than an entire career.

THE ERROR OF LIFETIME TENURE

The constitutional principle of lifetime tenure during good behavior for federal judges is noteworthy, especially given the fact that almost all of the fifty states appoint or elect their judges for limited terms. The state judicial terms range from four years for judges on the Kansas Superior Court to fourteen-year terms for judges on the New York Supreme Court, with the average term being approximately seven years. In nearly every case these terms are renewable through reappointment or reelection. In twenty-seven states, there is a mandatory retirement age, ranging from seventy (in twenty states) to seventy-two (in four states) to seventy-five (in three states).[14] Interestingly, there is far less controversy about the judiciary in the states than there is at the federal level. No doubt, this is partly because many controversial questions are constitutional ones that must be resolved in the federal court system. But it is also true that state courts are closer to the publics they serve, and structurally more responsive to the community standards they are charged with upholding.

Not all state-based ideas are worth replicating at the federal level. The practice of electing judges in twenty-two states (and especially in the eight states that have partisan contests)[15] is highly questionable. These races have become increasingly vicious, forcing judicial candidates to get down in the muck and attack their opponents on personal character matters. Partisan judicial battles can also produce a real conflict of interest by pushing future judges to take positions, while stumping, on issues coming before their courts later on. Even worse, in 2004, judicial candidates for state supreme courts raised $47 million, primarily from the business interests and lawyers with a direct stake in their rulings. This sum skyrocketed from past elections.[16] Arguably, judicial elections completely remove the independence necessary for judges to make unpopular decisions, and encourage the kind of political pandering we associate more with the executive and legislative branches.

Fortunately, we have no such problem at the federal level, where all judges are appointed—nominated by the president and confirmed (or rejected) by the Senate. This is true at the lowest level of federal judgeships (the district court level, where 642 judges serve in ninety-four individual districts),[17] the appellate court level (where 167 judges hear appeals from the lower courts and serve in eleven multistate districts),[18] and at the nation's highest court, where final appeals are heard. Yet in recent years, the federal courts have become divisive for different reasons. Some extremely controversial decisions have been made by the Supreme Court and lower federal courts: *Bush v. Gore* in 2000, the temporary banning of "under God" in the Pledge of Allegiance, a series of rulings on gay rights and abortion, the abolition of the death penalty for juveniles, the prohibition on prayer in many public places, the ban on medical marijuana, easing the rules for local governments to seize private property for semipublic uses, a ruling striking down laws requiring online publishers to protect children from accessing obscene material, and a series of decisions lowering the threshold for police searches. These rulings have produced a strong backlash against the national judiciary from both left and right.[19] The federal courts are seen as being out of touch with reasonable community mores, insufficiently restrained, and too inclined to issue decisions based upon personal whim and opinion rather than real constitutional principle.

The "least political branch," a variation on Hamilton's description of the judiciary often used by the civic texts, has become exceptionally political. How else to explain why every appointment now receives the kind of intense scrutiny formerly reserved for presidents, senators, and governors? Citizens resent it when the courts make decisions on sensitive social matters that they believe ought to be left to the executive and legislature, whose members are on the ballot and can be reelected or defeated. The people often have no recourse with court decisions but to accept them or face severe legal consequences. Public resentment has begun to manifest itself in reduced respect for the judicial system, whether measured by public opinion polls or commentary on a wide range of blogs.[20] The undermining of popular support for the federal judiciary ought to be of great concern, since voluntary compliance stemming from respect for the rule of law is critical to the courts' success.

Some solutions can be found in the states, and several common practices there ought to be applied to the federal judiciary. First, lifetime tenure should be abolished. Some observers already insist that federal judges are not guaranteed lifetime tenure by the Constitution, which states only that judges should "hold their Offices during good Behaviour."[21] Others have noted that the president or Senate could request a commitment from any nominee to serve a limited term; but any such commitment would not be legally binding, and it is difficult to see a set of circumstances that would compel a president or Senate to request a term limit.

In fact, early in his career as a Reagan White House lawyer, our current chief justice, John G. Roberts Jr., argued for a fifteen-year limit on Supreme Court service.[22] The founders "adopted life tenure at a time when people simply did not live as long as they do now," noted Roberts. "A judge insulated from the normal currents of life for 25 or 30 years was a rarity then but is becoming commonplace today. Setting a term of, say, 15 years would ensure that federal judges would not lose all touch with reality through decades of ivory tower existence."[23] Roberts's take on the issue was raised at his confirmation hearings for chief justice in September 2005; however, he demurred, his views having changed. (Where one stands depends on where one sits.)

In truth, the custom of lifetime tenure is now so entrenched that only a change in the Constitution can alter the practice. The late chief justice William H. Rehnquist once defined "during good Behaviour" as "mean[ing], for all practical purposes, for life."[24] Because of this, and as the judiciary has become almost as polarized along partisan lines as the elective branches, presidents have been seeking out younger and younger judgeship appointees at every level of the judiciary, hoping to influence the courts long after they leave the White House. The data on length of judicial service also clearly show that Supreme Court justices are serving in their positions longer, too. The first chief justice, John Jay, stayed a mere five years, and his two immediate successors had even shorter tenures.[25] Compare that with the thirty-three years served on the Court by the late chief justice William Rehnquist. It is true that the fourth chief justice, the great John Marshall, set the precedent for Rehnquist by staying on the Court for thirty-four years, but Marshall was the great exception in the Republic's first century. The first ten justices stayed on the Supreme Court, on average, a bit under eight years each, and the first ninety justices left the pre-1970 Court, on average, after fifteen years at age sixty-eight.[26] By contrast, tenure of twenty-plus years has now become the norm. As one Court observer calculated, justices who left the Supreme Court in the period 1971 to 2000 served an average of 25.5 years![27] Further, the average age of departing justices over that period increased considerably, from about age seventy to approaching the age of eighty.

The insularity produced by lifetime tenure, combined with youthful appointment and long service, often means that senior judges represent the views and outlooks of past generations better than the current day. Therefore, a nonrenewable, lengthy term of fifteen years is an attractive innovation, and the limit would apply to *all* federal judges, from the district courts all the way up to the Supreme Court.[28] At the district and appellate levels only, judges approaching the fifteen-year limit could apply to the Senate for a five-year extension. These judgeships, while important, are a great deal less critical and powerful than the Supreme Court posts, so the prospect of five extra years for those judges who wish to apply for the extension seems reasonable and might ease somewhat the confirmation burden on the Senate. One suspects that many lower-court judges, nearing retirement or preferring to rejoin the more lucrative private legal sector, probably would not request an extension. For those who ask for another five years, the Senate would need to reconfirm the judges by the customary majority vote. Much as we observe in the process of reconfirmation at the state level, though, many judges would be extended in office without controversy and with a streamlined procedure, given the short length of the extension. The ones who are weeded out might well follow the state pattern; that is, overwhelmingly, the only judges not reelected or reconfirmed by the legislatures are those who have demonstrated serious personal problems or have proven tone-deaf to ethical challenges during their terms.

Undoubtedly, given the partisanship in the modern U.S. Senate, other judges would be denied extensions by being in the minority party in the Senate, assuming that party control of the upper chamber had switched in the fifteen years since first appointment. This is not a bad thing, since one of the arguments for term-limiting judges is to ensure that the judiciary more accurately reflects the current makeup of the nation. After all, a single laggard branch can stymie reforms that the American people have decisively voted for; a Republican-dominated Supreme Court overturned much of Franklin D. Roosevelt's New Deal efforts to combat the Great Depression, for example.[29] Still, with some exceptions, the Senate would be unlikely to tie itself in knots about short-term extensions for most lower-court judges, even if partisan control of the Senate has changed hands over the fifteen-year period. Far more pressing business would normally take precedence.

Supreme Court slots are far more critical to the nation, and for that reason, the fifteen-year limit should be absolute—a lifetime limit. This is a long time to serve—nearly four current presidential terms, or about a third of the average American's working life.[30] At the same time, it is short enough to prevent justices from becoming too detached and generationally removed from the American mainstream. And as noted earlier, it is about the length of time the first ninety justices served (on average) in the Republic's first eighteen decades. Fifteen years is also long enough to permit both institutional memory and collective wisdom to develop within the Court, yet short enough to deter most justices from evolving a dramatically different philosophy or deteriorating beyond tolerable limits. The term might also ensure that presidents—and the rest of us—get what they have bargained for, whether a liberal or a moderate or a conservative. With the notable and rare exception of a justice like David Souter, who started affiliating with the liberals on the Supreme Court just a few years after his appointment as a supposed conservative, ideological evolution of justices usually takes considerable time, somewhat longer than a decade. While it is their right to evolve, there is also a touch of arrogance involved, not to mention the complete lack of accountability. Judicial independence must be honored and valued, but not to extremes.

Tremendous authority has been concentrated in the federal courts' hands, especially in the Supreme Court, so much so that it is hard to believe that the founders would not have limited them in some ways had they realized what the courts would become in time. It is now appropriate to carry forward the founders' preferences for checks on *all* centers of great power by making these constitutional changes in the Supreme Court and lower courts. It is time to bring the judiciary down from Mount Olympus—not to sea level but to an elevated pedestal within sight of the America they are sworn to serve.

FIXED TERMS

How exactly would the fifteen-year term work? First, it is worth noting that the United States, with the highest per capita population of attorneys in the world,[31] has a deep bench of legal talent that could ably serve in the judiciary. The fifteen years would be a lifetime limit; that is, no one could be reappointed after the passage of a few years to yet another fifteen-year term. The chief justice should be no different in this regard. Even if a president should choose to nominate an existing Court member as chief, his or her term on the Court would end on schedule at the end of the fifteen-year limit. A chief newly nominated to the Court would serve a full fifteen-year term in the post. Staggered terms to "phase in" the fifteen-year term would not be necessary. As we transition from lifetime appointments, new justices would be selected as vacancies occur, on an irregular basis, on the old Court. Similarly, deaths and resignations from the Court would inevitably scramble the schedule of appointments. In the case of the Supreme Court, uncertainty about the schedule of appointments is mainly a good thing, just as it is today under lifetime tenure. Some presidents would get several appointments, and a few would get none, as fortune dictates.

A fifteen-year nonrenewable term would have another benefit: It might encourage presidents to choose the best qualified of the available candidates, even if he or she was older. Increasingly, presidents have searched for younger potential jurists, and while nothing is intrinsically wrong with Supreme Court justices and lower-court judges who are fifty and younger,[32] there is something to be said for the leavening influence of judges with more age and experience under their belts. As talented and intelligent as Chief Justice John Roberts was upon appointment to the Supreme Court at the age of fifty in 2005, for example, he had had a very narrow, constrained legal career, never having argued a case in a court below the Supreme Court nor done many of the practical tasks one associates with a well-rounded lawyer.[33] Roberts became the youngest chief justice since John Marshall was confirmed at age forty-five in 1801, and not by accident. President Bush clearly sought a youthful appointee to place his stamp on the Court for a generation or longer, just as President Clinton had done with the appointment of Stephen Breyer at age fifty-five in 1994 and President George H. W. Bush had done with the selection of Clarence Thomas at age forty-three in 1991. Older candidates for the Court are practically ruled out today, even if they might have the most to offer. For example, will the Supreme Court ever again see a justice like the widely admired Lewis F. Powell Jr., appointed to the Court in 1971 by President Nixon at the age of sixty-four? It is not likely under the prevailing political polarization, as long as lifetime tenure is at stake.

NOT-SO-EARLY RETIREMENT

Several Supreme Court justices have long overstayed their welcome, remaining in office well into their eighties and even nineties. For every Oliver Wendell Holmes, who stayed mentally sharp and retired from the Court at age ninety, there is a William O. Douglas, who clearly went infirm and had to be nudged off the Court at age seventy-seven.[34] More recently in 2005, Chief Justice William H. Rehnquist insisted upon staying on the Court despite a fatal diagnosis of thyroid cancer; he died, still on the Court, having missed months of Court work, intermittently, for almost a year. Scholars of the Court can point to well over a dozen Supreme Court justices whose tenure exceeded their physical and mental abilities to serve.[35] No doubt the intellectual stimulation of the Court's work has helped to keep some jurists alert and alive, but very few human beings at advanced ages retain all their stamina and faculties, and it is questionable whether the "supersenior Supremes" can really be in touch with the ever-changing norms of a dynamic society. While no specific age should be mentioned in the Constitution, given the wonders of modern medical science in gradually extending the life span, the Congress should be given the constitutional authority to set a reasonable retirement age for the robed ones on all federal courts. At least from the perspective of the year 2007, retirement with full pension at seventy-five or, at most, eighty would seem logical.[36] The public appears to be quite supportive of a mandatory retirement age. A recent random-sample survey found that Americans back it by the wide margin of 66 percent to 28 percent.[37] Our own survey, reported in chapter 6, demonstrates even greater backing for mandatory retirement.

The introduction of a retirement age would nicely complement the fifteen-year term for the federal courts, with the term and retirement age serving as the new institutional checks on the judiciary's role in American life. Note that neither innovation would limit the authority of the courts overall. All of their powers would remain intact. But these constitutional bookends would ensure that the courts' members, while still independent, were more representative of, and responsive to, the country's prevailing political and social culture. For all of the judges' insistence that the laws and Constitution alone determine their decisions, it is abundantly clear to observers of every ideological stripe that the values and backgrounds of the men and women who serve on the courts influence their judicial outlooks. Just as the electorate "refreshes" the executive and legislative branches at regular intervals, so too should the judicial branch be refreshed more frequently by means of some added constitutional limits.

A BALANCED BENCH

A third change is also desirable. The size of the Supreme Court should be expanded from nine to twelve. As the power of each member of the Court, and the Court as a whole, has grown in recent decades, so too has the need for greater diversity and representation in the membership of the Court. The latter goal is more difficult to achieve with a Court of nine than a Court of twelve. The additional three members would permit increased diversity in race, gender, ethnicity, religion, age, background, and ideological leanings. At the same time, three more justices would not be enough to reduce the cozy amiability of Court deliberations or transform some of the welcome traditions that help the Court to function collegially. Moreover, the Court's expansion would reduce a bit the critical importance of each member. Might this not lower the temperature by a few degrees in the confirmation process? Incidentally, an expansion is not unprecedented. Since the dimension of the Court is not specified in the current Constitution and is left to the discretion of Congress,[38] the Supreme Court has been of various sizes throughout the centuries; for example, there were ten justices between 1863 and 1866.[39]

To prevent unwanted political manipulation, such as FDR's attempted court-packing scheme in 1937, the flexibility of the constitutional language should be reduced in this one case to lock in the precise number of justices in the text, rather than letting Congress determine the Supreme Court's size by statute. Is it wise to permit the size of the Court to be changed at any time, at the whim of a president and Congress seeking to accomplish some short-term political ends? That seems doubtful. A numerical specification in the Constitution would actually help to protect the independence of the Court. Under the present rules of lifetime tenure and no retirement age, such a change might be ill-advised since it would eliminate possible leverage to move a recalcitrant Court. But with fairly frequent turnover ensured with the establishment of the fifteen-year term and mandatory retirement age, the country could afford to balance those new checks with a further guarantee of Court autonomy.

An even number of justices is proposed for a good reason. There is no doubt that the Court will deadlock 6 to 6 on many occasions. This is actually a good thing, given the concern many Americans have about the Court becoming a super-legislature. A tie vote simply would uphold the appellate court ruling, without setting a national precedent. Since fewer national precedents would mean less judicial intervention, a larger Supreme Court would take a somewhat smaller role in national life—which is probably a good thing for it and the country.

Note, too, that an even number would make it much more difficult for a single justice to become the key "swing justice," such as Justice Sandra Day O'Connor was for much of the 1990s and the first half decade of the new century, and Justice Anthony Kennedy has become since O'Connor's retirement. It is not healthy for one justice, in effect, to become the Supreme Court's brain, deciding most of the divisive cases with her lone choice of sides. A Court of twelve would likely have more complex factions that would mix and remix in interesting and not always predictable ways.

POWER OF THE PURSE

Just as we should guarantee judicial independence by eliminating possible executive and legislative manipulation of the Court's size, we also ought to give the Supreme Court and inferior courts true constitutional independence in the matter of their salaries. After much debate, the original Constitutional Convention decided to grant Congress the right to set judicial salaries, though the legislature was prohibited from decreasing judges' pay. The problem here is that judges must, with some regularity, go hat in hand to Congress, begging for cost-of-living increases. These requests can potentially affect their decisions regarding congressional actions. Yet another rejected proposal by James Madison has promise for us today. Madison was concerned about the use of the purse to incite "cabal and corruption," and he suggested that the salaries of judges be fixed using a standard of "wheat or some other thing of permanent value."[40] All judges ought to be constitutionally guaranteed annual cost-of-living increases, similar to those of Social Security recipients. Congress should retain the power to *raise* base salaries more substantially from time to time in order to attract the best and the brightest to the judiciary from the lucrative legal profession.

By the way, for many consecutive years, the chief justices have issued an end-of-the-year "state of the judiciary" report, calling for dramatically increased pay for judges. Citing an alleged "brain drain" of the most qualified jurists from the bench back to the lucrative private sector, Chief Justice Roberts claimed in December 2006 that the situation has "now reached the level of a constitutional crisis and threatens to undermine the strength and independence of the federal judiciary."[41] Terming the matter a "constitutional crisis" seems overblown, especially since the annual salaries of judges range from $165,000 at the district court level up to $203,000 for the Supreme Court (and $212,000 for the chief justice). Nonetheless, the fifteen-year term limit actually helps here. This fixed period will involve less financial sacrifice for those called to the high honor of serving on the federal courts—again, if one can see these high salaries as painful.[42]

*

As with the presidency and the Congress, revising the judiciary would involve mixing and matching constitutional means and ends. Just as the founders wisely determined, each branch should have the powers necessary for it to perform its vital function, yet no branch should possess so much power as to be overweening. Each branch must check the others. There is no change here to this brilliant design, only some fine-tuning. We have recommended that the executive and the legislature be rebalanced in some ways, and similarly, the judiciary has been altered with care. The goal is never to strengthen or weaken one branch with respect to the others, but actually to bolster the operation of all three branches by helping them to function better internally and to work responsibly with the others.

We have only one advantage over the framers in redesigning the Constitution: the experiences of the past 220 years. Given all this history, practice, and controversy, good and bad, it would be odd if we could not find some ways to tweak and polish the Constitution. In the chapters on the Congress, the presidency, and the Supreme Court, I have avoided radical change—such as the transition to a parliamentary democracy—and focused instead on moderate ways to improve a system that is already sound in the basics (separation of powers, checks and balances, and individual liberties). But there are several reforms that mark a clear departure from past practice, and it is to those ideas that we now turn in the next several chapters.

CHAPTER FOUR

★

POLITICS: AMERICA'S MISSING CONSTITUTIONAL LINK

IT'S MANIFESTLY OBVIOUS. The last thing the United States needs is more politics. Or so those Americans who hate politics believe. On this point, however, they are very wrong. It's not that citizens are off course in disliking the excessive length of campaigns, the sky-high cost of elections, the almost irrational methods we employ to choose presidential nominees, and the archaic way the Electoral College functions. In all of these fashions, the American political system is inequitable and doesn't work very well. But it is unfair and doesn't work well because the Constitution does not contain workable rules to govern it. If we wanted to point fingers, we could place the blame for this deficiency squarely on the shoulders of the founders. Yet that would also be unfair. The demands of their time were very different; we now need to redesign the Constitution to accommodate the political needs of our time.

Most would argue that, in many respects, today's political system is broken, and there is currently no reasonable prospect of fixing it. Our schedule of presidential primaries and caucuses is a mess, giving too much power to an unrepresentative few with undue influence over the party nominees. Because it would require taking on entrenched interests, the Congress, the parties, and the states refuse to tackle reform of the nominating system, and plenty of other key parts of politics as well. Our scheme of campaign financing incorporates the worst of several worlds and deteriorates further with each passing election cycle. Our partisan procedure for drawing legislative districts encourages vicious polarization rather than promoting moderation and compromise. In the end, all these disasters can be traced back to the Constitution—not so much what was included in the text, but some items excluded from it.

The founders preferred to think of themselves as statesmen, not politicians, and in the statecraft of their times there was remarkably little *formal* role for politics. Even more than in the current day, politics was viewed as a disreputable business, and the perfidies of "factions" (the founders' name for political parties) were detested and dreaded. George Washington famously warned the new nation against them in his farewell address.

> However combinations or associations of the above description may now and then answer popular ends, they are likely, in the course of time and things, to become potent engines, by which cunning, ambitious, and unprincipled men will be enabled to subvert the power of the people and to usurp for themselves the reins of government, destroying afterwards the very engines which have lifted them to unjust dominion.[1]

But as the years rolled by, even during Washington's own administration, most of the founders came to understand that politics and its institutions were necessities for a successful republic. Adams and Jefferson helped to create rival political parties. Their Electoral College deadlock in the 1800 presidential contest led to a constitutional amendment that acknowledged the inevitable political relationship between the president and vice president. Citizens grew restive at elite rule and began demanding the opportunity to cast popular ballots for president to instruct their electors. And the American system, in fits and starts and the occasional piecemeal constitutional adjustment, adapted to include these political changes.

The essential problem, though, has never been corrected. The Constitution was written by the founders when they had not yet realized the vital necessity of politics and parties in the process of our elections. Further, the enormous transformation of politics from the part-time avocation of "public-spirited gentlemen" to the multibillion-dollar enterprise of electoral institutions in a rich, diverse, continental republic has not been matched by constitutional adaptation. The absence of modern politics in the Constitution—from the structure of presidential selection to the manner of congressional elections to some critical aspects of electioneering, such as redistricting and campaign finance—has caused no end of difficulties, which can only be corrected by the inclusion of thoughtful provisions on these subjects in a new twenty-first-century Constitution. Critics of this constitutional approach may insist that the political inadequacies of our system are best handled through statutory means, the better to make adjustments as needed from time to time. And partly, this point of view has merit. The constitutional provisions on the political system should be kept only as specific as absolutely required to cure the ills we will discuss in this chapter. Congressional and state statutes—the regular law-making process in the various legislatures—can supplement mandates in the Constitution.

However, the chances for serious, widespread political reform at this late date are virtually nil without constitutional prodding. Yes, a state here or there may enact a useful reform plan for a piece of the puzzle. But the nation is desperately in need of widespread change and dramatic updating for the political system. Ingrained interests would fight and stop most or all of the reforms outlined in this chapter. The United States now has a massive superstructure of almost untouchable procedures and traditions with powerful beneficiaries: incumbents, wealthy groups and individuals, even specific states (think Iowa and New Hampshire in the presidential selection process).

A new revolution is required to revitalize America's antique politics. The occasional initiative or referendum that usually fails due to campaign spending by special interests must give way to a wide-ranging approach in the national interest. We need to seek a comprehensive solution that will be as permanent as the Constitution can promise. We should start by overhauling the inadequate and sometimes destructive methods we employ for picking a president.

OF PARTIES, PRESIDENTIAL POLITICS, AND THE QUADRENNIAL ORGY

Once avoided in their entirety by the founders and the Constitution, political parties have become the sine qua non of American democracy. This was obvious by the time of Andrew Jackson, if not before. Woodrow Wilson declared parties to be utterly essential to the functioning of both elective branches—the institutions holding together the government of the United States in the face of so many internal, dividing checks and balances.

> Government is not a machine, but a living thing . . . No living thing can have its organs offset against each other as checks, and live . . . The way in which the several branches of the federal government have been separately organized and given efficiency in the discharge of their own functions has only emphasized their separation and jealous independence . . . It is for that reason that we have had such an extraordinary development [outside of the Constitution] of party authority in the United States and have developed

> outside the government itself so elaborate and effective an organization of parties. [The political parties] are absolutely necessary to hold the things thus disconnected and dispersed together and give some coherence to the action of political forces.[2]

Wilson also suggested the government was subject to Darwinian evolutionary forces, and he was correct again. Over many decades, the parties have evolved to meet the organizational needs of government. Along the way, though, the constitutionally ungoverned parties have also changed to serve their own needs better—and some of those selfish purposes have begun to override those of the citizenry's. Most people think the political parties are nationally run by the Democratic and Republican national committees. To a limited degree, especially in the administration of the national party conventions every four years, that is true. But fundamentally, parties are and have always been state-based, because there are no federal constitutional guidelines and strictures on them. The state party committees, in conjunction with the state legislatures, actually set many of the rules for presidential selection, such as whether a primary or a caucus is held in a particular state, and how those events are actually run. With no one at the national level truly in charge, the fifty state political parties on each side (Democratic and Republican) squabble among themselves, initiating internecine battles about who can go first, and second, and tenth, in presidential selection every four years. Sometimes, the Democratic Party and the Republican Party in some states cannot even agree on a common date for the primary or caucus, so the voters in those states are treated to two separate nomination campaigns within the span of a few weeks or months. In doing so, the state parties promote and serve individual state or party interests over the national interest. The federal Constitution has been preeminent over the state constitutions since the days of Chief Justice John Marshall, but not so among the political parties, which live in a no-man's-land—a Wild, Wild West—in law and practice: nationally organized but state-based, fundamentally private associations of like-minded people yet groups with vital public functions (such as the nomination of our highest elected officials). Darwinian evolution is fine for the origin of species, but it is past time for the necessary political institutions called parties to be governed by some sort of federal intelligent design. Only the Constitution can achieve this aim.

If any ongoing disaster can prove the point, surely it is the quadrennial orgy of the presidential primary process.

Imagine that a convention of clowns met to design an amusing, crazy-quilt schedule to nominate presidential candidates. The resulting system would probably look much as ours does today. The incoherent organization of primaries and caucuses, and the candidates' mad-dash attempts to move around the map, would be funny if the goal—electing the leader of the free world—weren't so serious.

In 1968 there were fifteen presidential primaries, a manageable number spread out over about three months, from March until June.[3] The voters could focus on their task, and often there was enough time between primaries (a couple of weeks or so) for midcourse corrections in the selection of a party nominee, that is, enough time between contests for the momentum of the first primary winner to die down so that voters in the next state could take a fresh look at the contenders. In 2004 there were thirty-six primaries, not counting the ones in D.C. and for "Americans Abroad,"[4] stretching from January through June—a six-month period of intense politicking, preceded by at least a year of equally intense, headline-grabbing candidate maneuvering. In 2008 forty-one state presidential primaries are scheduled at the time of this writing.

To make matters worse, in a phenomenon called *front-loading*, a majority of the states are rushing to the start of the calendar, in order to maximize their impact on the choice of the party nominees. The financial and other benefits are great in securing one of the early spots: The candidates spend millions on advertising and staff support, while the news media add millions more in free publicity for the picturesque spots in the state. The problem here is that the states are now bunched together so tightly that the winner of the first primary or caucus often wins the second, and the third, and the entire nomination simply because of the big momentum generated off the first victory. Some call it a "steamroller," others a "slingshot," but the effect is clear: a lightning-quick nomination of that initial victor. The primaries scheduled later in the calendar become pro forma events, with low voter turnout and little media attention. To add insult to injury, the already-crowned candidates often do not even show up to campaign. Moreover, the front-loading means that the candidates must start their campaigns at least a full year in advance of the first nomination contest, in order to become known around the country and raise the huge sums needed to compete. This elongation of the full-throttle campaign is welcomed only by political consultants and other paid election staffers, certainly not by the average voter, who becomes bored with the permanent campaign.

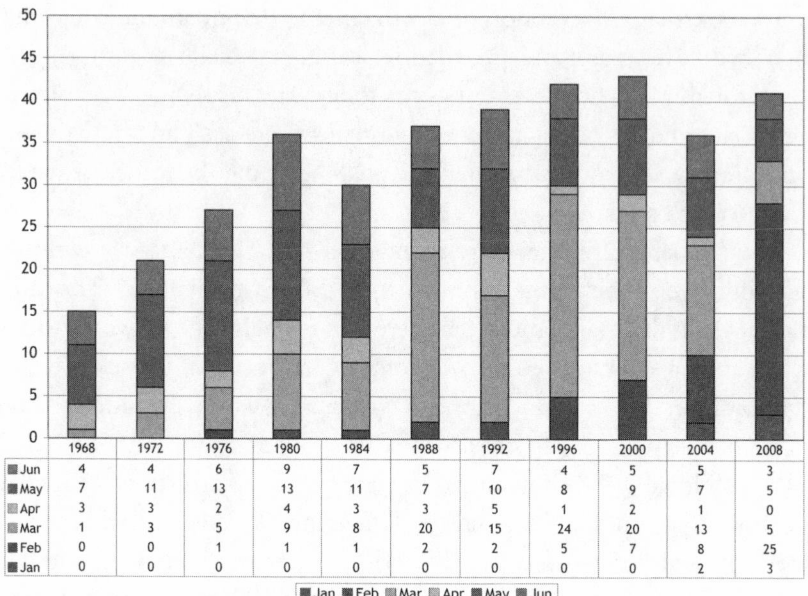

	1968	1972	1976	1980	1984	1988	1992	1996	2000	2004	2008
Jun	4	4	6	9	7	5	7	4	5	5	3
May	7	11	13	13	11	7	10	8	9	7	5
Apr	3	3	2	4	3	3	5	1	2	1	0
Mar	1	3	5	9	8	20	15	24	20	13	5
Feb	0	0	1	1	1	2	2	5	7	8	25
Jan	0	0	0	0	0	0	0	0	0	2	3

FIGURE 4.1. NUMBER OF PRESIDENTIAL PRIMARIES BY MONTH, 1968–2008

Front-loading has become endemic over the last thirty years. While only one state had a primary or caucus in January or February of 1980, by 2000 that number was nine (including seven primaries) and by 2004, nineteen (including ten primaries).* The 2008 schedule is guaranteed to break 2004's record by a wide margin; at the time of this writing, forty-three states (including twenty-eight primaries) were on the calendar with contests before the start of March. In 1976, a typical year in that era, the midpoint of the presidential primary season—the date when half of the primaries had been held and half had yet to be staged—was May 18, but in 2008 the primary midpoint will be in early February.[5] In the presidential system, the old axiom that "the first shall be last, and the last shall be first" doesn't apply. With only a couple of modern exceptions (1976 on the Republican side and 1984 in the Democratic contest),[6] the presidential nominees have been known well in advance of the party conventions, and usually the first handful of primary and caucus contests determine the winners.

Few want to go back to the bad old days when party "bosses" chose

* Note that these monthly totals include primaries *and* caucuses. The totals in Figure 4.1 represent only primaries.

presidential candidates in smoke-filled rooms. (Yes, the bosses did reasonably well by selecting nominees such as Franklin Roosevelt, but they also picked the disastrous Warren G. Harding.) Primaries and caucuses are now fundamental to our conception of popular democracy in presidential selection. But there is such a thing as ineffective popular democracy, especially when it is hopelessly disorganized.

Every attempt to bring order out of chaos has failed, and there have been many attempts to do so.[7] Recently, national Republican leaders at the 2000 GOP Convention in Philadelphia, where George W. Bush was nominated for president for the first time, tried to pass a plan to give states incentives to hold *later* primaries and caucuses in an attempt to slow front-loading, but the plan failed to pass muster with the convention delegates.[8] For 2008, the Democratic National Committee is attempting to bring about some reasonable reordering of the early contests by designating a handful of more diverse small states to go first, but the attempt to dilute the impact of Iowa and especially New Hampshire is turning out to be less than successful.[9] Democrats have chosen Nevada, with its relatively large Hispanic population, and South Carolina, with its sizable African American electorate, to join Iowa and New Hampshire at the front of the line in January 2008, and other states such as Florida and Wyoming are jumping into January on their own. Not surprisingly, Iowa and New Hampshire are balking and appear determined to go first—national party rules be damned. Moreover, since a majority of the parties' convention delegates will be selected by early February, the nomination battles will likely be over in record time—before voters have had an opportunity to reconsider the fifty states' candidate choices. The presidential general election of 2008 will almost certainly be the longest and most intense in American history.

As suggested above, a good-size piece of the problem can be labeled "Iowa and New Hampshire." These two states seem to assume that the Constitution guarantees that they should go first, but a close reading of the text finds no such clause. The New Hampshire primary was initiated in 1920, and it has arguably been very influential since 1952, when it played a role in both the decision of President Truman not to seek reelection and Dwight Eisenhower's successful quest for the GOP nomination.[10] New Hampshire reprised its 1952 incumbent-toppling when Minnesota senator Eugene McCarthy came within a few percentage points of President Lyndon Johnson in the 1968 Democratic primary, leading in part to LBJ's decision shortly thereafter not to seek another term.[11] The Iowa caucus has only played a role since 1968, and its true national debut came in 1972, when George McGovern scored well there on his way to a surprise, ill-fated Democratic nomination. Just four years later, the Iowa caucus propelled a little-known former Georgia governor, Jimmy Carter, to the Democratic nomination and the presidency, assisted also by Carter's subsequent narrow victory in New Hampshire. In both the Hawkeye and Granite states, Carter received less than 30 percent of the votes, but in a crowded Democratic field of candidates, this low percentage was enough to prevail.[12]

All early-voting states benefit, as I suggested before, but the presidential selection process is a special bonanza for both Iowa and New Hampshire—an industry that produces tens of millions of dollars in spending from the campaigns. Candidates and their staffs often practically move into these states, and they bring thousands of reporters with them over time. The television and radio stations, the hotels, and the restaurants of Iowa and New Hampshire make a killing off the business generated by their claim to political supremacy. Moreover, all the candidates—and thus the eventual president—learn about their problems and needs—an educational process that cannot hurt the states in the spending decisions of the next administration. Plus, the elected president knows he will have to start his reelection effort in the same two states—further incentive to assist them. The presidential selection process is a gravy train for the Hawkeye and Granite states, and they know it. The citizens of the lead-off states take their job as presidential screeners seriously, but then what state given this important task would not? The presidential candidates fully understand the game they are playing, and the absurdity of it. For example, Michael Dukakis, the 1988 Democratic presidential nominee, had this to say about Iowa: "I spent 85 campaign days in the state of Iowa alone. Now, Iowa is a great state . . . and they did very well by Mike Dukakis. But, 85 full campaign days in one state . . . really doesn't make a hell of a lot of sense, does it?"[13]

Why should two small, heavily white, disproportionately rural states have a hammerlock on the making of the president? Together, Iowa and New Hampshire comprise a mere 1.4 percent of the U.S. population, and about 40 percent of their residents are rural—double the national proportion. Their average African American plus Hispanic/Latino population is 3.6 percent, while the nation as a whole is 24.6 percent minority. Even if one assumes, incorrectly, that the two states are somehow representative of their Northeast and Midwest regions, the burgeoning South and West (containing 55 percent of the country's people) are mainly left out of the critical opening window of presidential selection.

The truth is that Iowa and New Hampshire have a franchise they are determined to keep at all costs. New Hampshire even has a law that requires its secretary of state to do whatever is necessary to keep its primary first,[14] and Secretary William Gardner has threatened, if needed, to move the New Hampshire primary back into *the calendar year before the presidential election* to fulfill his mandate. No doubt Iowa would do the same. And we think the process takes too long already?

Without a constitutional requirement, there is simply no solution to a situation that deteriorates every four years. Try as they might, the national party committees cannot orchestrate a fix. In the end, they can only punish a recalcitrant Iowa and New Hampshire in minor ways, by cutting the size of their convention delegations or giving the delegates bad hotels and seating at the party conclaves. The candidates who campaign in states holding contests earlier than permitted can also be penalized by having the national parties deny them any delegates they may win in those states. But a handful of lost delegates is trivial compared to the whirlwind of positive publicity secured by victory in early states. These penalties, light as they are, may not even materialize. By the time of the national conventions, the parties are unlikely to want to alienate swing states such as Iowa and New Hampshire as the general election campaign begins. Every electoral vote matters in this closely divided era, and the results in Iowa and New Hampshire have been among the closest in the nation in the 2000 and 2004 presidential elections. Nor will the parties want to aggravate their candidates by penalizing them at a time when they are attempting to fully unify their forces at the convention.

Congress has some power to intervene in the state-based, party-centered nominating process, yet the federal legislature would be highly unlikely to step into that briar patch.[15] Presidential nominating reform has never been a priority for Congress, in part because of the traditional rights of the states and the parties to organize this sector of politics. It is highly doubtful that Congress will generate the will to clean up the nomination mess anytime soon. For one thing, the senators and representatives from Iowa and New Hampshire would be willing to do anything to stop congressionally sponsored reform, quite possibly with assistance from colleagues who would see their own presidential ambitions at stake. A senator who becomes a hero in Iowa and New Hampshire for saving the caucus and primary would be halfway to a presidential nomination! And realizing this, most or all of the senators with presidential aspirations would jump to back the Iowa/New Hampshire status quo. (It's a rare ambitious senator who doesn't get up in the morning and see a president in the mirror.)

Thus, the only possible, comprehensive answer is likely to be a constitutional one. In the twenty-first century we the people need to do what the founders didn't even perceive as necessary in their pre-party, pre-popular-democracy age. The guiding principle should be one that all citizens, in theory, can readily embrace: Every state and region ought to have essentially an equal chance, over time, to influence the outcome of the parties' presidential nominations, and thus the selection of presidents. We are one nation, and simple equity demands that all of us, regardless of our state of residence, should have the opportunity at some point to influence the selection of presidential nominees by filling one of the precious, early voting slots.

Beyond the equal-influence-over-time rule, the presidential selection process also ought to enable the states to spread out the contests over several months, thereby reducing front-loading and the low voter turnout in the primaries that follow. In most recent cycles, the nominations have been all but decided by the first few weeks of voting, leaving large majorities of voters and states effectively disenfranchised. In 2000, for example, both Vice President Al Gore and Governor George W. Bush had all but clinched their party's nominations before thirty-three states, including many of the largest, had even held their primaries. Understandably, this fact led an alienated public to tune out the process before they could become engaged and learn about all the men and women who would be president. In 2000 again—the last time both parties had multi-candidate, highly competitive fields running for the presidency—a mere 17.7 percent of the adult population turned out to vote in all primaries and caucuses, in both parties and all states combined. This is a miserable showing, and it also contributes to the control of both parties' nominating machinery by those well over on the left (Democrats) and the right (Republicans). The majority of the public that is gathered around the ideological center has become discouraged and disconnected in the past few decades, assisting the polarization that bedevils American politics. The construction of a nominating process that is inclusive and rational may contribute a great deal to broadening the level of participation in the primaries and caucuses.

That nominating process ought also to be moved back into the four months leading up to the party conventions. Presidential politics now takes fully one fourth of a president's four-year term—whether he is running for re-election or not—and with front-loading accelerating, it soon may consume even more of it. Not only is this bad for the presidency as an institution, but it causes the electorate to tire of the never-ending political campaign. It should be possible to create a system that flows from the first primaries and caucuses beginning in March or April directly into August party conventions, and then into the Labor Day kickoff for the autumn general election. Not only is this not rocket science; it doesn't even qualify as elementary mathematics. It is easy, if the will and the means are present. The electorate must supply the will, and the Constitution should outline the means.

There have been dozens of proposals to revamp the primary scheme,[16] though none has been offered as a constitutional fix. Clearly, that is both because the Constitution currently ignores the politics of the system almost entirely and because a constitutional insertion—virtually written in stone—would have to be as fair and foolproof as possible. The following plan, the product of much discussion and thought, is proposed in that spirit.

THE REGIONAL LOTTERY PLAN FOR THE NEW CONSTITUTION

The Congress should be constitutionally required to designate four regions of contiguous states (with contiguity waved for Alaska and Hawaii, and any other stray territories that may one day become states). The regions would surely look something like the ones in figure 4.2, with natural boundaries denoting the Northeast, South, Midwest, and West.[17] All of the states in each region would hold their nominating events in successive months, beginning in April and ending in July. The two major-party conventions would follow in August. This schedule, all by itself, would cut three months off the too-long process currently prevailing in presidential years.

The presidential nominating system would still be state-based, so each state party would be free to choose any date it wished within the region's month, and further, it would be free, as currently, to choose either the primary or the caucus method of selecting delegates.[18] Of course, all the states in a region might try to front-load their contests on the first possible day, but that actually would make little sense, except perhaps for the first region in the series. Even in that first region, a state might have more influence coming later in the month, perhaps standing alone on a particular day—a situation that would encourage presidential candidates to spend time and money in the stand-alone state. After all, the post-primary headlines would belong solely to the candidate who won that stand-alone state. If there were ten states on a particular day, the headlines as well as the candidates' time and money would be split ten ways. Note, too, that the regional system would concentrate the candidates within a single region for a month. They would have a better opportunity to get to

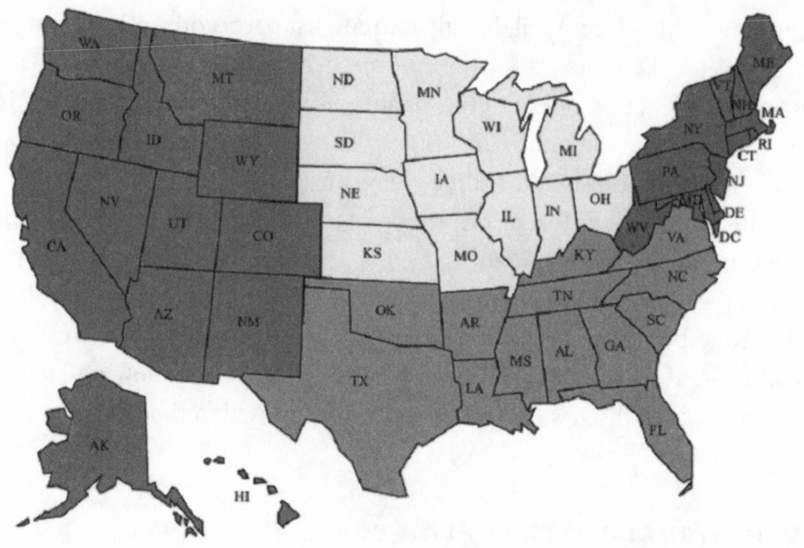

FIGURE 4.2. PROPOSED REGIONAL MAP

know the problems and peoples of the region and its states, and the geographic proximity of the campaigning would cut down on the wear and tear on the candidates, to some degree anyway.

But how would the order of the regions be determined? In many cases, there would still be a bonus in going first. The establishment of a U.S. Election Lottery, to be held on New Year's Day of the presidential election year, would yield fairness and also add an element of drama to the beginning of a presidential year. One of the nation's famous lottery machines with the pop-up ping-pong balls would finally find a purpose beyond bestowing untold riches on people who can't handle it. Four color-coded balls, each representing one of the regions, would be loaded into the machine, and in short order—the length of a ten-second lottery TV drawing—the regional primary order would be set. Since none of the candidates would know in advance where the political season would begin, part of the permanent presidential campaign would be dismantled. After all, even a very wealthy candidate wouldn't waste the money necessary to organize all fifty states in advance, and the four-year-long homesteading in Iowa and New Hampshire would be gone forever. Much more important, the "law" of averages would give every state and each region, over time, the precious opportunity of going first. Clearly, there is no guarantee that a particularly lucky region would not be repeatedly chosen to start the process, but the equal-access principle is key to the fairness in this plan. These new constitutional provisions would "repeal" the nonexistent constitutional right to go first that Iowa and New Hampshire have appropriated for themselves.

Another benefit of the Regional Lottery Plan would be the reasonable spacing between contests, allowing candidates potentially to recover from setbacks in one region and to regroup prior to the next set of contests. Today's front-loading nearly ensures that the entire competition for the party nominations is over within a few weeks, whereas under the Regional Lottery Plan regional pride and loyalties might demand that the race continue through two or three, and maybe all four, sections of the nation. The news media and voters in each region would certainly be on the same page on this critical matter, demanding their fair share of attention.

One additional facet should be added to the plan in order to enhance its effectiveness. The best argument made for Iowa and New Hampshire is that their small populations allow for highly personalized campaigning. The candidates are able to meet individual citizens for lengthy and sometimes repeated conversations about the issues, and these voters are able to size up potential presidents at eye level, without the candidates having the protection of the usual large retinue of image makers and staffers. In that sense, lightly populated states can serve as a useful screening committee for the rest of us. The United States is a continental country, after all, and each large region is still enormous in size.

There is a way to combine the advantages of small-state scrutiny of candidates with the inherent fairness of round-robin regional primaries. We can achieve the best of both worlds by adding a second lottery on January 1. The names of all states with four or fewer members in the U.S. House of Representatives (at present, twenty states)[19] would be placed in a lottery machine, and two balls would be selected. This plan excludes the island territories, which are far-flung and don't influence the November presidential outcome, since they have no electoral votes. The District of Columbia *should* be included, however, and this would mean twenty-one jurisdictions would have a chance to be selected in the second lottery. With a larger population than Wyoming, and with three electoral votes assigned in November, the District's citizens—currently and shamefully without full voting representation in either house of Congress—would no doubt relish and deserve this opportunity, should Lady Luck in the lottery deliver it to them.

The two small states (or D.C.) with relatively low populations would lead off the regional contests, and they would be held on or about March 15—at least two full weeks before the initial contests would begin in the first region. These two states would be free to stage a primary or a caucus, and the candidates would be free to participate in none, one, or both. As a practical matter, most candidates would choose both, unless a prominent candidate hailed from one of the lead-off states. Traditionally, a home candidate gets deference and is sometimes unopposed for the state's delegate votes. Of course, the other party can still have a full-fledged fight in the state's primary or caucus.

No doubt, all the candidates would rush to these lead-off states right after the lottery on January 1, and they would have two and a half months to campaign. But there would be no permanent, four-year campaigns there, and personalized, one-to-one campaigning would be a large part of the effort. In other words, the two states would offer all the advantages of Iowa and New Hampshire, without having to always be Iowa and New Hampshire. Additionally, the guarantee of at least two weeks of decompression after the lead-off states make their choices gives voters in the first region a chance to evaluate the results and reevaluate the winners—and possibly to make different choices.

In sum, the Regional Lottery Plan would achieve many good things simultaneously for a selection process that currently makes little sense. The election campaign would be shortened and focused, a relief to both candidates and voters. All regions and states would get an opportunity to have a substantial impact on the making of the presidential nominees. A rational, nicely arranged schedule would build excitement and citizen involvement in every corner of the country, without sacrificing the personalized scrutiny of candidates for which Iowa and New Hampshire have become justly known. And all of this can *only* come about by putting the politics of nominations and elections in its proper place—the United States Constitution.

THE ELECTORAL COLLEGE: MEND IT, DON'T END IT

The second half of the presidential electoral process is also in need of constitutional reform. The 2000 election cliffhanger between George W. Bush and Al Gore was only the latest crisis to beset the constitutional mechanism for the election of a president, the Electoral College. There have been other Electoral College controversies, including the presidential elections of 1800 (Thomas Jefferson, John Adams, and Aaron Burr),[20] 1824 (John Quincy Adams, Andrew Jackson, and others),[21] 1876 (Rutherford B. Hayes versus Samuel Tilden),[22] and 1888 (Grover Cleveland versus Benjamin Harrison).[23] In 1824, 1876, and 1888—just as in 2000—the popular vote winner was denied the presidency because of a contrary Electoral College vote. In 1800, 1824, and

1876—just as in 2000—there were political shenanigans of various sorts that further clouded the results.

Moreover, there have been a number of near misses in American presidential history, cases where the nation narrowly avoided great controversy in the final results. In the lifetimes of many Americans, for example, the 1968 and 1976 contests teetered on the edge. In 1968 the 46 electoral votes secured by the segregationist George Wallace of Alabama in Deep South states might well have decided the tight election between Richard Nixon (R) and Hubert Humphrey (D). In the end, Nixon edged Humphrey slightly in the popular vote and secured a modest majority in the Electoral College so that Wallace could not have determined the winner by throwing his electoral votes to one of the candidates.[24] Imagine the consequences had a race-baiter like Wallace been the one to pick a president![25] In 1976 an addition of just 11,117 votes in Ohio and 7,373 votes in Hawaii for the Republican ticket would have produced a four-year term for President Gerald Ford (R), even though Jimmy Carter (D) would have won the popular vote by a massive 1.7 million.[26] Even in a more decisive popular-vote election like 2004, when President George W. Bush won by 3 million votes nationally and an Electoral College vote of 286 to 252 over the Democrat John F. Kerry,[27] a switch of only 60,000 votes in Ohio would have given Kerry the Buckeye State's 20 electoral votes and 272 electoral votes overall—and thus, the presidency.[28]

Many analysts and observers of American politics say that this record, and the very real potential for more mayhem in the future, calls for outright abolition of the Electoral College in the next constitutional revision.[29] But these critics ignore some important advantages of the Electoral College—which endures, albeit unloved—and deserves more respect than it gets. At the same time, the current system is inadequate to the needs of the modern Republic, so a proper approach is "Mend it, don't end it."

The Founding of a College

Adopted in 1789, before the establishment of political parties and before most citizens had the right to vote, the Electoral College was created for a variety of reasons—some purely political, others based upon principle. At the heart of the college was compromise, producing a republican, though undemocratic, system designed to give all states a voice in the selection of the nation's leader. The men drafting the Constitution found it very difficult to believe that a national mandate, like that naturally possessed by George Washington, would be attainable for candidates in the future. The framers wanted the

Electoral College to serve as a reliable gatekeeper, a richly endowed "nominating committee" that would send the top vote-getters to the U.S. House for a final choice, without any reliance on the will of the general public. George Mason, cited in James Madison's notes, "conceived it would be as unnatural to refer the choice of a proper character for chief Magistrate to the people, as it would, to refer a trial of colours to a blind man. The extent of the Country renders it impossible that the people can have the requisite capacity to judge."[30]

Once instituted, it did not take long for the Electoral College to stir controversy. In 1796 John Adams defeated Thomas Jefferson for the presidency by just three electoral votes, with Jefferson becoming vice president due to his second-place finish. Four years later, Jefferson ran again, against incumbent President Adams. This time around, Jefferson and his ticket mate, Aaron Burr, came out on top in the Electoral College. At that time, each elector voted for two men, and the top two vote-getters were supposed to serve as president and vice president. But the Jefferson electors had voted for both men, so Jefferson and Burr each had 73 of 138 electoral votes. While Burr had been the choice for vice president and not president, his political ambition kept him from stepping aside. It took thirty-six ballots in the U.S. House of Representatives—with votes cast by state delegations as a whole, not by individual members—to select Thomas Jefferson as our third president. This fiasco prompted the Twelfth Amendment to the Constitution, which, among other provisions, requires electors to vote for presidential and vice presidential candidates separately.

More than two centuries later, despite the many controversies that have engulfed presidential elections, the Twelfth Amendment still marks the most significant change to the Electoral College in all of American history—a fact that alone suggests that some rethinking may be in order. In the 1960s, the Twenty-third Amendment granted three electoral votes to the District of Columbia. Other amendments have primarily altered the timing of the electoral vote tabulation and the way in which individual states choose to allocate their electors.[31]

Despite these small changes, the Electoral College today works much as it has since the 1800s. Each state receives a number of electors equal to the size of its delegation to the U.S. Congress (the number of U.S. representatives as determined by the decennial census, plus two electors for the two U.S. senators from the state). Anyone except a federal public officeholder[32] can serve as an elector. The state political parties select their electors—usually faithful party workers—in the spring or summer of the presidential election year and submit their list to the board of election in each state. The electors appear on the ballot in November, as a slate, under the names of their party's candidates for president and vice president; we voters are actually choosing a slate of electors who are pledged to our preferred nominees for the top national offices. The electoral slate receiving a plurality of the popular vote—at least one vote more than the other electoral slates—in the November general election meets in the state capitol in early December for a formal ceremony whereby they cast their ballots for president and vice president. While pledged to their party nominees, they have the right to vote for absolutely anyone who meets the constitutional qualifications for either position (at least thirty-five years of age, natural-born citizen, etc.)[33] whether the individual appeared on the ballot or not.

Those electors who do not follow their pledge are called *faithless electors.*[34] Given the considerable freedom that electors have to ignore the mandate of the voters, it is easy to understand why the political parties do their best to carefully select their elector candidates, trying to pick only the most loyal activists. Still, the parties can only hope that their electors will remain steadfast. Human beings can be unreliable and unpredictable, and an elector might be genuinely put off by a pledge made by his or her party's presidential candidate during the autumn campaign. Fortunately for the parties, there is a real stigma attached to the label of faithless elector, and anyone acquiring it can forget about a successful future career in politics.[35] In any event, the tally of the electors' ballots from the fifty state capitols is sent to the Congress, and in a simple but moving ceremony in January, the incumbent vice president—the president of the Senate—opens and reads the ballot tallies before a joint session of Congress. (In modern times, somewhat jarringly, Vice President Richard Nixon in 1961, Vice President Hubert Humphrey in 1969, and Vice President Al Gore in 2001 had to read the electoral tallies and announce their opponents, John F. Kennedy, Richard M. Nixon, and George W. Bush respectively, as having been elected president.)

As long as one presidential ticket has received an absolute majority of the electoral votes, the election is over. If no one has received a majority for president and/or for vice president—remember, the Twelfth Amendment requires the separate counting of ballots for each office—then the House of Representatives gathers to elect a president and the Senate to elect a vice president. An absolute majority of the House state delegations, with each delegation voting as a unit and every state—regardless of size—having a single vote, is required to elect a president, and an absolute majority of the Senate is required to elect a vice president.[36]

Whatever one thinks of its origins, development, and complicated operation, the Electoral College has become a fundamental component of our presidential selection system. Campaigns base their strategies upon it, but its impact extends far beyond presidential politics. Should the nation seriously consider altering or eliminating this system, it must carefully examine the true benefits and disadvantages of our current system versus the consequences of any reform proposals. Let's look first at the positive side of the ledger for the Electoral College.

Advantages of the Electoral College

The Electoral College has served as a stabilizing force in American politics by limiting fragmentation through the emergence of multiple parties.

This benefit exists because of the winner-take-all allocation of electors in all states but Maine and Nebraska.[37] Simply put, Americans are encouraged to vote for one of the two major parties' presidential tickets so as not to "throw their vote away." Either the Democrats or the Republicans have won the presidency since the election of 1856,[38] and prior to that year, the Democrats and the Whigs had dominated presidential politics since 1836.[39] To vote for a third party or an independent candidate was to "waste" one's vote, since victory was deemed impossible for these minor contenders. Such a belief was encouraged by the two major parties, of course, but also by the system the framers created in the Electoral College, since only the top two competitors have any real chance of winning a majority of the electoral votes and therefore the White House. Thus, by pushing Americans toward the two top parties, the Electoral College can be said to forge consensus and encourage coalition building.

A two-party system, buttressed by the Electoral College, has protected the American system against the fragmentation of multiparty representation often seen in other nations, where any party securing as little as 5 percent of the national vote can find representation in the parliament. If the bar is set that low, third parties will almost certainly proliferate, and when multiple parties develop, they often do so along single-issue, ethnic, socioeconomic, religious, and regional lines. This can prove quite divisive, and especially so in a heterogeneous nation such as the United States. Also, when many small parties or factions participate independently in the process, majorities are very difficult to build, and small groups often attain disproportionate power, because they are the key to a majority, governing coalition. If small parties were suddenly able to play a continuing, major, and decisive role in presidential politics, they would likely begin to see greater success at the local, state, and national levels, perhaps changing the face of our Congress and transforming the legislatures in all of the states. Advocates of third parties would welcome this, but the United States is not Belgium or Italy, and it can be argued that the world's premier superpower cannot afford to increase its internal quarrels to the point of frequent, ungovernable destabilization.

*

Candidates must pay some attention to lightly populated states and regions with substantial, cumulative electoral votes, and not simply run campaigns focused entirely on large population centers that could produce a popular-vote majority.

Without the Electoral College, the half of the states with small populations would stand little chance of seeing much of the presidential candidates. Instead, the contenders would inevitably concentrate their time and travel in the top twenty urban areas, such as New York and Los Angeles, where candidates can shop for votes much more efficiently. We are one country, and would-be presidents must become acquainted with the whole of it to govern well. Waging a national campaign is one vital means to that good end.

*

The Electoral College undergirds federalism and reinforces the role of states in our representative democracy.

The college derives its power from the various states, dampening the tyranny of the majority so feared by the founders. Although the Electoral College is arguably a ceremonial body, which convenes at the end of an election after the president-elect has been known for some time, it symbolizes the integral role the fifty states play in the American system. All matters concerning elections, from holding the primary contests to selecting electors, rest with the states, and the college underlines and augments this.

These three arguments are strong ones, but the history of the Electoral College points out some clear disadvantages, too.

Concerns with the Current Electoral College

The winner of the popular vote does not necessarily win the presidency.

Admittedly, some observers do not see this as a problem, believing as the founders did that the popular vote is at best secondary to the selection of a federal president. But surely in the modern age, when virtually all other democracies around the globe choose their leaders by pure popular vote, the world's foremost democracy ought to serve as an example of majority rule. In addition, as measured by public opinion polls, most Americans now believe that the candidate with the most votes should win, and the Electoral College be damned.[40] The support of the people is essential for the success of any electoral system, after all.

*

When it comes to the presidency, the votes of individuals in each state do not count equally.

The basis of the Electoral College (much like the foundation of the U.S. Senate) is a far cry from "one person, one vote." This is due primarily to the allocation of two senatorial bonus electors to every state, regardless of size. So giant California receives two, and tiny Rhode Island also gets two. Several states also have excess population that does not quite merit an additional representative, and those tens or hundreds of thousands of people are discounted in the electoral count (at least until the next census). Perhaps some unfairness in allocating electors within a federal system is inevitable, but the inequity seems exaggerated in the existing arrangement. Electors, and not individual voters, pick presidents, and this fundamental fact in itself is somewhat undemocratic. The system of allocating electors adds to the undemocratic nature of the Electoral College.

*

Faithless electors can cast votes that do not correspond with the results of the election in their state.

This is historically rare and has never played a role in deciding an election. However, one can easily imagine a situation in which a group of such electors could significantly impact a close election. This prospect is especially troubling, considering that most voters do not even know the names of the electors they choose, let alone trust in their judgment to select the president. A few examples: a Washington, D.C., elector cast a blank ballot in the extremely close contest of 2000 to protest the lack of voting rights in the District of Columbia; a West Virginia elector cast her ballot backward in 1988, picking Lloyd Bentsen for president and Michael Dukakis for vice president, a switched ticket to indicate her personal preference; a Minnesota Democratic elector did precisely the same thing in another reasonably close race, that of 2004, giving an electoral vote to John Edwards instead of John Kerry; and in 1968, a North Carolina man cast his vote for Alabama governor George Wallace instead of Richard Nixon.[41]

*

The college is susceptible to a tie.

There are dozens of ways that the Electoral College can tie, and in this age of very tight elections, it is entirely conceivable that a tie will one day occur. In that case, the U.S. House of Representatives would select the president, but in the odd way mentioned earlier: Each state, regardless of size or population, would cast a single vote. Furthermore, if a state's House delegation tied (split evenly) between the contenders, the state's one vote for president would not be cast at all—potentially disenfranchising millions of people in the determination of the next president. This would be unfortunate for the people of any state, but imagine if the House delegations in just three states (California, Florida, and Texas) were deadlocked: Over one quarter of the nation's population would get no say in the identity of the next president. Add to this mix one other distasteful ingredient. Given the horse-trading that might well ensue in the House, it is safe to predict most Americans would find this an unpalatable way to choose our chief executive. Although there is no way to say for sure how the representatives would vote, the selection of the president would likely rest in the hands of the party controlling a majority of delegations in the House of Representatives. Here again, the president chosen by the House method might easily have lost the popular vote.

Reforms That Abolish the Electoral College

Many groups and individuals, including the League of Women Voters, most academics in the field, many members of Congress from both parties, and past presidential candidates such as the Independent John Anderson and the Democrat Michael Dukakis, insist that the Electoral College should be abolished altogether, in favor of a direct popular vote, perhaps with a runoff between the top two contenders if no candidate receives at least 40 percent of the national vote.[42] Polls since the 1970s consistently show approximately 60 percent of Americans agree with this assessment.[43]

At first glance, the notion of switching to a direct popular vote for president would appear to address the problems associated with the Electoral College. Most people would find it implicitly more democratic—all voters would know that their vote was counted equally—and the notion of faithless electors would be a historical footnote.

However, defenders of the Electoral College believe abolishing it would lead to fundamental change in our political system. Candidates would be inclined to run airport "tarmac" campaigns, jetting from population center to population center and focusing advertising dollars on large urban areas with many voters, virtually ignoring vast swaths of the nation where there are relatively few voters. More important, a free-for-all national direct election would certainly encourage a multiparty system. In time, the country might well see a dozen or more serious or semiserious candidates on the ballot, each pitching a big issue or basing his or her campaign on race, ethnicity, religion, region, or some other splintering characteristic. Every presidential candidate would simply hope to secure one of the runoff spots with another candidate who would be deemed less acceptable. One of the United States already has experienced the possible results, and it is a cautionary tale for the nation. In 1975 Louisiana established just such a free-for-all system for its gubernatorial contests,[44] and in a 1991 runoff for governor between the top two finishers in the first election, the state ended up with a choice between a crook, the frequently indicted former governor Edwin Edwards, and a KKK white racist, David Duke. As the famous bumper sticker of the time noted, VOTE FOR THE CROOK. IT'S IMPORTANT. Louisianans did, to deny Duke. Edwards later went to jail after yet another corrupt term in office.[45] This is hardly the ideal model for the nation's presidential elections.

Reforms That Mend the Electoral College . . . but Have Unintended Consequences

Many proposals for changing the Electoral College, without abolishing the institution, have been made over the centuries. Even James Madison had developed serious doubts about various aspects of the college by 1823 and proposed reform of it.[46] Most of these accumulated proposals are intellectually stimulating, but many are inadequate, with hidden, unintended consequences. A few are even dangerous to the American Republic. Here are three such unwise plans.

Congressional District Allocation

A frequently mentioned reform proposal, district allocation of electors, has been on the table since the 1890s.[47] Under this system, electors would be apportioned one to each congressional district, with the presidential winner in each district collecting the elector, and the two extra senatorial electors going to the statewide winner. (As mentioned earlier, only Maine and Nebraska have adopted this method of elector allocation.) Interestingly, an earlier version of the Twelfth Amendment, which barely failed ratification, called for electors to be allocated by "electoral districts."[48] The states currently have the power to put the district plan into effect, just as Maine and Nebraska have done. Yet the large states have no desire to do so, since breaking up their electors would dilute the impact of their large Electoral College prizes. So a constitutional mandate would be required if this plan is to be universal.

One positive outcome of the congressional district method of assigning electors is that it might expand the campaign's playing field. Many strongly "Red" and "Blue" states have at least one congressional district that is competitive for the minority party; the large states have several each. Therefore, a Democratic presidential nominee would spend time in some Texas and North Carolina districts, while the Republican nominee would find his or her way to parts of New York, Illinois, and California. It would be a good thing for more states to see the candidates up close and personal during the general election. This would be a welcome antidote to the current winner-take-all system's result, whereby thirty or more states are all but decided months ahead of time and thus avoided by time-pressed candidates.

Despite this salutary effect, though, the district plan creates more problems than it solves. The impact it would have had on previous elections is mixed. Would Gore supporters who blame the Electoral College system for depriving their popular-vote winner of the presidency jump for joy if electors were counted by congressional district? Hardly. A study by the independent analyst Rhodes Cook found the winner still to be George W. Bush, with a more clear-cut 288 to 250 Electoral College win than the 271 to 266 victory he actually secured. The broader distribution of Republican votes would help all GOP presidential candidates, while Democrats might be penalized for the urban concentration of their support. Gore, for example, won all 22 Illinois electors in 2000. But under the district plan, Bush would have picked up 9 of those 22 votes.[49] Similarly, Richard Nixon would have won the 1960 presidential election if the electoral votes were allotted under the district plan.[50]

More important, this plan could alter the future dynamics of our political system in unexpected ways. Lowering the winner-take-all bar from the state level to the congressional district level might allow more parties to win electoral votes. There is great risk for our democracy in the possible fragmentation of the Electoral College, with purely sectional or highly ideological third parties and independent candidates grabbing electoral votes here and there across the map. Should this happen, probably producing no majority in the college for any candidate, the nation might be faced with the two major-party candidates engaged in postelection pandering to smaller parties in order to secure the minimum number of electoral votes for the presidency. What promises would be made, what secret deals would be concluded, to produce a college majority? Even if the major candidates were not surreptitiously engaged in these disreputable activities, many Americans would assume they were. Their suspicions would no doubt be fueled by speculative news reports and partisan attacks. With persistent questioning of the integrity of the president-elect nearly guaranteed, that helpful period known as the "honeymoon" for the nation's new leader would be difficult to achieve.

Also, imagine a multitude of Florida 2000–like disputes that could arise in any close election, as campaigns jockey for individual electoral votes by contesting tallies district by district across the nation. Every single congressional district where the candidates were separated by a thousand or fewer votes would likely be targeted, and teams of lawyers would descend on these unfortunate areas to fight over every vote. Partisan passions in these districts would be inflamed, and angry demonstrations—again, think of South Florida in 2000—would ensue. Local, state, and federal courts would be jammed with election law cases around the nation, and judges would replace voters as the arbiters of the election results. Americans would not have much confidence in the outcome, especially since varying election law standards existing in the fifty states and thousands of localities would be applied differently from place to place.

Proportional Allocation

This proposal would have each state's electoral votes divided in the same proportion as that state's popular vote, rounded to the nearest elector. This method of distributing electors presents a few benefits. Depending upon the exact method of implementation, the plan could have the effect of forcing candidates to campaign in places they currently ignore. It would certainly make decisions by the campaigns about where to stump much more complex. Unlike allocation by congressional district, this option could also boost voter enthusiasm, especially in areas that lean heavily toward one party, since everyone's vote would count in the ultimate proportional allocation of electors. (If you belong to the minority party in an area sure to vote for the majority party, you have less incentive to show up at the polls—unless proportional allocation is in effect.)

However, this approach—which could again be adopted without changing the Constitution—is even more problematic than the congressional district method because it would inevitably lead to the fragmentation of multiple parties. Every third party, whether it were organized around a charismatic individual, a hot-button issue, sectional concerns (a South-based party or a Rocky Mountain party), or some general philosophy of life (Libertarians, Greens, and so on), would have an incentive to jump into the presidential contest in at least a few states in order to grab some electoral votes. The goal would be to deny either major-party nominee a majority of the Electoral College in order to become "the tail that wags the dog," by providing the extra electoral votes required for a majority—in exchange, of course, for a series of concessions on policy and appointments by the winner-to-be. Imagine the corrupt, backroom deals that could become common in presidential elections. After all, as long as an election is reasonably close between the two major-party candidates (as most of them are), a couple of dozen electoral votes secured by third parties would make all the difference. A proportional system of electoral vote allocation (even if there is a cutoff—say 5 percent of a state's vote, below which a party would get no electors) nearly guarantees that any muscular third party would secure some electors. Presidential elections might turn into a fearsome bazaar in the period between the November election day and the December casting of electoral votes. And if the electoral votes were made automatic, as we have recommended above, then many presidents would end up being selected by the House of Representatives (and vice presidents by the U.S. Senate). This is not a prospect that would be welcomed by most Americans. Essentially, we would have shifted the critical choice of national leaders from the people to the Congress in quite a few election years.

As if these prospects were not enough to warn us off any system of proportional allocation of electoral votes, there are practical problems galore in determining just how many electors each party would get per state. Exactly how should popular vote percentages be converted into smaller electoral vote totals in each state? For example, in a state with three electoral votes, how would the votes split up in an election where both candidates get close to 50 percent? How would they split in an election with multiple candidates? Endless controversies and charges of unfairness would await us if we were to go down this road—which we obviously should not.

Electoral College with Superelectors

Under this third proposal, candidates would continue to compete for electors on a state-by-state, winner-take-all basis, but the winner of the national popular vote would be awarded a set of bonus electors. The historian Arthur Schlesinger Jr. suggested this reform in an editorial published in the wake of the 2000 elections.[51] Schlesinger argued that 102 electors go to the general election popular vote winner—two for each state and the District of Columbia. The major advantage of the Schlesinger system, other than guaranteeing that the popular vote winner (if clear) becomes president, would be to give voters in heavily "Red" or "Blue" states incentive to cast their ballots; even though the outcomes were clear in advance in their states, these voters would be contributing to the popular vote total for their candidate and helping him or her to win the national superelectors.

Still, the Schlesinger model would be nothing more than an abolition of the Electoral College in disguise, and the substitution of a pure popular vote system. What would happen if the national vote is very close, as it was in the election of 1960, when Schlesinger's candidate, John F. Kennedy, secured a bare plurality of less than 119,000 votes out of about 70 million cast, based in large part on possibly fraudulent returns in Illinois and Texas?[52] JFK was lucky to have had a healthy Electoral College margin (303 to Richard Nixon's 219), which gave his presidency legitimacy despite the near tie in the popular vote. If the superelectors had been the difference between victory and defeat in 1960, Nixon might well have been inclined to seek a recount and to investigate possible shenanigans in the Land of Lincoln and the Lone Star State (and elsewhere). A recount in every state and locality, with the accompanying court disputes in a continental nation, would freeze the process far more than in the disputed 2000 election, when the recount was isolated to one state. Do we want the world's only superpower in crisis, with an acting president (probably the Speaker of the House of Representatives, whose direct popular mandate is limited to his or her tiny congressional district) running the United States for months or years while the election result is litigated and sorted out?

Reform Approaches That Mend the Electoral College . . . and Can Work

Having made their way through this thicket of unwise reforms, diligent readers must wonder whether *any* changes can both improve the Electoral College *and* avoid the unintended consequences that have plagued the earlier proposals. In fact, there are three approaches that, together, can constitute a workable and progressive reform package.

Elimination of Faithless Electors

While faithless electors have not previously posed a serious threat to the electoral process, just one could throw a wrench into the machinery in a close election. The new Constitution must include a reform that prevents this possibility, while maintaining the party-building advantages of electors: Make the position of elector a strictly honorary one. The political parties could still offer these posts to their staunchest members, but the individuals would not need to make a trek to the statehouse (except perhaps for some sort of ceremony) and they would not cast an actual vote. Instead, each state's electoral votes would be cast automatically for the winner of the certified popular vote in the state. Surely, this is one change that cannot be very controversial. The political parties will be able to keep these prestigious patronage posts to reward loyal party activists—the honorary position of elector will remain a résumé enhancer for those selected—but the nation need not worry about an illegitimate president produced by electors who arbitrarily decide to abandon their solemn pledge to back the people's candidate.

Elimination of the Unit Rule in the House of Representatives

The second reform, which would also be nearly universally welcomed, would apply whenever the election of a president is thrown into the U.S. House of Representatives, due to the failure of any candidate to secure a majority of electoral votes. Fortunately, this unwelcome event has only occurred twice in American history, in the presidential elections of 1800 and 1824. Both were highly controversial contests. In 1800 the nation narrowly avoided being deprived of the signal presidency of Thomas Jefferson, and having Aaron Burr substituted instead.[53] In 1824 the machinations in the House resulting in the election of John Quincy Adams as president literally ruined Adams's one term. Having lost both the popular vote and the electoral vote to Andrew Jackson, Adams gained the White House in a "corrupt deal" with a third candidate, Henry Clay—or so Jackson insisted until his dying day. Clay's appointment as Adams's secretary of state appeared to confirm the deal. With a hostile public and many critics in Congress, Adams accomplished little during his frustrating stay in the executive branch, ending with his landslide defeat by Jackson in the election of 1828.[54] (Adams was far more successful in his second career as a crusading antislavery member of the U.S. House from Massachusetts.)

In modern times, America has faced the prospect of a nasty repeat of 1824 in several close elections (including 1968 and 2000). Most citizens are suspicious enough of Congress in good times; one can only try to imagine the deep cynicism that might be engendered should the House pick the president today. But the worst aspect of the House selection process is the *unit rule,* which mandates that each state shall cast one vote for president, irrespective of the state's size, with a majority of states (twenty-six) being required for the election of a chief executive. So Wyoming (population 505,887) would have the same weight as California (population 35,842,038) in selecting the occupant of the White House for four years. This news would not likely be well received in California—or in any of the populous states. (I call it *news* because 90 percent or more of the American public is unaware of this procedure, last used over 180 years ago.) Even worse, some states would not get to cast a ballot at all, since they would be deadlocked. In most cases, all it would take to produce a deadlock is an equal number of Democrats and Republicans in a state's delegation.[55]

The easiest, most sensible reform is to abolish the unit rule, and let every U.S. representative cast a ballot as he or she sees fit—a ballot for which each member of the House will be held accountable by the constituency at the next election.[56] A good case can be made for preserving the Electoral College as a bulwark of federalism, but the House unit rule in presidential elections is federalism taken to a destructive extreme.[57] Interestingly, James Madison had perceived the antidemocratic nature of the House unit rule as early as 1823, and he urged that each member of the House should be permitted to vote individually for a presidential candidate in the case of Electoral College deadlock. As Madison wrote to his friend George Hay, the House unit rule was too "great a departure from the Republican principle of numerical equality" and was "so pregnant also with a mischievous tendency in practice, that an amendment of the Constitution on this point is justly called for by all its considerate & best friends."[58]

Growing the Electoral College

By now, it should be clear that the Electoral College serves some useful functions and ought to be preserved, especially considering the distasteful alternatives. Yet the college's status quo is not acceptable either. There is too great a chance that the popular vote winner could lose the election, and the lightly populated states have too great a cumulative edge in the Electoral College, mainly due to the automatic two senatorial bonus electoral votes allocated to each state, regardless of size.

Should the changes to the U.S. Senate advocated in chapter 1 be adopted, with larger states gaining U.S. senators, then the tally in the Electoral College would automatically change in the correct direction.[59] This reallocation of Senate seats would add electoral votes to the heavily populated states and thus help to maximize the opportunity for the popular-vote winner to capture the presidency—while preserving the wonderful college advantage of isolating recounts in close elections to one or a few states. In that sense, expanding the Senate to account for population would send two birds—both outdated constitutional pterodactyls—into well-deserved extinction. The Senate would become more representative of the electorate, and the Electoral College simultaneously would as well. Our earlier proposal to increase the size of the House to 1,000 members would have no net effect on the apportionment of electors, since the number of House members per state—currently and under the reform's scheme—is a function of each state's population.[60] The proposal would simply grow each state's House delegation, and number of electors, in proportion to the state's due by merit of population.

If the expansion of the Senate proves politically or constitutionally impossible, there is another sound means to accomplish the very same goal in the Electoral College.[61] The college itself could be directly enlarged, and the new electoral votes distributed among the heavily populated states to more closely reflect actual population. In addition to the 538 electoral votes currently allocated among the nation's fifty states and the District of Columbia, this proposal would give states additional electoral votes based on their percentage of the national population.

To see the practical implementation of this plan, take a look at table 4.1. A state that has less than 0.5 percent of the national population would keep its current electoral vote total. But states that possess more of the country's population would be given additional electors. Each state that claims between 0.5 to 2.0 percent of the national population would receive one more elector. An additional electoral vote would also be allocated for each additional percent (rounded to the nearest percentage point) of the national population over 2.0 percent. For instance, Alabama (currently possessing nine electoral votes) has 1.5 percent of the nation's population. Since it falls between 0.5 and 2.0 percent, the state would be allotted one more electoral vote, for a total of ten electors. Florida boasts 5.9 percent of the national population, so it would get five additional electoral votes, for a total of thirty-two electors. As you can see from the table, a large majority of the fifty states (thirty-eight) would gain electoral votes in this fashion, while no state would lose any electoral votes it currently has. This should facilitate passage of the college reform,

TABLE 4.1. GROWING THE ELECTORAL COLLEGE IN 2004

State	Population	% of National Population	Current No. of Electors	Extra Electors	Total No. of Electors
Alabama	4,525,375	1.5	9	1	10
Alaska	657,755	0.2	3		3
Arizona	5,739,879	2.0	10	1	11
Arkansas	2,750,000	0.9	6	1	7
California	35,842,038	12.2	55	11	66
Colorado	4,601,821	1.6	9	1	10
Connecticut	3,498,966	1.2	7	1	8
Delaware	830,069	0.3	3		3
District of Columbia	554,239	0.2	3		3
Florida	17,385,430	5.9	27	5	32
Georgia	8,918,129	3.0	15	2	17
Hawaii	1,262,124	0.4	4		4
Idaho	1,395,140	0.5	4		4
Illinois	12,712,016	4.3	21	3	24
Indiana	6,226,537	2.1	11	1	12
Iowa	2,952,904	1.0	7	1	8
Kansas	2,733,697	0.9	6	1	7
Kentucky	4,141,835	1.4	8	1	9
Louisiana	4,506,685	1.5	9	1	10
Maine	1,314,985	0.4	4		4
Maryland	5,561,332	1.9	10	1	11
Massachusetts	6,407,382	2.2	12	1	13
Michigan	10,104,206	3.4	17	2	19
Minnesota	5,096,546	1.7	10	1	11
Mississippi	2,900,768	1.0	6	1	7
Missouri	5,759,532	2.0	11	1	12
Montana	926,920	0.3	3		3
Nebraska	1,747,704	0.6	5	1	6
Nevada	2,332,898	0.8	5	1	6
New Hampshire	1,299,169	0.4	4		4
New Jersey	8,685,166	3.0	15	2	17

State	Population	% of National Population	Current No. of Electors	Extra Electors	Total No. of Electors
New Mexico	1,903,006	0.6	5	1	6
New York	19,280,727	6.6	31	6	37
North Carolina	8,540,468	2.9	15	2	17
North Dakota	636,308	0.2	3		3
Ohio	11,450,143	3.9	20	3	23
Oklahoma	3,523,546	1.2	7	1	8
Oregon	3,591,363	1.2	7	1	8
Pennsylvania	12,394,471	4.2	21	3	24
Rhode Island	1,079,916	0.4	4		4
South Carolina	4,197,892	1.4	8	1	9
South Dakota	770,621	0.3	3		3
Tennessee	5,893,298	2.0	11	1	12
Texas	22,471,549	7.7	34	7	41
Utah	2,420,708	0.8	5	1	6
Vermont	621,233	0.2	3		3
Virginia	7,481,332	2.5	13	2	15
Washington	6,207,046	2.1	11	1	12
West Virginia	1,812,548	0.6	5	1	6
Wisconsin	5,503,533	1.9	10	1	11
Wyoming	505,887	0.2	3		3
TOTAL	**293,656,842**	**100.0**	**538**	**74**	**612**

Source: Population totals from U.S. Census, 2004.

and voters in the thirty-eight states gaining electors would surely feel a sense of increased empowerment. In all, 74 electors would be added to the 538 in the existing Electoral College, for a total of 612. Budget hawks need not be concerned about the college's expansion since no monies are expended in the process. And the possibility of "faithless electors" would not be multiplied because electoral votes—under this new system—would be cast automatically. In fact, the political parties would have dozens more honorary posts to bestow upon their most faithful activists.

In 2004 this new version of the Electoral College would have closely paralleled President Bush's 3-million vote plurality over Democratic senator

John Kerry with an electoral victory of 325 to 286. But the real test would have come four years earlier. How would this system have worked in the squeaker election of 2000? It would have produced an Electoral College result that more closely reflected the popular vote. With slightly different calculations than those of table 4.1, due to the fact that the 1990 census allocations of electors were still in effect, the Electoral College would have produced a one-vote victory for Democrat Al Gore over Republican George W. Bush, by 306 to 305.[62] After all, Gore won the popular vote by 540,000, and I have promised that this new method will more accurately reflect the will of the people.[63]

ADDING SOME POLITICAL RULES OF THE GAME FOR THE TWENTY-FIRST CENTURY

The American political system would be significantly improved if we could add these two categories of constitutional reform, one for the presidential nominating process and the other for the Electoral College. The absence of the first and the antiquated design of the second have caused no end of problems as the modern Republic has emerged.

By no means, however, do these two big reforms exhaust the possible agenda for political change. A new Constitutional Convention should take up the issue of campaign finance, even though it is full of sticky threats to First Amendment freedoms.[64] Still, the current prohibition on any spending limit for the wealthy in their own campaigns—which stems from a Supreme Court interpretation of the First Amendment[65]—would be a fit subject for convention discussion. Should the rich be able to spend freely and, in some cases, buy high office, as so many have done in both parties?[66] Same reasonable limitation on the wealthy's campaign spending would be welcome, by capping the total donations they could make to their own candidacy. A revised Constitution should give Congress the power to do just that. Public financing of congressional campaigns, partial or full,[67] is also the only real alternative to the lobbyist and private interest-group financing that has produced scandal after scandal in Washington and the state capitals.[68] Congress already has the constitutional authority to exact public financing, though as yet they have not exercised it.

Finally, a Constitutional Convention may want to ask a basic question about the most precious right to vote: Have we finally reached the point in the United States where we should move to automatic voter registration of all citizens? Most other advanced democracies already have such a system.[70] By contrast, in the United States, a citizen must first take the initiative to register well in advance of election day,[71] then take the initiative again, later on, to cast a ballot. If we assume that advanced technology or a national identification card would limit or eliminate the potential for fraud (no minor consideration),[72] why should we place an extra barrier in the way of broader participation at the ballot box? Libertarians despise national ID cards, but should we ever adopt the practice for security reasons, there could be a side benefit at the polls.

And it really does matter whether people vote or not. The simple act of voting connects a person to the political process, gives him or her some skin in the game, and encourages a citizen to pay attention. We need to do everything we can, within reason, to get more Americans participating regularly in elections. Even in supposedly "high turnout" presidential contests, 40 to 50 percent of adults fail to show up at the polls in November. The turnouts for state and local offices are even more abysmal. No democracy can truly be termed healthy when so many millions abstain from the most basic duty of citizenship.

*

In sum, politics will never be popular, and its practitioners will always be maligned, but a well-designed dose of politics is essential for the health of the American Republic. The founders mainly avoided the topic in the Constitution, and in their times, little harm was done. This is not true any longer. The absence of a modern political framework in the Constitution for presidential nominations and elections has made the U.S. system one of the least sensible in the world. We can and must do better.

CHAPTER FIVE

★

A CITIZENSHIP OF SERVICE: ASKING WHAT WE CAN DO FOR OUR COUNTRY . . . AND OURSELVES

NO ADULT AMERICAN alive on January 20, 1961, will ever forget the stirring words of President John F. Kennedy in his inaugural address: "Ask not what your country can do for you; ask what you can do for your country." The nation's young leader thus captured the spirit of a new generation finally gaining real power—a generation that, along with their parents, had successfully conquered the Great Depression, won World War II, and believed that America could accomplish anything through personal initiative and shared sacrifice. Kennedy's Peace Corps, established that same year, became the early focus for idealistic young people determined to meet the president's challenge.[1]

Today a hardened and cynical generation that has endured Vietnam, Watergate, 9/11, and other soul-depressing events since JFK's assassination still accepts the promise of personal initiative, but shared sacrifice has become a lesser-known concept for many. We have it within our power to change this, and to go back to the future. A new Constitution can fuel America's transformation into a society that once again fulfills Kennedy's vision.

The best means available would be a constitutional requirement that all able-bodied Americans devote at least two years of their lives to the service of their nation. The charge must be broad, and the civilian and military options—which I will outline in this chapter—must be many, to accommodate the varied talents of the population and the diverse dictates of conscience. But the principle must be immutable: Enjoying the benefits of living in a great democracy is not a God-given right. In exchange for the privileges of American citizenship, every individual has obligations to meet, promises to their fellow citizens and posterity to keep.

Universal National Service (UNS) would be a kind of Bill of Responsibilities, a useful complement to the Bill of Rights. A simple but powerful constitutional clause would decree that "all citizens of the United States, who are of sound mind and body, shall be required to give two years of service to their country, in a manner prescribed by law." Normally, the service would be discharged between the ages of eighteen and twenty-six, but Congress could provide for delay for reasons of health or special family situations.

Libertarians find this proposal especially objectionable, insisting that governmental power over the individual must be kept to an absolute minimum. The philosophy of libertarianism has much to recommend it on some topics, including personal lifestyle issues. But in this case, the libertarian approach ignores the substantial benefits not just for society but for the individual in the commitment to service.

Americans appreciate and jealously guard their constitutional rights. At the same time, most acknowledge their responsibilities to the social contract that has guaranteed their rights. Taking inspiration from the British philosopher John Locke,[2] the founders understood that people create a country through a social contract, that is, citizens agree to give up some of their rights and submit to a government's authority in order to secure for themselves and their descendants the blessings of liberty. Among those blessings is the freedom to build a better society by individual initiative and group action. Ideally, that better society would be assembled solely through voluntary efforts. However, volunteerism—while essential to happy, healthy communities—is rarely sufficient to accomplish all that needs to be done. Even more important, everyone should have the opportunity to take part. In a country of America's size and complexity, that argues for a grand, well-organized enterprise, precisely what UNS is envisioned to be. We are at our best when challenged to do great things, to move beyond our familiar comfort level. A universal service clause in the new Constitution will help all of us to adopt the U.S. Army's famous imperative, to "be all that you can be," so that our nation can be all that it can be, too.

Not long ago, after a late afternoon discussion with some University of Virginia students about the possible addition of a national service clause to the Constitution, I received the following e-mail from a bright graduate student, Karim Kai Logue: "I think people would support national service because we're all looking for reasons to be better, more selfless, more giving, and less afraid."[3] Karim nicely captures the beautiful idealism of youth, the yearning to give and to serve. Yet this instinct is more than youthful; it is

American. A cultural sociability and an outgoing spirit, coupled with innate optimism and enthusiasm, infuses the American people. We believe deeply that we can make a difference—each one of us—and the most amazing part of it is that most individuals participate in service activities not out of obligation but as volunteers.

When great commitment becomes necessary, Americans traditionally respond to the call—or sometimes without a call at all. America's wars have always resulted in a flood of citizen-warriors at enlistment offices. Peacetime needs have also produced a harvest of volunteers. In April 1995 hundreds of Americans drove long distances to help with cleanup and comfort the residents of Oklahoma City after the Alfred P. Murrah Federal Building was blown up by home-grown terrorists. In September 2001 so many people, on their own, drove cross-country to assist New York City in the wake of the World Trade Center's destruction that the authorities could not utilize them all. In September 2005 after Hurricane Katrina devastated Louisiana and Mississippi, a human tide of good Samaritans replaced the storm tide. This is the way Americans are.

At the same time, it is obvious that—except perhaps in some wars—we have not been able to capture and channel the full energy of America's volunteer spirit as well as we could have. A constitutional clause can finally achieve the goal universally. Nothing will revitalize American democracy from the ground up like UNS, giving the young a hands-on civics lesson that will show them the way to get involved, and keep many involved for life in their chosen activities. Nothing can do more to make America a better, fairer nation, with everyone pulling his or her own weight. Just as the youth of the World War II era learned service from shared sacrifice, so too can every generation begin adult life by contributing its full share to building America and helping other people around the globe.

There is no serious question that universal service would be in the short- and long-term interests of the young. Their worldview would be broadened enormously, and their lives would be far richer for the perspective they gain. They would understand, early on, one of life's most precious lessons: There is no greater privilege than the call to serve, and no greater joy than the fulfilling of it. For the individual American, UNS would mold constructive and humane citizens. For the United States as a whole, UNS would unleash enormous energy for good at home and abroad. This new constitutional provision can make America, even more than ever before, an exemplar of idealism and a beacon of hope for people everywhere.

AN AMERICAN HISTORY OF SERVICE: MILITARY CALLS AND CIVILIAN SUPPLEMENTS

Alexis de Tocqueville was one of the first to record the propensity of Americans to help one another by joining private organizations and associations.[4] The economic philosophy of *laissez-faire*—government should not interfere with private markets—prevailed for most of American history. So the federal government was not greatly involved in meeting the needs of its citizens until the New Deal, and the poor, sick, and immigrants had to rely on these private groups, as well as the political parties, for their sustenance.[5]

Militarily, it was a different story, of course, and the government took the lead in raising its armies. For most of the nation's wars, there was rarely a shortage of volunteers.[6] Conscription in the Civil War was not always popular, and the wealthy could pay to have someone else take their place, but there was sometimes a social stigma placed on those who refused to do their part.[7] From the Revolutionary War and the Mexican War to the Spanish-American War and World War I,[8] men (and some women as well) flocked to join the armed forces, many out of patriotism and a sense of adventure, though some sought to escape grinding poverty and joblessness.

A critical moment arrived in the reluctant preparation for America's entry into World War II. After a long debate in the summer of 1940, Congress passed the first peacetime draft in history, and in August of 1941, the U.S. House of Representatives voted to extend the service period for draftees and ensured that the U.S. military was prepared when the attack on Pearl Harbor ultimately occurred.[9] Military service among young adult men was nearly universal from 1941 to 1945, since citizens backed the war effort with fervor and close to unanimity. With the war's end came the decision to continue the draft indefinitely.[10] As the preeminent world power, the United States would have obligations of leadership for many decades to come. The Korean War, the Cold War, and the Cuban Missile Crisis only underlined this reality, and opposition to the draft was mild to nonexistent in most of the country during the late 1940s, the 1950s, and the early 1960s. Then came the Vietnam War. This disastrous war left the nation torn apart and many of the young in a state of rebellion. The end of the draft became a political inevitability, and President Nixon officially announced the phase-in of the all-volunteer armed forces in April of 1970.[11] The phase-out of the draft had the desired effect of reducing opposition to the Vietnam War, which was also gradually winding down.

The United States has never returned to a draft, despite all the stresses on the military since Vietnam, in good part because the public has not indicated any support for it. One wonders what would have happened after 9/11 had President Bush called for this kind of shared sacrifice. The draft likely would have been reinstituted by an agreeable Congress that passed all the other major Bush requests, including controversial ones such as the Patriot Act.[12] While not everyone would have welcomed a new draft, there is considerable evidence to suggest that America's youth were willing to heed the call to national service in the wake of the terrorist attacks. On September 11, 2001, online registration for the Selective Service Act topped six thousand—more than three times the daily average.[13] Moreover, in the first months after 9/11, applications for the federal government's AmeriCorps jumped 50 percent, applications for the Peace Corps doubled, and those for the nonprofit group Teach for America tripled.[14]

Whatever might have been, the nation has fought wars in Afghanistan and Iraq, and maintained substantial forces around the world, with the volunteer army. Still, the military has been stretched thin, and many critics of the Iraq War have convincingly insisted that additional troops for the invasion and the critical first year of the war might have been able to quell the vicious insurgency that has followed.[15]

Moreover, something special has been lost with the end of the draft. For three decades, almost every able-bodied man was stripped of privilege and compelled to serve in the ultimate top-down organization. They received meager wages, they endured poor conditions and hardships, and they bonded across social class (if not, sadly, racial lines for most of that time). When Congress funded U.S. wars, many legislators thought about their own sons in the military.

Today, only a handful of members of Congress have had children fight in either Afghanistan or Iraq,[16] and Congress itself has seen the proportion of military veterans in its ranks fall from a high of more than two thirds in the 1970s to a mere 24 percent in 2007. The decline has been particularly precipitous in the House of Representatives, with the proportion of veterans plummeting from a high of 75 percent in 1971 to only 23 percent today.[17] More important is that average Americans have lost a remarkable tie that bound them together with their contemporaries: military service. Foreign wars are even more distant to most people than the miles demand, and there is a disturbing disconnect between a sizable majority of citizens and the professional soldiers who fight the wars and die in them. That useful tie can and should be restored.

What about the domestic side of governmental service in American history? Interestingly, the military plays a large role here, too. Just as soldiers in ancient Rome built roads and aqueducts throughout the Empire during peaceful times,[18] so too has the American military and National Guard become a resource in times of great need. Hurricane relief in the United States and tsunami aid abroad are but two examples.

In addition to the efforts of the armed forces, much of the domestic service need in America has been left to private nonprofit groups, including organizations like the Red Cross and the country's largest philanthropic organization, the Bill and Melinda Gates Foundation.[19] Compulsory civil service has been mainly restricted to jury duty and work assigned to conscientious objectors to the draft, when it existed.

Very occasionally, though, the federal government has launched broad initiatives for public service. These examples are useful for our inquiry, for they suggest what has worked and what has not in the field of governmental public service. The programs that I will discuss—the Civilian Conservation Corps, the Peace Corps, Volunteers in Service to America (VISTA), the "Thousand Points of Light" initiative, and AmeriCorps—were all designed to tap into the idealism of the young or the desperate need for employment in hard times. Thus, the motives for joining have been mixed, and signing up has been voluntary. The positions have mainly been full-time, and they have been subsidized, though not lavishly, from taxpayer funds. Perhaps most important, the participants in all five programs have something vital in common: They prove that youthful service activity produces solid citizens, solves problems for the country, and can simultaneously lift up the individuals who serve and the nation that is served.

FDR's Civilian Conservation Corps

Possibly the most popular program in the New Deal, the Civilian Conservation Corps (CCC) had one overriding goal in mind: to put people to work at the height of the Great Depression. As President Franklin D. Roosevelt explained the CCC in a May 1933 "fireside chat" on radio:

> First, we are giving opportunity of employment to one-quarter of a million of the unemployed, especially the young men who have dependents, to go into the forestry and flood prevention work. This is a big task because it means feeding, clothing and caring for nearly twice as many men as we have in the regular Army itself. In creating this civilian conservation corps we are killing two birds with one stone. We are clearly enhancing the value of our natural resources and second, we are relieving an appreciable amount of actual distress.[20]

Over the decade of the CCC's existence (1933–42), more than four thousand camps were established across all forty-eight states and the Alaskan and Hawaiian territories. These camps were run by the U.S. Army, with about three thousand reservists serving as "camp directors." Each camp had a governmental sponsor, usually a unit of the Department of Interior or Agriculture, and that unit trained the camp foremen. Participants worked forty hours a week with a wage of thirty dollars a month, with twenty-five dollars a month required to be sent home to participants' families. The army provided just about everything the men needed, from equipment, housing, and groceries to doctors and chaplains.

A great deal of good resulted—and not simply the employment of thousands and the financial support of their families. Soil erosion control, national park construction, the installation of power and phone lines, and wildfire prevention were just a few of the CCC's achievements. In the evenings, many of the camps also offered participants training in other skills and even the opportunity to become literate.

In the beginning the CCC limited enrollment to men between the ages of eighteen and twenty-five whose fathers had registered as unemployed, with exceptions made for veterans. By 1937 Congress had dropped the "unemployment registration" requirement and adjusted the ages to seventeen through twenty-three. Participants signed up for six-month terms, renewable for up to two years. About six in ten of those who enrolled were uneducated, malnourished, and desperate, with few personal possessions and no health care. The CCC was literally a lifesaver for many of them, and even though there was no penalty for desertion, high morale and lack of alternatives kept the desertion rate to less than 2 percent per month. No strikes or revolts were ever recorded in any camp, and the threat of a "dishonorable discharge" kept the discipline tight. The CCC gave participants many things, but above all, hope. "This is a training station. We're going to leave morally and physically fit to lick 'Old Man Depression,' " read a newsletter from one North Carolina camp.

The Great Depression finally lifted with the onset of World War II, and of course, the CCC's target audience was being drafted into the military as of 1940. With the pool of men shrinking, all CCC efforts were transferred to army bases, and funding for the CCC ended in 1942 (though some camps were used for alternative service for conscientious objectors during the war). This magnificent social experiment had been extraordinarily successful, by all accounts. One shudders to imagine America without the CCC in the 1930s.

Many of those young men, and their families back home, might well have starved to death. Instead, the United States trained hundreds of thousands to be productive citizens, and just in time for World War II, when their new skills would be most needed.

JFK's Peace Corps

On October 14, 1960, nearing the conclusion of the presidential campaign, Democratic candidate John Kennedy arrived at the campus of the University of Michigan. Despite the late hour—about two a.m.—Kennedy was astonished to find a crowd estimated at ten thousand enthusiastic students. Speaking extemporaneously, JFK challenged the young to devote part of their lives to living and working in Asia, Africa, and Latin America. The response was highly positive, with the Michigan students launching a petition drive in support of the idea. In his brief but stirring speech, JFK asked his young audience:

> How many of you who are going to be doctors, are willing to spend your days in Ghana? Technicians or engineers, how many of you are willing to work in the Foreign Service and spend your lives traveling around the world? On your willingness to do that, not merely to serve one year or two years in the service, but on your willingness to contribute part of your life to this country, I think will depend the answer whether a free society can compete.[21]

The idea for the Peace Corps went back many decades. The philosopher William James called for the establishment of a "peace army" in 1904, and politicians such as Senator Hubert H. Humphrey (D-MN) had championed the cause.[22] President Kennedy was able to bring it to fruition not simply because it was attractive altruism but also because the United States needed to take a tough-minded but friendly-faced approach to the threat posed by international communism.

In Kennedy's initial 1961 executive order, supplemented by the subsequent congressional legislation, the Peace Corps was charged with three lofty goals.

1. To help the people of interested countries and areas in meeting their needs for trained workers.

2. To help promote a better understanding of Americans on the part of the peoples served.

3. To help promote a better understanding of other peoples on the part of Americans.[23]

Later approved by Congress as a permanent agency of the State Department, the Peace Corps was eventually folded into an umbrella agency known as ACTION, a clearinghouse for national service programs created by President Nixon in 1971. President Carter later granted the corps autonomy as an independent agency in 1979.[24] It is true that the Peace Corps' peak enrollment of 15,000 was achieved in 1966, in the wake of JFK's assassination, yet interest has been sustained for a remarkable forty-six years, with 7,810 Americans serving as of 2006. As the Peace Corps approaches the half-century mark, a total of 182,000 Americans have joined its ranks for at least one stint, serving in 138 countries since the corps' founding. With only a minimal subsistence stipend, these Americans—mostly in their twenties but as many as 6 percent over the age of fifty—have proven over and over that Kennedy was right in his inaugural address when he claimed that "the torch has been passed to a new generation . . . and the glow from that fire can truly light the world."[25]

LBJ's VISTA

President Lyndon B. Johnson sought to expand Kennedy's Peace Corps to the domestic front. JFK had earlier failed to get Congress to create a national service corps, but as in so many other spheres, LBJ used Kennedy's death to create the Volunteers in Service to America (VISTA) program in 1964.[26] VISTA was a piece of LBJ's "War on Poverty," with the volunteer members of the program serving for one year helping the poor in selected locations throughout the United States. Each VISTA worker was paid wages just above the local poverty level, a strategy intended to help participants understand the daily struggles faced by the disadvantaged. By 1967, more than 3,000 Americans were VISTA volunteers, helping their fellow countrymen in 412 antipoverty projects nationwide. By mid-1968, VISTA had received 70,000 applications from would-be volunteers (and due to budgetary restraints was only able to accept about 20 percent). To date, more than 177,000 Americans have served their country by volunteering through VISTA or its successor, AmeriCorps*VISTA.[27]

George H. W. Bush's "Thousand Points of Light"

So far, the examples of national service have been provided by Democratic presidents—no accident, given the activist, more liberal, larger-government nature of their administrations. Yet Republicans also support some forms of national service. Since Kennedy, five GOP chief executives have continued, in some form, the Peace Corps and VISTA.[28] But more important, Republicans believe that individual initiative should take precedence over governmental action, and also that privately run service is more effective and efficient than D.C.-sponsored efforts.

With this philosophy in mind, President George H. W. Bush launched his "Thousand Points of Light" initiative in 1989. Bush had used the phrase often throughout the 1988 presidential campaign. During his acceptance speech at the Republican National Convention, Bush told his audience that he would "keep America moving forward, always forward—for a better America, for an endless enduring dream and a thousand points of light."[29] President Bush expanded on the idea more fully in his inaugural address.

> I have spoken of a Thousand Points of Light, of all the community organizations that are spread like stars throughout the Nation, doing good. We will work hand in hand, encouraging, sometimes leading, sometimes being led, rewarding. We will work on this in the White House, in the Cabinet agencies. I will go to the people and the programs that are the brighter points of light, and I'll ask every member of my government to become involved. The old ideas are new again because they're not old, they are timeless: duty, sacrifice, commitment, and a patriotism that finds its expression in taking part and pitching in.[30]

The 1989 initiative created a "Points of Light Foundation" which worked to support grassroots-level, community service organizations across the country. In particular, the Points of Light initiative sought to promote youth leadership and peer-to-peer training, focusing on the notion that individuals should strive to "connect" to their communities and engage in the lives of others on a one-to-one basis.[31] President Bush's commitment to the principles of national service helped keep the idea on the national agenda. Bush's successor as president was able to capitalize on this precedent, and national service became one of the central proposals of the Clinton administration.

Bill Clinton's AmeriCorps

By most accounts, Bill Clinton's political hero was John F. Kennedy, whom the future president famously met at the White House in July 1963 while a youthful Arkansas leader of Boys' State.[32] Unsurprisingly, Clinton sought to imitate some of JFK's initiatives. With the Peace Corps in mind, President

Clinton quickly secured the National and Community Service Trust Act from the Democratic Congress during his first year in office (1993). The starring role in this act belonged to AmeriCorps.[33]

AmeriCorps brought together 2,100 nonprofit groups, religious institutions, and public agencies committed to community service, under the aegis of a three-part bureaucracy: AmeriCorps*State and National, which provide grants to community service organizations across the country, AmeriCorps*VISTA, which continues the mission of President Johnson's VISTA program by providing services to low-income individuals and communities across the country, and AmeriCorps*National Civilian Community Corps (AmeriCorps*NCCC), which is a full-time residential program deploying young people to aid in conservation efforts and national disaster relief.

Since its inception, AmeriCorps has been the most energetic and sustained force for youth national service in the country's history. More than 400,000 Americans have served in the corps since its founding, with 75,000 full and part-time volunteers participating in AmeriCorps programs in 2005 alone.[34] AmeriCorps volunteers give back to their communities in diverse and creative ways, including projects aimed at education, economic development, public health, job training, and housing-related activities.[35] Full-time volunteers receive a modest subsistence stipend, and those who complete a one-year service commitment receive a $4,725 education award.[36]

In this politically polarized time, it could be expected that AmeriCorps would become controversial, and it has. The Clinton presidency's sharp partisan divisions, which have persisted throughout George W. Bush's presidency (with the exception of the 9/11 period), have contributed to the dichotomous views of AmeriCorps. Immediately after 9/11, Senator John McCain (R-AZ) and Senator Evan Bayh (D-IA) proposed the Call to Service Act of 2001, which would have expanded AmeriCorps to a total force of 250,000 over several years.[37] President Bush went in a very different direction. By 2007, the Bush budget proposed a massive funding cut for AmeriCorps*NCCC, from $27 million to $5 million, with the ultimate goal of eliminating this program altogether.[38] In this critical respect, AmeriCorps is very unlike JFK's Peace Corps, which despite initial skepticism has come to be supported by major figures in both parties from its inception until the present day.[39]

Supporters of AmeriCorps point to the logical gains produced by such a program. The concrete projects achieved, such as organizing food programs, rehabilitating vacant public housing units, improving landscaping in urban areas, and providing parenting classes to low-income families, have been judged favorably in absolute terms and also in economic cost-benefit analysis.[40] AmeriCorps participants clearly gain substantially as well, developing skills in crisis handling, time management, and critical thinking, and improving on personal, professional, and social measurements.[41] Advocates also have demonstrated that the volunteers are diverse in race, class, and gender, and that their involvement assists in building ties across these all-too-daunting barriers in human society.

Opponents of AmeriCorps are just as insistent that the program has fatal flaws.[42] The federal funding mechanism had unintended consequences, for example. AmeriCorps funds are divided into thirds. The first third of the more than $250-million budget is distributed to states and localities using an automatic population formula.[43] Another third is awarded to groups nominated by the states and selected in a competitive process at the national level. The final third is given to countrywide organizations, institutions of higher learning, and multistate groups, and this is also based on a national competition. The problem here is simple: The states have "gamed" the system by funding marginal, less productive projects through the formula grant while sending only their best projects to the actual competitions. Moreover, federal funding has often *replaced* local funding instead of *adding to* local resources, thus defeating the purpose of the new federal war chest. Then there is the overall cost. Critics maintain that every AmeriCorps participant drains thousands of dollars from the taxpayers.[44] Finally, despite a prohibition against funding organizations that participate in partisan activities, a few liberal groups have slipped through and secured money, making AmeriCorps all the more controversial with Republicans in Congress.[45]

By no means do the dilemmas and downsides of AmeriCorps lead a fair-minded person to conclude that a national service mandate cannot work, but they do suggest some vital qualifiers for a successful service requirement. AmeriCorps is more about groups than individuals, centered on federal funding every bit as much as service. Despite some decentralized management and attempts to hold down the price, AmeriCorps may still be too "top-down" and expensive to succeed in a country that often says it prefers small government. And AmeriCorps can be subject to partisan whims, manipulation, and controversy. The keys to designing an effective universal national service program can be found in successfully dealing with such issues.

THE CASE FOR UNIVERSAL NATIONAL SERVICE (UNS)

There is no time in life quite like the late teens and early twenties. Many young people are bursting with energy, a sense of adventure, and an idealistic determination to make the world a better place. Not yet careworn, rarely cynical, and infused with a belief (sometimes naïve, sometimes accurate) that they can find a better way, the young seek out opportunities to make a difference. As a college teacher for three decades, I can personally and happily testify to this reality.

But the most motivated and capable of the young—at least those who choose the path of higher education—are also highly competitive, insistent on keeping up with their peers and finding success. Lest they be left behind, they push themselves quickly from high school to undergraduate college to graduate school to a good job. Public service is restricted in most cases to a bit of volunteer work in extracurricular activities. There is no expectation in our society now that any significant service is owed. Yet in the decades of the draft, until the debacle of Vietnam, millions of young men willingly accepted the mandate of military service and planned their private lives and future careers around it. The expectation of national service, once the mandate is reestablished, can again become part of the rhythm of life for the young. The adjustment will be far easier than critics imagine, because of both the adaptability and idealism of youthful Americans.

The keys to a successful mandate for national service are:

- True universality
- Flexibility of timing
- Wide choice of service opportunities to fit every taste, with a mixture of government service corps (military and nonmilitary) and private, nonprofit sector activity
- Appropriate incentives and rewards, especially for military service
- Special provisions for older Americans and new immigrants.[46]

True Universality

Fairness in a system of national service is essential, and fairness begins with ensuring that all young people of sound mind and body participate. Americans who remember the military draft in the late 1960s still recall the inequities in a process distorted by a highly unpopular war. Layers of student, family, and medical deferments often gave unjust advantage. Doctors were "available" to those with knowledgeable guides and money to discover a trick elbow or knee, resulting in absolution from the draft. Draft boards applied different standards in different localities, some draconian but perhaps more fair, others undemanding on those with connections.

Universality means just that: Everyone should be included. Exceptions should be rare, and close to nonexistent. Every young citizen can do something. Physical and mental illness of a serious nature should result in deferral, not elimination, of the service duty; when a person's physical and mental state permit, the service years can be fulfilled. This principle should even apply to the temporarily incarcerated; some activities defined as service could be performed behind bars, but for those eventually released from prison, national service must be performed. Given the CCC precedent during the New Deal, the often transformative nature of experiences like this may impart skills and discipline that can help set lives on a constructive course.

Flexibility of Timing

The rhythm of life varies from person to person, and national service should accommodate this reality. For some young people, national service right after high school graduation would make the most sense. Some will not be going to college, and others will not be ready for higher education quite yet. National service can add maturity and experience, better preparing some citizens for university study or careers. Every youth has to "find him/herself," and national service will be a lost-and-found for many. Still others will discover that a mid-college break is appropriate. While this will not be common, except among those attending two-year community colleges, it fits some lifestyles. Every college instructor has had students who "burn out" halfway through a four-year degree study program—individuals who would benefit from a change of pace and focus. Perhaps a majority of the young would choose to perform their national service right after obtaining their undergraduate degree. Graduate school administrators have long known that students who take a couple of years between undergraduate life and graduate education to do something else perform at a higher level in many courses of study. Post-B.A., students could spread their wings and learn a bit more about the "real world" that many have avoided or been sheltered from. Finally, some would prefer to obtain their graduate degree first. These later national service enrollees would be especially valuable, since medical, nursing, business, science, and other advanced training will be sought after by many of the national service agencies and activities.

Under this proposal, all young people would register for national service when they turn seventeen years of age (replacing draft registration at age eighteen). High schools could help to secure compliance. Early registration would be essential since approximately one third of all high school graduates do not go on to college.[47] National service would be especially beneficial for youths who stop at, or drop out of, high school. They would receive on-the-job training in their service assignment, which would likely make them more employable in the future. Troubled young people—those who have fallen prey to gangs and drugs, for example—should receive counseling and as much help as possible during their UNS term so that they could overcome debilitating problems that might keep them out of the job market. For the young in this threatened category, then, UNS could turn out to be a lifesaver, and certainly a circuit breaker from the bad habits acquired in dangerous company or deteriorated home environments. This maturing experience could even help them return to school, with financial assistance provided after their UNS term. If UNS is structured correctly, no group of youths will gain more than those in the greatest need. Of course, society will gain even more in the long run from their progress.

Whether poor or rich, registered youths would receive all the information they need from the government about the various avenues of national service—and they could also be recruited by the agencies selected to participate in the program. Much of this could be done inexpensively across the Internet. All young people would make two decisions for themselves. First, they could choose to begin to serve their years of national service at any point from the ages of eighteen to twenty-six. Second, they could seek to perform their service in the agency of their choice, if space is available and if the agency picks them. No doubt, many would have to settle for their second or third choices, but at least choice would be involved. Considering the vast array of agencies and groups that would likely qualify to recruit service volunteers, most youths would also have the choice of working off their requirement close to their family or far away. Some would prefer the comforts of home and to improve their own community in some way, but many others would indulge their sense of adventure and fly the nest to other states and countries, thus broadening their perspective.

The "draft board" concept would also need to be fully reactivated. Draft boards still exist as part of the machinery of the Selective Service system for a potential military draft, but only in a standby mode.[48] These "national service boards" would ensure that all eligible young people register for UNS and are placed in an appropriate, available slot. The boards would also consider appeals of various sorts, from the rare request to be excused from national service, to entreaties to delay service because of serious family circumstances and the like. Any such delays would be temporary. Lastly, the boards would supervise all enrolled young people, to ensure not only that the full UNS term is served but also that the term is fruitful for participants. The national director of UNS and his or her agency—which again would be adapted from the current Selective Service setup—would coordinate all the thousands of local boards. Perhaps the most vital function of the national agency would be to evaluate the program on a continual basis to maximize its positive impact for everyone involved.

Wide Choice of Service Opportunities

If national service were a reality today, about 37 million young people from eighteen to twenty-six would need to find opportunities to serve over the next eight years.[49] This is an enormous number, but so are the needs in the nation and around the world. Let's start with the military option. The four branches have had difficulty in meeting volunteer recruitment goals in recent years, as the Iraq War has grown more controversial. Their problems would be at an end with national service in place. Even if only 10 percent of the young select the military, that number would be 3.7 million over the next eight years, compared with a total force of 1.4 million today.[50] And the percentage could be expanded well beyond 10 percent with the right set of incentives, as discussed in the next section. Moreover, the military would have a much wider universe of applicants from which to choose under UNS. Many would already be college educated, some graduate school trained. The pool of military volunteers would be enriched accordingly, and even though national service is a requirement, it would still be a volunteer army. No young person would be forced to choose the military option.

If not the military, then what? The accompanying chart lists some of the organizations, governmental and nongovernmental, that could qualify as national service options. These are obvious choices, but there are many, many more at both the national and local levels. Here is where the federal government could play an essential coordinating role. Reasonable standards would have to be adopted to qualify an organization for national service, among them the ability to deliver high-quality service to a target

ORGANIZATIONS THAT COULD SATISFY UNS REQUIREMENT

United States Army	Save the Children
The Army National Guard	Shelter for Abused Women
United States Navy	Shriners Hospitals for Children
United States Air Force	ASPCA
United States Marine Corps	Volunteer Fire and Rescue
United States Coast Guard	Teach for America
Peace Corps	Habitat for Humanity
AIDS/HIV Services Group	Suicide Prevention Action Network USA
ALS Association	Big Brothers/Big Sisters
Boys and Girls Club	Special Olympics
Doctors without Borders USA	Red Cross and Red Crescent
Meals on Wheels	Civilian Conservation Corps[a]
Feed the Children	Urban Environmental Corps[a]
Humane Society	National Disaster Strike Force[a]
Make-A-Wish	
Reading Is Fundamental	

Note: This is a very partial listing of possibilities, just to give the flavor of groups that would or could qualify for UNS. Many of these groups have state and local chapters, sometimes numbering in the hundreds. UNS can be performed at the local level just as easily as at the national level. Almost every sizable city or county has dozens of nonprofit organizations that could apply to use UNS enrollees. The alternatives are practically limitless.

[a] New idea to be developed, or in the case of the CCC, to be revived for UNS participants.

population, the capacity to train and use national service volunteers, and the strength of the group's internal accounting and auditing systems. Nongovernmental organizations could apply for approval for a set number of volunteers directly, and states and localities could also request volunteers for a wide variety of service-delivery functions and even state units of the National Guard.

Organizations that focus on political activity, such as major and minor political parties, would not be able to use national service volunteers. Some nonprofit groups that are primarily service-oriented might have incidental political involvements, but in no case should national service volunteers be used for any partisan purpose.[51] Religious organizations would present a special challenge, but if national service volunteers were used specifically for the nonreligious community service arms of various denominations, their inclusion might be permissible and constitutionally acceptable.[52]

No doubt, the federal government agency established to administer national service would have to monitor and reevaluate its choices at regular intervals. But there would truly be something for everyone. The imagination is the only limit for the kinds of governmental and nongovernmental tasks these young volunteers can perform. The Civilian Conservation Corps could be revived, for instance, or an Urban Environmental Corps could be formed to spruce up selected localities, from removing litter and graffiti to adding appropriate artwork. A National Service Disaster Strike Force could be trained in the thousands to go into areas devastated by hurricanes, tornadoes, or earthquakes to provide some immediate hands-on assistance as well as long-term rebuilding help for residents. One only has to think about the Gulf Coast in the wake of Hurricane Katrina. The government at all levels, private organizations, and insurance companies were as overwhelmed as the residents themselves, and even years later they are struggling to rebuild. Groups of student volunteers from around the country used their college spring breaks to travel to the affected areas and do what they could to help. Even in small doses, their youthful energy, hard work, and endurance were a tonic to the handful of people lucky enough to get a hand. Tens of thousands of trained young people could do much more in such situations.

Appropriate Incentives and Rewards

Each young person would have the responsibility to arrange for his or her own national service and the freedom to choose among the options he or she can secure. Nonetheless, there could be differences among the incentives and rewards offered for various types of national service. Most, possibly all, private or nonprofit organizations would be paid a lump sum per volunteer by the government for training and administrative costs, and each volunteer would be paid a minimum wage for a forty-hour week (with some adjustments needed for service opportunities that require a greater weekly commitment of time). The national service minimum wage might or might not be as high as the federal minimum wage at any given time, with the obligation to give young volunteers enough money to meet their basic needs, but no more. Financial inducements would actually detract from the service spirit of the commitment. The minimum wage (and modest benefits such as basic health care, life insurance, and disability coverage)[53] would also hold down costs for the taxpayers. If funding permits, though, educational assistance ought to be provided on the basis of need to young people who want to go to college after they complete their UNS term. The maturing effect of UNS might give new ambition to young people of lesser means who might not have had a college-educated person in their family to serve as a model. Education is the key to prosperity not just for the individual but for American society, so UNS potentially could give a critical push to millions to advance their education and status in life—and the overall well-being of the United States, too.

Having established the principle of subsistence-level wages and benefits, we should make a few exceptions. The most significant and obvious exception would be military service. Only in the case of the armed forces should wages and benefits exceed the minimum by a substantial amount. It is not just that military volunteers are offering to risk their lives for their country—a service far in excess of those performing other functions, however valuable they may be. The training would be more intense and long-lasting than almost all other assignments, and the hardships probably much greater. Therefore, it is appropriate to offer increased incentives, such as college and graduate school expenses for those who have not already enjoyed these privileges, as well as forgiveness of some or all student loans for those who have already been to college. Complete heath care coverage and major death and injury benefits for the volunteers and their immediate families should also be guaranteed.

Given the length of training necessary to produce useful soldiers, the term of national service for the military volunteers should be extended by a year, maybe two, so that they are enlisting for either three or four years. In addition to augmented benefits such as those just mentioned, the pay in years three and four should be substantially greater than in the first two years. The risks assumed by members of the armed forces would unquestionably reduce enrollments, whatever the higher pay and incentives. Yet, as noted earlier, mandatory service would yield a large pool of potential recruits, and each military branch would likely have to be expanded in order to accommodate all capable, qualified volunteers. The Pentagon has, for example, been exploring a "citizen-soldier" short-term enlistment program which allows volunteers to sign up for fifteen months of active-duty service followed by twenty-four months of reserve duty, instead of traditional four- and five-year active-duty enlistments.[54] Looking around the world at U.S. commitments in this frightening age of terrorism, does anyone really doubt that we can use the augmented forces? Frequent natural disasters (tsunamis, earthquakes, famines, and so on) will also require the help of a well-trained and impressively equipped volunteer military.

It is reasonable to suspend repayments on student loans during the period of national service for all participants, whether in the military or not. As noted above, military service could result in partial or full loan forgiveness, and Congress might, from time to time, designate other specific national service duties as worthy of some loan forgiveness, in addition to the educational assistance for the poor and lower middle class that I mentioned earlier. This is a powerful incentive that the Congress can use to steer young people into the most needed branches of national service.

Special Provisions for Older Americans and New Immigrants

Properly structured and implemented, Universal National Service would change the face of America. Its attractiveness would not be limited to Americans between the ages of eighteen and twenty-six. Especially in its first decades, UNS would appeal to some older Americans who missed their opportunity in a pre-UNS era. The law passed by Congress to implement the new constitutional clause should include a provision for the participation of qualified volunteers who have passed the age of twenty-six. Many retirees may find UNS appealing. Over the years the Peace Corps has utilized hundreds of Americans over age sixty.[55] For example, former president Jimmy Carter's mother, Lillian Carter, volunteered for the Peace Corps at the age of sixty-eight in 1966, and she spent nearly two years working with lepers in India. It is easy to imagine senior citizens devoting some of their retirement careers to causes in the UNS universe.

Immigrants, too, should be included in the UNS family. It is often said that all Americans, except those descended exclusively from Native Americans, are the children of immigrants. Immigrants have always infused the United States with new ideas, rich culture, and entrepreneurial spirit, and legal immigrants should be fully integrated into the nation in every possible way. Youthful immigrants can perform national service at the regular age, but older immigrants should be encouraged to participate in UNS at some point after taking the oath of citizenship. Obviously, most senior immigrants are in a different stage of life, and it may not be possible, given their family and career responsibilities, for them to take part. Nonetheless, some might welcome the service years as an opportunity to serve their new nation.

Costs and Benefits

In this age of enormous budget deficits and unrestrained government spending, most of us have an instinctive reaction whenever a new federal program is proposed. How much will it cost? Can we really afford it? As I will demonstrate in this section, the benefits that will accrue as a result of Universal National Service will far outweigh the annual price tag for the federal Treasury.

First and foremost, it is admittedly difficult to run a cost-benefit analysis of a Universal National Service program. Many of the variables are difficult to quantify; how does one measure, for example, the value of an enhanced sense of civic duty? At the same time, many of the details of a UNS program would be left up to Congress, since the constitutional provision creating UNS would be appropriately broad. With these challenges in mind, the best available model for UNS is the AmeriCorps program already in existence. I discussed earlier how AmeriCorps has its own challenges, which a UNS program would need to address in order to be successful. AmeriCorps does, however, represent a nationwide, largely decentralized, sustained effort to engage young people in full-time national service. As such, it provides us with the best available data by which to consider the costs and benefits of a UNS program.

There have been seven cost-benefit analyses of AmeriCorps programs since its founding over a decade ago. In all, AmeriCorps averaged a total cost-benefit ratio of 1 to 1.95, meaning that AmeriCorps programs generated almost two dollars in benefits for every dollar invested—an investment return of nearly 100 percent.[56] Imagine the economic benefit to the U.S. economy with millions of young people engaged in this kind of national service.

What about the absolute cost to the federal Treasury? Administering a UNS program, complete with subsistence-level stipends and benefits for millions of young participants, as well as maintenance of the necessary bureaucracy, would generate substantial expenses. There have been several estimates over the years about precisely how much. One expert estimated the total cost of UNS at approximately 115 percent of the full-time minimum wage per participant.[57] With an average of 4.1 million young people becoming eligible for UNS every year, that amounts to an annual total cost of approximately $49.6 billion. A UNS authority with Clinton White House experience, Professor William Galston of the University of Maryland, estimated the total cost of administering UNS at $60 billion annually.[58] Finally, the Office of Management and Budget estimated the annual per-participant cost of AmeriCorps programs to be approximately $16,000, from which we can extrapolate a total yearly cost for UNS of about $65.7 billion.[59]

These are admittedly huge sums of money, but they are more than worth the benefits to the nation of creating a UNS program. It is helpful to remember that all government spending is a question of priorities. Consider the recent huge federal expenditure for the Iraq War. The government had spent $378 billion on the war as of March 2007, and experts estimate the total

TABLE 5.1. COMPARING UNS COSTS TO THE COST OF THE IRAQ WAR

Estimate	Total Cost	Cost per Citizen
UNS Estimate 1	$49.6 billion annually	$166
UNS Estimate 2	$60 billion annually	$201
UNS Estimate 3	$65.7 billion annually	$220
Iraq War Spending as of March 2007	$378 billion*	$1,267
Iraq War total cost, estimate 1	$750 billion	$2,517
Iraq War total cost, estimate 2	$2 trillion	$6,711

* See Amy Belasco, "The Cost of Iraq, Afghanistan, and Other Global War on Terror Operations Since 9/11," *Congressional Research Service* (14 Mar. 2007): p. 3. Available online at http://www.fas.org/sgp/crs/natsec/RL33110.pdf.

price for the war will eventually be somewhere between $750 billion and $2 trillion.[60] Compare the cost of a UNS program to the costs of the Iraq War in table 5.1.

As the reader can see, Americans have already spent, per citizen, almost six times as much on the Iraq War as on the most costly estimate of an annual one-year UNS program, and the Iraq War might end up costing as much as thirty times more per American than a UNS program.[61] And while Americans may receive benefits down the road from a democratized Middle East (and it remains a big "if"), national service has a proven, positive cost-benefit ratio. The contrast is stark between expenditures for Iraq, and a UNS program that could generate $120 billion in economic benefits every year.

Additionally, these simple economic models cannot capture the most potent benefits derived from UNS: an entire generation with a strong sense of civic engagement, an appreciation for service to others, a connection to one another across class, race, and economic lines, and a deeper respect for the privileges of American citizenship. These are not abstract concepts. Longitudinal studies of AmeriCorps participants reveal that even three years after leaving the program, participants are two and a half times more likely to volunteer in their local communities and substantially more likely to have jobs in public service.[62] Universal National Service can generate lifelong volunteerism and community building—a bold step toward a brighter future for our politics and our civic culture.[63]

UNIVERSAL NATIONAL SERVICE AND AMERICA'S FUTURE

The idea of national service already seems to have a special and enduring attraction in the United States. Americans are drawn to volunteer service in larger numbers than residents of many other countries.[64] Perhaps recognizing this, members of Congress from both houses and both parties have proposed various forms of national service with considerable frequency—though the concept has not yet received enough attention to spark a true national debate.[65]

Now, more than at any time since the 1960s, my college faculty colleagues and I sense a hunger among the young for constructive challenges. Conservatives and liberals alike in this marvelously energetic and idealistic age group want to create a happier, healthier, saner, safer country and world. They are awaiting an appeal to the better angels of their nature, and Universal National Service would be just such a clarion call. UNS could electrify the nation and give special purpose and meaning to a new Constitutional Convention. The idea of citizenship would be expanded to create a broader pact of rights and responsibilities that are mutually reinforcing.

Post-convention, once UNS had become part of the fabric of American society, it would be a *force multiplier* for civic activity. Force multiplier is a military term, defined by the Defense Department as "a capability that, when added to and employed by a combat force, significantly increases the combat potential of that force and thus enhances the probability of [a] successful mission." UNS would qualify as a force multiplier because participants in service programs have been shown to be particularly effective at recruiting many additional people for community work. For example, trained AmeriCorps activists have engaged over a quarter of a million more volunteers in construction of housing for Habitat for Humanity.[66]

In addition to the case already made for Universal National Service, an equally powerful argument can be put forth—the moral one. A society dedicated entirely to individual pursuits, without concern for the welfare of the whole body of citizens, is soulless. Volunteers in a wide variety of programs and activities have made a difference, yet many vital needs remain unmet, since volunteers can only do so much. The truth is that, given human nature, a purely voluntary regime of service means a few will give a lot, a fair number will give some, and many will contribute nothing. The unfairness of this situation is obvious, yet it is easy to overlook even more serious consequences.

Take the American military. The overall quality of the troops is high, and they are unquestionably well trained, but the all-volunteer system has resulted in a highly unrepresentative group of citizens constituting the armed forces. As the authors Kathy Roth-Douquet and Frank Schaeffer have convincingly argued, the best-educated and wealthiest young people—those who will comprise the governing class eventually, and whose parents and grandparents already do—are virtually absent from today's military.[67] Many of the Ivy League schools ban ROTC outright and totally prevent military recruiters from meeting with students on campus. The parents of privileged youths, and many of their teachers and advisers too, discourage these students from entering military service. Many poor and lower-middle-class kids flock to the military, by contrast, since it represents a way up, with substantial educational benefits unavailable to them in any other venue. So today's armed forces have less connection than ever before to Congress and other governing elites.

Why does this matter? For one thing, simple justice requires that the heaviest burdens of national defense should be shared equitably by all social classes. For another, it is always easier to send other people's children off to war than one's own. In the twenty-first century, the ultimate price—death or severe maiming in combat—is paid by an unrepresentative and often invisible slice of the nation. Nobody can honestly say that this is right. Universal National Service would guarantee that a much more representative group of young Americans was on the front lines. Just as important, the governing class of the future would contain a considerable number of military veterans who would understand what combat is and means.

The moral dimension of UNS extends far beyond military service. Equity in society demands that the burdens of citizenship be fairly distributed. The political scientist William Galston properly notes that an "all-volunteer jury" would be disastrous to the cause of justice, eliminating the "jury of our peers" and substituting a jury of those with nothing better to do.[68] Some burdens of citizenship must be compulsory, necessarily limiting personal liberty in order to ensure fairness. Americans accepted and backed military conscription for much of the twentieth century for precisely this reason. In the post-9/11 world, when sacrifice is again manifestly required, they can be persuaded to support it again.[69]

Critics of national service often adopt the libertarian credo that "the right to be left alone" is paramount in a free democratic society. However, the patriarch of libertarianism, John Stuart Mill, wrote that "everyone who receives the protection of society owes a return for the benefit . . . This consists . . . in each person's bearing his share . . . of the labors and sacrifices incurred for defending the society or its members from injury and molestation."[70] Ironically,

Mill's reasoning is a powerful antidote to libertarian excess. Those who question UNS also contend that it will inevitably become another massive government bureaucracy full of waste and fraud.[71] Granted, anything government touches can develop major flaws. The greedy would discover ways and means to steal, and those reluctant to serve would find or create loopholes to avoid their duty. Such is human nature when applied to a vast enterprise. But these difficulties could be surmounted or limited through proper supervision, and they should not be permitted to subvert the overwhelming positive good that UNS can accomplish.

UNS is less about governmental authority and more about a renewal of personal citizenship through sustained individual commitment to improving the nation. Here, we return to the young. That they and the nation need this civic renewal is unquestioned. What surprises many is that most young Americans quickly warm to the idea of UNS. They sense that something vital is missing from their own pressured lives, where they are hurried from one private achievement to the next, with barely a breath taken. They yearn for a broadening, unselfish experience shared by all in their age group. It is quite possible that a new generation of young Americans will one day ask one another with pride, "Where did you do your national service?" just as the "greatest generation," who fought and won World War II, traded stories throughout their lives of common youthful sacrifice and service. Those early trials shaped their worldview, one reflected by Winston Churchill, who once observed, "We make a living by what we get; we make a life by what we give."[72] Many veterans of the Second World War took Churchill's philosophy to heart and were consistently civic oriented and community minded—a passion they passed down to their children.[73] Through UNS, and its prominent placement in a new Constitution for the twenty-first century, we can light that fire again and pass the torch from generation to generation.

CHAPTER SIX

VOX POPULI: WHAT DO THE PEOPLE THINK OF CONSTITUTIONAL CHANGE?

VOX POPULI, THE voice of the people, matters enormously in all things constitutional. For here the people rule. No change in the Constitution will happen if the public is opposed to it. So what do Americans think of the reforms advocated in this book?

There is no simple answer to the question. Many of the reforms proposed in these pages are entirely new, and most citizens have never given a moment's thought to the subjects. Some of the ideas are complex, and not easily translated into short opinion poll queries that busy Americans will actually take the time to respond to. Critics could legitimately point out that we are creating public opinion where it does not exist merely by asking questions, or asking the questions in a certain way (however well balanced and neutral may be the wordings).

Most important of all, real constitutional change will be a carefully deliberative, painfully slow process, with thorough discussion of every reform proposal. The debate may stretch across a generation or more. Surely, the place where many thoughtful people start out in their views on the substance of a Constitutional Convention almost certainly will not be the place where they end up.

Despite these handicaps, natural curiosity led to testing out the ideas presented in this volume. I wanted to get a sense about whether Americans are sufficiently open to new ideas, or fed up with the unworkable aspects of the current system, that they would consider fundamental change. Alternately, are citizens so convinced of the infallibility of the founders, or fearful of unleashing the forces of reform, that they would be unwilling to open what they might perceive to be a dangerous door?

To find out, we engaged a noted public opinion firm—one that had a remarkably accurate record in the campaigns of 2006—to poll a sizable random sample of Americans.[1] On September 10, 2006, Rasmussen Reports conducted a telephone survey of 981 Americans on the topic of potential changes to the Constitution. Respondents were asked twenty-six substantive questions about their reaction to various proposals, and they ranked each proposal on a standard favorability scale (from "strongly favor" to "strongly oppose"). Of the twenty-six questions, seventeen were focused on ideas that I have actually proposed in the book, while nine concerned other possible constitutional changes not advocated here. Some in the latter category were designed to elicit strongly favorable responses, and others were phrased to produce outrage. This is a standard polling technique that permits useful comparisons as the results are evaluated.

The results help to clarify the attitudes of the American public about constitutional possibilities, and hence they provide a revealing starting point for a national debate. It is worth noting that nothing like this has been done before; while some of the individual queries have been asked occasionally, no similar set of questions has ever been recorded or reported in public opinion research. If we are going to take the idea of constitutional change seriously, though, precisely this kind of empirical analysis and good-faith experimentation will be necessary to move the country forward.

In general, these survey results bode well for the promise of serious debate about constitutional change. Of the seventeen reform proposals made in this book that are included in the Rasmussen poll, eight already draw majority support without benefit of extended debate. At the same time, Americans display a healthy degree of initial skepticism about many proposed alterations to their founding document. Some major changes, such as restructuring the Electoral College and the creation of Universal National Service, do not yet achieve majority backing in our survey. And yet, many of the boldest proposals outlined in this book were received favorably by between one third and one half of all respondents, which indicates that a considerable portion of the American electorate is willing to at least entertain the notion of major reform.

This provides precisely the foundation from which we can build a national dialogue and gradually move toward a Constitutional Convention. It is reasonable to assume that detailed discussion and debate over many years' time would encourage growing acceptance of at least some currently alien constitutional reform ideas. Inarguably, additional debate would sink others or cause still more creative proposals or compromises to be floated and accepted. All of this is to be expected in the normal course of events leading to a Constitutional Convention.

THE CAUTION LIGHT BLINKS STEADILY

Our country may have been born in revolution, but, on the whole, Americans are instinctively cautious. The United States' economy, government, and society are relatively strong, so proposed change is often viewed with a jaundiced eye. Why mess with success? Thus, as we will discuss in chapter 7, it is no accident that the United States has one of the lowest rates of constitutional amendment of any democracy worldwide—a testament both to the great difficulty of passing an amendment but also to the enduring faith that Americans have in their basic blueprint for government.

Unsurprisingly, then, our survey found that proposals that would most radically alter America's constitutional machinery were met with more skepticism from the public. (See table 6.1. The exact questions are listed in the appendix at the end of this chapter.) Therefore, the notion of a more representative Senate earned a 74 percent disapproval rating (though, for reasons we will discuss later, the idea of a more representative Electoral College was greeted much more favorably). In part because the idea of a renewed Constitution has barely been broached with the public, 71 percent rejected the notion that we should make undefined "major changes" to the Constitution, and a majority of Americans turned down the idea that the Constitution needs to be "brought up to date." This makes perfect sense. Major constitutional change is not a conclusion that moderate, prudent Americans would reach instantly when questioned over the telephone by an anonymous pollster. We have survived and prospered with the current Constitution, so the burden of the argument, as yet unheard by the public, must rest with the advocates of change. Citizens also associate many constitutional amendment proposals with controversial, divisive social issues that generate upheaval and animosities. As a country, we have enough urgent problems on our plate, it would seem at first blush, without inviting additional turmoil with "unnecessary" constitutional tampering.

There is no doubt that the push for a major overhaul in government will be a slow, uphill, perhaps generational battle—and that is exactly as it should be. Stability is essential, and a majority of the public must be convinced over a long period of time that each and every constitutional change is worth making, that the gain of reform is greater than the pain experienced in the run-up to reform. The public's response in our poll, then, is exactly the right one.

However—and this is encouraging for the reformers among us—the Rasmussen poll also established that there are numerous aspects of the American system that the public views as inadequate, and thus, areas where

TABLE 6.1. AMERICA'S REACTION TO PROPOSALS FOR CONSTITUTIONAL CHANGE

Proposal	% in Favor	% Strongly in Favor	% Opposed	% Strongly Opposed
	Most highly rated reform proposals			
Judges retire at 75	77	55	20	10
Approval from Congress for war	71	55	27	13
Limits on personal/family donations	71	55	25	12
Congressional term limits	66	43	30	17
Judicial term limit (15 years)	56	31	41	20
Free TV advertising	54	26	40	25
Regional presidential primaries	51	23	38	19
House term of 3 years	50	23	46	27
	Less highly rated reform proposals			
Mandatory public service	43	26	53	36
Expand Supreme Court to 12 members	37	20	55	36
More representative Electoral College	37	18	57	35
Public funding for all campaigns	35	15	57	33
Increase size of Congress	33	13	59	40
Presidential term of 6 years plus referendum for 2-year extension	31	11	64	41
Foreign-born president	30	12	68	48
Constitutional Convention—bring up to date (split sample for special wording—see appendix to this chapter)	28	17	66	52
Constitutional Convention—make major changes (split sample for special wording—see appendix to this chapter)	25	8	71	57
More representative Senate	24	9	74	58
	Control ideas (not among the recommendations in this book but used for testing purposes)			
Direct election of president	69	51	27	18
Raise age of president to 40	48	27	50	31
Ban TV advertising	33	18	63	36
House term of 1 year	28	11	81	60

Proposal	% in Favor	% Strongly in Favor	% Opposed	% Strongly Opposed
Lower age of president to 30	20	10	79	59
Tax on nonvoters	19	10	79	66
Decrease Supreme Court to seven members	14	6	78	59
Lower voting age to under 18	8	3	91	76

Source: This table is based on data from a random sample telephone poll of 981 adult Americans taken on September 10, 2006. The margin of error is plus or minus 3 percent with a 95 percent level of confidence. The survey was conducted specifically for this book by Rasmussen Reports. See the appendix at the end of this chapter for a complete listing of questions and response rates.

change would be embraced by a majority. These areas of reform can initiate a dialogue about change that can eventually lead to the larger undertaking of a new Constitutional Convention.

DISSATISFACTION WITH THE STATUS QUO

Unsurprisingly, adult Americans living today are unhappiest about the constitutional provisions (or absence of them) that have been linked to contemporary problems. Our citizens particularly dislike congressional corruption, hubristic presidential war making, judicial adventurism, and embarrassing election practices.

Americans have long had a fascination with term limits as one solution for congressional and state legislative excesses. Sure enough, Americans expressed hearty support for congressional term limits in our survey (the question suggested six years in the House and twelve years in the Senate), with 66 percent in favor.

The disaster of the Iraq War, so reminiscent of a similar quagmire in Vietnam, has created anew a desire for clear, continuous congressional sanctioning of America's foreign wars (71 percent approval). Judging by the results of the 2006 midterm elections, this is a firmly held view and perhaps a generational lesson to be drawn from Iraq. In fact, 55 percent of our sample *strongly* favored the congressional war-making role—tied for top place in the "strongly favored" category for all questions in the survey.

The inadequacies of the political process in the United States produced public assent for considerable change. By a margin of 51 percent in favor to

38 percent opposed, respondents liked the idea of replacing the current presidential nomination system, in which Iowa and New Hampshire play a dominant role, with "a series of four regional primaries, held one per month from March to June." For the general election, perhaps remembering the Electoral College "misfire" in the 2000 presidential contest, 69 percent wanted the president directly elected "so that whoever gets the most votes nationwide would become president." This book's less radical proposal to preserve the Electoral College by making it "more representative of the people by giving more electoral votes to the largest and medium-sized states" secured 37 percent backing, with 57 percent opposed. Clearly, Americans appear to have soured on the Electoral College, and if we are to "mend it, not end it," the federalist undergirding and recount-isolation advantages originally embedded in the college will have to be thoroughly explained to the public in a most convincing manner.

Skyrocketing campaign spending and the inevitable compromising of elected officials' independence to pass laws in the national interest led the public to back some of the constitutional campaign reforms mentioned in chapter 4, including caps on currently unlimited personal and family donations to the campaigns of wealthy candidates (71 percent approval) and some "free or heavily discounted" TV advertising for candidates (54 percent approval). Also, weariness with every-other-year House elections appears to have generated narrow support (50 percent yea to 46 percent nay) for extending the House term to three years. This counts as a mild surprise. People are willing to give members of the House an extra year on each term, even though the public's dislike of Congress is intense, with disapproval usually hovering around two thirds or more of the voters.

The judiciary came in for a certain amount of reformist zeal among the public, too. In fact, the proposal that garnered the most support of any in the survey was to require a mandatory retirement age for judges at seventy-five years (77 percent approval). Interestingly, this idea was backed by more than 80 percent of those aged sixty-five or older, precisely those who most understand the natural limitations of age—and perhaps, too, those who most comprehend the unwise hesitancy of some seniors to make way for a younger generation in the top jobs. The fervor for term limits also carried over to the argument for a fifteen-year term limit for federal judges (56 percent support). Probably, some respondents were expressing dislike for judicial lawmaking, while others simply preferred to avoid the hubris that comes with long tenure in any position of great power.

Some of our reform proposals did not garner majority support in our survey, but the backing was substantial enough to suggest that minds could be changed in the debate. Our signature proposal for Universal National Service secured a surprisingly large 43 percent support, with 53 percent opposed. With the Iraq War raging at the time of the poll, it is encouraging that so many would approve of UNS (though we did stress that service could be in "either military or civilian activities"). Concerning the expansion of the Supreme Court from nine to twelve, 37 percent of our sample favored this while 55 percent opposed it. Given the mood of national crisis that descends upon the Capitol every time a Court vacancy occurs, the public's caution is understandable. The suggested increase in size for the U.S. House of Representatives was heavily opposed by 59 percent and favored by just 33 percent. However, to be fair to the proposal, none of the arguments in support of the idea were made in the necessarily brief question, and people likely imagined that the costs, staffs, and salaries in Congress would skyrocket along with the number of legislators. (Our proposal dictates otherwise, and it is simply an attempt to make representation more personal.)

This book's scheme for a six-year presidential term with a referendum option for a two-year term extension was opposed 64 percent to 31 percent. It will clearly take a lot of coaxing to make this acceptable to a majority. In an era when immigration is highly controversial, the fact that the provision to allow non-native-born Americans to become president after a period of at least twenty years' citizenship failed to draw much support (30 percent yea, 68 percent yea) was not unexpected. Maybe Arnold Schwarzenegger, who would directly benefit, could turn the public around! Even he would have great difficulty reversing the tide of opinion on a "more representative" U.S. Senate, at least to judge from our poll. The question was straightforward enough: "As you know, every state in the Union gets two senators. A proposal has been made to give the largest states two more Senate seats and medium-sized states one more Senate seat." Yet only 24 percent approved, with 74 percent saying no (58 percent strongly opposed). Many residents of large and medium-sized states that would have benefited under the proposal refused to go along. Perhaps Americans simply do not want more senators. Or maybe the American predisposition toward fairness is at work again: Every state should have only the two senators provided for in the Constitution, though the survey question did not emphasize that just 17 percent of the American people produce a majority of the Senate.

To round out the survey, we included some truly bad ideas not endorsed in this book as a kind of "test control" for reform. Almost all of them were overwhelmingly opposed by the public, including giving the vote to those between the ages of thirteen and seventeen, reducing the House term to only one year, shrinking the Supreme Court to seven members, and banning all TV advertising by candidates. Interestingly, far more Americans (48 percent) were willing to lift the threshold age for the presidency from thirty-five to forty, than to lower it from thirty-five to thirty (20 percent). My favorite no-go proposal was the idea to "impose a special tax" on those who do not vote (which is actually done in Switzerland, Australia, and several other democracies). Nearly 80 percent of our sample said they were opposed, finding it to be distinctly un-American, since this nation's traditions generally honor individual choice.[2]

LOOK WHO'S TALKING

Before leaving this very early gauge of public opinion for the new Constitution, it would be useful to examine some of the demographic breakdowns. Table 6.2 gives the overall average backing for the ideas tested in our survey for seven classifications of respondents (gender, age, political party affiliation, race, ideology, income level, and occupation). The average of all 981 respondents clocked in at close to 41 percent backing for the various reforms.

Overall, the variations in backing are not enormous from category to category, with some specific exceptions. For example, Republicans are much more opposed to any alteration of the Electoral College than are Democrats or Independents. While 86 percent of Democrats and 72 percent of Independents would do away with the college altogether, only a bare majority (51 percent) of Republicans would do the same. Surely, Democratic and GOP partisans remember the role of the college in electing George W. Bush in 2000 despite his loss of the popular vote, and that one event has in good part shaped contemporary perceptions of the college's worth. The same phenomenon is at work in the two parties' very different evaluations of restrictions on the president's war powers. Ninety percent of Democrats and 70 percent of Independents would require the president to seek explicit authorization from Congress before going to war, whereas only 52 percent of Republicans believe such a requirement is necessary. This is in part a reflection of opinions on Bush and Iraq. It is quite possible that if this survey were being taken during the Clinton presidency, the partisan numbers would be reversed.

Looking beyond the specifics of individual proposals, however, some interesting trends emerge as to what extent various demographic groups favor constitutional change more or less than others.

TABLE 6.2. BREAKING DOWN THE PUBLIC'S OPENNESS TO CONSTITUTIONAL CHANGE

Demographic	Average Favorability (%)	Adjusted Average (%)
Gender		
Male	37	–3.2
Female	43	2.4
Age		
18–29	38	–2.3
30–39	39	–2.2
40–49	42	0.9
50–64	40	–0.6
65+	44	3.1
Political Party		
Republicans	36	–4.4
Democrats	46	5.4
Other	38	–2.4
Race		
White	41	0.1
Black	42	1.5
Other	37	–3.3
Ideology		
Conservative	37	–3.6
Moderate	43	2.2
Liberal	42	1.3
Not sure	40	–0.3
Income Level		
Under 20k	50	9.6
20k–40k	40	–0.3
40k–60k	39	–1.9
60k–75k	41	0.3
75k–100k	36	–4.4
100k+	41	–0.2
Not sure	36	–5.2

TABLE 6.2 (continued)

Demographic	Average Favorability (%)	Adjusted Average (%)
Occupation		
Government	35	–5.4
Entrepreneur	40	–0.5
Private sector	40	–1.1
Retired	43	2.3

Note: This chart compares survey results by demographic, obtaining an adjusted average for each demographic surveyed. First, an average is taken for all questions as to how many respondents responded that they "strongly favor" or "somewhat favor" a proposal. That's the *overall average*, which comes in at 40.7 percent. Then, for each demographic, an average is taken across all twenty-six questions as to the total percentage favoring the proposal. This is the *average favorability*. That number is subtracted from the overall average to yield the *adjusted average*.

It is obvious that Democrats favor constitutional change a great deal more than Republicans. Democrats register an average favorability rating of 46 percent to proposals for change—a full 10 percent higher than Republicans and 5.4 percent above the overall average. As a group, Republicans and Independents are less likely than the average American to support proposals for constitutional reform. This is partly a function of ideology, not just party. Conservatives are less likely to favor constitutional change, while liberals and moderates are more likely to do so—though the ideological distinctions are less pronounced than the partisan ones in these highly polarized times.

At the same time, there are some noteworthy exceptions. For instance, Republicans are more likely than Democrats to favor Universal National Service. Perhaps this result reflects the lingering opposition to the military draft among some baby boomers. During the Vietnam War, antagonism toward the draft was disproportionately Democratic in the final years of the draft (the late 1960s and early 1970s), before the nation converted to the all-volunteer armed forces.

Beyond the distinctions of party and ideology, we can see that gender, race, income, age, and occupation also have certain impacts. Women are more open to change than men. It isn't a Venus-to-Mars-size gap, but it is measurable—more than 5 percentage points. African Americans are more likely than whites to respond positively to suggestions for reform, whereas other minorities are substantially less likely than whites to support major change. We can only offer tentative hypotheses for why this might be so. Perhaps "other" minorities, mainly first- or second-generation Hispanic, Latino, and Asian Americans, are less willing to question the system they have more recently embraced, while African Americans have consistently pushed for change and struggled for centuries to make the Constitution live up to its promises. Fairness—or the lack of it in the Constitution—would naturally resonate with blacks.

Somewhat correlated to race is income, of course. Those making less than $20,000 per year (disproportionately black but also including millions of whites and those of other races) supported the idea of major change at an average rate of 50 percent—almost 10 percentage points higher than the overall average. Those who are economically besieged, ranking at the bottom of the income ladder, might have seen the idea of constitutional reform as hope for a brighter future and a better break.

Perhaps most surprising are the demographic breakdowns by age. Intuitively, we might expect young people to be the most enthusiastic about the idea of constitutional reform, since they are perceived as more idealistic and less invested in the current system. We might also expect the elderly to be less favorable to reform, having supposedly become more conservative and resistant to change over time. In fact, just the opposite occurred. Those between the ages of eighteen and twenty-nine are *less* likely than the average American to react favorably to constitutional reform, whereas those aged sixty-five or older are *more* likely than the average citizen to support reform by a substantial margin. The same pattern emerges when comparing respondents by occupation. Retirees are more likely to support reform than entrepreneurs or private and public sector employees. (The public sector employees, with the greatest investment in the governmental status quo, are the most resistant to constitutional change.)

How do we explain such a counterintuitive pattern among our age cohorts? Perhaps, on reflection, it makes sense that young people would react more suspiciously to constitutional change. They have just passed through a decade or more of civic education predicated on the heroics of the founding fathers and the unquestioned success of the Constitution. Conversely, in the course of their lengthy lives, the elderly have observed decades of scandal, witnessed several deeply unpopular foreign wars, and seen firsthand the inadequacies of many parts of the American political system.

*

The framers would likely have looked askance at this attempt to use public opinion to shape constitutional reform. They feared the "tyranny of the majority"—the possible dilution of minority rights according to the whim of a majority of the public. While favoring democracy, the framers were suspicious that too much democracy would lead to "mob-ocracy," with the thoughtless, ill-educated masses determining the country's direction. Perhaps in their time, these concerns were at least partly justified.

Conditions in the twenty-first century could not be more different. Many Americans may sincerely believe that various elites (elected officials, campaign donors, lobbyists, and the news media) control what happens in the nation's government. But the more one studies contemporary American democracy, the more one is reassured that little of consequence can occur without the support—or at least the acquiescence—of the general public. This conclusion is certain with respect to constitutional change. Unless and until the American people are ready to embrace a new Constitution, it will not happen. This is why a lengthy, thorough national conversation about the subject is a requirement to produce change. This book, hopefully, is a step toward that conversation.

APPENDIX: RASMUSSEN POLL ON THE PROPOSED NEW CONSTITUTION

Rasmussen Reports conducted a random sample telephone survey of 981 adult Americans on September 10, 2006. The survey was conducted specifically for this book. Interviewees were asked twenty-six questions and given a choice of four responses for each: strongly favor, somewhat favor, somewhat oppose, and strongly oppose. The results (in percentages) are listed below. The margin of error is plus or minus 3 percent with a 95 percent level of confidence. Additional questions on demographics (age, income, race, and so on) were also asked, but they are not included in this summary. Questions designated by the term *split sample* were put to one half of the total sample, with the other half receiving a different version of the question.

1. *Presidents are currently limited to two four-year terms in office. A proposal has been made to elect the president for a single six-year term, with an up-or-down "confirmation election" for a two-year extension.*

11% Strongly favor
20% Somewhat favor

23% Somewhat oppose
41% Strongly oppose
5% Not sure

2. *A proposal has been made that would require the president to get approval from Congress before going to war.*

55% Strongly favor
16% Somewhat favor
14% Somewhat oppose
13% Strongly oppose
2% Not sure

3. *The Constitution currently prevents anyone who is not a natural-born citizen from serving as president. Some have suggested that this be changed so that anyone who has been a U.S. citizen for at least twenty years can be eligible to serve as president.*

12% Strongly favor
18% Somewhat favor
20% Somewhat oppose
48% Strongly oppose
3% Not sure

4. [Split Sample] *The Constitution currently requires that one must be at least thirty-five years old in order to become president. A proposal has been made to raise the minimum age for presidents to forty.*

27% Strongly favor
21% Somewhat favor
19% Somewhat oppose
31% Strongly oppose
2% Not sure

5. [Split Sample] *The Constitution currently requires that one must be at least thirty-five years old in order to become president. A proposal has been made to lower the minimum age for presidents to thirty.*

10% Strongly favor
10% Somewhat favor
20% Somewhat oppose
59% Strongly oppose
1% Not sure

6. *As you know, every state in the union gets two senators. A proposal has been made to give the largest states two more Senate seats and medium-sized states one more Senate seat.*

9% Strongly favor
15% Somewhat favor
16% Somewhat oppose
58% Strongly oppose
3% Not sure

7. [Split Sample] *Members of the House of Representatives must run for reelection every two years. A proposal has been made to lengthen the term of office to three years.*

23% Strongly favor
27% Somewhat favor
19% Somewhat oppose
27% Strongly oppose
3% Not sure

8. [Split Sample] *Members of the House of Representatives must run for reelection every two years. A proposal has been made to shorten the term of office to one year.*

11% Strongly favor
7% Somewhat favor
21% Somewhat oppose
60% Strongly oppose
2% Not sure

9. *A proposal has been made to place term limits on members of Congress so that no one can serve longer than six years in the House or twelve years in the Senate.**

43% Strongly favor
23% Somewhat favor
17% Somewhat oppose
13% Strongly oppose
3% Not sure

10. *Federal judges are currently appointed for life. Do you strongly favor, somewhat favor, somewhat oppose, or strongly oppose a proposal to limit judges to serving for fifteen years?*

31% Strongly favor
25% Somewhat favor
20% Somewhat oppose
21% Strongly oppose
3% Not sure

11. *Do you strongly favor, somewhat favor, somewhat oppose, or strongly oppose a proposal that would require federal judges to retire at age seventy-five?*

55% Strongly favor
22% Somewhat favor
10% Somewhat oppose
10% Strongly oppose
2% Not sure

12. [Split Sample] *Do you strongly favor, somewhat favor, somewhat oppose, or strongly oppose a proposal to increase the number of justices on the Supreme Court from nine to twelve?*

20% Strongly favor
17% Somewhat favor

---

* In the interest of question simplicity—a key element of polling over the telephone—this question did not specify whether the listed term limits would be consecutive years or total years. It was designed to elicit a quick reaction to the concept of term limits, and nothing more.

19% Somewhat oppose
36% Strongly oppose
7% Not sure

13. [Split Sample] *Do you strongly favor, somewhat favor, somewhat oppose, or strongly oppose a proposal to reduce the number of justices on the Supreme Court from nine to seven?*

6% Strongly favor
8% Somewhat favor
19% Somewhat oppose
59% Strongly oppose
8% Not sure

14. *As you know, every presidential election primary season starts out in two small states, Iowa and New Hampshire. A proposal has been made to change this and replace it with a series of four regional primaries, held one per month from March to June.*

23% Strongly favor
28% Somewhat favor
19% Somewhat oppose
19% Strongly oppose
12% Not sure

15. *A proposal has been made to place a constitutional limit on the amount of money candidates and their close relatives can donate to their own campaigns.*

55% Strongly favor
16% Somewhat favor
13% Somewhat oppose
12% Strongly oppose
5% Not sure

16. *A proposal has been made to guarantee free television advertising or greatly discounted television airtime for candidates for national office.*

26% Strongly favor
28% Somewhat favor

15% Somewhat oppose
25% Strongly oppose
5% Not sure

17. *A proposal has been made that would make it illegal for candidates to buy television advertising time for their campaigns. Only groups with positions on important issues would be allowed to buy television advertising.*

18% Strongly favor
15% Somewhat favor
27% Somewhat oppose
36% Strongly oppose
5% Not sure

18. *A proposal has been made to provide public funding to all candidates for Congress.*

15% Strongly favor
20% Somewhat favor
24% Somewhat oppose
33% Strongly oppose
8% Not sure

19. *A proposal has been made that would require every able-bodied American between the ages of eighteen and twenty-six to devote at least two years to the service of the nation, either in military or civilian activities.*

26% Strongly favor
17% Somewhat favor
17% Somewhat oppose
36% Strongly oppose
4% Not sure

20. [Split Sample] *A proposal has been made to do away with the Electoral College and move to a direct election so that whoever gets the most votes nationwide would become president.*

51% Strongly favor
18% Somewhat favor

9% Somewhat oppose
18% Strongly oppose
3% Not sure

21. [Split Sample] *A proposal has been made to make the Electoral College more representative of the people by giving more electoral votes to the largest and medium-sized states.*

18% Strongly favor
19% Somewhat favor
22% Somewhat oppose
35% Strongly oppose
6% Not sure

22. *Currently, members of Congress represent about 600,000 people in their district. A proposal has been made to increase the size of Congress so that each member would represent only 50,000 people in their district.*

13% Strongly favor
20% Somewhat favor
19% Somewhat oppose
40% Strongly oppose
8% Not sure

23. [Split Sample] *A proposal has been made to hold a new Constitutional Convention so that we can make major changes to our Constitution.*

8% Strongly favor
17% Somewhat favor
14% Somewhat oppose
57% Strongly oppose
5% Not sure

24. [Split Sample] *A proposal has been made to hold a new Constitutional Convention so that we can bring our Constitution up to date after the passage of more than 200 years.*

17% Strongly favor
11% Somewhat favor

14% Somewhat oppose
52% Strongly oppose
6% Not sure

25. *A proposal has been made to change the Constitution and give teenagers under the age of eighteen the right to vote.*

3% Strongly favor
5% Somewhat favor
15% Somewhat oppose
76% Strongly oppose
1% Not sure

26. *Some people say that in order to get more people to participate in voting, we should impose a special tax on people who do not vote.*

10% Strongly favor
9% Somewhat favor
13% Somewhat oppose
66% Strongly oppose
2% Not sure

CHAPTER SEVEN

CALLING THE TWENTY-FIRST-CENTURY CONSTITUTIONAL CONVENTION

The States will never agree in their plans, and the Deputies to a second Convention coming together under the discordant impressions of their Constituents, will never agree. Conventions are serious things, and ought not to be repeated.

—*Charles Cotesworth Pinckney, 1787*[1]

I strongly believe that, as a practical matter, holding an Article V Convention . . . would be a needless and perilous undertaking—one likely to generate uncertainties where confidence is indispensable, one likely to invite division and confrontation where unity and cooperation are critical, one likely to thwart rather than vindicate the will of the American people and damage rather than mend the Constitution.

—*Laurence Tribe, 1979*[2]

[The Constitution] has, to put it plainly, become in many respects obsolete. The succeeding generations still living within its directives are confronted with conditions radically different from those known to the original framers. . . . Does anyone believe that if the Constitution in its entirety should be submitted to referendum now, and relieved somehow of its traditional sanctity, it would be ratified? If it would not, and if constitutional government is desirable, then it follows that an acceptable one ought to be devised. This simple logic seems irrefutable; actually it is universally evaded. It is even widely regarded as reprehensible to make such a suggestion.

—*Rexford Tugwell, 1976*[3]

THE FEAR OF the "common people" that drove America's founders had obvious results in the Constitution. Presidents were elected by a small Electoral

College without a popular vote, the Senate was filled with the choices of state legislatures and not the people, and the electorate was kept tiny and discriminatorily select. Indirect representative democracy held pure democracy at bay.

Given the lack of broad-based education, the widespread poverty of eighteenth-century America, and the absence of any successful contemporary democratic precedents, perhaps the founders' fears were at least partly justified. None of those conditions prevails today, however. Never in the history of mankind have a people been so well educated, with so many sources of information available at instant command. Indirect quasi-democracy has long since given way to direct election of U.S. senators, nearly universal suffrage, a massive popular vote that almost always determines the identity of the president of the United States, and dozens of annual popular referendums and initiatives that decide key public policies in states in every region.

Instead of fearing the people, it is time to trust the people, for another Constitutional Convention is long overdue. The founders themselves would have been the first to express amazement, and puzzlement, that their country had not had the self-confidence to reexamine their labors at regular intervals. Now, at long last, is the time to begin to do so.

THE FOUNDERS' DARING—AND OUR TIMIDITY

Consider for a moment the daring of our founders. They had risked life, limb, fortune, and birthright to revolt against their mother country, determined to stand on principle. Against the odds, they succeeded and created a new nation, only to fail at their first attempt at constitution making in the Articles of Confederation. After a frustrating decade of painful efforts to make the articles work, they had the wisdom to recognize the articles' fatal structural weaknesses. Despite the risks, they took decisive action in calling a Constitutional Convention to remake the shaky system undergirding the fragile Republic. Knowing full well that the new design was potentially as fraught with dangers and miscalculations as the old articles, these nation builders provided many means of constitutional change, adaptation, and amendment. As the proceedings of the convention make clear, the writers of the Constitution of the United States hoped and intended that it would be a living document—sturdy, yes, but also a foundation upon which changes would be constructed with regularity.[4]

Unquestionably, the founders would have been delighted and amazed to learn that their creation would survive for centuries and produce one of the most accomplished nations in human history. But they might also have been surprised and disappointed that future generations of Americans would be unable to duplicate their daring and match their creativity when presented with new challenges. The evidence today that parts of the Constitution do not work well is just as overwhelming as the proof in the founder's day that the Articles of Confederation were inadequate to the needs of the growing United States.

Most of our Constitution is a living document that still works well in the twenty-first century. But selected parts of it—the ones I have focused on in this volume—are museum pieces. Far from being a fragile instrument of government, the Constitution is strong, and it will actually benefit from wise scrutiny, adaptation, and alteration. As the political scientist Donald Lutz has documented, the U.S. Constitution has one of the lowest rates of amendment of any such document in the world, and its process of amendment is among the most cumbersome in the world.[5] Defenders of the status quo would no doubt insist that this is evidence of great success, that the Constitution has not been much amended because it has a higher level of perfection than exists elsewhere. The dominance of the United States economically and militarily, they would contend, is Exhibit A for their case. Yet the case for reform is powerful, and America can be more effective in many sectors with a more up-to-date Constitution.

Expecting change with some frequency, the founders provided for two means of constitutional reform.[6] The first is the one with which all Americans are familiar. The Congress can pass a constitutional amendment with a two-thirds affirmative vote in both houses, and then the amendment must be ratified by three quarters of the state legislatures (currently, thirty-eight of fifty). The second method of constitutional change is virtually unknown. Two thirds of the state legislatures (thirty-four of fifty) may submit "applications" to Congress for the calling of a convention to revise the Constitution, at which point the Congress "shall" call such a convention. Following the convention, Congress has the choice of submitting proposed amendments either to the state legislatures or to special state-ratifying conventions, and three fourths of either the legislatures or conventions must approve the amendments to achieve ratification. (It is the prerogative of Congress to choose which method is employed, and all states must follow the congressional mandate.)

It's always possible that Congress could be persuaded to propose the reforms advocated in these pages, using the direct constitutional amendment method. Some ideas already have scattered backing among the members in both houses. However, Congress has mainly been a graveyard for constitutional amendments over the decades, defeating more than nine thousand of them since the Constitution's ratification in 1789.[7] Without question, most of these thousands of proposed amendments were trivial, unwise, or poorly timed—but certainly not all of them. There exists a powerful inertial bias within Congress against constitutional reform, and that is unlikely to change. First, the current constitutional arrangement elected all the sitting members of the House and the Senate—proof positive for most members of Congress that the system works. Second, Congress is an exceptionally busy institution where the circuits always appear to be overloaded with pressing measures. What can be delayed—and even much of what cannot—is put off to another day. Antonin Scalia, now a Supreme Court Justice, made the case well in 1979 when he observed, "The Founders inserted this alternative method of obtaining constitutional amendments because they knew the Congress would be unwilling to give its attention to many issues the people are concerned with, particularly those involving the government's own power. The Founders foresaw that and they provided the Convention as a remedy."[8]

Therefore, one can make a strong argument that it may finally be time to utilize the second method of constitutional adaptation. In fact, it is difficult to imagine that the kind of sweeping, institution-by-institution reform advocated in this book could happen any other way. One of the first keen observers of the Constitution, Henry St. George Tucker,[9] wrote in 1803 about the two methods of constitutional revision, noting that a full-blown convention "will probably never be resorted to, unless the federal government should betray symptoms of corruption, which may render it expedient for the states to exert themselves in order to the application of some radical and effectual remedy."[10] Tucker's feared corruption has come in many stultifying forms, from extreme partisan gerrymandering to the unresponsiveness of the political system produced by ossification over the centuries.

Only a new Constitutional Convention would be likely to take on the difficult tasks of tinkering with the presidency, the Congress, the Supreme Court, the Electoral College, the presidential nominating system, nonpartisan legislative redistricting, and the concept of universal national service simultaneously. The reforms I am advocating are not just dramatic in many cases, but they also interconnect. Congress will never have the flexibility to suspend most other business and debate at great length the intricate puzzle pieces, one after another, discussed in this volume. The reforms cannot make as much sense unless their interconnectivity is discussed and analyzed. It will take a deliberative conclave of able delegates who are representative of the states' full diversity to accomplish such completely absorbing, time-consuming work. In other words, revising and updating the U.S. Constitution requires a gathering of the most talented statesmen and the best minds in the country, not unlike the original Convention in 1787.

Impossible, some say. America had the good fortune or the divine inspiration in its beginning to benefit from an extremely rare collection of men that will never be duplicated again. And we have idealized the founders to the degree that most might agree with that assessment. I beg to differ. The United States today boasts the most educated, professional electorate and the most thoroughly representative, mentally sharp group of politically active citizens in its history. The diverse men and women who are likely to be elected by the people as delegates to the new Constitutional Convention would be, for the most part, exceptionally prepared for the job. Mass communications media unavailable in the 1700s or even a decade ago—the potent combination of the Internet, satellite conferencing, and multichannel cable TV—would be available to involve everyone in the debate surrounding the convention. Schools at all levels could join in the process, while news organizations of every description, from the networks to the papers and magazines to the blogs, could inform their readers and viewers and generate discussion and involvement. We could have a participatory, deliberative nationwide undertaking that is unmatched in the history of constitution writing. To be sure, this new convention would be quite different from the elite, somewhat isolated one of 1787; quiet compromises arrived at in the backrooms would be more difficult. On the other hand, the extensive debate and media attention that would accompany the work of the new conclave could enlighten both the delegates and the citizenry, and produce a thoroughly vetted document.

Before turning to how a convention could play out, however, we should examine the constitutional option of the convention to see how this would work in practice.

THE LEGAL NETHERWORLD SURROUNDING A NEW CONVENTION

It is not a simple matter to outline the ground rules for a new Constitutional Convention, due in large part to the vagueness of Article V, which reads in relevant part:

> The Congress, whenever two thirds of both Houses shall deem it necessary, shall propose Amendments to this Constitution, or, on *the Application of the Legislatures of two thirds of the several States, shall call a Convention for proposing*

> *Amendments,* which, in either Case, shall be valid to all Intents and Purposes, as part of this Constitution, when ratified by the Legislatures of three fourths of the several States, or by Conventions in three fourths thereof, as the one or the other Mode of Ratification may be proposed by the Congress. (Italics added.)

In this amendment we have the miserly sum and substance of the founders' decision about a Convention.[11] Three aspects of this are straightforward: Congress has no choice but to call a Convention after thirty-four or more states petition for one; convention amendments are subject to the same ratification requirements (three quarters of the state legislatures or conventions giving assent) as congressionally sponsored amendments; and the president has no role whatsoever in the convention or amendment process.[12] However, since a Constitutional Convention has never been held under Article V, dozens of vital questions about the convention's possible organization remain unanswered.

The country has come close in several instances to getting some answers. First, Congress chose state ratifying conventions to ratify the Twenty-first Amendment overturning Prohibition in 1933, but this was a special case, with the method chosen mainly to expedite the process, and no national convention was held.[13] Second, when Congress received a large number of state applications in the second decade of the twentieth century for the purpose of switching to popularly elected U.S. senators, it decided against calling a convention and instead wrote the Seventeenth Amendment itself, submitting it to the states for ratification.[14]

Then, about a half century later, the states rebelled after Supreme Court rulings requiring "one person, one vote" in state legislative elections—the controversial redistricting decisions in the 1960s that required every legislative district be composed of approximately the same number of citizens. Especially noxious to the states was a Court decision in 1964 that both houses of the state legislatures had to be apportioned by population, despite the national precedent set by the geographically based U.S. Senate.[15] Thirty-two states demanded a convention to return to the status quo ante, but no more applied after March 1967, two states short of the required thirty-four. (The remaining state legislatures got cold feet, mainly about the undefined idea of a convention.) Two decades later, in the latter 1980s and early 1990s, the states rose up in arms about the consistent lack of a federal balanced budget and the accumulation of a large national debt. Once again, thirty-two states applied to Congress for a convention by April of 1992.[16] Just as with reapportionment, the fervor waned as states faced up to the great unknown of a convention, and no more states made application for a Balanced Budget Amendment.

The amendments sought by the bold thirty-two in each case may or may not have been wise, but had the process gone forward, some intriguing aspects of Article V would at last have been clarified, such as those contained in a list of questions with "unknowable" answers about a new convention, compiled by Professor Laurence Tribe of Harvard Law School.[17]

1. The Application Phase
   a. Must both houses of each state legislature take part in making application for a convention to Congress?
   b. By what vote in each house of a state legislature must application to Congress be made? Simple majority? Two-thirds?
   c. May a state governor veto an application to Congress?
   d. When, if ever, does a state's application lapse?
   e. May a state insist in its application that Congress limit the Convention's mandate to a specific amendment?
   f. Must a state's application propose a specific amendment, or may a state apply to revise the Constitution generally?
   g. By what criteria are applications proposing related but slightly different subjects or amendments to be aggregated or set apart?
   h. May a state rescind its application? If so, within what period and by what vote?
   i. What role, if any, could a statewide referendum have in mandating or forbidding an application or a rescission?

2. The Selection and Function of Delegates
   a. Who would be eligible to serve as a delegate?
   b. Must delegates be specially elected? Could Congress simply appoint its own members?
   c. Are the states to be equally represented, as they were in the 1787 Convention, or must the one-person, one-vote rule apply, as it does in elections for all legislative bodies except the United States Senate?
   d. Would delegates be committed to cast a vote one way or the other on a proposed amendment? Could they be forbidden to propose certain amendments? Would delegates at a Convention enjoy immunity parallel to that of members of Congress?
   e. Are delegates to be paid? If so, by whom?

f. Could delegates be recalled? Could the Convention expel delegates? On what grounds?

3. The Convention Process
   a. May Congress prescribe any rules for the Convention or limit its amending powers in any way?
   b. How is the Convention to be funded? Could the power to withhold appropriations be used by Congress to control the Convention?
   c. May the Convention remain in session indefinitely? May it agree to reconvene as the need arises? May it choose not to propose the amendment for the purpose of which it was convened?

4. Ratification of Proposed Amendments
   a. To what degree may Congress, under its Article V power to propose a "Mode of Ratification," or ancillary to its Article V power to "call a Convention," or pursuant to its Article I power under the Necessary and Proper Clause, either refuse to submit to the states a proposed amendment for ratification or decide to submit such an amendment under a severe time limit? What if Congress and the Convention disagree on these matters?
   b. May Congress permit or prohibit rescission of a state's ratification vote? May the Convention? What if Congress and the Convention disagree?

Tribe and others, including the American Bar Association[18] and, separately, Professor Michael Paulsen of the University of Minnesota Law School,[19] have suggested some answers, though it would inevitably be up to Congress to provide the statutory guidance in the event of a new Constitutional Convention. In this legal and constitutional netherworld, the following offers a synthesis of prior ideas as well as some new interpretations in order to create the framework for a convention that can achieve the great purposes of a modern Constitution.

SETTING THE GROUND RULES PRIOR TO THE CONVENTION

What Will Be the Convention's Scope?

One of the fundamental prerequisites to calling the convention would be the determination of the convention's scope. Could a convention be restricted in its subject matter, or is the scope essentially unlimited and left to the discretion of those who are chosen to serve as delegates? This matters greatly, since if the states and Congress could not focus the convention on an agreed-upon agenda, the convention would have less chance of ever being called. Many would raise the specter of a "runaway" conclave that could rewrite the Bill of Rights or try to abolish personal liberties.

This concern is exaggerated, of course, since anything coming out of the convention would still have to be ratified by thirty-eight states—a difficult hurdle in any circumstance. The abolition of precious freedoms would certainly never secure the requisite number of states' approval. In addition, the runaway scenario is a nightmarish suggestion that presupposes the state legislatures or the voters throughout the land would have taken leave of their senses in the selection of convention delegates. Still, there would be far less risk if the convention's goals could be carefully laid out in advance.

Not surprisingly, given the theoretical nature of the discussion, legal scholars are divided on the subject. Some, such as the longtime Columbia and Yale professor Charles Black, insist that Article V must be read literally, and so "a Convention for proposing Amendments" ought to be interpreted as "a convention for proposing amendments as that convention decides to propose."[20] Black has presented evidence that, throughout the nineteenth century, states understood fully that when they submitted applications for a convention for whatever purpose, the convention itself—once called—would be general in purpose.[21] Professor Walter Dellinger of Duke University has offered historically based information that seems to support Black.[22] The founders included a state-initiated constitutional amendment option precisely because they wanted to circumvent Congress as much as possible. Congress, it was feared, might refuse to act on amendments with which it disagreed or which limited legislative power.[23]

However, from a purely practical vantage point, there is little doubt that a convention would be guided by its mandate from Congress and the states.[24] Its work would be pointless, otherwise, with ratification of its document guaranteed to fail once submitted to the states. In their petitions to Congress requesting a convention, states could mention varying topics, and not every petition would be identical. It is here that Congress could legitimately bring order out of potential chaos. Logically, the convention would be called to consider only those items mentioned in thirty-four state petitions. This has been the position of most lawmakers who have attempted to codify Article V standards, such as former senator Sam Ervin (D-NC) and Senator Orrin

Hatch (R-UT).[25] Senator Ervin correctly argued that if no limitations (such as a prohibition on changing the Bill of Rights) could be placed on a new convention, then a new convention would never be called.[26] The American Bar Association has supported this interpretation, noting that without clear purposes having been outlined for a convention, citizens or state legislatures would be unable to select their convention delegates in an environment where the pertinent issues were understood and the delegate-candidates would be able to state their positions.[27] Some legal scholars have reinforced the ABA's view,[28] and certain state court decisions on the subject also bolster the case for a limited convention.[29]

With so many power centers—not to mention attorneys—involved, nothing would be simple, of course. Congress could play games and claim that state petitions were not identical because of slight wording differences, thus delaying or denying a convention, or Congress could refuse to submit for ratification some convention-drawn amendments, on the pretext that they were outside the legislatively determined boundaries for the convention. For example, let's say the convention was charged with considering a Balanced Budget Amendment, and in the course of doing so, decided to add limitations on taxation and spending. They are related subjects, for sure, but a balky Congress could argue that the latter was outside the mandate for the former. Still, the Congress is composed of elected officials, and if there were enough public support for the proposed amendments, sooner or later legislators would submit them to the states lest their constituents take revenge on them at the ballot box. The key words are "enough public support," of course, since Congress has many ways to change the subject of public debate or sidetrack popular measures without fingerprints. The states might well be forced to appeal to the Supreme Court, which could act as a referee in some of these disputes between Congress and the states.[30]

No doubt, there would be some internal pressure within any convention to move beyond the boundaries set by Congress. The justification for this is not provided by modern legal authorities as much as by the founders themselves. As Professor Akhil Amar of Yale University has shown, our original constitutionalists believed that a convention was, and always would be, the highest form of national assemblage, closest to the reality of popular sovereignty.[31] James Wilson, a delegate to the 1787 convention, asserted:

> Perhaps some politician, who has not considered with sufficient accuracy our political systems, would answer that, in our governments, the supreme power

> was vested in the constitutions . . . This opinion approaches a step nearer to the truth, but does not reach it. The truth is, that, in our government, the supreme, absolute, and uncontestable power *remains in the people* . . .
>
> The consequence is, that the people may change the constitutions whenever and however they please. This is a right of which no positive institution can ever deprive them.[32]

So where does all this argumentation leave us? The states would be the source of the subject matter to be considered by the convention, but Congress would shape the convention's charge by summarizing and giving structure to thirty-four state petitions calling for the convention. The states and Congress could place limitations on the convention's mandate, but they could not really control what would happen at the convention. Once called and in session, the convention would be a "free agency"[33] that would propose whatever it chose. Yet one would hope that a wise convention, full of the best and brightest that the nation has to offer, would adhere closely to its actual mandate. To do otherwise would nearly guarantee rejection of its proposals and bring its members into disrepute. In the end, common sense, and perhaps the political ambitions of delegates to a high-profile Constitutional Convention, would be the most significant check on bad behavior.

Which State Applications Count?

The most amazing event in the history of American constitutional amendments occurred in 1992, when the Twenty-seventh Amendment—prohibiting any congressional pay raise from taking effect until after a new election for the House had intervened—was ratified.[34] What made it remarkable was that the amendment was originated by James Madison in 1789! Six states approved it within two years of Madison's authorship, but it had lain dormant until a college student from Texas, Gregory Smith, rediscovered and revived the ratification process in 1982.[35] Ten years later, 203 years after the text was written, the thirty-eighth state (Alabama) ratified the pay raise codicil so it could take its place, at last, in the roll call of constitutional amendments.

Many constitutional experts questioned whether an amendment could be brought back from the dead, or the comatose, after such a passage of time. They pointed to the Supreme Court's decision in *Dillon v. Gloss* in 1921,[36] when the Court had ruled favorably on the constitutionality of Prohibition's Eighteenth Amendment. A convicted bootlegger had asked the Court to declare invalid the Eighteenth Amendment, the first of its kind to include a time limit (seven years) on ratification. His attorneys' argument was that there was no provision for time limits in Article V. But in part, the Court held in *Dillon*, "We conclude that the fair inference or implication from Article V is that the ratification must be within some reasonable time after the proposal [is made]."[37] Essentially, the Court established a kind of "contemporary consensus" rule in this case.

But the Court reached quite a different conclusion in a case in 1939, *Coleman v. Miller*,[38] when it was asked to impose an arbitrary time limit on a proposed constitutional amendment concerning child labor. Recognizing the sticky problem of standardless line-drawing, and realizing it had no basis on which to say that an amendment had to be ratified in seven or twenty or fifty years, the Supreme Court threw up its collective hands and declared, "Whenever Congress has not exercised that power [to set a time limit], the Court should [not] take upon itself the responsibility of deciding what constitutes a reasonable time."[39]

This decision created a wholly separate dilemma, often called the *Eternal Amendment*, or *Terminator* problem.[40] Proposed amendments apparently never die; like the movie character the Terminator, they survive indefinitely on the shelf and can fulfill their mission centuries later if eventually ratified.

Of course, this is a man-made, or more accurately, a congressionally created, difficulty. Under all the relevant Court decisions, Congress has the power to set a time limit on any constitutional amendment and, by inference, on the durability of state applications for a new Constitutional Convention. The confusion that exists today is due to the fact that Congress has never passed legislation setting deadlines for the state applications for amendments or conventions. Professor Michael Paulsen of the University of Minnesota has suggested a sensible model for the legislation, which would also include a provision permitting Congress to repeal a constitutional amendment, by a two-thirds vote of both houses, before it is ratified.[41] States would also be free to repeal their ratification of an amendment before it reached the thirty-eight-state approval mark. In other words, as Paulsen argues, "An amendment results, once and for all, whenever there concurrently exists a valid, un-repealed enactment of thirty-eight state legislatures ratifying that proposal . . . A good way of describing Article V's requirements is 'concurrent legislation' adopted by Congress (by two-thirds supermajorities) and separately adopted by three-fourths of the state legislatures."[42]

With this model, each state can be thought of as having an "on or off light" for an amendment or a Constitutional Convention. When a state ratifies an amendment, or submits to Congress an application for a convention, it turns its light on. Before the critical number of states is reached to ratify an amendment (thirty-eight) or call a convention (thirty-four), each state has the right to rescind its ratification or application, thus turning its light off. A state could also set a time limit on its approval, say, giving the process seven years to work its will across the country; at the end of the seven years, if the critical number had not been attained, the state's light would turn from on to off.

Having slogged through this short-form version of a complicated area in constitutional law, readers will now come to a surprising conclusion. Remember that (1) thirty-four state applications are needed to call a Constitutional Convention; (2) unless a state specifies a time limit on its application, or it has explicitly rescinded a previous call for a second convention, the state's light is on; and (3) Congress has not passed any legislation contradicting the logical, insightful Paulsen principles. Therefore, by Paulsen's meticulous accounting, forty-five state lights were turned on as of 1993, when he wrote his article—far more than the thirty-four required to call a convention immediately![43]

For example, Virginia submitted an application for a Constitutional Convention in 1788, one of three states[44] to request a second immediate convention to rectify errors it believed existed in the product of the first convention. Virginia has never rescinded its application (nor submitted another one), so the Old Dominion's light is on for a new Constitutional Convention. Is this so different from the process whereby the Twenty-seventh Amendment was ratified gradually, over two full centuries?

Since Paulsen's work was published, three states (Arizona, Idaho, and Utah) have passed resolutions explicitly rescinding all their previous applications for a Constitutional Convention, thereby bringing the total of states with on lights down to forty-two, still eight more than needed to call a convention.[45]

There is no doubt that this basic question of when a state's Constitutional Convention light is on would have to be litigated before a convention could be called. Would the Supreme Court agree with Paulsen's regimen, or our modifications of it, or establish some other standard? Or would Congress resolve the matter by legislation first, attempting to eliminate some state petitions by time limit, subject matter, or other means? No one knows the answers, though it seems highly improbable that the Court would order a Constitutional Convention on the basis of Paulsen's accounting. My point here is the loopholes in the current system are numerous—and that state applications for a convention have been more numerous than most people would expect.

It is also crystal clear that Congress must establish a statutory framework for considering state applications, some of which have been poorly worded or even demanded unconstitutional action.[46] Incredibly, Congress does not even keep up-to-date records of the state applications it receives. The federal legislature has established no standardized form for state application submissions, and it maintains no clearinghouse or database of these significant exercises of the states' constitutional authority.[47]

All of these preliminaries are fascinating and relevant, but they pale in comparison to the core task at hand: If a new Constitutional Convention were to be called, how should it unfold?

CALLING THE CONVENTION

How Will the Delegates Be Chosen?

Most legal experts agree that Article V empowers Congress to determine many of the convention's particulars, including its time, place, duration, and the composition of the delegates.[48] But the same authorities, including the American Bar Association, caution that Congress will be on shaky ground should it try to dictate the internal operating rules of the convention. After all, the convention of 1787, and nearly two hundred state constitutional conventions that have taken place since the Republic's founding, have established their own procedural rules.[49]

The delegates to the 1787 convention were appointed by the various state legislatures.[50] But just about everyone who has examined this subject agrees that the delegates to a twenty-first-century convention should be elected by the people, and Congress would be likely to agree. Popular democracy is well established today, and the voters would have far less confidence in the convention if they had not had a hand in shaping it. Also, the election campaigns by delegate-candidates would help to educate the electorate about the issues to be discussed at the convention and in turn would frame the debate through the election of delegates with particular views on controversial subjects or perhaps certain philosophical approaches to Constitution making.[51]

Furthermore, there is little question that delegates should be apportioned to the states according to the "one person, one vote" principle (that is, delegate slots should be allocated to each state in proportion to its percentage of the nation's population).[52] The Supreme Court has suggested as much in a 1970 decision, *Hadley v. Junior College District*,[53] ruling that "one person, one vote" applies to the election of all key officials who carry out major governmental functions. So ingrained now is "one person, one vote" that it is doubtful states could even be apportioned delegates along the lines of the current Electoral College—that is, with each state, regardless of population, receiving two extra "at-large" votes.[54] Rather, the logical way to apportion delegates is simply to have one delegate elected per congressional district (435 total) plus an additional, voting delegate for the District of Columbia. This Constitutional Convention of 436 delegates is a manageable size, far smaller than the national party presidential conventions, which usually have two or three thousand delegates apiece.[55] At the same time, a gathering of 436 is large enough to represent the diversity of America by region, race, ethnicity, gender, and so on.[56]

It is worth noting that a "one person, one vote" apportionment of delegates by states cannot result in a pure equality of representation across states. This is because several small states do not have enough population to fully merit their one delegate, just as those same states lack the population to completely earn their one U.S. House member.[57] However, the federal system and the Constitution properly mandate representation for all states, and the cumulative total of malapportioned delegates is quite small. Alternative systems of delegate election, such as equalization formulas to add delegates to larger states or the creation of special elective districts that cross state lines, are complex, confusing, and ultimately counterproductive.[58]

Should sitting members of Congress be welcomed as convention delegates, or should there be an "exclusionary rule" banning federal legislators from seeking the delegate slots? Good arguments can be marshaled on both sides of this question. On the one hand, voters ought to have the widest possible choice on their ballots, and they have access to their member of Congress and may know his or her views reasonably well. Also, the current Constitution's Article I, Section 6, which bans members of Congress from holding any other "civil Office under the Authority of the United States," does not apply to a new convention, since those prohibited offices must be created under the presidential appointment provisions of Article II. Moreover, several delegates at the convention of 1787 were members of the Continental Congress, so the precedent for participation is there.[59]

Nonetheless, it would probably be unwise to permit sitting congressmen or -women to run for convention delegate.[60] They might well have large stakes in preserving the status quo of their branch of government (for example, insisting on the continuance of partisan gerrymandering of House districts, if an amendment were brought to prohibit this), and simultaneously they might wish to change the status quo of the other branches (possibly to weaken their rivals, the presidency, or the courts). This conflict of interest would be redoubled if the delegate districts were precisely the same as the House districts. Many entrenched incumbent members of Congress could easily engineer their elections to the new, prestigious post of delegate. State legislators and local officials do not face the same serious conflicts, and so they should be permitted to seek the delegate office.

A fair number of these lower-level elected officials would almost certainly win delegate slots, thus providing to the convention the experience that only elected leadership can lend. At the same time, grassroots politics would likely yield the election of citizen-delegates in many places, well-respected and -established individuals who would not normally seek elective office but would offer their names for this temporary, historically significant post. This mix of seasoned and fresh perspectives in the convention could be catalytic and creative.[61]

In the call to a convention, Congress would specify the date or a range of dates for the election of delegates in the various states. While states might be given a choice of several dates within a specified month, it is more likely that Congress would pick a particular date for the election, to be held simultaneously everywhere. This might be the wiser course, since it would focus national media attention on a single, critical election day that would be uniform throughout the fifty states. And surely, for this greatest of all public tasks, we can have *nonpartisan* elections. If they must, the political parties, along with interest groups of all varieties, can endorse delegate candidates, but no party labels should appear on the ballot. With the specifics again determined by Congress in the call to convention, each delegate candidate would qualify for the ballot by collecting perhaps one thousand signatures of registered voters in the district and paying a small nominal filing fee to defray election costs (say, $250). Constitutionally, private contributions to the delegate candidates cannot be banned from the election as a matter of First Amendment free-speech rights,[62] but it might make sense to provide a reasonable level of public funding to all delegate candidates who can demonstrate, through polls or petitions, at least 15 percent support among registered voters in their district.[63] If public funding is provided, Congress could attach a useful requirement that, in exchange for the acceptance of public money, delegate candidates would have to debate one another at least twice during the course of the campaign. The campaign's length will depend on Congress's setting of the election date, but certainly not fewer than three months should be allotted for this critical election.

After the elections for delegates and during the potentially lengthy convention, vacancies caused by resignation and death will arise. Rather than special elections consuming months, which may leave some districts unrepresented during critical debates, it makes sense to have state governors fill the vacancies promptly.[64] Similarly worthwhile will be provisions in the congressional call to convention for adequate delegate compensation (a comfortable per-diem salary equal to prorated congressional pay, plus travel expenses)[65] and privileges similar to those enjoyed by members of Congress, such as freedom from arrest or questioning except in cases of "treason, felony, and breach of the peace."[66]

How Will the Convention Be Organized?

With the exceptions of designating the convention's presiding officer and specifying the basic voting procedure to be used at the convention, Congress should leave the internal procedures of the convention to the delegates assembled. Perhaps most important would be the level of majority required to send an article or amendment to Congress for transmission to the states (simple majority, three fifths, two thirds, three quarters, or something else). Obviously, the higher the majority in the convention, the more likely the proposal would be widely acceptable and thus win eventual approval. The delegates should debate this issue as one of their first tasks, not least because it would be a useful "shakedown cruise" for the assemblage and test their mettle on a procedural question before divisive substantive topics came to the fore.

The identity of the convention's initial presiding officer and the choice of the basic voting procedures to be used at the convention will be among the most critical decisions made by Congress in designing the conclave. Senator Hatch has urged that the first stages of a convention be led jointly by the Senate's president pro tempore and the Speaker of the U.S. House of Representatives.[67] However, this two-headed hydra might not work well if these two politicians were not in concert, and besides, Article V took the form it did partly because the framers wanted to minimize the ability of the Congress to suppress state-initiated constitutional reform. Senator Ervin once suggested that the vice president would be the logical early presiding officer.[68] The vice president has some experience in the art of presiding, being the designated president of the U.S. Senate. Moreover, despite this role in the Senate, the vice president is an executive branch official, and thus more acceptable under the terms of the founders' preferences since that branch has no formal role in the constitutional amendment process. While the vice president is an acceptable choice, the chief justice of the United States might be an even better one. A chief justice would be much farther removed from the partisan politics of the day than a vice president, and he would be used to serving in ceremonial roles that require studied neutrality and engender widespread respect. Once the convention is fully organized and the delegates have adopted the body's operating rules—a period of a couple of weeks, probably—the delegates can elect their own presiding officer from among their ranks, and the chief justice can return to his duties in Washington. The delegates may also decide to keep the chief justice as the ceremonial presiding officer, and ask him to return to the chair at important moments during the convention.

As to the voting procedures to be designated, Congress would have several choices.[69] Each state delegation as a whole could receive a single vote; this "unit voting" system was employed in the original convention of 1787. Or a kind of Electoral College model could be used, whereby on every question, each state would poll its delegation, with a majority within each delegation determining how the state's entire bloc of votes should be cast. Third, each delegate could simply be given a single vote to cast independently on each issue before the convention.

The advantage of unit voting is that the 1787 precedent would be preserved, and ratification might be advanced if proposals had to win state-based support—just as they would have to once they were eventually submitted to the state legislatures. Similarly, the Electoral College model could prepare the way for state ratification. Yet in the twenty-first century, neither of these voting procedures would likely find favor with the public. In a "one-person, one vote" world, which would probably serve as the basis for the election of delegates, a subsequent adoption of rules that would dramatically malapportion the convention floor votes and permit delegate majorities to be overridden would be certain to cause great controversy. This would be no way for the convention to begin its work, which would be intensely scrutinized by the news media and public.[70] There is only one politically acceptable choice for Congress here, and that is to choose "one person, one vote" for delegates on all matters coming before the convention. In 1787 the United States may have been little more than a "league of friendship" entered into by thirteen semiautonomous states. After more than two centuries, though, it is a well-integrated nation that respects state powers and traditions but acts as a unified whole.[71]

What about the convention's funding and general authority? Without question, the convention would be distinctly federal since it would derive its authority from Article V of the U.S. Constitution.[72] Therefore, Congress should appropriate all necessary monies for the convention's operations. But what if Congress, at some point, disagreed with the decisions of the delegates and wanted to pull the plug by failing to further fund the convention? Once again, we can see the wisdom of the framers' desires that Congress be as separate as possible from a future effort at constitutional revision. It is essential that the initial enabling legislation for the convention include a fallback provision that would permit costs to be assessed to the states, on a population basis, should Congress stop the flow of money at any point in the process. This standby source of dollars should preserve the convention's integrity and minimize any attempt by Congress to use its appropriations authority as political leverage on the convention.[73]

Lastly, the convention as a whole must be given subpoena power over all those in the federal government, including the top officers of the executive, legislative, and judicial branches as well as the constituent agencies and departments of those branches. A wisely led convention would use the subpoena power sparingly; this would not be a show trial, after all. Yet the delegates would want to research their proposals thoroughly, and that might require that the convention see some information possessed, and hear some opinions held, by those in elective and appointive federal office.[74]

AFTER THE CONVENTION: RATIFICATION AND ITS AFTERMATH

This second Constitutional Convention would be uncharted territory in most ways. There is no way to know how long it would actually last, though Congress would almost certainly set a maximum time limit for it. (Presumably, the convention could request an extension from Congress if needed, which the federal legislature might or might not grant.) It is also impossible to guess whether the deliberations would be congenial or disruptive, unifying or divisive. The subject matter and the convention's leadership would have great influence on the outcome here, and this is yet another reason why great care would have to be taken in drawing up the call to convention and in electing the convention's delegates.

Substantively, the convention might end up rewriting large portions of the original Constitution or proposing only a limited number of amendments. Which road is taken would depend upon three variables: the convention's mandate of organization, the consensus that emerged in its deliberations, and the actual votes taken in the conclave's sessions. Clearly, this volume has advocated a package of wholesale reforms, but American politics being as multidimensional as it is, only the most naïve author would expect a convention's product to resemble one man's concept. The convention's alterations to the U.S. Constitution could range from the technical to the dramatic. At one extreme, the convention could adopt a mega-amendment which would read, "Section One. The 1787 Constitution of the United States is hereby repealed. Section Two. We the People of the Twenty-First Century United States . . . ," though this is so improbable the Las Vegas bookies would not even take bets on it!

More reasonably, the convention might focus on some of the areas identified in this book, and "package" amendments together for the consideration of the states and the people. For instance, it would be unwise to strengthen one branch of the federal government while weakening the others. The proposals herein made have reshuffled the powers of all three branches a bit, but with no clear "winner" in the power game. Thus, regardless of whether a convention agreed with this reshuffling or chose another kind of power swap, textual provisions should be included in any amendments affecting the executive, legislature, or judiciary, mandating that "this amendment shall not be operative as a part of the Constitution unless amendments X and Y are also ratified." A Constitutional Convention would almost certainly have the latitude to do so in drawing up its amending texts.[75]

The convention might also want to encourage the individual states to hold an "advisory referendum"—an opportunity for the registered voters in each state to vote yea or nay on all the proposed constitutional charges—before the state legislatures or the ratifying conventions voted on the amendments. The amendments should be voted on separately, rather than as a package, in order to secure a more precise view of the public's opinion on each individual reform. Since the holding of such state referendums did not take place at the time of the original Constitution, given the framers' fears about excessive popular democracy, and since there is no mention of referendums in Article V, this call would be merely a suggestion, and not a mandate. However, if it were to be followed, the legislatures or conventions in the several states would have a better basis on which to proceed in making the ratifying decisions. The history of the referendum in the United States is a decidedly mixed one,[76] and the process could be just as akin to sausage making as the actions of state and federal legislatures. Still, major constitutional change is as serious a matter as a nation can consider, and popular involvement in various forms would be essential.[77]

Another useful addendum to all the convention's amendments would be a "sunset provision," requiring that each amendment be ratified in every state within a set number of years (perhaps seven to ten). Otherwise, "the

Terminator" would return with a vengeance.[78] Few would disagree that the states and people should have a reasonable, even lengthy, period in which to consider the amendments for a thumbs-up or thumbs-down decision, but the situation involving the Twenty-seventh Amendment is best not repeated. Eternal life should be reserved for the afterlife.

In the same vein, the convention should consider including a Jefferson-inspired amendment that a new Constitutional Convention be called with each turn of a century. While the exact year in each new century should be at the discretion of the states and the Congress, the New Century Convention would convene within a decade of the start of each hundred years (2100, 2200, and so on). The convention might or might not choose to propose a package of amendments, but the delegates would review the Constitution from the perspective of all the social, cultural, political, and technological changes that had occurred in the ten decades since the previous convention. Jefferson may have preferred constitutional revision every generation, but given the effort required for such an undertaking, the century mark is a better goal and is very much in keeping with Jefferson's idea.

Whether the convention's handiwork was minimal or maximal, the dangers to the Republic would be quite limited. Antonin Scalia, one of the most conservative Supreme Court justices, has asserted, "I have no fear that . . . extreme proposals would come out of a constitutional convention . . . I think [a new convention] is necessary for some purposes, and I am willing to accept what seems to me a minimal risk of intemperate action."[79] Three quarters of the states would have to ratify any amendment, and for that to happen a large majority of the American public would have to be convinced that an amendment was worth the risk of change. The public's voices would have been heard during the convention debate via the mass media and communications with delegates, and post-convention, Americans would not prove shy about transmitting their views to state legislators. Amendments that were highly controversial among the people would be exceedingly unlikely to win legislative backing; the legislators themselves would be back on the campaign trail seeking votes in due course. Even if the public were strongly in favor of the amendments, there would be no guarantee that the state legislatures (or alternately, state ratifying conventions) would assent in sufficient numbers. Opposition might be concentrated in only the thirteen most lightly populated states, just enough to defeat a new amendment. Moreover, we are not really a change-oriented society. In part, this is because modern society forces us to accept many revisions in our lives and communities as a matter of course, and so we hold on to the status quo as a lifeline. So the standard for ratification would be quite high, and that is as it should be.

There would unavoidably be legal bumps on the road to possible ratification. For example, Congress might strongly object to one or more proposed amendments and stubbornly refuse to formally submit them to the states. In such a circumstance, the Supreme Court would have to intervene. In *Coleman v. Miller*,[80] the Supreme Court appeared to say that Congress was the sole arbiter of the amendment process under the Constitution and that the Court had no role to play in answering many of the intractable questions surrounding a convention or the ratification process,[81] but since 1920 a consensus has emerged both that the *Coleman* ruling was confused and ignored key precedent, and that judicial review on these critical constitutional matters is both necessary and desirable.[82] While legal experts believe that the courts should intervene only in "egregious" cases when Congress has clearly ignored the essence of Article V,[83] even recent legislation sponsored by Senator Orrin Hatch permits states to sue for relief as a matter of original jurisdiction under the Constitution should Congress not submit a convention amendment to the states.[84] The enabling legislation for the convention (that is, the call to the convention) ought to include Hatch's provision. Even if the legislation is silent on this matter, it is highly likely that the courts will have jurisdiction over convention and amendment matters.

Another example of a legal road bump involves the proposal for expansion of the U.S. Senate in chapter 1, which suggested adding senators for the more populous states (two more senators for the ten largest states and one more for the next fifteen largest states) to correct the current inequity—the fact that just 17 percent of the people of the United States can elect a majority of the Senate. Further, "national senators"—all of the former presidents and vice presidents of the United States—would be added to the voting rolls in the Senate. On top of all the usual challenges in securing ratification of such a major change, there is the part of Article V that reads, "Provided that . . . no State, without its Consent, shall be deprived of its equal Suffrage in the Senate." This actually could mean that a proposed amendment that alters equal state representation in Congress's upper chamber would have to be ratified by all fifty states, rather than the usual thirty-eight. Were that to be true, ratification would be nearly impossible, given that a lightly populated state such as Wyoming with about a half million people, fewer than the population of the District of Columbia, depends heavily on its Senate clout for federal influence. A no vote from Wyoming alone could stymie this amendment, as could any of the other six states in Wyoming's general category (Alaska, Delaware, Montana, North Dakota, South Dakota, or Vermont).

Of course, one could make a counterargument that if the framers had meant that this portion of the Constitution could not be amended without unanimous consent, they could and should have specified this. Since they did not, perhaps we can assume that the normal procedure applies. If it does not, then the Constitutional Convention could propose an amendment removing the Senate proviso from Article V. Once that amendment were ratified, a separate amendment expanding the Senate could take effect. But could the same Constitutional Convention propose an amendment modifying Article V *and* altering equal representation in the Senate? And if so, would the amendment modifying equal representation only have the force of law if the amendment modifying Article V was ratified first? Alternatively, what if the amendment modifying representation in the Senate was ratified first, and the amendment modifying Article V ratified months (or even years) later? Could the representation amendment lay dormant, part of the Constitution but inoperative under the Senate proviso until activated by a change in Article V, or would the amendment never become part of the Constitution in the first place?

This shows the complexity involved in constitutional revision. The courts, ultimately the Supreme Court, would have to decide this question (probably after Wyoming or another small state mounted a challenge to the proposed Senate amendment),[85] and other dilemmas would have to be similarly resolved judicially. As the founders could have told us, Constitution making is thorny and perilous. Yet all of the most vital and rewarding elements of nation building are thorny and perilous. Let's remember that the founders of the Republic undertook the job under far more difficult conditions and without the benefits of an educated electorate and modern marvels of communication and composition. Surely, then, with all our blessings of wealth, training, and technology, we can endeavor to make some modern improvements on their work.[86]

CONCLUSION

✶

GETTING THERE FROM HERE

> The warmest friends and the best supporters the Constitution has, do not contend that it is free from imperfections; but they found them unavoidable and are sensible, if evil is likely to arise there from, the remedy must come hereafter; for in the present moment, it is not to be obtained; and, as there is a Constitutional door open for it, I think the People (for it is with them to Judge) can as they will have the advantage of experience on their Side, decide with as much propriety on the alterations and amendments which are necessary [as] ourselves. I do not think we are more inspired, have more wisdom, or possess more virtue, than those who will come after us.
>
> —*George Washington in retirement, November 1797*[1]

GEORGE WASHINGTON'S ASTUTE and forward-looking advice to posterity on constitutional revision, posed just a few months after leaving the presidency, has been mainly lost to history, but it is a fitting way to begin this book's conclusion.

Perhaps in honoring Washington, and the other founders and framers, we have chosen to idealize their work beyond how they saw it during their lifetimes. Not surprisingly, Washington and his distinguished contemporaries had a better fix then than we do now on the virtues and flaws of the Constitution. Far from writing a document that was intended to stand untouched for all of human history, they understood that they were drawing up a blueprint designed to meet the needs of their present. The framers' skill and brilliance were such that their 1787 blueprint enabled Americans to build a durable mansion. But the most beautiful, sturdy houses eventually need repair. We are at that moment, and we ought to embrace the challenge Washington presciently gave us. Our job is far less revolutionary than that of the founders because the tools we need for adaptation are contained in the Constitution itself. With these gifts from the founders, we can modify some rooms in the American manor and construct others anew, in order to meet the needs of our dynamic twenty-first-century society.

Originalists in the legal community and their allies in the academy and media[2]—people who believe that the original text of the Constitution is nearly perfect, or divinely inspired, or good enough so that we must avoid the dangers of revisionist upheaval—will vigorously oppose any effort to move toward a convention or even to revise the Constitution by congressional amendment. At the other end of the spectrum, some true radicals will insist that the reforms suggested in this book are too timid, and that a massive transformation to a parliamentary system or some form of democratic socialism is the only change worth fighting for. These two polarized camps cannot be reconciled to any moderate program of reform. While the more sweeping theorists and their followers on the left comprise only a few percent of the American people, the originalist conservatives are a considerably larger group with far greater clout. In our system, those who oppose change can usually carry the day since the current Constitution requires extraordinary majorities to coalesce at the national and state levels before the status quo can be altered. So while constitutional amendments and conventions are possible under the right conditions, the odds are almost always not in their favor.

One type of reform can do quite well in the American system, however: change that is positioned between the extremes, change that originates in, and satisfies, the broad middle of the ideological spectrum. By almost any measure, a large majority of Americans are gathered around the center, and therefore effective change must recognize that. The proposals in this book are neither radical nor reactionary, and they comprise a moderate program of reform. They are mainly structural in nature, designed to improve upon but not replace any of the founding principles of American government and politics. A few ideas could be characterized as leaning a bit to the left, a few others as tilting slightly right, yet on the whole the book's agenda seeks only to help America move forward and create a fairer society.

When I undertook to write this book, I hoped that it would help to focus citizens on their Constitution, a dazzling piece of statecraft. None of the criticisms of it expressed herein can detract from its genius. For more than two centuries America has survived crisis after crisis, foreign test after domestic stress, in no small measure due to the Constitution's flexible design. Indeed, it has been so successful that contemporary Americans take it for granted and thus know next to nothing about what it provides for every American, day in and day out. This condition affects even well-educated citizens who contribute to their communities regularly and correctly consider themselves both politically astute and deeply patriotic. Consider the following facts culled from modern studies of the public's ignorance of the Constitution.

- Only a bare majority of Americans can name even one basic purpose of the Constitution, many asserting that it was written to declare independence from Great Britain or to create the original thirteen states. Just four out of ten know that the Bill of Rights is the first ten amendments. Somewhat amusingly, about half of U.S. adults think the Marxist credo, "from each according to his ability, to each according to his need," is a part of the U.S. Constitution. Close to two thirds mistakenly think the Constitution declares English to be the official language. Perhaps of greatest concern, half believe that the president, acting alone, can suspend the Constitution in times of war or national emergency. No doubt, presidents would like to have that power; will public ignorance one day encourage a power-hungry chief executive to attempt it?[3]

- A survey of teenagers conducted by the National Constitution Center found that while 71 percent could name the first three letters of any Web address (www), just 35 percent knew the first three stirring words of the Constitution, *We the People*. And by a margin of three to one, teens could identify the city denoted by the zip code 90210 (Los Angeles), rather than the City of Brotherly Love, where the Constitution was written.[4]

- A Zogby International poll revealed that the "Three Stooges" can be named by 78 percent of Americans, while just 42 percent knew the names of the three constitutional branches of government.[5]

- Studies in individual states are equally discouraging. For example, fully 44 percent of the citizens of Colorado did not know the number of U.S. senators allotted to each state. The House fared worse. More than two thirds of the state's residents had no idea that the length of a House term is two years.[6]

- Nearly four in ten Americans (38 percent) think it is acceptable for the president to ignore a Supreme Court ruling if the president believes disregarding it will protect the country from terrorist attacks.[7]

- In a 1997 poll about American's knowledge of the Constitution,[8] the National Constitution Center found that some of the poll's participants asserted some unusual "facts" about our system, including the following responses.
  - The Constitution was written in France.
  - The first ten amendments to the Constitution are called the Pledge of Allegiance.
  - One of the rights guaranteed by the First Amendment is "freedom from fear."
  - Only the rights of judges and lawyers are protected by the Constitution.
  - There are a total of seven U.S. senators in the Congress.
  - The Constitution was written in 1892.

There are plenty more depressing numbers in the annals of recent public opinion research, which speak to the lack of civic education in the United States. This situation is less than ideal for the country and for individual Americans. Citizens will never truly feel a part of the system unless they comprehend it. A society is stronger when a great many of its citizens are participating in its basic institutions and processes, but participation is very difficult until one knows the rules of the game. Perhaps most important, the occasional dangerous man or woman who is elected—a Huey Long (D) or a Joseph McCarthy (R)[9]—can easily manipulate people who lack an understanding of their democracy's essentials.

Perhaps this book can encourage Americans to read the text of their Constitution as a starting point to entering the dialogue about revising some of its provisions. The entire text of the Constitution, the Bill of Rights, and all other amendments is provided in the appendix to this book. The Center for Politics at the University of Virginia has taken to giving out thousands of pocket-size Constitutions to young people in schools across the country, and many other organizations do the same.[10] And of course the Constitution is easily available on the Internet. Reading the full text is an exercise we all need to undertake more frequently. Some of the language is archaic, but even the unfamiliar words make sense in the context of the stirring phrases that define

American life (from "the Blessings of Liberty" to "the equal protection of the laws"). A careful review gives anyone renewed respect for our system and reveals the sophistication of thought and ingenious balance undergirding the American system. A half hour with the Constitution demystifies the document, revealing it to be a vibrant entity, not a stone tablet, showing its splendor in the many adaptations to political reality—and inviting more of our own today.

The primary purpose of this book is to generate debate about possible revisions in the Constitution in every place thoughtful citizens gather: in colleges and high schools, at senior centers, and across the Internet. It is the discussion that is vital, and agreement with this book's proposals is certainly not required. No one person is likely to agree with all of the reforms, precisely as formulated, in these pages. The brightest minds and the collective wisdom of the American people would no doubt do better in a generational process of constitutional change. If you believe our system of government needs refurbishing, this volume can start the progression by stimulating a mental exercise for each one of us—a process that follows one of life's best questions: What if? Framing these twenty-three proposals for revising the Constitution has been an intellectually challenging exercise for me, and I hope, whether you agree with them or not, that thinking about them will be the same for you. (See the accompanying list for a chapter-by-chapter recap of these proposals.)

PROPOSALS FOR REVISING THE CONSTITUTION

Chapter 1. Creating a Capital Congress

1. Build a more representative Senate by granting the ten states with the greatest population two additional senators and the next fifteen states one additional senator each. Under this proposal, the District of Columbia would also finally receive its own voting representation in the Senate.

2. Appoint all former presidents and vice presidents to the new office of "national senator."

3. Mandate nonpartisan redistricting for House elections. This single reform, if properly implemented, could significantly enhance electoral competition.

4. Change congressional terms by lengthening House terms to three years and setting all Senate terms to coincide with each presidential election. The entire House and Senate would be elected anytime the presidency was contested on the ballot.

5. Expand the size of the House to approximately 1,000 members so that representatives can better get to know and represent smaller constituencies. The staffing and budget levels for the House would remain the same (plus an inflation factor) over the years, thereby greatly reducing the resources available to each member in the larger House. The reduced resources will keep many incumbents from creating impregnable fiefdoms. This will level the playing field with their challengers at each election, thereby increasing the competitiveness of elections.

6. Establish generous term limits for representatives and senators, thus restoring the founders' favored principle of frequent rotation in office.

7. Add a Balanced Budget Amendment, with appropriate safeguards and escape clauses, in order to encourage fiscal fairness to future generations.

8. Create a Continuity of Government procedure that would: allow for the gubernatorial appointment of deceased representatives to the House until a special election can be held; permit the temporary appointment of replacement legislators if elected representatives and senators are incapacitated; and require members of Congress to draw up a "succession list" upon their election from which their replacement would be drawn to avoid unhelpful political maneuvering at a time of national crisis.

Chapter 2. Perfecting the Presidency

9. Establish a new six-year presidential term, including a fifth-year extension referendum—that is, an up-or-down confirmation election—which could result in an additional two years in office for the president. In the event of a no-confidence vote from the American public, a new national election featuring candidates from both political parties would be held.

10. Limit some presidential war-making powers and expand Congress's oversight of war making, particularly through extending, toughening, and incorporating into the Constitution the kind of regime envisaged by the War Powers Resolution of 1973. As the Iraq War has shown anew, the resolution as currently written statutorily has been largely ineffective at curtailing executive military adventurism. This new proposal, requiring renewed congressional assent to ongoing wars at regular intervals, is one of the most far-reaching ever made on the topic, but few constitutional subjects have proven to be so troublesome and in need of dramatic reform.

11. Give the president a line-item veto to remove specific items from appropriations bills.

12. Replace the unfair constitutional prohibition against non-natural-born presidents with a requirement that a candidate for the presidency or vice presidency need only have been a U.S. citizen for twenty years.

Chapter 3. The New Courts—Supreme but Not Eternal

13. Eliminate lifetime tenure in favor of a single, nonrenewable term of fifteen years for all federal judges.

14. Grant Congress the power to set a mandatory retirement age for federal judges, including Supreme Court justices.

15. Expand the size of the Supreme Court bench from nine to twelve to allow for a more representative high court.

16. Give federal judges more financial independence with guaranteed cost-of-living increases. Congress would retain the power to raise judicial base salaries as well.

Chapter 4. Politics: America's Missing Constitutional Link

17. Write a new, separate constitutional article specifically for the *politics* of the American system. The framers chose to avoid this topic, having not yet realized the importance of political parties to the structure of our

elections. By creating a rational presidential selection process and adding other needed political changes, the revised Constitution can bring some much needed order out of the chaos that currently exists due to the lack of any substantive political guidance in the basic document of state.

18. Adopt a regional lottery system for presidential party nominations to avoid the destructive front-loading of primaries. The order of state nominating contests will be determined on January 1 of the election year, thus ending part of the permanent campaign for the White House. The primary process would also be restricted to the four months preceding the August nominating conventions, thereby sparing voters a yearlong, all-out campaign.

19. Mend rather than end the Electoral College by granting more populated states additional electors (essentially in proportion either to their population or to their enhanced U.S. Senate representation). This preserves the salutary effects of the Electoral College, such as isolating postelection recounts, while minimizing the chances that a president will win the office without a plurality of the popular vote. In addition, faithless electors should be eliminated by making the position honorary, and the exceptionally inequitable "unit-voting" rule in the U.S. House for breaking electoral ties would be abolished in favor of "one congressperson, one vote."

20. Reform campaign financing by permitting Congress to pass reasonable limitations on campaign spending by the wealthy from their family fortunes, and mandate partial public financing for general election House and Senate campaigns.

21. Adopt an automatic registration system for all qualified American citizens, thereby guaranteeing that the right to vote shall not be abridged because of unnecessary bureaucratic requirements.

Chapter 5. A Citizenship of Service

22. Create a constitutional requirement that all able-bodied young Americans devote at least two years of their lives to the service of their nation. This universal civic duty would be, in essence, a Bill

of Responsibilities to accompany the Bill of Rights. A wide array of civilian and military options would be provided.

Chapter 7. Calling the Twenty-first-Century Constitutional Convention

23. In order to adopt the other twenty-two ideas, the country should convene a new Constitutional Convention, using the state-based mechanism left to us by the framers in the current Constitution.

It is possible for some of these reforms to be considered separately, such as the restructuring of the presidential nominating system, the redistricting proposal, or Universal National Service. But most ideas fit together as an integral whole and could not be individually adopted without doing damage to the American system, including the changes in term lengths for Congress and the presidency. Thinking about all these ideas as a package is the best approach, and that almost certainly would require a deliberative convention.

Again, while you are unlikely to buy into all of these ideas, I would be surprised if none of them appeals to you. Certainly, our Rasmussen poll about citizen attitudes suggested solid interest in beginning the discussion that could lead to a new Constitutional Convention. But how do we transform a generalized openness to change into a national convention? In other words, how do we get there from here?

Let's stipulate two principles from the outset in any dialogue over a new convention. First, the run-up to the convention must be done carefully, gradually, and deliberately. While I believe there is urgency in many of the needed reforms advocated in these pages, the greater danger lies in rushing and not thinking through the process, which will lead either to a failed reform effort or to amendments that do not work as intended. Many years of discussion and debate will be needed to prepare the way for a convention. In this sense, the new Constitution will be more evolutionary than revolutionary, and this fits the American mood today. Speedy revolution was required to rid the nation of British colonialism in the eighteenth century, but the modern United States is far more comfortable with gradual transformations. From early proposals through discussion, debate, and the actual Conventional Convention itself, the process could easily take a generation or more.

Second, the only real chance for a successful convention will come if interested, involved citizens in every state and region are given the opportunity to reach a reasonable consensus about a revised Constitution. Inevitably, much of the political establishment and commentariat will oppose any real change, since the status quo has proved beneficial for them and change might threaten their position. But if the people are engaged early and step forward to run the process, they can overcome the inertia of the elites. Cynics forget that the collective votes of millions of average citizens still determine the country's direction. Therefore, constitutional change must grow from the grass roots. An Astroturf movement that produces amendments dictated by officeholders or powerful interest groups or media pooh-bahs will never take root to blossom into a convention. This bottom-up method of constitutional development is a dramatic departure from the top-down promulgation of the eighteenth-century original, but bottom-up fits our participatory, Internet-driven times.

There is already a bottom-up example of major constitutional change. The Progressive movement in the first two decades of the twentieth century involved thousands of citizens in every state and yielded an astonishing array of political reforms at the federal and state levels. Nationally, Amendments Sixteen (the income tax—1913), Seventeen (popular election of senators—1913), and Nineteen (women's suffrage—1920) were all products of Progressive fervor.[11] Interestingly, a second Constitutional Convention nearly served as an additional monument to Progressivism. By 1912, as noted in the previous chapter, nearly enough states had submitted petitions to Congress to trigger a second convention under Article V. One probable reason a second convention failed to materialize then is that the Senate, after years of ignoring the public's demand, finally agreed to send the Seventeenth Amendment to the states for ratification.[12]

There is no current movement like Progressivism that could power a comprehensive agenda of change into the Constitution. But there is a magnificent modern tool available for both discussion and organization: the World Wide Web. That is the logical place to begin. A national Web site for this purpose, amoreperfectconstitution.com, is a useful starting point, and it can serve as a countrywide clearinghouse of ideas for the revised Constitution, while linking to other related Web sites and chat rooms. Let the debate begin, not in a convention hall but among the wired community of interested citizens from coast to coast. There are national conventions of bloggers, too, such as the annual gathering of liberals organized by DailyKos,[13] the blog begun by the Democratic activist Markos Moulitsas Zuniga. Conservatives gather at Townhall and many similar civic blogs. On a daily basis there are hundreds of thousands of engaged citizens kibitzing about public affairs via blogs, and their debates can continue for months or years.[14] Constitutional reform is tailor-made for just such extended treatment.[15]

Of course, change in the basic document of state is so fundamental that it must reach a broader population than those online. Schools at all levels are ideal forums. The Center for Politics at the University of Virginia designed a curriculum called the Youth Leadership Initiative (YLI), encouraging civic education and participation among the young, that is now used in more than seventeen thousand schools and by thirty thousand elementary and secondary teachers in all fifty states and in American schools around the world. Lesson plans via the World Wide Web; the largest Internet mock election anywhere; and even an interactive CD-ROM on running a campaign form the heart of YLI.[16] Each of these components can be adapted to lessons on constitutional revision. For example, a DVD with hundreds of possible constitutional proposals, featuring the pros and cons of each one, could be a hit in high schools and colleges. Other superb civic organizations that are oriented to the young could be enlisted to help.[17] Classroom and interschool debates at the high school and college levels will be prime testing grounds for constitutional proposals.[18] I have tried this in my own five-hundred-person introductory class in American politics at the University of Virginia, and few lectures or topics have stirred original student thought like constitutional change. Most students have written term papers on this topic; some of their opinions and arguments altered my own. This can happen at hundreds of colleges and universities in thousands of courses, year after year.

Within a few years, widespread talk should lead to some early concrete actions. Mock conventions are the logical next step. Since we have chosen the 435 congressional districts (plus D.C.) as the basis for delegate election to the eventual, real convention, it makes perfect sense for interested citizens, organized and funded through foundation grants, to pull together a "community convention" in each district. These weekend-long sessions, with professional facilitators acting as chairpersons, could host discussions about the wide variety of possible reforms. One goal of each district's community convention would be to elect up to a half dozen delegates to a "state mock convention," where the discussions could continue during a future weekend in each state capital. After the same process had unfolded in the fifty state conventions, a National Mock Constitutional Convention should be staged in Washington or another, more central location. With one delegate representing each congressional district plus the District of Columbia, and the agenda at least partially determined by the community and state mock conventions, this National Mock Convention could be a dry run for the real conclave to come.[19]

Media coverage would undoubtedly be extensive (as it would have been on the state and local levels earlier). PBS, C-SPAN, the History Channel, the Discovery Channel, and all the network news departments and twenty-four-hour news channels could both televise the proceedings and hold spin-off versions of their own, such as focus groups of diverse citizens reacting to what they see at the conventions—not unlike the regular television accompaniments to presidential debates and State of the Union addresses.

Would mock conventions lead to a Constitutional Convention? That would be up to the citizenry, of course. If the process was unsatisfying, or the reforms put forward too radical or dubious, probably the worst that could happen would be a strengthening of civic education and participatory democracy, possibly including a long-term increase in voter turnout. Or individual ideas could take hold, leading to constitutional amendments proposed in Congress and submitted to the states for ratification under the regular process. By contrast, if people liked what they saw, the delegates from all the mock conventions as well as intrigued rank-and-file voters presumably would lobby their state legislatures to petition Congress for a convention. The legislatures would listen if the people eagerly wanted to explore the possibilities of a revised Constitution, since every member of every state legislature is elected, or defeated, by those same people.

There would be ferment if the convention process catches on, and that could lead to chaos or creativity or both. But the original Constitutional Convention wasn't always orderly, and heated debate forged the document hailed by most Americans and welcomed by Washington, Jefferson, Madison, and other framers. They would have been the first to insist that the Constitutional Convention of 1787 was not a once-in-human-history's gathering of great minds, never to be matched or exceeded. They would have been prominent among those admitting that the first Constitution, a welter of temporary compromises suited to the needs of an agricultural nation of just 4 million people gathered almost entirely along a small strip of land hugging the eastern seaboard, could not fulfill the best interests of a complex continental country of 300 million that is at the same time the world's leading democracy.

Washington, Jefferson, and Madison would see all this easily. Can we?

APPENDIX

*

UNITED STATES CONSTITUTION AND AMENDMENTS

THE CONSTITUTION

***We the People** of the United States, in Order to form a more perfect Union, establish Justice, insure domestic Tranquility, provide for the common defense, promote the general Welfare, and secure the Blessings of Liberty to ourselves and our Posterity, do ordain and establish this Constitution for the United States of America.*

Article I

Section 1

All legislative Powers herein granted shall be vested in a Congress of the United States, which shall consist of a Senate and House of Representatives.

Section 2

The House of Representatives shall be composed of Members chosen every second Year by the People of the several States, and the Electors in each State shall have the Qualifications requisite for Electors of the most numerous Branch of the State Legislature.

No Person shall be a Representative who shall not have attained to the Age of twenty five Years, and been seven Years a Citizen of the United States, and who shall not, when elected, be an Inhabitant of that State in which he shall be chosen.

Representatives and direct Taxes shall be apportioned among the several States which may be included within this Union, according to their respective Numbers, which shall be determined by adding to the whole Number of free Persons, including those bound to Service for a Term of Years, and excluding Indians not taxed, three fifths of all other Persons. The actual Enumeration shall be made within three Years after the first Meeting of the Congress of the United States, and within every subsequent Term of ten Years, in such Manner as they shall by Law direct. The Number of Representatives shall not exceed one for every thirty Thousand, but each State shall have at Least one Representative; and until such enumeration shall be made, the State of New Hampshire shall be entitled to chuse three, Massachusetts eight, Rhode-Island and Providence Plantations one, Connecticut five, New-York six, New Jersey four, Pennsylvania eight, Delaware one, Maryland six, Virginia ten, North Carolina five, South Carolina five, and Georgia three.

When vacancies happen in the Representation from any State, the Executive Authority thereof shall issue Writs of Election to fill such Vacancies.

The House of Representatives shall chuse their Speaker and other Officers; and shall have the sole Power of Impeachment.

Section 3

The Senate of the United States shall be composed of two Senators from each State, chosen by the Legislature thereof for six Years; and each Senator shall have one Vote.

Immediately after they shall be assembled in Consequence of the first Election, they shall be divided as equally as may be into three Classes. The Seats of the Senators of the first Class shall be vacated at the Expiration of the second Year, of the second Class at the Expiration of the fourth Year, and of the third Class at the Expiration of the sixth Year, so that one third may be chosen every second Year; and if Vacancies happen by Resignation, or otherwise, during the Recess of the Legislature of any State, the Executive thereof may make temporary Appointments until the next Meeting of the Legislature, which shall then fill such Vacancies.

No Person shall be a Senator who shall not have attained to the Age of thirty Years, and been nine Years a Citizen of the United States, and who shall not, when elected, be an Inhabitant of that State for which he shall be chosen.

The Vice President of the United States shall be President of the Senate, but shall have no Vote, unless they be equally divided.

The Senate shall chuse their other Officers, and also a President pro tempore, in the Absence of the Vice President, or when he shall exercise the Office of President of the United States.

The Senate shall have the sole Power to try all Impeachments. When sitting for that Purpose, they shall be on Oath or Affirmation. When the President of the United States is tried, the Chief Justice shall preside: And no

Person shall be convicted without the Concurrence of two thirds of the Members present.

Judgment in Cases of Impeachment shall not extend further than to removal from Office, and disqualification to hold and enjoy any Office of honor, Trust or Profit under the United States: but the Party convicted shall nevertheless be liable and subject to Indictment, Trial, Judgment and Punishment, according to Law.

Section 4

The Times, Places and Manner of holding Elections for Senators and Representatives, shall be prescribed in each State by the Legislature thereof; but the Congress may at any time by Law make or alter such Regulations, except as to the Places of chusing Senators.

The Congress shall assemble at least once in every Year, and such Meeting shall be on the first Monday in December, unless they shall by Law appoint a different Day.

Section 5

Each House shall be the Judge of the Elections, Returns and Qualifications of its own Members, and a Majority of each shall constitute a Quorum to do Business; but a smaller Number may adjourn from day to day, and may be authorized to compel the Attendance of absent Members, in such Manner, and under such Penalties as each House may provide.

Each House may determine the Rules of its Proceedings, punish its Members for disorderly Behaviour, and, with the Concurrence of two thirds, expel a Member.

Each House shall keep a Journal of its Proceedings, and from time to time publish the same, excepting such Parts as may in their Judgment require Secrecy; and the Yeas and

Nays of the Members of either House on any question shall, at the Desire of one fifth of those Present, be entered on the Journal.

Neither House, during the Session of Congress, shall, without the Consent of the other, adjourn for more than three days, nor to any other Place than that in which the two Houses shall be sitting.

Section 6

The Senators and Representatives shall receive a Compensation for their Services, to be ascertained by Law, and paid out of the Treasury of the United

States. They shall in all Cases, except Treason, Felony and Breach of the Peace, be privileged from Arrest during their Attendance at the Session of their respective Houses, and in going to and returning from the same; and for any Speech or Debate in either House, they shall not be questioned in any other Place.

No Senator or Representative shall, during the Time for which he was elected, be appointed to any civil Office under the Authority of the United States, which shall have been created, or the Emoluments whereof shall have been encreased during such time; and no Person holding any Office under the United States, shall be a Member of either House during his Continuance in Office.

Section 7

All Bills for raising Revenue shall originate in the House of Representatives; but the Senate may propose or concur with Amendments as on other Bills.

Every Bill which shall have passed the House of Representatives and the Senate, shall, before it become a Law, be presented to the President of the United States: If he approve he shall sign it, but if not he shall return it, with his Objections to that House in which it shall have originated, who shall enter the Objections at large on their Journal, and proceed to reconsider it. If after such Reconsideration two thirds of that House shall agree to pass the Bill, it shall be sent, together with the Objections, to the other House, by which it shall likewise be reconsidered, and if approved by two thirds of that House, it shall become a Law. But in all such Cases the Votes of both Houses shall be determined by Yeas and Nays, and the Names of the Persons voting for and against the Bill shall be entered on the Journal of each House respectively. If any Bill shall not be returned by the President within ten Days (Sundays excepted) after it shall have been presented to him, the Same shall be a Law, in like Manner as if he had signed it, unless the Congress by their Adjournment prevent its Return, in which Case it shall not be a Law.

Every Order, Resolution, or Vote to which the Concurrence of the Senate and House of Representatives may be necessary (except on a question of Adjournment) shall be presented to the President of the United States; and before the Same shall take Effect, shall be approved by him, or being disapproved by him, shall be repassed by two thirds of the Senate and House of Representatives, according to the Rules and Limitations prescribed in the Case of a Bill.

Section 8

The Congress shall have Power To lay and collect Taxes, Duties, Imposts and Excises, to pay the Debts and provide for the common Defence and general Welfare of the United States; but all Duties, Imposts and Excises shall be uniform throughout the United States;

To borrow Money on the credit of the United States;

To regulate Commerce with foreign Nations, and among the several States, and with the Indian Tribes;

To establish an uniform Rule of Naturalization, and uniform Laws on the subject of Bankruptcies throughout the United States;

To coin Money, regulate the Value thereof, and of foreign Coin, and fix the Standard of Weights and Measures;

To provide for the Punishment of counterfeiting the Securities and current Coin of the United States;

To establish Post Offices and post Roads;

To promote the Progress of Science and useful Arts, by securing for limited Times to Authors and Inventors the exclusive Right to their respective Writings and Discoveries;

To constitute Tribunals inferior to the supreme Court;

To define and punish Piracies and Felonies committed on the high Seas, and Offences against the Law of Nations;

To declare War, grant Letters of Marque and Reprisal, and make Rules concerning Captures on Land and Water;

To raise and support Armies, but no Appropriation of Money to that Use shall be for a longer Term than two Years;

To provide and maintain a Navy;

To make Rules for the Government and Regulation of the land and naval Forces;

To provide for calling forth the Militia to execute the Laws of the Union, suppress Insurrections and repel Invasions;

To provide for organizing, arming, and disciplining, the Militia, and for governing such Part of them as may be employed in the Service of the United States, reserving to the States respectively, the Appointment of the Officers, and the Authority of training the Militia according to the discipline prescribed by Congress;

To exercise exclusive Legislation in all Cases whatsoever, over such District (not exceeding ten Miles square) as may, by Cession of particular States, and the Acceptance of Congress, become the Seat of the Government of the

United States, and to exercise like Authority over all Places purchased by the Consent of the Legislature of the State in which the Same shall be, for the Erection of Forts, Magazines, Arsenals, dock-Yards, and other needful Buildings;—And

To make all Laws which shall be necessary and proper for carrying into Execution the foregoing Powers, and all other Powers vested by this Constitution in the Government of the United States, or in any Department or Officer thereof.

Section 9

The Migration or Importation of such Persons as any of the States now existing shall think proper to admit, shall not be prohibited by the Congress prior to the Year one thousand eight hundred and eight, but a Tax or duty may be imposed on such Importation, not exceeding ten dollars for each Person.

The Privilege of the Writ of Habeas Corpus shall not be suspended, unless when in Cases of Rebellion or Invasion the public Safety may require it.

No Bill of Attainder or ex post facto Law shall be passed.

No Capitation, or other direct, Tax shall be laid, unless in Proportion to the Census or enumeration herein before directed to be taken.

No Tax or Duty shall be laid on Articles exported from any State.

No Preference shall be given by any Regulation of Commerce or Revenue to the Ports of one State over those of another; nor shall Vessels bound to, or from, one State, be obliged to enter, clear, or pay Duties in another.

No Money shall be drawn from the Treasury, but in Consequence of Appropriations made by Law; and a regular Statement and Account of the Receipts and Expenditures of all public Money shall be published from time to time.

No Title of Nobility shall be granted by the United States: And no Person holding any Office of Profit or Trust under them, shall, without the Consent of the Congress, accept of any present, Emolument, Office, or Title, of any kind whatever, from any King, Prince, or foreign State.

Section 10

No State shall enter into any Treaty, Alliance, or Confederation; grant Letters of Marque and Reprisal; coin Money; emit Bills of Credit; make any Thing but gold and silver Coin a Tender in Payment of Debts; pass any Bill of Attainder, ex post facto Law, or Law impairing the Obligation of Contracts, or grant any Title of Nobility.

No State shall, without the Consent of the Congress, lay any Imposts or Duties on Imports or Exports, except what may be absolutely necessary for executing its inspection Laws: and the net Produce of all Duties and Imposts, laid by any State on Imports or Exports, shall be for the Use of the Treasury of the United States; and all such Laws shall be subject to the Revision and Controul of the Congress.

No State shall, without the Consent of Congress, lay any Duty of Tonnage, keep Troops, or Ships of War in time of Peace, enter into any Agreement or Compact with another State, or with a foreign Power, or engage in War, unless actually invaded, or in such imminent Danger as will not admit of delay.

Article II

Section 1

The executive Power shall be vested in a President of the United States of America. He shall hold his Office during the Term of four Years, and, together with the Vice President, chosen for the same Term, be elected, as follows:

Each State shall appoint, in such Manner as the Legislature thereof may direct, a Number of Electors, equal to the whole Number of Senators and Representatives to which the State may be entitled in the Congress: but no Senator or Representative, or Person holding an Office of Trust or Profit under the United States, shall be appointed an Elector.

The Electors shall meet in their respective States, and vote by Ballot for two Persons, of whom one at least shall not be an Inhabitant of the same State with themselves. And they shall make a List of all the Persons voted for, and of the Number of Votes for each; which List they shall sign and certify, and transmit sealed to the Seat of the Government of the United States, directed to the President of the Senate. The President of the Senate shall, in the Presence of the Senate and House of Representatives, open all the Certificates, and the Votes shall then be counted. The Person having the greatest Number of Votes shall be the President, if such Number be a Majority of the whole Number of Electors appointed; and if there be more than one who have such Majority, and have an equal Number of Votes, then the House of Representatives shall immediately chuse by Ballot one of them for President; and if no Person have a Majority, then from the five highest on the List the said House shall in like Manner chuse the President. But in chusing the President, the Votes shall be taken by States, the

Representation from each State having one Vote; A quorum for this purpose shall consist of a Member or Members from two thirds of the States, and a Majority of all the States shall be necessary to a Choice. In every Case, after the Choice of the President, the Person having the greatest Number of Votes of the Electors shall be the Vice President. But if there should remain two or more who have equal Votes, the Senate shall chuse from them by Ballot the Vice President.

The Congress may determine the Time of chusing the Electors, and the Day on which they shall give their Votes; which Day shall be the same throughout the United States.

No Person except a natural born Citizen, or a Citizen of the United States, at the time of the Adoption of this Constitution, shall be eligible to the Office of President; neither shall any Person be eligible to that Office who shall not have attained to the Age of thirty five Years, and been fourteen Years a Resident within the United States.

In Case of the Removal of the President from Office, or of his Death, Resignation, or Inability to discharge the Powers and Duties of the said Office, the Same shall devolve on the Vice President, and the Congress may by Law provide for the Case of Removal, Death, Resignation or Inability, both of the President and Vice President, declaring what Officer shall then act as President, and such Officer shall act accordingly, until the Disability be removed, or a President shall be elected.

The President shall, at stated Times, receive for his Services, a Compensation, which shall neither be increased nor diminished during the Period for which he shall have been elected, and he shall not receive within that Period any other Emolument from the United States, or any of them.

Before he enter on the Execution of his Office, he shall take the following Oath or Affirmation:—"I do solemnly swear (or affirm) that I will faithfully execute the Office of President of the United States, and will to the best of my Ability, preserve, protect and defend the Constitution of the United States."

Section 2

The President shall be Commander in Chief of the Army and Navy of the United States, and of the Militia of the several States, when called into the actual Service of the United States; he may require the Opinion, in writing, of the principal Officer in each of the executive Departments, upon any Subject relating to the Duties of their respective Offices, and he shall have Power to grant Reprieves and Pardons for Offences against the United States, except in Cases of Impeachment.

He shall have Power, by and with the Advice and Consent of the Senate, to make Treaties, provided two thirds of the Senators present concur; and he shall nominate, and by and with the Advice and Consent of the Senate, shall appoint Ambassadors, other public Ministers and Consuls, Judges of the supreme Court, and all other Officers of the United States, whose Appointments are not herein otherwise provided for, and which shall be established by Law: but the Congress may by Law vest the Appointment of such inferior Officers, as they think proper, in the President alone, in the Courts of Law, or in the Heads of Departments.

The President shall have Power to fill up all Vacancies that may happen during the Recess of the Senate, by granting Commissions which shall expire at the End of their next Session.

Section 3

He shall from time to time give to the Congress Information of the State of the Union, and recommend to their Consideration such Measures as he shall judge necessary and expedient; he may, on extraordinary Occasions, convene both Houses, or either of them, and in Case of Disagreement between them, with Respect to the Time of Adjournment, he may adjourn them to such Time as he shall think proper; he shall receive Ambassadors and other public Ministers; he shall take Care that the Laws be faithfully executed, and shall Commission all the Officers of the United States.

Section 4

The President, Vice President and all civil Officers of the United States, shall be removed from Office on Impeachment for, and Conviction of, Treason, Bribery, or other high Crimes and Misdemeanors.

Article III

Section 1

The judicial Power of the United States shall be vested in one supreme Court, and in such inferior Courts as the Congress may from time to time ordain and establish. The Judges, both of the supreme and inferior Courts, shall hold their Offices during good Behaviour, and shall, at stated Times, receive for their Services a Compensation, which shall not be diminished during their Continuance in Office.

Section 2

The judicial Power shall extend to all Cases, in Law and Equity, arising under this Constitution, the Laws of the United States, and Treaties made, or which shall be made, under their Authority;—to all Cases affecting Ambassadors, other public Ministers and Consuls;—to all Cases of admiralty and maritime Jurisdiction;—to Controversies to which the United States shall be a Party;—to Controversies between two or more States;—between a State and Citizens of another State;—between Citizens of different States;—between Citizens of the same State claiming Lands under Grants of different States, and between a State, or the Citizens thereof, and foreign States, Citizens or Subjects.

In all Cases affecting Ambassadors, other public Ministers and Consuls, and those in which a State shall be Party, the supreme Court shall have original Jurisdiction. In all the other Cases before mentioned, the supreme Court shall have appellate Jurisdiction, both as to Law and Fact, with such Exceptions, and under such Regulations as the Congress shall make.

The Trial of all Crimes, except in Cases of Impeachment, shall be by Jury; and such Trial shall be held in the State where the said Crimes shall have been committed; but when not committed within any State, the Trial shall be at such Place or Places as the Congress may by Law have directed.

Section 3

Treason against the United States, shall consist only in levying War against them, or in adhering to their Enemies, giving them Aid and Comfort. No Person shall be convicted of Treason unless on the Testimony of two Witnesses to the same overt Act, or on Confession in open Court.

The Congress shall have Power to declare the Punishment of Treason, but no Attainder of Treason shall work Corruption of Blood, or Forfeiture except during the Life of the Person attainted.

Article IV

Section 1

Full Faith and Credit shall be given in each State to the public Acts, Records, and judicial Proceedings of every other State. And the Congress may by general Laws prescribe the Manner in which such Acts, Records and Proceedings shall be proved, and the Effect thereof.

Section 2

The Citizens of each State shall be entitled to all Privileges and Immunities of Citizens in the several States.

A Person charged in any State with Treason, Felony, or other Crime, who shall flee from Justice, and be found in another State, shall on Demand of the executive Authority of the State from which he fled, be delivered up, to be removed to the State having Jurisdiction of the Crime.

No Person held to Service or Labour in one State, under the Laws thereof, escaping into another, shall, in Consequence of any Law or Regulation therein, be discharged from such Service or Labour, but shall be delivered up on Claim of the Party to whom such Service or Labour may be due.

Section 3

New States may be admitted by the Congress into this Union; but no new State shall be formed or erected within the Jurisdiction of any other State; nor any State be formed by the Junction of two or more States, or Parts of States, without the Consent of the Legislatures of the States concerned as well as of the Congress.

The Congress shall have Power to dispose of and make all needful Rules and Regulations respecting the Territory or other Property belonging to the United States; and nothing in this Constitution shall be so construed as to Prejudice any Claims of the United States, or of any particular State.

Section 4

The United States shall guarantee to every State in this Union a Republican Form of Government, and shall protect each of them against Invasion; and on Application of the Legislature, or of the Executive (when the Legislature cannot be convened), against domestic Violence.

Article V

The Congress, whenever two thirds of both Houses shall deem it necessary, shall propose Amendments to this Constitution, or, on the Application of the Legislatures of two thirds of the several States, shall call a Convention for proposing Amendments, which, in either Case, shall be valid to all Intents and Purposes, as Part of this Constitution, when ratified by the Legislatures of three fourths of the several States, or by Conventions in three fourths thereof, as the one or the other Mode of Ratification may be proposed by the Congress; Provided that no

Amendment which may be made prior to the Year One thousand eight hundred and eight shall in any Manner affect the first and fourth Clauses in the Ninth Section of the first Article; and that no State, without its Consent, shall be deprived of its equal Suffrage in the Senate.

Article VI

All Debts contracted and Engagements entered into, before the Adoption of this Constitution, shall be as valid against the United States under this Constitution, as under the Confederation.

This Constitution, and the Laws of the United States which shall be made in Pursuance thereof; and all Treaties made, or which shall be made, under the Authority of the United States, shall be the supreme Law of the Land; and the Judges in every State shall be bound thereby, any Thing in the Constitution or Laws of any State to the Contrary notwithstanding.

The Senators and Representatives before mentioned, and the Members of the several State Legislatures, and all executive and judicial Officers, both of the United States and of the several States, shall be bound by Oath or Affirmation, to support this Constitution; but no religious Test shall ever be required as a Qualification to any Office or public Trust under the United States.

Article VII

The Ratification of the Conventions of nine States, shall be sufficient for the Establishment of this Constitution between the States so ratifying the Same.

The Word, "the," being interlined between the seventh and eighth Lines of the first Page, the Word "Thirty" being partly written on an Erazure in the fifteenth Line of the first Page, The Words "is tried" being interlined between the thirty second and thirty third Lines of the first Page and the Word "the" being interlined between the forty third and forty fourth Lines of the second Page.

Attest William Jackson Secretary

Done in Convention by the Unanimous Consent of the States present the Seventeenth Day of September in the Year of our Lord one thousand seven hundred and Eighty seven and of the Independence of the United States of America the Twelfth. In witness whereof We have hereunto subscribed our Names,

G°. Washington
Presidt and deputy from Virginia

Delaware
Geo: Read
Gunning Bedford jun
John Dickinson
Richard Bassett
Jaco: Broom

Maryland
James McHenry
Dan of St Thos. Jenifer
Danl. Carroll

Virginia
John Blair
James Madison Jr.

North Carolina
Wm. Blount
Richd. Dobbs Spaight
Hu Williamson

South Carolina
J. Rutledge
Charles Cotesworth Pinckney
Charles Pinckney
Pierce Butler

Georgia
William Few
Abr Baldwin

New Hampshire
John Langdon
Nicholas Gilman

Massachusetts
Nathaniel Gorham
Rufus King

Connecticut
Wm. Saml. Johnson
Roger Sherman

New York
Alexander Hamilton

New Jersey
Wil: Livingston
David Brearley
Wm. Paterson
Jona: Dayton

Pennsylvania
B Franklin
Thomas Mifflin
Robt. Morris
Geo. Clymer
Thos. FitzSimons
Jared Ingersoll
James Wilson
Gouv Morris

THE BILL OF RIGHTS AND OTHER AMENDMENTS TO THE CONSTITUTION

Amendment I

Congress shall make no law respecting an establishment of religion, or prohibiting the free exercise thereof; or abridging the freedom of speech, or of the press; or the right of the people peaceably to assemble, and to petition the Government for a redress of grievances.

Amendment II

A well regulated Militia, being necessary to the security of a free State, the right of the people to keep and bear Arms, shall not be infringed.

Amendment III

No Soldier shall, in time of peace be quartered in any house, without the consent of the Owner, nor in time of war, but in a manner to be prescribed by law.

Amendment IV

The right of the people to be secure in their persons, houses, papers, and effects, against unreasonable searches and seizures, shall not be violated, and no Warrants shall issue, but upon probable cause, supported by Oath or affirmation, and particularly describing the place to be searched, and the persons or things to be seized.

Amendment V

No person shall be held to answer for a capital, or otherwise infamous crime, unless on a presentment or indictment of a Grand Jury, except in cases arising in the land or naval forces, or in the Militia, when in actual service in time of War or public danger; nor shall any person be subject for the same offence to be twice put in jeopardy of life or limb; nor shall be compelled in any criminal case to be a witness against himself, nor be deprived of life, liberty, or property, without due process of law; nor shall private property be taken for public use, without just compensation.

Amendment VI

In all criminal prosecutions, the accused shall enjoy the right to a speedy and public trial, by an impartial jury of the State and district wherein the crime shall have been committed, which district shall have been previously ascertained by law, and to be informed of the nature and cause of the accusation; to be confronted with the witnesses against him; to have compulsory process for obtaining witnesses in his favor, and to have the Assistance of Counsel for his defence.

Amendment VII

In Suits at common law, where the value in controversy shall exceed twenty dollars, the right of trial by jury shall be preserved, and no fact tried by a jury, shall be otherwise re-examined in any Court of the United States, than according to the rules of the common law.

Amendment VIII

Excessive bail shall not be required, nor excessive fines imposed, nor cruel and unusual punishments inflicted.

Amendment IX

The enumeration in the Constitution, of certain rights, shall not be construed to deny or disparage others retained by the people.

Amendment X

The powers not delegated to the United States by the Constitution, nor prohibited by it to the States, are reserved to the States respectively, or to the people.

Amendment XI

Ratified February 7, 1795

The Judicial power of the United States shall not be construed to extend to any suit in law or equity, commenced or prosecuted against one of the United States by Citizens of another State, or by Citizens or Subjects of any Foreign State.

Amendment XII

Ratified June 15, 1804

The Electors shall meet in their respective states and vote by ballot for President and Vice-President, one of whom, at least, shall not be an inhabitant of the same state with themselves; they shall name in their ballots the person voted for as President, and in distinct ballots the person voted for as Vice-President, and they shall make distinct lists of all persons voted for as President, and of all persons voted for as Vice-President, and of the number of votes for each, which lists they shall sign and certify, and transmit sealed to the seat of the government of the United States, directed to the President of the Senate;—the President of the Senate shall, in the presence of the Senate and House of Representatives, open all the certificates and the votes shall then be counted;—The person having the greatest number of votes for President, shall be the President, if such number be a majority of the whole number of Electors appointed; and if no person have such majority, then from the persons having the highest numbers not exceeding three on the list of those voted for as President, the House of Representatives shall choose immediately, by ballot, the President. But in choosing the President, the votes shall be taken by states, the representation from each state having one vote; a quorum for this purpose shall consist of a member or members from two-thirds of the states, and a majority of all the states shall be necessary to a choice. [And if the House of Representatives shall not choose a President whenever the right of choice shall devolve upon them, before the fourth day of March next following, then the Vice-President shall act as President, as in case of the death or other constitutional disability of the President.—]* The person having the greatest number of votes as Vice-President, shall be the Vice-President, if such number be a majority of the whole number of Electors appointed, and if no person have a majority, then from the two highest numbers on the list, the Senate shall choose the Vice-President; a quorum for the purpose shall consist of two-thirds of the whole number of Senators, and a majority of the whole number shall be necessary to a choice. But no person constitutionally ineligible to the office of President shall be eligible to that of Vice-President of the United States.

Amendment XIII

Ratified December 6, 1865

Section 1

Neither slavery nor involuntary servitude, except as a punishment for crime whereof the party shall have been duly convicted, shall exist within the United States, or any place subject to their jurisdiction.

Section 2

Congress shall have power to enforce this article by appropriate legislation.

Amendment XIV

Ratified July 9, 1868

Section 1

All persons born or naturalized in the United States, and subject to the jurisdiction thereof, are citizens of the United States and of the State wherein they reside. No State shall make or enforce any law which shall abridge the privileges or immunities of citizens of the United States; nor shall any State deprive any person of life, liberty, or property, without due process of law; nor deny to any person within its jurisdiction the equal protection of the laws.

Section 2

Representatives shall be apportioned among the several States according to their respective numbers, counting the whole number of persons in each State, excluding Indians not taxed. But when the right to vote at any election

* Superseded by Section 3 of the Amendment XX.

for the choice of electors for President and Vice-President of the United States, Representatives in Congress, the Executive and Judicial officers of a State, or the members of the Legislature thereof, is denied to any of the male inhabitants of such State, being twenty-one years of age, and citizens of the United States, or in any way abridged, except for participation in rebellion, or other crime, the basis of representation therein shall be reduced in the proportion which the number of such male citizens shall bear to the whole number of male citizens twenty-one years of age in such State.

Section 3

No person shall be a Senator or Representative in Congress, or elector of President and Vice-President, or hold any office, civil or military, under the United States, or under any State, who, having previously taken an oath, as a member of Congress, or as an officer of the United States, or as a member of any State legislature, or as an executive or judicial officer of any State, to support the Constitution of the United States, shall have engaged in insurrection or rebellion against the same, or given aid or comfort to the enemies thereof. But Congress may by a vote of two-thirds of each House, remove such disability.

Section 4

The validity of the public debt of the United States, authorized by law, including debts incurred for payment of pensions and bounties for services in suppressing insurrection or rebellion, shall not be questioned. But neither the United States nor any State shall assume or pay any debt or obligation incurred in aid of insurrection or rebellion against the United States, or any claim for the loss or emancipation of any slave; but all such debts, obligations and claims shall be held illegal and void.

Section 5

The Congress shall have the power to enforce, by appropriate legislation, the provisions of this article.

Amendment XV

Ratified February 3, 1870

Section 1

The right of citizens of the United States to vote shall not be denied or abridged by the United States or by any State on account of race, color, or previous condition of servitude—

Section 2

The Congress shall have the power to enforce this article by appropriate legislation.

Amendment XVI

Ratified February 3, 1913

The Congress shall have power to lay and collect taxes on incomes, from whatever source derived, without apportionment among the several States, and without regard to any census or enumeration.

Amendment XVII

Ratified April 8, 1913

The Senate of the United States shall be composed of two Senators from each State, elected by the people thereof, for six years; and each Senator shall have one vote. The electors in each State shall have the qualifications requisite for electors of the most numerous branch of the State legislatures.

When vacancies happen in the representation of any State in the Senate, the executive authority of such State shall issue writs of election to fill such vacancies: *Provided*, That the legislature of any State may empower the executive thereof to make temporary appointments until the people fill the vacancies by election as the legislature may direct.

This amendment shall not be so construed as to affect the election or term of any Senator chosen before it becomes valid as part of the Constitution.

Amendment XVIII

Ratified January 16, 1919

Section 1

After one year from the ratification of this article the manufacture, sale, or transportation of intoxicating liquors within, the importation thereof into, or the exportation thereof from the United States and all territory subject to the jurisdiction thereof for beverage purposes is hereby prohibited.

Section 2

The Congress and the several States shall have concurrent power to enforce this article by appropriate legislation.

Section 3

This article shall be inoperative unless it shall have been ratified as an amendment to the Constitution by the legislatures of the several States, as provided in the Constitution, within seven years from the date of the submission hereof to the States by the Congress.

Amendment XIX

Ratified August 18, 1920

The right of citizens of the United States to vote shall not be denied or abridged by the United States or by any State on account of sex.

Congress shall have power to enforce this article by appropriate legislation.

Amendment XX

Ratified January 23, 1933

Section 1

The terms of the President and the Vice President shall end at noon on the 20th day of January, and the terms of Senators and Representatives at noon on the 3d day of January, of the years in which such terms would have ended if this article had not been ratified; and the terms of their successors shall then begin.

Section 2

The Congress shall assemble at least once in every year, and such meeting shall begin at noon on the 3d day of January, unless they shall by law appoint a different day.

Section 3

If, at the time fixed for the beginning of the term of the President, the President elect shall have died, the Vice President elect shall become President. If a President shall not have been chosen before the time fixed for the beginning of his term, or if the President elect shall have failed to qualify, then the Vice President elect shall act as President until a President shall have qualified; and the Congress may by law provide for the case wherein neither a President elect nor a Vice President shall have qualified, declaring who shall then act as President, or the manner in which one who is to act shall be selected, and such person shall act accordingly until a President or Vice President shall have qualified.

Section 4

The Congress may by law provide for the case of the death of any of the persons from whom the House of Representatives may choose a President whenever the right of choice shall have devolved upon them, and for the case of the death of any of the persons from whom the Senate may choose a Vice President whenever the right of choice shall have devolved upon them.

Section 5

Sections 1 and 2 shall take effect on the 15th day of October following the ratification of this article.

Section 6

This article shall be inoperative unless it shall have been ratified as an amendment to the Constitution by the legislatures of three-fourths of the several States within seven years from the date of its submission.

Amendment XXI

Ratified December 5, 1933

Section 1

The eighteenth article of amendment to the Constitution of the United States is hereby repealed.

Section 2

The transportation or importation into any State, Territory, or Possession of the United States for delivery or use therein of intoxicating liquors, in violation of the laws thereof, is hereby prohibited.

Section 3

This article shall be inoperative unless it shall have been ratified as an amendment to the Constitution by conventions in the several States, as provided in the Constitution, within seven years from the date of the submission hereof to the States by the Congress.

Amendment XXII

Ratified February 27, 1951

Section 1

No person shall be elected to the office of the President more than twice, and no person who has held the office of President, or acted as President, for more than two years of a term to which some other person was elected President shall be elected to the office of President more than once. But this Article shall not apply to any person holding the office of President when this

Article was proposed by Congress, and shall not prevent any person who may be holding the office of President, or acting as President, during the term within which this Article becomes operative from holding the office of President or acting as President during the remainder of such term.

Section 2

This article shall be inoperative unless it shall have been ratified as an amendment to the Constitution by the legislatures of three-fourths of the several States within seven years from the date of its submission to the States by the Congress.

Amendment XXIII

Ratified March 29, 1961

Section 1

The District constituting the seat of Government of the United States shall appoint in such manner as Congress may direct:

A number of electors of President and Vice President equal to the whole number of Senators and Representatives in Congress to which the District would be entitled if it were a State, but in no event more than the least populous State; they shall be in addition to those appointed by the States, but they shall be considered, for the purposes of the election of President and Vice President, to be electors appointed by a State; and they shall meet in the District and perform such duties as provided by the twelfth article of amendment.

Section 2

The Congress shall have power to enforce this article by appropriate legislation.

Amendment XXIV

Ratified January 23, 1964

Section 1

The right of citizens of the United States to vote in any primary or other election for President or Vice President, for electors for President or Vice President, or for Senator or Representative in Congress, shall not be denied or abridged by the United States or any State by reason of failure to pay poll tax or other tax.

Section 2

The Congress shall have power to enforce this article by appropriate legislation.

Amendment XXV

Ratified February 10, 1967

Section 1

In case of the removal of the President from office or of his death or resignation, the Vice President shall become President.

Section 2

Whenever there is a vacancy in the office of the Vice President, the President shall nominate a Vice President who shall take office upon confirmation by a majority vote of both Houses of Congress.

Section 3

Whenever the President transmits to the President pro tempore of the Senate and the Speaker of the House of Representatives his written declaration that he is unable to discharge the powers and duties of his office, and until he transmits to them a written declaration to the contrary, such powers and duties shall be discharged by the Vice President as Acting President.

Section 4

Whenever the Vice President and a majority of either the principal officers of the executive departments or of such other body as Congress may by law provide, transmit to the President pro tempore of the Senate and the Speaker of the House of Representatives their written declaration that the President is unable to discharge the powers and duties of his office, the Vice President shall immediately assume the powers and duties of the office as Acting President.

Thereafter, when the President transmits to the President pro tempore of the Senate and the Speaker of the House of Representatives his written declaration that no inability exists, he shall resume the powers and duties of his office unless the Vice President and a majority of either the principal officers of the executive department or of such other body as Congress may by law provide, transmit within four days to the President pro tempore of the Senate and the Speaker of the House of Representatives their written declaration that the President is unable to discharge the powers and duties of his office. Thereupon Congress shall decide the issue, assembling within forty-eight hours for that purpose if not in session. If the Congress, within twenty-one days after receipt of the latter written declaration, or, if Congress is not in session, within twenty-one days after Congress is required to assemble, determines by two-thirds vote of both Houses that the President is unable to discharge the powers and duties of his office, the Vice President shall continue to discharge the same as Acting President; otherwise, the President shall resume the powers and duties of his office.

Amendment XXVI

Ratified July 1, 1971

Section 1

The right of citizens of the United States, who are eighteen years of age or older, to vote shall not be denied or abridged by the United States or by any State on account of age.

Section 2

The Congress shall have power to enforce this article by appropriate legislation.

Amendment XXVII

Ratified May 7, 1992

No law, varying the compensation for the services of the Senators and Representatives, shall take effect, until an election of representatives shall have intervened.

ACKNOWLEDGMENTS

I owe much to many, for I was assisted in this revolutionary task by some of the ablest people to be found. It was my good fortune to attract two agents who cared as much about the content of the book as the particulars of the publishing contract. To Susan Rabiner and Sydelle Kramer of the Susan Rabiner Literary Agency, thank you for your close attention to every nuance. You were with me all the way, just as you promised. Similarly, this author was lucky to find an editor, George Gibson, publisher of Walker & Company, who was genuinely enthusiastic about the book's purpose and goals, and determined to make this project a success. The care he took in editing the manuscript was extraordinary, and he significantly improved the text substantively and stylistically. A book needs an advocate, too, and in Gene Taft of GT/PR, I gained a superb one. Gene found ways to get busy professionals in the media and elsewhere to take a serious look at my arguments—a prerequisite for publishing success.

No author has ever been more blessed by such able research assistants. Two absolutely superb University of Virginia students worked with me daily over two years' time. First came Benjamin Sachs, whose love of the Constitution won him a coveted position at the University of Virginia's School of Law. Then Ben handed off the project in an orderly way to his chosen successor, Daniel T. Young, one of only six politics honors students in twenty-seven years to achieve highest honors at graduation. They both headed up UVA's national championship Mock Trial team and penned background memos for me that could have been published instantly. Holidays? Weekends? What are these things? Ben and Daniel certainly made no such distinctions on their calendars. What a joy it will be to watch these two brilliant young minds scale legal mountains in the exceedingly productive careers that await them. A third University of Virginia student, politics doctoral candidate Drew

Kurlowski, moved into the project in its final stage. His editing eye for detail added measurably to the manuscript. I can already see his inevitable success as a scholar, teacher, and writer.

Furthermore, the book could never have happened without the dedication, hard work, and loyalty that I have come to expect from my staff at the University of Virginia's Center for Politics. Michael Baudinet, my executive assistant, efficiently performed many tasks and kept the trains running on time in the long run-up to this publication. Chief of Staff Ken Stroupe managed all the book-related activities with his usual consummate skill. My heartfelt appreciation also goes to the entire staff, including Mary D. Brown, Megan Davis, Kristen Durst, Vanessa Freeman, Meg Heubeck, Daman Irby, Reggie Jackson, Jenny Merrill, Jennifer Page, Danelia Robinson, Reed Saul, Tara Saylor, Joshua Scott, Matt Smyth, Bruce Vlk, David Wasserman, and Isaac Wood. I also wish to thank my colleague Professor Paul Freedman and well-known pollster Scott Rasmussen for their critical assistance in designing the survey research that provided the basis for chapter 6.

Finally, a grateful instructor should mention his students. For three decades I have been teaching courses on the fundamentals of American politics and government to some of the brightest young people in the nation. Semester after semester, these University of Virginia students have asked good questions that made me think deeply about our system. The young are like that: They don't know what can't be done. Some have reacted to the ideas proposed in this book and found flaws or offered suggestions. Several are acknowledged in the notes to the various chapters, but I thank every student who took the time to make his or her views heard. Truth is, many of my reforms have been classroom generated. Learning is a two-way street.

With so much aid in so many forms, I have less excuse than most authors for errors, but no doubt there are some. I accept the customary responsibility for the mistakes that remain in these pages.

NOTES

Preamble

1. Just to cite one example, president after president pushes ethanol subsidies for Iowa as a payback to the state that votes first. Ethanol has its defenders as a gasoline substitute, but many other energy experts view it as an overpriced, inadequate alternative to fossil fuels.
2. This estimate of Americans ineligible for the presidency is explained in chapter 2. There is a legal dispute about which citizens are actually excluded from the White House, though the number is unquestionably in the millions.
3. There is no denying that slavery was at the heart of many of the compromises reached at the Constitutional Convention. Perhaps the nation could not have been forged without these agreements in 1787, but it is impossible to study the subject without deep sorrow that so many were in bondage for so long, with the permission of the Constitution. See Lawrence Goldstone, *Dark Bargain: Slavery, Profits, and the Struggle for the Constitution* (New York: Walker, 2005). Redemption came after the bloody Civil War, and there is no better account of the partial absolution that came with the Fourteenth Amendment, which made the former slaves into full citizens, than Garrett Epps, *Democracy Reborn: The Fourteenth Amendment and the Fight for Equal Rights in Post–Civil War America* (New York: Holt, 2006).
4. Justice Samuel Alito, speaking at the University of Virginia, Charlottesville, Virginia, on February 7, 2007.
5. Roberts noted that even "law professors, judges, [and] law students," not just "normal everyday citizens" fail to read the Constitution. The interview with Roberts was conducted by Brian Lamb of C-SPAN in August 2006. A partial transcript was published by the *Washington Post* on September 18, 2006.
6. Full Inscription: "Author of the Declaration of Independence, of the Statute of Virginia for Religious Freedom, and the Father of the University of Virginia." Note that the list does not include Jefferson's service as a two-term president of the United States. How many of our modern presidents could survive as even a paragraph in the history books without that title? Dwight David Eisenhower, the supreme Allied commander during World War II, is probably the only one.
7. Jefferson chose nineteen years for a generation's length, drawing upon actuarial data assembled by the Comte de Buffon, whose actual generational estimation was eighteen years and eight months. See Peter S. Onuf, "Who Are 'We The People'? Bruce Ackerman, Thomas Jefferson, and the Problem of Revolutionary Reform," *Constitutional Political Economy* 10.4 (1999): 397–404. Jefferson's time in France was

very productive, and it permitted him to watch the French Revolution from a front-row seat. Reportedly, because of the high esteem in which he was held, Jefferson would sometimes leave his residence and ride in his carriage to observe directly the rioting in the streets. The rioters would politely make way for Jefferson, before returning to their rampages and hunts for the next victims of the executioner's blade. See Dumas Malone, *Jefferson and the Rights of Man,* vol. 2 (Boston: Little, Brown, 1951), pp. 225–26.

8. On February 4, 1790, James Madison responded from New York to Jefferson's letter. Madison wrote in support of the principle that the Constitution was meant to be examined critically and improved over time, affirming the "general importance of [the principle] in the eye of the philosophical Legislator." Madison continued, "It would give me singular pleasure to see [this principle] first announced in the proceedings of the U. States, and always kept in their view, as a salutary curb on the living generation from imposing unjust or unnecessary burdens on their successors." After reading both letters in concert with other writings of Jefferson and Madison, Adrienne Koch described this exchange as "one of many convincing proofs that although [Madison] was a constitution-maker, he was not a constitution-idolater." See Adrienne Koch, *Jefferson and Madison, the Great Collaboration* (Gloucester, MA: Peter Smith, 1970), p. 74.
9. By no means am I alone in making the general argument about the need for basic constitutional reform. See, for instance, the following three books: Donald L. Robinson, ed. *Reforming American Government: The Bicentennial Papers of the Committee on the Constitutional System* (Boulder, CO: Westview Press, 1985); Daniel Lazare, *The Frozen Republic: How the Constitution Is Paralyzing Democracy* (New York: Harcourt Brace, 1996); and Sanford Levinson, *Our Undemocratic Constitution: Where the Constitution Goes Wrong (And How We the People Can Correct It)* (Oxford: Oxford University Press, 2006). The reform agendas in these books have some overlap, but not a great deal. Similarly, while my own book echoes some of the arguments made by these earlier authors, most of my proposals are quite original, for better or worse. The fact that the four of us, among others, could examine the American system and come up with such separate programs for change only underlines the difficulty we will have in securing the kind of broad consensus needed for a successful second Constitutional Convention. Hope springs eternal, of course.
10. The method of using conventions to alter the Constitution was employed only once: to ratify the Twenty-first Amendment, which ended Prohibition by repealing the Eighteenth Amendment. The text of the amendment called for "conventions in the several States." Advocates for repeal of Prohibition believed that conventions, which would permit average citizens more control over ratification, would be more likely to produce a repeal of the Eighteenth Amendment. Many state legislators of the time had long since committed to back Prohibition, and they were loath to break their pledges and offend well-organized "dry" groups. See David E. Kyvig, *Repealing National Prohibition* (Kent, OH: Kent State University Press, 2000), p. 171.
11. "Amendments: Thousands Proposed, Few Ratified," *Congressional Quarterly Weekly*, February 28, 2004, p. 533.
12. *Populist* has been used to describe a wide range of politicians and platforms. "Capital-P" Populism began as the Populist Party in the 1880s, but over many decades the term's meaning has broadened. Modern populists have perhaps one principle in common: They want to give average citizens a powerful voice in decision making. In *Populism* (New York: Harcourt Brace Jovanovich, 1981), Margaret Canovan

divides populism into two broad forms: agrarian populism, which focused on the needs of farmers, especially in the South, and political populism, which refers to government "by the people and for the people," including such measures as the referendum and the initiative. The legacy of American populism is mixed, of course. Two infamous populists, "Pitchfork" Ben Tillman of Georgia and the Ku Klux Klan's David Duke of Louisiana, preached a noxious brand of white supremacy in the South more than a century apart. Others associated with a nonracial populism have made more positive, though often controversial, contributions. Included in this number are past presidential candidates William Jennings Bryan (Democratic Party), Ross Perot (Reform Party), and Ralph Nader (Green Party).

13. Letter from Jefferson to John Adams, written from Monticello, October 14, 1816.

14. Letter from Jefferson to the Republican Citizens of Washington County, Maryland, March 31, 1809.

15. These ideas are discussed in far greater detail in many of the following volumes. For a study of the Constitutional Convention, both the issues and the personalities that were at work in 1787, see Jack R. Rakove, *Original Meanings: The Politics and Ideas in the Making of the Constitution* (New York: Knopf, 1996) and Calvin C. Jillson, *Constitution Making: Conflict and Consensus in the Federal Convention of 1787* (New York: Agathon Press, 1988). For a thoughtful analysis of the "Father of the Constitution," see Robert J. Morgan, *James Madison on the Constitution and the Bill of Rights* (New York: Greenwood Press, 1988). Many studies focus on the political and historical trends that molded the Constitution over time; for example, see David M. O'Brien, *Constitutional Law and Politics*, 5th ed., 2 vols. (New York: Norton, 2003). Similar topics are covered in a thorough textbook-style reference by Richard S. Randall, *American Constitutional Development*, 2 vols. (New York: Addison Wesley Longman, 2002). For essays on the judiciary's role in interpreting the Constitution, see Robert A. Goldwin and William A. Schambra, ed., *The Constitution, the Courts, and the Quest for Justice* (Washington, DC: American Enterprise Institute for Public Policy Research, 1989).

Others books written mainly for academics, practicing attorneys, and law students focus more heavily on constitutional law and theory rather than historical trends or perspectives. See Alpheus Mason and Donald Grier Stephenson Jr., *American Constitutional Law: Introductory Essays and Selected Cases*, 14th ed. (Upper Saddle River, NJ: Pearson Education, 2005). For an almost exclusively case-driven analysis of constitutional law, see Jerome A. Barron et al., eds., *Constitutional Law, Principles and Policy: Cases and Materials*, 6th ed. (Newark, NJ: LexisNexis, 2002) and Louis Fisher, *American Constitutional Law*, 6th ed. (Durham, NC: Carolina Academic Press, 2005).

16. With some frequency, modern observers of the American system dream about converting the United States to parliamentary government, and this sentiment has historical roots. For example, Woodrow Wilson began writing about the inefficiencies and constraints of the separation of powers as early as the 1870s, calling for a cabinet government where legislators would serve and perform executive functions. See Ronald J. Pestritto, ed., *Woodrow Wilson: The Essential Political Writings* (Lanham, MD: Lexington Books, 2005), especially pp. 127–40. Charles Haines cited the "almost universal tendency of European nations to unite . . . legislative and executive functions" to conclude that "our present system, a disjointed and indirect system of legislative and executive relations, should be revised." See Charles Grove Haines, "Ministerial Responsibility Versus the Separation of Powers," *American Political Science Review* 16.2 (May 1922): 194–210. More recently, Bruce Ackerman described

the American system as working "well enough at home [but] nothing less than disastrous abroad," instead suggesting a mixing of the British and American systems as "constrained parliamentarianism." See Bruce Ackerman, "A New Separation of Powers," *Harvard Law Review* 113.3 (Jan. 2000): 633–729.

17. Nearly all states have some form of direct democracy, from popular approval of constitutional amendments to statutory initiatives, and the numbers have only been increasing. Many of these shifts have caused drastic, sometimes dangerous, results, such as when California voters approved Proposition 13, slashing property taxes and sending California's fiscal policy into turmoil. For an analysis of direct democracy in states, along with proposed reforms, see Larry J. Sabato, Howard R. Ernst, and Bruce A. Larson, *Dangerous Democracy? The Battle over Ballot Initiatives in America* (Lanham, MD: Rowman and Littlefield, 2001). The trend toward direct democracy has not been exclusive to the United States; citizens around the world are exerting greater direct control over their laws, often with troubling consequences. See David Butler, and Austin Ranney, ed., *Referendums around the World: The Growing Use of Direct Democracy* (Washington, DC: American Enterprise Institute for Public Policy Research, 1994).
18. This is the entire Section 2 of Article I, Bill of Rights, of the Virginia Constitution of 1776.
19. Excerpt of Section 3, Article I, ibid.
20. Number of constitutional overhauls by state for the original thirteen colonies: Connecticut, 1; Delaware, 3; Georgia, 8; Maryland, 3; New Hampshire, 2 (including the 1792 recodification); New Jersey, 2; New York, 3; North Carolina, 3; Pennsylvania, 3; Rhode Island, 1; South Carolina, 5; Virginia, 6. As noted in the text, Massachusetts is the only state of the original thirteen colonies that has had just one constitution over its history. The remaining states and the number of major constitutional overhauls by state: Alabama, 4; Alaska, 0; Arizona, 0; Arkansas, 3; California, 1; Colorado, 0; Florida, 4; Hawaii, 0; Idaho, 0; Illinois, 3; Indiana, 1; Iowa, 1; Kansas, 3; Kentucky, 3; Louisiana, 8; Maine, 0; Michigan, 3; Minnesota, 0; Mississippi, 3; Missouri, 3; Montana, 1; Nebraska, 1; Nevada, 0; New Mexico, 0; North Dakota, 0; Ohio, 1; Oklahoma, 0; Oregon, 0; South Dakota, 0; Tennessee, 2; Texas, 4; Utah, 0; Vermont, 2; Washington, 0; West Virginia, 1; Wisconsin, 0; Wyoming, 0. See Richard E. Berg-Andersson, "Constitutions of the Several States," *The Green Papers* (updated Dec. 5, 2004, accessed July 8, 2005), http://www.thegreenpapers.com/.
21. Alexis de Tocqueville, *Democracy in America*, trans. George Lawrence, ed. J. P. Mayer (New York: Harper and Row, 1966), p. 642.

1. Creating a Capital Congress

1. This pro–King George Tory lyric was published in 1776 in the *Pennsylvania Evening Post*, among other places. Its first stanza reads: "Ye Tories all rejoice and sing/Success to George our gracious king;/The faithful subjects tribute bring/And execrate the Congress." See Niall Ferguson, *Empire* (New York: Basic Books, 2003).
2. These numbers exclude nonvoting congressional delegates. See Associated Press, "A Numeric Profile of the New Congress," *Washington Post*, January 4, 2006. The freshman House class also includes the first Muslim and the first two Buddhists to serve in Congress. See also "Ethnic Minorities in the New Congress," *Congressional Quarterly Weekly*, November 13, 2006.
3. Using population estimates from the July 2006 census. In states where only one senator voted in favor of the motion, half the total population of the state went into the

calculation. The resulting grand total: Senators voting in favor of the motion represent 184,353,878 Americans, or approximately 62 percent of the total population.

4. According to the U.S. Census Bureau, Virginia's population in 1790 was recorded as 747,550 people, whereas Delaware had a mere 59,096. Estimates of population for July 1, 2006, put California's population at 36,457,549 people and Wyoming's at 515,004.
5. According to population estimates for 2006 published by the U.S. Census Bureau, the fifty-one senators required to comprise a majority can represent as little as 16.9 percent or as much as 84.3 percent of the nation's more than 300 million people—arguably, a disparity too great for the Senate's institutional well-being and the country's political health.
6. See Lynn A. Baker and Samuel H. Dinkin, "The Senate: An Institution Whose Time Has Gone?" *Journal of Law and Politics* 21.13 (Winter 1997): pp. 23–29. See also Daniel Patrick Moynihan's introduction to Herman B. Leonard and Jay H. Walder, eds., *The Federal Budget and the States: Fiscal Year 1999* (Taubam Center for State and Local Government, JFK School of Government, Harvard University and office of Senator Moynihan). In addition, two political scientists have developed a formal model for predicting the Senate's funding decisions. On average, the smallest state will receive about $120 per capita in federal funding compared to just $82 for the largest state—a huge gap in dollars when multiplied by the populations of these states. See Frances E. Lee and Bruce I. Oppenheimer, *Sizing Up the Senate: The Unequal Consequences of Equal Representation* (Chicago: University of Chicago Press, 1999).
7. July 2006 estimates, U.S. Census Bureau.
8. The Virginia Plan pioneered by Madison called for a bicameral legislature with both houses having representation "to be proportioned to the Quotas of contribution [of federal taxes] or to the number of free inhabitants." See Anderson Thornton, *Creating the Constitution: The Convention of 1787 and the First Congress* (University Park, PA: Pennsylvania State University Press, 1993), p. 51. Since the Articles of Confederation called for equal representation for each state, the large states faced an uphill battle. The small states merely had to defend the status quo, while the large states would have to persuade the small states to accept less representation. The task proved to be insurmountable. See also Jack N. Rakove, *James Madison and the Creation of the American Republic* (New York: HarperCollins, 1990), p. 57.
9. Texas and California together have a population of 59,965,332, while Wyoming and Vermont collectively have a mere 1,138,912, according to 2006 estimates released by the U.S. Census Bureau.
10. According to U.S. Census data, the mid-2006 U.S. population was 299,398,484, 67.7 percent more than the 1960 figure of 178,554,916. As of the dawn of 2007, the U.S. population was estimated to be about 300,922,550, or 68.5 percent more than in 1960.
11. The budget bill for legislative branch appropriations in the 2005 fiscal year called for $725,067,000 for the expenses of the Senate. Even if this figure increased by 35 percent with the introduction of thirty-five senators—which is unlikely—this would only cost the taxpayers $253 million, less than a dollar per citizen.
12. Young gloated that he stuffed the August 2005 appropriations bill "like a turkey," including a $231-million expense for a bridge in Anchorage to be named "Don Young's Way." See Stephen Slivinski, "Don Young's World," *Cato Institute*, August 17, 2005.
13. It is impossible to prove this statement with absolute certainty, since we cannot know the results of elections for extra seats that do not currently exist. But given the partisan predilections of the states that would gain representation under the new scheme, as well as the strong Democratic trend that manifested itself in November 2006, it appears very likely that enough antisurge senators would have been elected

to accomplish what is arguably the main public mandate from the 2006 election. This statement also assumes that the new Senate would maintain the 60 percent cloture rule to shut off filibusters. It is at least possible that the new, more representative Senate would choose to lower the percentage of senators needed to end filibusters, thus making it even easier to pass the antisurge resolution.

14. In the House, the twenty-five smallest states command just 16 percent of the 435 votes, whereas under the new plan for the Senate, the twenty-five smallest states would control 37 percent of the Senate's 135 votes.
15. The D.C. delegate to the House can vote in committees and can also cast some votes on the floor of the House—though if her vote makes the difference in a measure passing, it is discounted! This bizarre arrangement does not satisfy even the most basic requirements of representation in a democracy.
16. For more on the management of Washington, D.C., see "Democracy or Distrust? Restoring Home Rule for the District of Columbia in the Post-Control Board Era," *Harvard Law Review* 111.7 (May 1998): 2045–62.
17. Congress held extensive hearings on the question of D.C. statehood in the early 1990s. See Judiciary and Education Subcommittee of the House Committee on the District of Columbia, *Statehood for the District of Columbia*, hearing, July 28, August 5, and November 3, 1993, 103rd Cong., 1st sess., serial no. 103-6 (Washington: Government Printing Office, 1994). A commonly proposed alternative to statehood for the District would be for Maryland to take back the land it contributed to the city, as Virginia did in 1846. Called *retrocession*, this proposal would restore voting rights to all D.C. residents by making them citizens of Maryland. See Michael K. Fauntroy, Congressional Research Service (hereafter, CRS) Report for Congress no. RS20875, *District of Columbia Delegates to Congress* (updated Apr. 4, 2001). See also Mary Beth Sheridan, "Picking the Brains of the Founding Fathers," *Washington Post,* May 28, 2007.
18. Since 1983, thirteen bills for D.C. statehood have been introduced, though few made it out of committee. Statehood for the District of Columbia was defeated in the House of Representatives by a vote of 277 to 153 when last voted upon in 1993. One hundred fifty-two Democrats and just one lone Republican voted in favor of the bill, while 105 Democrats and 172 Republicans voted against. See U.S. Cong., House, 103rd Cong., 1st sess., *H.R. 51, New Columbia Admission* (introduced Jan. 5, 1993; floor vote Nov. 21, 1993). Note that in 1993 the Democrats controlled the House with a sizable majority. A similar vote now in a more closely divided, Democratic-run House might be even more overwhelmingly lost.
19. Numbers are based on 2006 Census Bureau estimates.
20. Italy includes its former presidents in its national Senate, for example. See Bruce Ackerman, "The New Separation of Powers," *Harvard Law Review* 113.3 (Jan. 2000): 633–729, note 121.
21. Pensions and office allowances are authorized under the Former Presidents Act of 1958, which delegated to the General Services Administration the task of allocating the funds for former presidents. The act provides for a furnished office in a location of the former president's choosing, a staff, franking privileges, Secret Service protection, transition expenses, travel expenses, and other needs. The dollar amounts authorized for former presidents by the General Service Administration have been increasing for every president, from about $540,000 for President Ford to $1,125,000 for President Clinton, not counting Secret Service protection, whose funds are not disclosed for security reasons. For more on presidential retirement benefits, see Stephanie Smith, CRS Report Order Code 98–249 GOV, *Former Presidents: Federal Pension and Retirement Benefits* (updated Apr. 27, 2005).

22. Under the Ethics in Government Act of 1978, senators are forbidden from receiving any honorarium (compensation for any appearance or writing related to their office), nor can they earn outside income of more than 15 percent of their annual senatorial salary. Book royalties are the exception, however, and there is no limitation in this category. Of course, all of these rules apply only to sitting senators, and after retirement from the Senate a former member can pursue private income without sanction or limit.
23. After leaving office, Reagan accepted more than $2 million for two twenty-minute speeches and a few public appearances in Japan in 1989. See the preface to the 2000 edition of Lou Cannon's *President Reagan: The Role of a Lifetime* (New York: Simon and Schuster, 1991). In the first couple of years after leaving office, former president Clinton earned more than $13 million in speaking fees. Despite this wealth, Clinton still asked for $3.5 million from the government to pay his legal fees from years-long battles over Whitewater and other business dealings—which he was entitled under the law to do.
24. Byrd was reelected to his ninth term in 2006 at the age of eighty-seven. Thurmond served eight terms, leaving in early 2003 at age one hundred. He died a few months later.
25. Look again at the case of our most recent former president, Bill Clinton. In the first six years after leaving office in early 2001, Clinton earned $40 million just in speaking fees at home and abroad. This is apart from the tens of millions of dollars in book royalties Clinton has made in his postpresidency. See John Solomon and Matthew Mosk, "For Clinton, New Wealth in Speeches," *Washington Post*, February 23, 2007.
26. Sadly, these numbers are not exceptional. In fact, the situation was even worse in 2004, when 62 House nominees ran unopposed by the other major party, and 293 other candidates secured 60 percent or more of the vote—a clear sign of inadequate competition.
27. Further, of the sixty-one contests in 2006 that were decided by a margin of 10 percent or less, only thirty-six of these were decided by 5 percent or less. As the text asserts, the state of competition was far worse in the prior 2004 House contests. Before the election, political observers saw no more than thirty-five to forty districts with any chance of a party turnover, and in the end, there were few real surprises. A mere five challengers in the entire United States managed to defeat incumbents in the 2004 House elections. Nearly eight in ten successful candidates for the House in 2004 won over 60 percent of the vote. The precise numbers are: 342 of 435 winners, or 78.6 percent, won more than 60 percent of the vote in 2004. See "2004 House," *Larry J. Sabato's Crystal Ball*, http://www.centerforpolitics.org/crystalball/2004/house/.
28. The franking privilege has been a part of American politics since the first Congress. Elected officials can write their name in lieu of a postage stamp for U.S. mail, though over time some limits on the practice have been put in place. The practice continued fairly steadily from the 1700s until serious problems developed in the early 1970s. With no clear guidelines on what sort of mail was "frankable," citizen-lawsuits popped up across the country, and the courts were loath to weigh in on the matter. In 1972 guidelines were set regarding the frank after members of Congress were perceived to be abusing the privilege for reelection campaigns. For instance, Representative Fletcher Thompson (R-GA) charged more than $200,000 in mail-outs to voters in his 1972 Senate campaign. In 2001 the total cost of the frank incurred by the House alone was more than $20 million. Data compiled by the National Taxpayers Union, http://www.ntu.org. See also Dan Greenberg, "Slashing Congressional Spending, Part I: Congressional Pay, Pensions, Perks, and Staff," *Heritage Foundation*, May 16, 1995.

For other data related to congressional spending, see the series *Vital Statistics on Congress* by Norman J. Ornstein and Thomas Mann (Washington, DC: AEI Press), published every two years.

29. Members of the House of Representatives receive three major allowances annually: a personnel allowance for employing a staff, an allowance for official office expenses, and a franking allowance. Under the personnel allowance, a member is entitled to $632,355 to hire up to eighteen permanent employees and four additional nonpermanent employees, such as temps and interns. The official office expense includes a base allowance of $127,724 plus two allowances for office space and travel, which vary from member to member. The amount of the franking allowance is effectively equal to the cost of sending three pieces of first-class mail to every residential address in a member's constituency; however, a member may pull from his or her other accounts to pay for additional franked mail if needed. As for senators, the law entitles them to between $1.7 and $2.7 million for personnel, depending on the size of the state being represented. Their official office expense accounts range from $128,102 to $474,426 per year, and, like the representatives, they are entitled to the franking privilege. See Paul E. Dwyer, CRS Report RL30064, *Salaries and Allowances: The Congress* (updated Nov. 22, 1999).
30. For example, in 2001, Democratic National Committee chairman Terry McAuliffe used $10 million in party funds to install state-of-the-art e-mail servers, television equipment, and satellite linkups in the DNC headquarters in Washington, barely beating the enactment date of the McCain-Feingold law that limited the use of so-called party soft money. The Republicans have been using such technology for years, even employing sophisticated computer programs to analyze car ownership registries and magazine subscriptions to form a list of 170 million potential "small-time" donors. See Adam Clymer, "The Donkey's Flush. Will the New DNC Chief Make Hay?" *Washington Post*, February 6, 2005. Members of Congress have benefited immensely from having access to these high-tech tools.
31. Numbers have been rounded and taken from disbursement reports released by the Federal Election Commission. Numbers before rounding: $428,079,289 for incumbents, $22,602,995 for challengers.
32. The nature of political man is a constant through the ages. As one scholar has shown, partisan redistricting had a major effect on the composition of the U.S. House throughout the post–Civil War era in the nineteenth century, at times even determining the controlling party in a highly competitive age. See Erik J. Engstrom, "Stacking the States, Stacking the House: The Partisan Consequences of Congressional Redistricting in the 19th Century," *American Political Science Review* 100.3 (Aug. 2006): 419–27. The rules at this time were less precise, and "one-person, one-vote" was a century away, yet more than half of the House districts were redrawn after the censuses of 1870, 1880, and 1890—mainly to score partisan advantage.
33. Hoping to keep Madison out of the House of Representatives in 1789, Patrick Henry and his Anti-Federalist allies gerrymandered Madison's Orange Country district to include the greatest possible number of Anti-Federalist voters and altered the election rules to enforce a longer residency requirement, making any move to another district impossible. Still, Madison was able to defeat his opponent, James Monroe, by 336 of the 2,280 votes cast in the February election. See Robert A. Rutland et al., ed., *The Papers of James Madison*, vol. 11 (Charlottesville, VA: University Press of Virginia, 1977), pp. 301–4.
34. For examples of bizarrely gerrymandered districts in American politics, see http://www.westmiller.com/fairvote2k/in_gerry.htm.

35. The 2002 House elections show some of the least competitive numbers in history. The average margin in any one election was almost 40 percent, with only four incumbents losing to challengers, the lowest number ever recorded. Three out of four incumbents who faced close elections in 2000 enjoyed much less competitive districts in 2002, thanks to partisan redistricting. See "Redistricting and Incumbent Protection in 2001–2002," *FairVote: The Center for Voting and Democracy*, http://www.fairvote.org/?page=715. For more on redistricting in the wake of recent Supreme Court cases, see Michelle H. Browdy, "Computer Models and Post-Bandemer Redistricting," *Yale Law Journal* 99.6 (Apr. 1990): 1379–98.
36. See Alan I. Abramowitz, "Don't Blame Redistricting for Uncompetitive Elections," *Larry J. Sabato's Crystal Ball* (May 26, 2005), http://www.centerforpolitics.org/crystalball/. See also the "Rethinking Redistricting" Symposium in *PS* 40.1 (Jan. 2006): 77–101. The exchange among Abramowitz, Thomas Brunell, Michael McDonald, and others is enlightening, and it suggests to a careful reader that while redistricting reform is definitely not the whole answer to increasing congressional competition, it can play a significant role in achieving this good end.
37. Iowa constitutionally requires that districts be contiguous, compact, and drawn without regard to partisan whims, but its system is unlike any other. An independent commission develops a redistricting plan after each census and submits it to the state legislature. The legislature must bring the plan to a vote expeditiously and may not amend it. If the plan is rejected, the commission delivers an alternate plan, which again may not be amended. If that too is rejected, a third plan is submitted, which can be amended like any other bill. In the 2002 election, when the redistricting standards were in full legal effect, Iowa had more competitive districts than New York and California combined. Arizona also uses an independent commission balanced across party lines to draw districts. The districts must be compact, contiguous, equal in population, and preserve "communities of interest." Hawaii, Idaho, Montana, New Jersey, and Washington also give independent commissions full autonomy over redistricting. Indiana allows an independent commission to resolve redistricting if legislators deadlock. See Gregory L. Giroux, "Iowa, Redistricting Without Rancor," *Congressional Quarterly Weekly*, April 7, 2001, p. 792, and more generally, see "Redistricting Commissions and Alternatives to the Legislature Conducting Redistricting," *National Conference of State Legislatures* (accessed June 23, 2005), http://www.ncsl.org/.
38. In a special election in November 2005, California voters turned down Proposition 77, Governor Arnold Schwarzenegger's attempt at balanced redistricting by employing a three-judge panel. See the California Secretary of State Web site at http://www.ss.ca.gov/. In Tennessee, only 10 state legislative seats of 435 were decided by less than five percentage points in 2004. Tennessee's own U.S. House members, led by the Union City Democrat John Tanner, have endorsed a state legislative bill, as yet unpassed, that would establish independent commissions to draw districts every ten years. See Mike Madden, "Take Politics out of Redistricting, Say Tennessee Congressmen," *Tennessean*, August 18, 2005. In Florida, a group called the Committee for Fair Elections collected more than two hundred thousand signatures to have its redistricting plan, which called for compactness and competitiveness in districts, go to referendum in 2006. It failed. See Joni James, "Reformers Forge On with Redistricting Referendum, Despite Wordy Ballot," *St. Petersburg Times*, August 25, 2005. Also calling for independent commissions, a proposal pushed by Reform Ohio Now qualified for the November 2005 ballot, but it too was defeated. See Dean E. Murphy, "Democrats and Labor Get Redistricting Vote on

Ohio Ballot," *New York Times*, September 7, 2005. Massachusetts may get a referendum as early as 2008 on a proposed constitutional amendment transparency in redistricting. See Jim O'Sullivan, "Redistricting Reform Coalition Confident," *State House News Service*, January 13, 2005. Many of these proposals faced legal challenges on everything from constitutional issues to the number of words in the proposals, as partisans worked successfully to keep power over their districts. See also Richard E. Cohen, "Boundary Wars," *National Journal* 26 (June 25, 2005): 2074–75.

39. According to one source, Democrats have already allocated an astonishing $17 million over the next five years solely for the purpose of fighting redistricting battles across the country. See Pamela M. Prah, "First Salvos Prepared for Statehouse Redistricting Battles," *Stateline.org*, August 24, 2006, http://www.stateline.org/live/details/story?contentId=136505.

40. The Voting Rights Act of 1965 (79 Stat 437), hereafter called the VRA, dismantled many of the most egregious methods of disenfranchisement in the South, and the broad statutes paved the way for a number of controversial Supreme Court decisions over the role of race in redistricting. The act banned literacy tests and allowed for judges to take an active role in coercing states to comply with the statutes, including measures that required certain states to submit laws affecting voting rights to a three-judge panel before they could be enacted by the legislature. The act has been renewed several times. In 1975 the act was expanded to protect language-minority citizens, such as Hispanics and Native Americans, and in 1985 the act was amended to allow for termination of coverage of the act for some states under certain conditions. See also major Supreme Court decisions on the VRA, such as *South Carolina* v. *Katzenbach* (383 U.S. 301 [1966]) and *Shaw v. Reno* (509 U.S. 630 [1993]). The bitter truth is that the mandate to create as many "minority-in-the-majority" districts as possible has contributed greatly to the crazy-quilt congressional maps. Where Democrats are in control in the states, minorities get these districts because most minorities disproportionately support Democratic candidates. Where Republicans are in control in the states, minorities get these districts because the GOP wishes to isolate as many minorities as possible in heavily black or Hispanic/Latino enclaves. This creates mostly white districts surrounding the enclaves, and a substantial majority of the white districts elect Republicans, especially in the South and border states.

41. For one defense of the maximization of majority-minority districts at any cost, including the total absence of compactness, see J. Morgan Kousser, "Colorblind Injustice: Minority Voting Rights and the Undoing of the Second Reconstruction," *Public Affairs Report* 40.3 (May 1999), http://www.igs.berkeley.edu/publications/par/2/kousser.html.

42. See David Wasserman, "To Better Draw a District: Objective Congressional Redistricting Standards for the 21st Century," distinguished politics major, thesis, University of Virginia, April 17, 2006.

43. See Dennis Polhill and Patrick Basham, "Policy Analysis: Uncompetitive Elections and the American Political System," *Cato Institute*, June 30, 2005, especially p. 12, as well as Mark Rush, *Does Redistricting Make a Difference? Partisan Representation and Electoral Behavior* (Baltimore, MD: Johns Hopkins University Press, 1993).

44. The Supreme Court has allowed states to limit the number of terms state legislators can serve, and fifteen states now have such limits. See *Bates v. Jones* (523 U.S. 1021 [1998]), cert. denied. Members of Congress, however, cannot have term limits imposed by their respective states, according to the Court's ruling in *U.S. Term Limits v. Thornton* (514 U.S. 779 [1995]). See also Kris W. Kobach, "Rethinking Article V:

Term Limits and the Seventeenth and Nineteenth Amendments," *Yale Law Journal* 103.7 (May 1994): 1971–2007. For specifics on the legislative term limits established by each state, see "Summary and Citations of State Term Limit Laws," *National Conference of State Legislatures*, May 5, 2004, http://www.ncsl.org.

45. *The Records of the Federal Convention of 1787*, ed. Max Ferrand, vol. 2 (New Haven, CT: Yale University Press, 1966), p. 644.
46. From U.S. Const., Art. I, Sec. 2: "The actual Enumeration shall be made within three Years after the first Meeting of the Congress of the United States, and within every subsequent Term of ten Years, in such Manner as they shall by Law direct. The Number of Representatives shall not exceed one for every thirty Thousand, but each State shall have at Least one Representative." What Washington was petitioning for, then, was a *smaller* minimum district size, meaning that Congress could (potentially) have a larger *maximum* size. Obviously this is never an issue today, with Congress having surpassed the thirty-thousand minimum quite some time ago. The first apportionment, based on the 1790 census, resulted in 105 members (http://www.census.gov/population/www/censusdata/apportionment/history.html).
47. James Madison, "No. 55: The Total Number of the House of Representatives," *The Federalist Papers*, ed. Clinton Rossiter (New York: Penguin Books, 1961), pp. 338–43.
48. Ibid.
49. George F. Will, "Congress Just Isn't Big Enough," *Washington Post*, January 14, 2001.
50. Briefly in 1958–1960, the House comprised 437 members with the admission of Alaska and Hawaii to the Union, each new state receiving one House member. With the election of 1962, the House returned to 435 members.
51. These are averages, and they obviously ignore the wide disparity in representation necessary in apportioning House members. For example, according to 2006 Census Bureau estimates, the congressman from Wyoming, the most lightly populated state, represents 515,004, while in Montana, currently entitled to just one representative, the congressman represents 944,632. These differences are inevitable in a state-based districting system, but they should be understood. For more information on congressional apportionment, see the U.S. Census Congressional Apportionment Web site, http://www.census.gov/population/www/censusdata/apportionment.html.
52. Mathew Cossolotto, "Fight for a Bigger House," *Hartford Courant*, October 7, 2001.
53. Supra at note 49. Also see Robert D. Novak, *Completing the Revolution: A Vision for Victory in 2000* (New York: Free Press, 2000), pp. 186–89.
54. Robert Novak wants to go further, with each congressman receiving a fraction of the current pay. To compensate, congressmen would be permitted to pursue their own professions without limit in law, business, medicine, teaching, and so on. The inevitable conflicts of interest would be judged not by an ethics committee but by the voters at the next election. Supra at note 53.
55. Detailed information regarding voter turnout is available through the Inter-University Consortium for Political and Social Research (ICPSR) in general and the American National Election Study (ANES) in particular. See, for example, University of Michigan, Center for Political Studies, American National Election Study. AMERICAN NATIONAL ELECTION STUDY, 2004: PRE- AND POST-ELECTION SURVEY [Computer file]. ICPSR04245-v1; Ann Arbor, MI: University of Michigan, Center for Political Studies, American National Election Study [producer], 2004; and Ann Arbor, MI: Inter-University Consortium for Political and Social Research [distributor], 2006-02-17. Additionally, the Yale political scientists Alan Gerber and Donald Green have done extensive research into what motivates voter turnout. See

Alan S. Gerber and Donald P. Green, "The Effects of Canvassing, Telephone Calls, and Direct Mail on Voter Turnout: A Field Experiment," *American Political Science Review* 94.3 (Sept. 2000): 653–63; Donald P. Green, Alan S. Gerber, and David W. Nickerson, "Getting Out the Vote in Local Elections: Results from Six Door-to-Door Canvassing Experiments," *Journal of Politics* 65.4 (Nov. 2003): 1083–96.

56. Cited in Gideon Doron and Michael Harris, *Term Limits* (Lanham, MD: Lexington Books, 2001), p. 3.
57. The principle of *rotation in office* rested on the notion that one individual holding on to any single office for an extended period of time was anathema to the mechanism of representative democracy. Consider Thomas Jefferson's worries about the lack of term limits in the 1787 Constitution: "I dislike, and strongly dislike . . . the abandonment in every instance of the principle of rotation in office and most particularly in the case of the President. Reason and experience tell us that the first magistrate will always be re-elected if he may be re-elected. He is then an officer for life." Thomas Jefferson to James Madison, 1787, *The Writings of Thomas Jefferson*, memorial ed., ed. Andrew A. Lipscomb and Albert Ellery Bergh (Washington, DC: Thomas Jefferson Memorial Foundation, 1903–04), vol. 6, p. 389. George Washington, of course, epitomized the principle of rotation in office by declining a third term. See Carl E. Prince, *The Federalists and the U.S. Civil Service* (New York: New York University Press, 1978). It should also be noted that Jefferson disproved his own argument, at least in part, by becoming the first challenger to defeat an incumbent president, when he ousted one-term chief executive John Adams in 1800.
58. Lord John Emerich Edward Dalberg Acton (1834–1902). More information, including a full biography, is available on the Acton Institute Web site, http://www.acton.org/publicat/randl/liberal.php?id=75.
59. Barbara Silberdick Feinberg, *Term Limits for Congress*? (New York: Twenty-First Century Books, 1996), p. 8.
60. Available online through the Yale Law School's Avalon Project at http://www.yale.edu/lawweb/avalon/states/va05.htm.
61. Cited in Doron and Harris, *Term Limits*, p. 5.
62. See, for example, George Will, *Restoration: Congress, Term Limits and the Recovery of Deliberative Democracy* (New York: Free Press, 1993), in which the virtue of the citizen-as-legislator is central to Will's argument.
63. Feinberg, *Term Limits*, p. 10.
64. May 31, 1797. Madison's notes on the debates at the Philadelphia Convention are available online through the Yale Law School's Avalon Project at http://www.yale.edu/lawweb/avalon/debates/531.htm.
65. In particular, see *The Federalist No. 52*, which discusses at length the necessity of frequent elections in a healthy republic. Available online at http://www.foundingfathers.info/federalistpapers/fed52.htm.
66. Feinberg, *Term Limits*, pp. 10–11.
67. Ibid. The year cited here is 1996.
68. 115 USC 1842 (1995).
69. H.J. Res. 2, 105th Cong., 1st sess. (1997). The missing seven votes were composed of absentees and seat vacancies.
70. Einer Elhauge, "Are Term Limits Undemocratic?" *University of Chicago Law Review* 64.1 (Winter 1997): 83–201, at 85.
71. Jeffrey A. Karp, "Explaining Public Support for Legislative Term Limits," *Public Opinion Quarterly* 59.3 (Autumn 1995): 373–91, at 376.

72. Ibid., p. 386.
73. Elhauge, "Are Term Limits Undemocratic?" pp. 85–86.
74. V. O. Key, *The Responsible Electorate: Rationality in Presidential Voting, 1936–1960* (Cambridge: Harvard University Press, 1966). "The perverse and unorthodox argument of this little book is that voters are not fools. To be sure, many individual voters act in odd ways indeed; yet in the large the electorate behaves about as rationally and responsibly as we should expect, given the clarity of alternatives presented to it and the character of the information available to it" (7).
75. Elhauge, "Are Term Limits Undemocratic?" pp. 170–77.
76. Richard A. Clucas, "California: The New Amateur Politics," in *The Test of Time: Coping with Legislative Term Limits* (hereafter referred to as *Test of Time*), ed. Rick Farmer, John David Rausch Jr., and John C. Green (Lanham, MD: Lexington Books, 2003), pp. 17–32.
77. See Nancy Vogel, "Election 2006: Same Party Mix, Different Flavor," *Los Angeles Times*, November 9, 2006.
78. Bruce E. Cain and Thad Kousser, "Adapting to Term Limits in California: Recent Experiences and New Directions," National Conference on State Legislatures, *Joint Project on Term Limits, 2004*. The full report is available online at http://www.ncsl.org/jptl/casestudies/CaseContents.htm.
79. Ibid.
80. James M. Penning, "Michigan: The End Is Near," in *Test of Time*, pp. 34–45.
81. Ibid., p. 44.
82. Eric Kelderman and Pamela M. Prah, "Report Chronicles Downside of Term Limits," *Stateline.org*, August 16, 2006. The most extensive information about the effect of term limits on state legislatures is available through the National Conference on State Legislatures, including a 2006 summary report, *Coping with Term Limits: A Practical Guide*, a three-year study which brought together government officials and political scientists from across the country. The 2006 report supports the conclusions about the effects of term limits outlined here. More information is available at http://www.ncsl.org/programs/legismgt/ABOUT/Termlimit.htm.
83. John M. Carey, Richard G. Niemi, and Lynda W. Powell, *Term Limits in the State Legislatures* (Ann Arbor: University of Michigan Press, 2000), p. 123. Not all term-limited states have registered increases in women legislators. Ohio and Michigan are among the exceptions. See Peter Slevin, "After Adopting Term Limits, States Lose Female Legislators," *Washington Post*, April 22, 2007.
84. Ibid., p. 125.
85. Kousser, Thad, *Term Limits and the Dismantling of State Legislative Professionalism* (Cambridge: Cambridge University Press, 2005), pp. 208–10.
86. Ibid.
87. *The Writings of Thomas Jefferson*, vol. 15, p. 23.
88. *Lochner v. New York* (198 U.S. 45).
89. George Washington's farewell address (1796) is available through the Yale Law School's Avalon Project at http://www.yale.edu/lawweb/avalon/washing.htm.
90. Kathy Gill, "Balanced Budget Amendment," *About.com Guide to U.S. Politics and Current Events*, March 17, 2006, http://uspolitics.about.com/od/thefederalbudget/i/balanced_budget.htm. By March 2007 the total national debt topped $8.82 trillion, and the nearly exact debt per American citizen amounted to about $29,400.
91. Ibid.
92. *Hearing before the Subcommittee on the Constitution to consider H.J. Res. 22, to propose an amendment to the Constitution to require a balanced federal budget*, 108th

Cong, 1st sess. (2003) (testimony of William Beach, director of the Center for Data Analysis at the Heritage Foundation).

93. *60 Minutes* profile of David Walker, head of the General Accounting Office and comptroller general of the United States, aired by CBS on March 4, 2007. Walker has assembled a collection of his speeches and presentations on the mounting national debt at the GAO Web site, http://www.gao.gov/cghome.htm. See, in particular, David Walker, "America in 2017: Making Tough Choices Today Can Help Save Our Future," University of Notre Dame, South Bend, Indiana, January 26, 2007.
94. Walker, "America in 2017," pp. 3–4.
95. BBAs come in a wide variety of shapes and sizes, though most share certain key structural formulations. The most recent BBA introduced in Congress, that of Representative Ernest Istook (R-OK) in February 2003, is a representative example. It includes provisions that would (a) limit outlays to receipts for a given fiscal year unless three fifths of each House voted to override, (b) direct the president to submit a balanced budget to Congress every fiscal year, and (c) provide a waiver in times of war or when both houses passed a resolution declaring that the United States "is engaged in military conflict which causes an imminent and serious military threat to national security." There are, of course, other versions. Many BBA's, for example, require a supermajority to raise taxes in addition to the balanced budget provisions outlined above.
96. See Michael Stokes Paulsen, "A General Theory of Article V: The Constitutional Lessons of the Twenty-Seventh Amendment," *Yale Law Journal* 103.3 (Dec. 1993): note 200 at p. 736.
97. Arizona, Utah, and Idaho have passed such "slate-clearing" resolutions rescinding all previous applications. See AZ: 149 *Congressional Record* S. 6976 (May 22, 2003); UT: 147 *Congressional Record* S. 10384 (Oct. 9, 2001); ID: 146 *Congressional Record* S. 739 (Feb. 23, 2000). For a more extensive discussion, see Paulsen, "A General Theory of Article V."
98. For one account, see "Budget Amendment Is Still One Vote Short," *St. Louis Post-Dispatch*, March 2, 1995. Several prominent Democrats pledged to vote against the measure at the last moment, citing concerns about Social Security in the face of massive budget cuts.
99. H.J. Res. 22, 108th Cong., 1st sess. (2003).
100. Poll quoted in Karen M. Paget, "The Balanced Budget Trap," *American Prospect*, November 1996–December 1996, p. 21.
101. Robert Greenstein, "The Balanced Budget Constitutional Amendment: An Overview," the Center on Budget and Policy Priorities, January 1997, http://www.cbpp.org/Bbaovrvw.htm.
102. All the states except Vermont have some legal requirement for a balanced budget. Some mandates are constitutional, some are statutory, and some have been derived from state judicial decisions concerning constitutional provisions about state indebtedness. See "State Balanced Budget Requirements: Executive Summary," National Conference of State Legislatures (updated April 12, 1999), http://www.ncsl.org/programs/fiscal/balreqs.htm. Also, a complete listing of the source of state balanced budget requirements (constitutional language, statutes, and judicial decisions) is available through the National Conference of State Legislatures, updated March 2004: http://www.ncsl.org/programs/fiscal/balbudb.htm.
103. Richard Briffault, "*Balancing Acts: The Reality Behind State Balanced Budget Requirements,*" Twentieth Century Fund, 1996.
104. Paget, "The Balanced Budget Trap."

105. Ibid.
106. Ibid.
107. "Why a Balanced Budget Amendment Must Include True Tax Limitation," the Heritage Foundation, January 24, 1995. http://www.heritage.org/Research/budget/bu237.cfm.
108. Greenstein, "The Balanced Budget Constitutional Amendment."
109. A study that explored the popularity of BBA proposals among voters found that the single greatest predictor of support for a federal BBA was conservative ideology. See David C. Nice, "State Support for Constitutional Balanced Budget Requirements," *Journal of Politics* 48.1 (Feb. 1986): 142.
110. Supra at note 107.
111. Daniel J. Mitchell, "Why a Tax Limitation/Balanced Budget Amendment Is Necessary to Control Spending," the Heritage Foundation, February 19, 1997, http://www.heritage.org/research/budget/BG1104.cfm.
112. Paget, "The Balanced Budget Trap."
113. Cited in Greenstein, "The Balanced Budget Constitutional Amendment."
114. Laurence H. Tribe, "Issues Raised by Requesting Congress to Call a Constitutional Convention to Propose a Balanced Budget Amendment," *Pacific Law Journal* 10 (1979): 629.
115. Ibid.
116. Laurence H. Tribe, "The Balanced Budget Amendment: An Inquiry into Appropriateness," *Harvard Law Review* 96.7 (May 1983): 1605.
117. *Lochner v. New York* (198 U.S. 45). See Howard Gillman, *The Constitution Besieged: The Rise and Fall of Lochner Era Police Powers Jurisprudence*. Durham, NC: Duke University Press, 1993.
118. Supra at note 88.
119. E. Donald Elliott, "Constitutional Conventions and the Deficit," *Duke Law Journal* 1985.6 (Dec. 1985): 1077–1110.
120. James Madison, *The* Federalist *No. 10*, quoted in ibid.
121. See, for example, David Mayhew, *Congress: The Electoral Connection* (New Haven, CT: Yale University Press, 2004). See also Morris Fiorina, *Congress, Keystone of the Washington Establishment* (New Haven, CT: Yale University Press, 1989).
122. Mancur Olson, *The Logic of Collective Action: Public Goods and the Theory of Groups* (Cambridge: Harvard University Press, 1971).
123. Elliott, "Constitutional Conventions," pp. 1091–92.
124. William Greider, "The Education of David Stockman," *Atlantic Monthly*, December 1981, p. 27.
125. Tribe, *Harvard Law Review*, supra at note 116.
126. Quoted in Greenstein, "The Balanced Budget Constitutional Amendment."
127. Gay Aynesworth Crosthwait, "Article III Problems in Enforcing the Balanced Budget Amendment," *Columbia Law Review* 83.4 (May 1983): 1065–1107.
128. Outlined in Bruce Kogan, "Enforcement of a Constitutional Balanced Budget Amendment: Questions without Answers," Center on Budget and Policy Priorities, January 6, 1997, http://www.cbpp.org/BBAENFRC.htm.
129. The federal budget was in surplus during fiscal years 1998 ($69.2 billion), 1999 ($122.7 billion), and 2000 (approximately $230 billion). See Kelly Wallace, "President Clinton Announces Another Record Budget Surplus," September 27, 2000, CNN.com, http://archives.cnn.com/2000/ALLPOLITICS/stories/09/27/clinton.surplus/.
130. An improving economy began lowering the deficit as of 2006, but even at a reduced level, its size remained breathtaking at $248 billion, added on top of the gigantic,

multitrillion-dollar, cumulative federal debt. See "Budget Management: Fiscal Discipline and Managing for Results," http://www.whitehouse.gov/infocus/budget/2007/index.html.

131. Estimate provided by the U.S. Department of the Treasury. The interest payments in 2007 will amount to $229 billion. This is 17 percent of the annual federal receipts of $2.54 trillion.
132. For a full account, see William M. Arkin, "Back to the Bunker," *Washington Post*, June 4, 2006. President Clinton's COG plan required every government department and agency to draw up a plan allowing it to restore critical functions within twelve hours of an emergency warning as well as to work from emergency facilities for up to thirty days. FEMA (Federal Emergency Management Agency) was charged with coordinating the COG plan—not necessarily a good choice.
133. For a harrowing account, see *The 9/11 Commission Report: Final Report of the National Commission on Terrorist Attacks upon the United States* (Washington, DC: Government Printing Office, 2004). The full report is available online at http://www.gpoaccess.gov/911/index.html.
134. The Continuity of Government Commission, *Preserving Our Institutions: The Continuity of Congress* (Washington, DC: AEI/Brookings, 2003). Available online at http://www.continuityofgovernment.org/pdfs/FirstReport.htm. Hereafter referred to as *COG Report.*
135. U.S. Const., Art. I, Sec. 5, Cl. 1.
136. *COG Report*, p. 9.
137. For example, Senator Carter Glass (D-VA) held on to his seat during a severe four-year-long illness until his death in 1946, even though he was unable to travel to Washington or to cast a vote on the Senate floor. Another sad instance occurred in the case of Senator Karl Mundt (R-SD), who never resigned his seat for two full years in the early 1970s despite being comatose after a stroke. There are many other cases, detailed at http://www.cqpolitics.com/2006/12/senate_has_history_of_lengthy.html. The most recent instance occurred when the South Dakota Democratic senator Tim Johnson had a severe strokelike episode in December 2006. Had he died, control of the closely divided Senate would have gone to the Republicans because the GOP governor of South Dakota would have appointed a Republican replacement. As it happened, Johnson lived, but he faced many months of rehabilitation and absence from the Senate.
138. A few states, including Oregon and Wisconsin, require Senate vacancies to be filled through special election rather than gubernatorial appointment. For a discussion of Senate-vacancy procedures, see Sula P. Richardson and Thomas H. Neale, "House and Senate Vacancies: How Are They Filled?" CRS Report for Congress, January 22, 2003, http://www.senate.gov/artandhistory/history/resources/pdf/Vacancies.pdf.
139. Hawaii and Wyoming currently have just such provisions in their laws governing gubernatorial appointments to the Senate. Of course, these existing statutes do not stop a governor from choosing a person who may be philosophically and ideologically different from the replaced incumbent, but at least the party identification of the Senate seat will remain the same. Later in this section, a new method will be proposed that guarantees the new appointee not only is of the same party but votes similarly to the replaced incumbent.
140. CPEC's Web site is at http://www.electcongress.org/.
141. The former House Judiciary chairman James Sensenbrenner (R-WI) is one such influential critic. Chairman Sensenbrenner personally helped to thwart any COG amendment in the 108th Congress, since these proposals were referred to the

Judiciary Committee in the House. See 108th Cong., 2nd sess., House Report 108–503, *Proposing an Amendment to the Constitution of the United States Regarding the Appointment of Individuals to Fill Vacancies in the House of Representatives*, available through the Library of Congress's THOMAS legislative information system. Sensenbrenner has written these words about the COG proposals: "Such proposals would deny the right to elected representation and accomplish what no terrorist could, by striking a fatal blow to what has always been 'The People's House.'" See James Sensenbrenner, "Preserving the 'People's House,'" *Washington Post*, June 2, 2004.

142. The *Federalist Papers* are available online at http://www.foundingfathers.info/federalistpapers/fedindex.htm.
143. *COG Report*, p. 24.
144. The following paragraphs are primarily drawn from the recommendations contained in the AEI/Brookings COG Commission, but they also include my own interpretations and suggestions.
145. As of August 2006, more than fifty members of Congress were relatives of other members. There were four sets of siblings, four widows, dozens of offspring, and spouses. See Jill Lawrence, "Congress Full of Fortunate Sons—and Other Relatives," *USA Today*, August 8, 2006.
146. Several COG amendments have been proposed since 9/11. Congresswoman Zoe Lofgren (D-CA) and Senator John Cornyn (R-TX) both offered amendments that would give Congress broad power to design replacement appointments. Congressman Brian Baird (D-WA) also introduced an amendment that would use the "replacement list" method outlined above. Whatever happens with COG, consideration should be given to applying the "replacement list" idea to all Senate vacancies. Why should a gubernatorial appointment be permitted to switch party control of the Senate, as probably would have happened had Senator Tim Johnson (D) died from his bleeding embolism in the brain in December 2006? Republican governor Mike Rounds of South Dakota would almost certainly have appointed a GOP replacement, turning the 51D-to-49R Senate into a 50–50 Senate with the ties broken by GOP vice president Dick Cheney.
147. For an excellent account of the fight for a COG amendment in Congress, see Thomas E. Mann and Norman Ornstein, "The Case of Continuity," chapter 6 in *The Broken Branch: How Congress Is Failing America and How to Get It Back on Track* (New York: Oxford University Press, 2006).

2. Perfecting the Presidency

1. Whether the presidents would have done so is unknowable, though one suspects they would have, based on their own comments at the time and afterward, as well as those of their key advisers.
2. The notes of the Constitutional Convention reveal that Edmund Randolph, then the governor of Virginia and a convention delegate, proposed that the "executive should consist of three members, to be drawn from different parts of the country," in order to ensure the independence of the executive from ambition and local politics. Still, he added, it would be "doubtful whether even a council will be sufficient to check the improper views of an ambitious man." William Paterson of New Jersey also suggested that a number of people should together comprise the executive. Roger Sherman of Connecticut believed that the executives "ought to be appointed and accountable to the Legislature only," suggesting that the number of executives

be left to the discretion of Congress. For more on the framers' comments at the Constitutional Convention, see Jane Butzner, ed., *Constitutional Chaff: Rejected Suggestions of the Constitutional Convention of 1787* (Port Washington, NY: Kennikat Press, 1970), especially p. 84.

3. Elbridge Gerry, a convention delegate from Massachusetts, suggested that a council be "annexed to the Executive in order to give weight and inspire confidence," even suggesting that the views of the council members be recorded so that the threat of impeachment would keep them accountable. Roger Sherman also supported the use of an advisory council "without which the first magistrate cannot act." See Butzner, *Constitutional Chaff*, p. 85.
4. From Jefferson's *Notes on the State of Virginia*, query 13, p. 245. Available online at http://etext.lib.virginia.edu/.
5. The Articles (Article IX) permitted a president to serve the one-year term and then be eligible for election again after having been out of the presidential office for at least two years. As it happened, no one was elected more than once to the presidency under the Articles. The other presidents after John Hanson were: Elias Boudinot, Thomas Mifflin, Richard Henry Lee, John Hancock, Nathan Gorman, Arthur St. Clair, and Cyrus Griffin. See http://www.marshallhall.org/hanson.html. See also http://www.yale.edu/lawweb/avalon/artconf.htm. It is vital to stress that, whereas the presidency we know today was established by the Constitution of 1787 and has always been the chief executive of a unified nation, the presidency envisioned by the Articles of Confederation was the executive officer of the Congress only. The Articles functioned more as a pact among sovereign states than as a unifying instrument, meaning that George Washington *was* the first president of the truly *United* States of America.
6. The term *elective kingship* dates back to Henry Jones Ford's *The Rise and Growth of American Politics: A Sketch of Constitutional Development* (New York: Macmillan, 1898), p. 293: "In the presidential office . . . American democracy has revived the oldest political institution of the race, the elective kingship. It is all there: the precognition of the notables and the tumultuous choice of the freemen, only conformed to modern conditions."
7. The president takes the power to receive ambassadors from Art. II, Sec. 3; the power to veto laws from Art. I, Sec. 7, Cl. 2; and the power of appointments from Art. II, Sec. 2, Cl. 2. The other six grants of power enable the president to act as commander in chief (Art. II, Sec. 2, Cl. 1), maintain order (Art. IV, Sec. 4), negotiate treaties (Art. II, Sec. 2, Cl. 2), faithfully execute laws (Art. II, Sec. 3), grant pardons (Art. II, Sec. 2, Cl. 1), and address Congress on the State of the Union (Art. II, Sec. 3).
8. While James Madison was not notably weaker than Thomas Jefferson, the successors to the other three presidents mentioned here, Martin Van Buren after Jackson, Andrew Johnson after Lincoln, and William Howard Taft after Theodore Roosevelt, respectively, certainly were less impressive chief executives.
9. The term *electronic throne* was first used by Fred Friendly in his foreword to *Presidential Television*, a book by Newton N. Minow, John Bartlow Martin, and Lee M. Mitchell (New York: Basic Books, 1973). Calling television a "miracle that American society has never learned to manage," Friendly added, "The drafters of the American Constitution strove diligently to prevent the power of the president from becoming a monopoly, but our inability to manage television has allowed the medium to be converted into an electronic throne."
10. See Arthur M. Schlesinger Jr., *The Imperial Presidency* (New York: Popular Library, 1974).

11. One should note that the 1973 law commonly referred to as the "War Powers Act" is officially called the "War Powers Resolution," Pub. L. no. 93-148, 87 Stat. 555 (1973) (codified at 50 U.S.C., Secs. 1541–48 [1982]). The official "War Powers Act" refers to a 1917 act that regulated trade with enemies of the United States during states of emergency. Besides the War Powers Resolution, Congress's other two attempts to retake ground occurred in the passage of the Congressional Budget and Impoundment Control Act of 1974 and the National Emergencies Act, each having limited success. The Congressional Budget and Impoundment Control Act was intended "to reassert the congressional role in budgeting, to add some centralizing influence to the Federal budget process, and to constrain the use of impoundments." More on the Congressional Budget and Impoundment Control Act of 1974 can be found in the 1993 final report of the Joint Committee on the Organization of Congress, S. Rept. no. 103-215, part 2, 103rd Cong., 1st sess. 32 (1993). The National Emergencies Act (Pub. L. no. 94-412, 90 Stat. 1255 [1976] [codified at 50 U.S.C., Sec. 1601 (1982)]) terminated many of the powers of the president held as a result of previous declarations of national emergency, many of which had been established decades earlier and never officially ended. The act also sets forth provisions for the president to report to Congress on the details of emergencies, when declared, but these provisions have often been sidestepped or simply ignored altogether. For more on the emergency powers of the presidency, see Jules Lobel, "Emergency Power and the Decline of Liberalism," *Yale Law Journal* 98.7 (May 1989): 1385–1433, especially 1412–18.
12. For books on the Iran Hostage Crisis, see David Harris, *The Crisis* (New York: Little, Brown, 2004); David Patrick Houghton, *US Foreign Policy and the Iran Hostage Crisis* (Cambridge: Cambridge University Press, 2001); and David Farber, *The Iran Hostage Crisis and America's First Encounter with Radical Islam* (Princeton, NJ: Princeton University Press, 2005).
13. The states that continued to allow the electors to be chosen by state legislatures in 1824 were Delaware, Georgia, Louisiana, New York, South Carolina, and Vermont. The major candidates were incumbent John Quincy Adams, Andrew Jackson, William Harris Crawford, and Henry Clay, with Jackson earning 99 electoral votes (151,271 popular votes), Adams earning 84 electoral votes (113,122 popular votes), Crawford winning 41 electoral votes (40,856 popular votes), and Clay winning 37 electoral votes (47,531 popular votes). The figures for popular votes obviously do not include the six states that had not yet instituted popular elections. For the first time since the passage of the Twelfth Amendment, no candidate received a majority of the electoral votes. Once the election was sent to the House, the campaign tricks and political maneuvering intensified. For more on the 1824 election, see Robert V. Remini, *John Quincy Adams* (New York: Times Books, 2002), pp. 62–74 and Everett S. Brown, "The Presidential Election of 1824–1825," *Political Science Quarterly* 40.3 (Sept. 1925): 384–403. For more on Andrew Jackson, see Richard E. Ellis, *Andrew Jackson* (Washington, DC: CQ Press, 2003) and Robert V. Remini, *The Election of Andrew Jackson* (Philadelphia, PA: Lippincott, 1963).
14. See Congressional Quarterly, *Guide to U.S. Elections* (Washington, DC: Congressional Quarterly, 1975), pp. 202–5, 263–66.
15. The switch from legislative choice of electors to popular choice was as much about the practical politics as it was democratic ideals. Just prior to the 1800 presidential election, Jefferson successfully persuaded his home state of Virginia to switch to popular choice of electors in order to ensure that he won Virginia's electoral votes in the upcoming election. In Maryland, state legislators campaigned on the issue, and

the state's Federalists pushed for legislative choice, knowing that such a move would secure their state's electoral votes for John Adams in his reelection campaign. But when the Democratic-Republicans took over Maryland's legislature, they opted for choice of electors by the voters in each congressional district separately. On election day, the districts split for Adams and Jefferson. Had the Federalists kept control of the legislature—and their electors—Adams would have won all ten of Maryland's electors and, therefore, reelection. See David F. Forte, "Marbury's Travail: Federalist Politics and William Marbury's Appointment as Justice of the Peace," *Catholic University Law Review* 45 (Winter 1996): 349–403, especially 394–96.

16. For more on political primaries, see pp. 3–5 of Larry J. Sabato, *The Democratic Party Primary in Virginia: Tantamount to Election No Longer* (Charlottesville, VA: University of Virginia Press, 1977). Also see Charles E. Merriam, and Louise Overacker, *Primary Elections* (Chicago: University of Chicago Press, 1928); Cortez A. M. Ewing, *Primary Elections in the South: A Study in Uniparty Politics* (Norman: University of Oklahoma Press, 1953); and Charles E. Merriam, *Primary Elections: A Study of the History and Tendencies of Primary Election Legislation* (Chicago: University of Chicago Press, 1909).
17. In some states, primaries were also required for U.S. Senate seats, even though the seats were still formally filled by the state legislatures, as required at the time by the U.S. Constitution. In that sense, the primaries were "advisory" elections, but state legislators who wanted to be reelected obviously were inclined to support their voters' choice.
18. The first presidential primaries were still generally controlled by party machinery. In 1912, thirteen states held primaries, and despite the fact that Teddy Roosevelt won nine, Taft used his political muscle to win the Republican nomination. Four years later, there would be twenty primaries, a number that fluctuated upward and downward a bit until the early 1970s. At that point, partly due to rules changes by the Democrats that encouraged primaries as an alternative to "boss-controlled" conventions, the number of primaries began to rise substantially. Regardless of the number held in any given year, primaries were used by candidates to show that they had popular support, since winning primaries did not mean a candidate would win the nomination. In 1952 the New Hampshire primary stole the spotlight for the first time, and Dwight D. Eisenhower's win over Senator Robert Taft helped give him the momentum to win the Republican nomination. John F. Kennedy used primaries to show that his religious beliefs were not an impediment to his electability. In 1972 George McGovern became the last candidate to win his party's nomination without winning a plurality of presidential primaries. A majority of states were holding primaries by 1976, and by 1988 Super Tuesday encompassed every southern state but South Carolina, helping make presidential primaries an even greater political and media event. See Rhodes Cook, *United States Presidential Primary Elections, 1968–1996: A Handbook of Election Statistics* (Washington, DC: CQ Press, 2000), time line on p. 8.
19. For more on the New Hampshire primary, see Niall A. Palmer, *The New Hampshire Primary and the American Electoral Process* (Westport, CT: Praeger, 1997) and Dante J. Scala, *Stormy Weather: The New Hampshire Primary and Presidential Politics* (New York, NY: Palgrave Macmillan, 2003).
20. The number of primaries varies every four years, as some states switch from primaries to caucuses, and vice versa. Over time, though, the trend has strongly favored an increase in the number of primaries.
21. In three recent instances, the nominees did not emerge until the final primaries were over and the convention held: 1972, with George McGovern (D); 1976, when

President Gerald Ford barely beat back an insurgent challenge from Ronald Reagan (R); and 1984, when former vice president Walter Mondale edged Senator Gary Hart at the Democratic convention. States have recently chosen to ignore these exceptions in their rush to the front of the pack every presidential election year. This phenomenon is discussed in chapter 4, on the election process.

22. The Democrats have added the Nevada caucus for the 2008 season, and the Silver State is scheduled to follow Iowa and precede New Hampshire, which remains the first primary. New Hampshire is resisting, and threatening to move up the date of its primary to early January 2008—or even December 2007. If this happens, the nominating period would be still earlier, of course.

23. In a letter to Elihu B. Washburne of Galveston, Texas, on March 25, 1880, Grant dismissed his friend's suggestion that he "authorize some one to say that in no event would Grant consent to ever being a candidate" for a third term, saying, "If they think my chances are better for election than for other probable candidates in case I should decline, I cannot decline if the nomination is tendered without seeking on my part." See *General Grant's Letters to a Friend, 1861–1880* (New York: Crowell), pp. 106–7. For other books on Grant, see Michael Korda, *Ulysses S. Grant* (New York: HarperCollins, 2004) and Josiah Bunting III, *Ulysses S. Grant* (New York: Times Books, 2004).

24. Wilson rejected pleas from his friends and political allies that he not run for a third term, and instead he often made public appearances that seemed to indicate he had every intention of seeking reelection. He often expressed reservations about the other candidates who might take his place, and pushed on with his desire for a third term even after he had collapsed from a stroke. See pp. 54–64 of Wesley M. Bagby's *The Road to Normalcy: The Presidential Campaign and Election of 1920* (Baltimore, MD: Johns Hopkins Press, 1968). Also see H. W. Brands, *Woodrow Wilson* (New York: Times Books, 2003).

25. Just after the election had been won, November 9, 1904, Roosevelt announced, "On the fourth of March next I shall have served three and a half years, and this three and a half years constitutes my first term. The wise custom which limits the President to two terms regards the substance and not the form. Under no circumstances will I be a candidate for or accept another nomination." This has often been referred to by Roosevelt historians and biographers as the biggest mistake of his political career, making him a lame duck almost immediately. See Mario R. Dinunzio, *Theodore Roosevelt* (Washington, DC: CQ Press, 2003), especially pp. 102–3. Also see Louis Auchincloss, *Theodore Roosevelt* (New York: Times Books, 2001).

26. With 41.8 percent of the popular vote, Wilson took 435 electoral votes, far more than the 266 required to win. Roosevelt's 88 electoral votes (27.4 percent of the popular vote) bested Taft's 8 electoral votes (23.2 percent of the popular vote), but added together, the Republican and Progressive votes would have produced the majority of electoral votes needed to win the White House. The candidate securing a plurality of the popular vote in a state wins all the electoral votes, of course. Had only Roosevelt, or only Taft, run, the GOP vote would not have been divided, and thus, the Republican candidate would have defeated Wilson in many of the states that the Democrat captured in a three-way race. Instead, the decision by Roosevelt to turn his back on his handpicked successor, Taft, produced a split that gave Wilson the election. See James Change, *1912* (New York: Simon and Schuster, 2004).

27. Serious speculation that Wilson and Theodore Roosevelt would go head-to-head in bids for a third term surfaced as early as 1918. Roosevelt had been criticizing Wilson throughout Wilson's years in office, and once Taft and Roosevelt reconciled their

differences stemming from the 1912 election, Roosevelt's name was at the top of nearly everyone's list as the potential Republican candidate for 1920. See Denunzio, *Theodore Roosevelt*, p. 17 and Bagby, *The Road to Normalcy*, p. 54.

28. Concerning Eisenhower's comments against the Twenty-second Amendment, see Sherman Adams's *Firsthand Report: The Story of the Eisenhower Administration* (New York: Harper, 1961), especially p. 296. Reagan began pushing for repeal of the Twenty-second Amendment during his second term, and he addressed the topic in his farewell address, saying, "I believe it's a preemption of the people's right to vote for whomever they want as many times as they want." The only Democratic president who might have been able to win reelection since the adoption of the Twenty-second Amendment, Bill Clinton, has also publicly called for its repeal. Clinton has additionally suggested that, if the amendment must be kept, it should apply only to two consecutive terms, so that a president could seek a third term after he had been out of office at least four years.
29. President Ford served more than half of President Nixon's second term from August 9, 1974, to January 20, 1977. Had Ford been elected in 1976, he could not have run for reelection in 1980.
30. See David Nice, "Party Realignment and Presidential Tenure: Some Implications for the Six-Year Term Proposal," *Policies Studies Journal* 13.2 (Dec. 1984): 295–302; James L. Sundquist, *Constitutional Reform and Effective Government* (Washington, DC: Brookings Institution, 1986); and Donald L. Robinson, ed., *Reforming American Government: The Bicentennial Papers of the Committee on the Constitutional System* (Boulder, CO: Westview Press, 1985), especially pp. 167–87.
31. For books on Watergate, see Carl Bernstein and Bob Woodward, *All the President's Men* (New York: Simon and Schuster, 1999); Bob Woodward, *The Secret Man: The Story of Watergate's Deep Throat* (New York: Simon and Schuster, 2005); Harry P. Jeffrey and Thomas Maxwell-Long, *Watergate and the Resignation of Richard Nixon: Impact of a Constitutional Crisis* (Washington, DC: CQ Press, 2004); and Keith W. Olson, *Watergate: The Presidential Scandal that Shook America* (Lawrence: University Press of Kansas, 2003).
32. The Presidential Appointee Initiative, begun by the Brookings Institution, has worked to review the problems of the nominating process and to propose reforms. This study can be found online at http://www.appointee.brookings.org. See especially *The Merit and Reputation of an Administration: Presidential Appointees on the Appointments Process,* a report jointly published by the Brookings Institution and the Heritage Foundation (Apr. 18, 2000).
33. *Democracy in America*, vol. I, book 1, chapter 8, online at http://xroads.virginia.edu. Quoted in Alice O'Connor, *So Great a Power to Any Single Person: The Presidential Term and Executive Power* (Washington, DC: Jefferson Foundation, 1984), pp. 11 and 22.
34. President Carter recognized precisely this point, citing pundits' criticisms that his actions were merely "campaign ploys" as burdening his work in the White House. Taking reelection out of the picture, Carter believed, would have "strengthened [his] hand with Congress." See James L. Sundquist, "Six-Year Presidential Term," *Encyclopedia of the American Presidency*, vol. 4 (New York: Simon and Schuster, 1993), p. 1374.
35. Former secretary of state Cyrus Vance understood this well, once commenting, "I do not at all doubt that a single six-year term would add important dimensions of continuity and stability to the conduct of our foreign relations [which are] affected by the preoccupation with presidential reelection." Quoted in O'Connor, *So Great a Power*, p. 23.

36. J. William Fulbright, *The Arrogance of Power* (New York: Random House, 1967), quotation taken from p. 3.
37. Twenty presidents sought and won reelection: Washington, Jefferson, Madison, Monroe, Jackson, Lincoln, Grant, Cleveland (in 1892), McKinley, Theodore Roosevelt, Wilson, Coolidge, Franklin D. Roosevelt, Truman, Eisenhower, Lyndon B. Johnson, Nixon, Reagan, Clinton, and George W. Bush. Ten lost in reelection campaigns: John Adams, John Quincy Adams, Van Buren, Cleveland (in 1888), Benjamin Harrison, Taft, Hoover, Ford, Carter, and George H. W. Bush. Note that Cleveland appears in both lists. Additionally, Tyler, Fillmore, Pierce, Andrew Johnson, and Arthur desired another term but did not actively run and earn the nomination of their party. It was clear to them in advance that they would not be successful, and so formal candidacies never materialized.
38. See Charles Peters, *Five Days in Philadelphia: Wendell Willkie, Franklin Roosevelt and the 1940 Election That Saved the Western World* (New York: Public Affairs, 2005).
39. For more on FDR's battle with polio, see Hugh Gregory Gallagher, *FDR's Splendid Deception* (New York: Dodd, Mead, 1985); Herman E. Bateman, "Observations on President Roosevelt's Health during World War II," *Mississippi Valley Historical Review* 23.1 (June 1956): 82–102; and William E. Leuchtenburg, ed., *Franklin D. Roosevelt: A Profile* (New York: Hill and Wang, 1967), especially pp. 34–44.
40. The reference here is to the twin Bush presidencies and the potential for twin Clinton presidencies. These two families have maintained a duopoly on the White House since 1989. At the state level, term limits have occasionally resulted in shenanigans we would prefer not to see at the national level. Forced out of the governor's office by a term limit in 1966, George Wallace of Alabama successfully ran his wife, Lurleen, to succeed him; he governed for her until her death from cancer in 1968. Then there is the example from Tennessee, where term-limited Democrats Frank Clement and Buford Ellington kept leapfrogging each other's terms, occupying the state's governorship consistently from 1953 to 1971. It is not hard to imagine something similar at the national level.
41. Occasionally, a presidential candidate may run specifically on a single, six-year-term pledge, akin to the one-term pledge taken by the successful presidential candidate James K. Polk (D) in 1844. Other presidents, like Rutherford B. Hayes (R), elected in a disputed vote count in 1876, may choose to serve only the six-year term and announce that decision early in the term, in order to promote unity and a relatively "nonpartisan" administration. For books on James K. Polk, see John Seigenthaler, *James K. Polk* (New York: Times Books, 2004) and Mark E. Byrnes, *James K. Polk: A Biographical Companion* (Santa Barbara, CA. ABC-CLIO, 2001). For Rutherford B. Hayes, see Hans L. Trefousse, *Rutherford B. Hayes* (New York: Times Books, 2002) and Ari Hoogenboom, *The Presidency of Rutherford B. Hayes* (Lawrence: University Press of Kansas, 1988).
42. Arthur M. Schlesinger Jr. described the painful transition period between Hoover and FDR as "the hiatus, the great void. The old regime's writ had run, while the new had no power to break the stagnation . . . and, suspended between past and future, the nation drifted as on the dark seas of unreality." See *The Age of Roosevelt: Crisis of the Old Order, 1919–1933*, 1st Mariner Books ed. (Boston: Houghton Mifflin, 2003), especially pp. 440–85. The Schlesinger quotation is found on p. 456.
43. That is, a vice president could succeed shortly after Inauguration Day, as Presidents John Tyler and Harry Truman did, following the deaths of, respectively, Presidents William Henry Harrison in 1841 and Franklin Roosevelt in 1945. If permitted

reelection after a successful confirmation vote, this president will have served nearly eight years in the first term, and possibly another eight years in the second term. Fifteen to sixteen consecutive years in the White House would strain any human being, and it would give pause even to ardent advocates of repeal of the Twenty-second Amendment.

44. The Twenty-second Amendment, adopted in 1951, reads in part, "no person who has held the office of President, or acted as President, for more than two years of a term to which some other person was elected President shall be elected to the office of President more than once." Thus, if a vice president succeeds to office anytime after noon on January 20 of the halfway point of a presidential term, he or she may run for two full four-year terms as president.
45. Republican U.S. Senator James Jeffords of Vermont, a moderate-liberal legislator unhappy with the conservative drift of the GOP, decided to switch to Independent status but vote with the Democrats to reorganize the Senate in May 2001. When his action took effect in June, the Senate switched from Republican control to Democratic control. The Senate had been tied, with 50 senators from each party; Vice President Cheney (R) had broken the tie in January 2001 to give the Republicans effective dominance of the Senate. With Jeffords's vote, the Democrats gained the upper hand by the thin margin of 51 to 49 in the 100-member body.
46. In 1932 thirty-three states held their gubernatorial elections during presidential election years. By 1980 only thirteen did so, and that number is now eleven. Usually, the states created special two-year gubernatorial terms to make the transition, and the same terms are applied to other statewide officers.
47. See also Sundquist, *Constitutional Reform and Effective Government* and Bruce Ackerman, "The New Separation of Powers," *Harvard Law Review* 113.3 (Jan. 2000): 633–727. By the way, should term limits for members of Congress be enacted, as advocated in chapter 1, then those "generous" limits would have to be slightly adjusted upward to fit the new House and Senate terms suggested here, with perhaps a maximum of sixteen years in each chamber instead of the twelve years that were prescribed earlier.
48. See especially John Hart Ely, *War and Responsibility: Constitutional Lessons of Vietnam and Its Aftermath* (Princeton, NJ: Princeton University Press, 1993), as well as Charles A. Lofgren, "War-Making under the Constitution: The Original Understanding," *Yale Law Journal* 81.4 (Mar. 1972): 672–702.
49. Ely, *War and Responsibility*, p. 3.
50. See James Madison's notes on June 19, 1787, from "The Debates in the Federal Convention of 1787."
51. After a lengthy study of this issue, Charles Lofgren concluded that "although the change from 'make' to 'declare' in the clause empowering Congress 'to declare War' was open to several interpretations among the members of the Philadelphia Convention, there is enough evidence . . . that the new Congress' power 'to declare War' was not understood in a narrow, technical sense but rather as meaning the power to commence war, whether declared or not." See Lofgren, "War-Making," p. 699.
52. Quotation from Gaillard Hunt, ed., *The Writings of James Madison*, vol. 6 (New York: G. P. Putnam's Sons, 1900–1910), pp. 312–14. Madison made the case that the executive could not launch a war without Congress at length in 1793, noting in part: "A declaration that there shall be war, is not an execution of laws. It does not suppose pre existing laws to be executed. It is not in any respect, an act merely executive. It is, on the contrary, one of the most deliberative acts that can be performed, and when performed, has the effect of repealing all the laws operating in a state of peace . . .

Another important inference to be noted is, that the powers of making war and treaty being substantially of a legislative, not an executive nature, the rule of interpreting exceptions strictly, must narrow instead of enlarging executive pretensions on those subjects." See James Madison, "'Helvidius' No. I," August 24, 1793. Thomas Jefferson clearly agreed with Madison, as he wrote in the same year of 1793 about the capture of a British vessel, "The making of a reprisal on a nation is a very serious thing. Remonstrance and refusal of satisfaction ought to precede; and when reprisal follows, it is considered as an act of war, and never yet failed to produce it in the case of a nation able to make war; besides, if the case were important enough to require reprisal, and ripe for that step, Congress must be called on to take it; the right of reprisal being expressly lodged with them by the Constitution, and not with the Executive." See Thomas Jefferson, "Opinion on the Capture of a British Vessel," 1793, as quoted in Andrew A. Lipscomb and Ellery Bergh, eds., *The Writings of Thomas Jefferson*, vol. 3 (Washington, DC: Thomas Jefferson Memorial Association, 1904), on p. 250.

53. From Abraham Lincoln to William H. Herndon from Washington, D.C., February 15, 1848. Herndon's letter to Lincoln defended Polk's actions in the Mexican-American War, when Polk used military muscle against the Mexican forces days shy of any formal resolutions from Congress. Lincoln was taking Herndon to task, and he concluded, "But your view destroys the whole matter, and places our President where kings have always stood."
54. See Louis Fisher, *Presidential War Power*, 2nd ed. (Lawrence: University Press of Kansas, 2004), especially p. 275. See also note 9, supra.
55. In Bush's "Letter to Congressional Leaders on the Deployment of United States Armed Forces to Saudi Arabia and the Middle East" on August 9, 1990, he told Congress that his deployment of forces was taken "pursuant to [his] constitutional authority to conduct our foreign relations and as Commander in Chief." Far from asking for Congress's consent, Bush told Congress, "[I am only providing] this report on the deployment and mission of our Armed Forces in accordance with my desire that Congress be fully informed and *consistent with* the War Powers Resolution." (Emphasis mine.) The wording of *consistent with* rather than *pursuant to* or *under* has been used by every president who deployed forces abroad since 1973. While the War Powers Resolution requires such a report be sent to Congress, each president has uniformly demonstrated his belief that the War Powers Resolution is illegitimate by refusing to say that he is governed by it, especially through the use of carefully chosen words such as these.
56. The Persian Gulf War Resolution passed the Senate (102 S.J. Res. 2) 52 to 47 and the House (102 H. J. Res. 77) 250 to 183 on January 12, 1991.
57. See "Authorization for Use of Military Force," Pub. L. no. 107-140, 115 Stat. 224 (2001).
58. See "Authorization for the Use of Military Force Against Iraq," Pub. L. no. 107-243, 116 Stat. 1498 (2002).
59. See Fisher, *Presidential War Power*, p. 262.
60. See David Gray Adler, "The Constitution and Presidential Warmaking: The Enduring Debate," *Political Science Quarterly* 103.1 (Spring 1988): 1–36, especially 34. See also Peter Irons, "War Powers: How the Imperial Presidency Hijacked the Constitution" (New York: Metropolitan, 2005).
61. At least in the current administration we can add the office of vice president to that of president in terms of zealous defense of executive authority. Vice President Dick Cheney has made a career of presidential empowerment, from his time as chief of staff to President Gerald Ford right up to the present day in the second Bush administration. See, for example, Charlie Savage, "Hail to the Chief: Dick Cheney's

Mission to Expand—or 'Restore'—the Powers of the Presidency," *Boston Globe*, (November 26, 2006).

62. Some want to go further than our suggestion here. For example, one legal scholar proposed a detailed constitutional amendment that puts Congress, not the president, in charge of military planning and execution. See Yonkel Goldstein, "The Failure of Constitutional Controls over War Powers in the Nuclear Age: The Argument for a Constitutional Amendment," *Stanford Law Review* 40.6 (July 1988): 1543–92, especially 1587. Other scholars, such as Louis Fisher, prefer that Congress assert itself using powers it already possesses. Fisher notes that Congress essentially ended the Vietnam War by means of its power of the purse in 1973, and in 1976 it stopped the Central Intelligence Agency from conducting military operations in the African nation of Angola. See Fisher, *Presidential War Power*, pp. 275–81.
63. The Gulf of Tonkin Resolution of 1964 was finally repealed by Congress on an overwhelming vote in both houses in 1970. The Nixon administration did not oppose the repeal, since withdrawal of American forces from Vietnam had already begun.
64. Jefferson's admonition is contained in Resolution IX of the "Resolutions Adopted by the Kentucky General Assembly in 1798–99." See *The Papers of Thomas Jefferson, Volume 30: 1 January 1798 to 31 January 1799* (Princeton University Press, 2003): pp. 550–56. See also http://www.princeton.edu/~tjpapers/kyres/kyadopted.html.
65. For articles on the line-item veto, see Glenn Abney and Thomas P. Lauth, "The Line-Item Veto in the States: An Instrument for Fiscal Restraint or an Instrument for Partisanship?" *Public Administration Review* 45.3 (May–June 1989): 372–77; Philip G. Joyce and Robert D. Reischauer, "The Federal Line-Item Veto: What Is It and What Will It Do?" *Public Administration Review* 57.2 (Mar.–Apr. 1997): 95–104; and Robert J. Spitzer, "The Constitutionality of the Line-Item Veto," *Political Science Quarterly* 112.2 (Summer 1997): 261–83. Also, for a case study of ten states in the South whose governors are empowered with a line-item veto, see Catherine C. Reese, "The Line-Item Veto in Practice in Ten Southern States," *Public Administration Review* 57.6 (Nov.–Dec. 1997): 510–16. For the full text of the Line Item Veto Act of 1996, see Pub. L. no. 104-130, 110 Stat. 1200 (1996) (codified at 2 U.S.C.A. Secs. 691 et seq. (Supp. 1997).
66. There are two other basic forms of item veto, *separate enrollment* and *expedited rescission*. Separate enrollment requires the enrolling clerk to break a spending bill into "minibills" for each spending item before presenting them to the president, allowing the president to veto any spending item using traditional veto power. Expedited rescission allows the president to propose cancellation of spending items and to impound the funds for a certain number of days; but it also requires that Congress approve the cancellation by vote.
67. David C. Slade, "The Power of the Purse," *World and I*, June 1, 1998. pp. 78–79.
68. Of the fifty state governors, forty-three have the power of line-item veto in some form. See Joyce and Reischauer, "The Federal Line-Item Veto," pp. 95–104. Former Wisconsin governor Patrick Lucey vetoed the word *not* in the phrase *not less than 50%* in a law concerning cooperative advertising, thus morphing what the legislature intended as a 50 percent floor to a 50 percent ceiling. See "The Partial Veto in Wisconsin," *State of Wisconsin Legislative Reference Bureau* (LRB–04–IB–1, Jan. 2004). Another former Wisconsin governor, Tommy Thompson, used his partial veto power to strike letters and numbers from bills, sometimes producing radically different laws than those intended by the legislature. For example, one budget bill—as written by the Wisconsin legislature—would have allowed courts to detain juveniles who violated certain court orders for "not more than 48 hours." The governor vetoed the phrase *48 hours* and then proceeded to cut parts of words from the

following sections until he had formed the words *ten days*. See Pet. Brief at 4-8, *State ex rel. Wisconsin Senate v. Thompson*, 144 Wis. 2d 429 (1988) (no. 87-1750-OA). The Wisconsin Supreme Court upheld the veto in that case, deciding that "the test in the veto of parts is simply whether what remains after the governor's veto is a complete and workable law." 144 Wis. 2d 429, 457. The voters of Wisconsin, however, put the brakes on such radical uses of the veto power by adopting a state constitutional amendment known as the "Vanna White Amendment," which bars the governor from creating "a new word by rejecting individual letters in the words of the enrolled bill."

69. The seventy-eight line-item vetoes cast by Clinton, constituting [savings of] $483.6 million, included thirty-eight from the military construction appropriations bill ($287 million); fourteen from Defense ($144 million); eight from Energy and Water ($19.3 million); seven from Veterans Administration/Housing and Urban Development ($14 million); three from Transportation ($6.2 million); and one from Commerce, Justice, and State ($5.0 million). From p. 758, fn. 8, of M. V. Hood III, Irwin L. Morris, and Grant W. Neeley, "Penny Pinching or Politics? The Line Item Veto and Military Construction Appropriations," *Political Research Quarterly* 52.4 (Dec. 1999): 753–66. The representatives losing the most from the vetoes were Steven Schiff, R-NM ($54 million); Brad Sherman, D-CA ($37.5 million); William Thomas, R-CA ($30 million); Owen Pickett, D-VA ($23.9 million); and John Murtha, D-PA ($23 million). Rick Rothacker, "Few Satisfied with Inaugural Use of the Line-Item Veto," *Legi-Slate News Service*, December 2, 1997, http://www.legislate.com/.
70. Figures from the Congressional Budget Office and the Bureau of the Public Debt, a division of the U.S. Department of the Treasury. Current numbers can be found online at http://www.publicdebt.treas.gov. In about the time it took to write this note, the nation's debt increased by an additional $2.5 million.
71. Hood et al., "Penny Pinching or Politics?" p. 765.
72. 524 U.S. 417 (1998).
73. From *Clinton v. City of New York:* "The Presentment Clause requires, in relevant part, that 'every Bill which shall have passed the House of Representatives and the Senate, shall, before it becomes a Law, be presented to the President of the United States; If he approves he shall sign it, but if not he shall return it,' U.S. Const., Art. I, Sec. 7, Cl. 2. There is no question that enactment of the Balanced Budget Act complied with these requirements: the House and Senate passed the bill, and the President signed it into law. It was only after the requirements of the Presentment Clause had been satisfied that the President exercised his authority under the Line Item Veto Act to cancel the spending item. Thus, the Court's problem with the Act is not that it authorizes the President to veto parts of a bill and sign others into law, but rather that it authorizes him to 'cancel'—prevent from 'having legal force or effect'—certain parts of duly enacted statutes." 524 U.S. 417, 463–464 (1998).
74. When the Line Item Veto Act initially passed, several congressmen—Senator Robert Byrd (D-WV), Senator Mark Hatfield (R-OR), Senator Carl Levin (D-MI), Senator Daniel Patrick Moynihan (D-NY), Representative David Skaggs (D-CO), and Representative Henry Waxman (D-CA)—sued in federal court to prevent its use. A federal court ruled in their favor, but the Supreme Court later reversed that decision on the grounds that the congressmen lacked standing—that is, because they had not been injured by the operation of the act, they had no grounds to bring a lawsuit (521 U.S. 811, 1997). The case in which the act was ruled unconstitutional, *Clinton v. New York*, was brought by the city of New York and several health care organizations which alleged that they had been injured when President Clinton

struck certain portions of the Balanced Budget Act of 1997. They were joined by Snake River Potato Growers, who argued they had suffered when President Clinton canceled portions of the Taxpayer Relief Act of 1997, which provided aid to farmers' cooperatives.

75. See the testimony of Akhil Amar, Southmayd Professor of Law and Political Science at Yale University, before the Senate Committee on the Judiciary in its hearing on "Maximizing Voter Choice: Opening the Presidency to Naturalized Americans," October 5, 2004.

76. See Jill A. Pryor, "The Natural-Born Citizen Clause and Presidential Eligibility: An Approach for Resolving Two Hundred Years of Uncertainty," *Yale Law Journal* 97.5. (Apr. 1988): 881–99, especially pp. 885–89.

77. Ibid.

78. Kissinger was born in Germany, Albright in Czechoslovakia, Chao in China, and Martinez in Cuba.

79. See U.S. Census Bureau 2004 American Community Survey, located at http://factfinder.census.gov/servlet/ADPTable?_bm=y&-geo_id=01000US&-qr_name=ACS_2004_EST_G00_DP2&-ds_name=&-redoLog=false&-format. This does not include 1.4 million Americans born in Puerto Rico or 167,000 born in U.S. island territories who are also not likely "natural-born" citizens. There are also 1.9 million Americans born to parents overseas whose status as "natural-born" is ambiguous at best. Keep in mind that the Census Bureau also estimates that 19.9 million foreign-born individuals are living in the United States—probably too low a figure given the high rate of illegal immigration and the tendency of these immigrants to do everything possible not to be found and counted. Over time, many of these individuals will find ways to become American citizens. A future immigration reform bill may also create a clear path for many to become citizens.

As with so many parts of the original Constitution, there is actually no legal agreement on what it means to be a "natural-born citizen." For example, as we will shortly discuss in the text, are the children of military servicemen and -women stationed abroad considered "natural-born"—or are they instead so-called citizens at law, a form of citizenry that does not have the same status as natural-born? If the former, these children could grow up to be president. If the latter, they could not. A Supreme Court decision may one day be necessary to decide this issue, and many others, if the current archaic constitutional provision is not changed. See Sarah Helene Dugene, and Mary Beth Collins, "Natural Born in the USA: The Striking Unfairness and Dangerous Ambiguity of the Constitution's Presidential Qualifications Clause and Why We Need to Fix It," *Boston University Law Review* 53.85 (Feb. 2005).

80. The arguments presented in this paragraph reflect those of Congressman John Conyers (D-MI), made in his remarks to the Senate Committee on the Judiciary in its hearing on "Maximizing Voter Choice: Opening the Presidency to Naturalized Americans," October 5, 2004.

81. Michigan governor George Romney, running for the Republican presidential nomination in 1968, was born in Mexico while his parents were on a Mormon Church missionary trip. The "native-born" qualification was of concern to some of his supporters, and if he had been successful in his quest for the GOP nod, Romney could easily have become the Court "test case" for this category of citizen that may fall under that provision of the Constitution. Of course, he lost the nomination to Richard Nixon. It is probably only a matter of time before someone else with a biography similar to Romney's runs for president and secures a major party nomination. At that point, perhaps the Court will clarify some of the constitutional particulars.

3. The New Courts: Supreme but Not Eternal

1. According to the Radio-Television Directors Association and Foundation, nineteen states generally allow cameras inside their courtrooms; fifteen states do so within certain limitations; and sixteen states do so with substantial restrictions, often allowing the filming of only appellate proceedings. For more information, see "Cameras in the Court: A State by State Guide," Radio-Television Directors Association and Foundation, 2005 (http://www.rtnda.org/foi/scc.shtml).
2. No federal courts allow the filming of trials, but federal appeals courts have the authority to decide on their own whether or not their oral arguments will be televised. Currently two of the thirteen appeals courts (the Second and Ninth Circuit Courts of Appeals) allow oral arguments to be filmed. See Lorraine H. Tong, *Televising Supreme Court and Other Federal Court Proceedings: Legislation and Issues*, Congressional Research Service, November 8, 2006, available online at http://www.fas.org/sgp/crs/secrecy/RL33706.pdf. In his confirmation hearings before the Senate Judiciary Committee, Justice Samuel Alito revealed he had voted to allow cameras to film the proceedings of the Third Circuit Court of Appeals—though the majority voted to keep cameras out. In the same hearings, Justice Alito said it would be "presumptuous" for him to comment on whether or not the Supreme Court should allow cameras to film oral arguments. See *Nomination of Samuel A. Alito, Jr. to be Associate Justice of the Supreme Court*, hearing of the Senate Judiciary Committee, January 11, 2006.
3. U.S. Cong., Senate, 110th Cong., 1st sess., *S. 352, Sunshine in the Courtroom Act of 2007* (introduced in the U.S. Senate January 22, 2007).
4. *NBC Nightly News*, February 14, 2007.
5. Justice Souter made the comments in a March 28, 1996, hearing before a House appropriations subcommittee while outlining the Supreme Court's budget for the upcoming fiscal year. See "On Cameras in Supreme Court, Souter Says, 'Over My Dead Body,'" *New York Times*, March 30, 1996.
6. As provided for in *H.R. 5576, Transportation, Treasury, Housing and Urban Development, the Judiciary, the District of Columbia and Independent Agencies Appropriations Act, 2007*, U.S. Cong., House, 109th Cong., 2nd sess. The Court's FY 2007 budget is an increase over the FY 2006 budget of $60.1 million.
7. From *The Federalist No. 78*: "Whoever attentively considers the different departments of power must perceive, that, in a government in which they are separated from each other, the judiciary, from the nature of its functions, will always be the *least dangerous* to the political rights of the Constitution; because it will be least in a capacity to annoy or injure them." Emphasis mine. See also Alexander Bickel, *The Least Dangerous Branch: The Supreme Court at the Bar of Politics* (New York: Bobbs-Merrill, 1962).
8. Judicial activism, in different ways, has taken hold of both liberal and conservative judges. For example, liberals on the Supreme Court swept aside the abortion laws of all fifty states with the breathtaking *Roe v. Wade* decision in 1973 (410 U.S. 113), which even many liberal scholars see as a reach, if not "indefensible," as one clerk for the author of the decision, Justice Harry Blackmun, called it. See Edward Lazarus, "After Two Days of Hearings on Supreme Court Nominee John Roberts, What Should Senate Democrats' Next Move Be?" *FindLaw Legal Commentary*, September 15, 2005. See http://writ.news.findlaw.com/lazarus/20050915.html. Yet conservatives on the Court in recent years have been much more likely to strike down congressional statutes—a clear measure of judicial activism. See Paul Gerwitz and Chad Golder, "So Who Are the Activists?" *New York Times*, July 6, 2005. See also an

excellent analytical essay on the forms of activism by Stuart Taylor, Jr., "What Kind of Justice?" *National Journal*, July 23, 2005: pp. 2352–57.

9. *Kelo v. City of New London*, 545 U.S. 125 S. Ct. 2655 (2005). The city of New London, Connecticut, invoked eminent domain authority to seize land from certain city residents, including Susette Kelo, to sell to developers as part of a larger economic development plan proposed by city officials. Kelo claimed that the takings clause of the Fifth Amendment, which allows the government to seize private land for "public use," only applies to cases where the land will be used for public property, such as a road or school. The Supreme Court ruled for the city of New London, claiming that the limitation of "public use" was intended to be broadly interpreted as "public purpose," and since the seizure was part of a larger economic development plan, the taking was constitutional.
10. In a speech at a meeting of the Clark County Bar Association in Las Vegas, Stevens said that allowing city officials broad seizure authority was *not* in the public's interest, but that he felt compelled to vote with the majority because such powers *were* authorized by the Constitution. Stevens suggested that it would be in the public's best interest to place stronger limits on the government's eminent-domain powers and allow free markets—rather than local officials—to decide who buys and who sells. See Linda Greenhouse, "Supreme Court Memo; Justice Weighs Desire v. Duty (Duty Prevails)," *New York Times*, August 25, 2005.
11. CBS News Poll, January 5–8, 2006, available online at http://pollingreport.com/Court.htm. The Supreme Court has historically enjoyed an approval rating of more than 70 percent, but in the midst of the politically charged nomination battles for President Bush's appointees, the Court's favorability rating reached a low of just 42 percent in June 2005, according to the Gallup Poll. In a CBS News/*New York Times* poll, 68 percent of people reported that they believed federal judges allow their political views to inappropriately influence their decisions at least half the time. See "Supreme Court's Image Declines as Nomination Battle Looms," *Pew Research Center for the People and the Press*, June 15, 2005. Like any other institution of government, the Supreme Court sees its popularity rise and fall with public reactions to new appointees and controversial cases, of course. Still, the Court has been the "storm center" of American life increasingly over the last half century, and the never-ending controversies over race, abortion, gay rights, and dozens of other matters have quite naturally taken a toll. See David M. O'Brien, *Storm Center: The Supreme Court in American Politics* (New York: Norton, 2005).
12. See Learned Hand, *The Spirit of Liberty: Papers and Addresses of Learned Hand* (Birmingham: Gryphon Editions, 1989). Hand served on the federal bench in New York's Southern District Court from 1909 to 1924 and then on the Second Circuit Court of Appeals until his death in 1961. Hand is widely considered to be the most influential judge in American history who never served on the Supreme Court.
13. The Holy Bible, revised standard version, Eccles. 1:2 (Philadelphia, PA: Westminster, 1952).
14. Only Rhode Island allows judges to sit for life. All other states have some limit on tenure, with most requiring regular reappointment or a retention election. Judges in New Jersey are subject to reappointment after seven years, but after reappointment they may serve without interference until mandatory retirement at age seventy. Massachusetts and New Hampshire allow judges to serve without reappointment or reelection, but they must retire at age seventy. For more on state judicial selection, visit the American Judicature Society at http://www.ajs.org/js/.

15. Alabama, Illinois, Louisiana, Michigan, Ohio, Pennsylvania, Texas, West Virginia, and Minnesota may soon be joining these erroneous eight.
16. Almost ten thousand "attack advertisements" aired on TV in the contests for state supreme court seats in 2004, with 43 percent appearing in a West Virginia race where an incumbent supreme court justice was unseated. See Kavan Peterson, "Cost of Judicial Races Stirs Reformers," *Stateline.org*, August 5, 2005, http://www.stateline.org/live/ViewPage.action?siteNodeld=136&languageId=1&contentId=47067.
17. These statistics are taken from the most up-to-date report available from the federal judiciary, current as of FY 2005 (http://www.uscourts.gov/judicialfactsfigures/Table101.pdf). Each state has at least one judicial district, though larger states can have as many as four districts. Districts do not cross state lines. In addition, there are district courts serving Puerto Rico, Guam, the U.S. Virgin Islands, the District of Columbia, and the Northern Mariana Islands.
18. In addition to the eleven numbered circuits, there is a court of appeals for the District of Columbia and a U.S. court of appeals for the Federal Circuit, which is not geographically bound and hears appeals on certain kinds of cases specified by statute, including those relating to patent law, international trade, and veterans' rights.
19. On the 2000 election, see *Bush v. Gore*, 531 U.S. 98 (2000). On the pledge of allegiance, see *Elk Grove Unified School District v. Newdow*, 542 U.S. 1 (2004). On sodomy laws, see *Lawrence and Garner v. Texas*, 539 U.S. 558 (2003). On abortion, see *Stenberg v. Carhart*, 530 U.S. 914 (2000). On the use of the death penalty for juveniles, see *Roper v. Simmons*, 125 S. Ct. 1183 (2005). On public prayer, see *Lee v. Weisman*, 505 U.S. 577 (1992) and, more recently, *Santa Fe Independent School Dist. v. Doe*, 530 U.S. 290 (2000). On medical marijuana, see *Gonzales v. Raich*, 125 S. Ct. 2195 (2005). On eminent domain, see *Kelo v. City of New London*, supra. at note 9. On the protection of children in public libraries from obscene content on the Internet, see *U.S. v. American Library Association*, 539 U.S. 194 (2003). On search and seizure, see *Illinois v. Wardlow*, 528 U.S. 119 (2000).
20. There are countless blogs devoted to law and legal issues, including Underneath Their Robes (http://underneaththeirrobes.blogs.com/main/), the American Constitution Society Blog (http://www.acsblog.org/), The Supreme Court Zeitgeist (http://judgejohnroberts.com/) and SCOTUSBlog (http://www.scotusblog.com/movabletype/). For a more complete directory of legal blogs, see http://www.blawg.com/.
21. Art. III, Sec. 1.
22. See Michael R. Blood, "Roberts Questioned Lifetime Appointments," *Associated Press Dispatch*, August 5, 2005.
23. This is an excerpt from a memo Roberts wrote to the White House counsel Fred Fielding on October 3, 1983, which is housed in the Reagan Presidential Library. Roberts concluded, much as we do here, "There is much to be said for changing life tenure to a term of years, without the possibility of reappointment."
24. Television interview with young people for educational purposes filmed with the chief justice in 1990, on the condition that it would not be aired until his death. ABC News first aired this excerpt on *World News Tonight*, September 12, 2005.
25. Jay's successor, John Rutledge, served a mere four months. Oliver Ellsworth next took over the chief justiceship for four years until December 1800. See http://www.supremecourtus.gov.
26. Stuart Taylor Jr., "Life Tenure Is Too Long for Supreme Court Justices," *National Journal*, June 26, 2005: pp. 2033–34.

27. Robert F. Bauer, "A Court Too Supreme for Our Good," *Washington Post*, August 7, 2005.
28. Two legal scholars, Paul D. Carrington of Duke Law School and Roger C. Cramton of Cornell Law School, proposed an eighteen-year term limit, with one Supreme Court appointment every two years to ensure that each president has the chance to put his stamp upon the Court. Endorsed by several dozen scholars of varying ideological stripes, it is an attractive though complex alternative to the simpler system we offer here. However, we believe the eighteen-year term is a bit too long to prevent judicial hubris—though there is no guarantee that a fifteen-year term will do so in all cases, either! See Carrington and Cramton, "The Supreme Court Renewal Act: A Return to Basic Principles," January 2, 2005, published online at http://zfacts.com/metaPage/lib/2005-SUPREME-COURT.pdf.
29. Several New Deal cases illustrate this point. See *Schechter Poultry Corp. v. U.S.*, 295 U.S. 495 (1935), striking down several sections the National Industrial Recovery Act, which empowered the president to set limits on employee wages and hours; *Louisville Joint Stock Land Bank v. Radford*, 295 U.S. 555 (1935), which struck down portions of an act that would have made it easier for farmers who defaulted on debts to seek relief in bankruptcy without losing their property; *Carter v. Carter Coal Company*, 298 U.S. 238 (1936), striking down the law intended to replace the NIRA, finding that labor relations were only indirectly related to interstate commerce and thus outside of the purview of Congress; and *Morehead v. New York Ex Rel. Tipaldo*, 298 U.S. 587 (1936), striking down a state law in New York prescribing a minimum wage for women. See also Daniel J. Hulsebosch, "The New Deal Court: Emergence of a New Reason," *Columbia Law Review* 90.7 (Nov. 1990): 1973–2016.
30. This approximation assumes that work begins at twenty-one and ends at sixty-five.
31. No matter how you measure it, the United States take the cake, with three times as many lawyers as our next biggest competitor, the United Kingdom. See George H. W. Bush, remarks at a Bush-Quayle fund-raising dinner in Dearborn, Michigan, April 14, 1992.
32. The minimum age for the presidency is thirty-five, but no such requirement is needed for the judiciary. There are hundreds of federal judgeships, so the judiciary can easily survive the inexperienced mistakes of a few young members, whereas the presidency—a singular office with tremendous concentrated power—would be seriously endangered by an immature chief executive. Similarly, the House of Representatives may even benefit from having a few members in their twenties, and the U.S. Senate by including a few in their thirties. Collective responsibility is a reasonable safeguard in Congress, and to a great extent, in the judiciary.
33. See Michael Grunwald, "Roberts Cultivated an Audience with Justices for Years," *Washington Post*, September 11, 2005.
34. Douglas served longer than any other justice with thirty-six years, seven months, on the bench. Despite a major stroke at age seventy-five, he refused to retire and let Gerald Ford, a Republican, appoint his successor. As his health continued to wane, seven of the eight remaining justices decided to refuse to hear any case whose outcome might be affected by the ailing Douglas. See Artemus Ward, "The Tenth Justice: The Retirement of William O. Douglas," *Journal of Supreme Court History* 25.3 (Nov. 2000): 296–312.
35. Among the recent jurists most often cited in this category are Frank Murphy, Charles Whittaker, Hugo Black, and Thurgood Marshall, in addition to Douglas. See Henry J. Abraham, *Justices, Presidents, and Senators: A History of the U.S. Supreme Court Appointments from Washington to Clinton* (Lanham: Rowman and

Littlefield, 1999) and Artemus Ward, *Deciding to Leave: The Politics of Retirement from the United States Supreme Court* (Albany, NY: State University of New York Press, 2003).

36. Under the "Rule of 80," a federal judge may retire from active status when his or her age plus years in service adds to at least eighty. To earn full salary, the judge must work a caseload roughly equal to one fourth the load of an active judge. If the judge submits a certificate of disability, the caseload requirement can be waived altogether. Note that retired Supreme Court justices would still be available to serve the judiciary and the nation under the "Rule of 80." See 28 U.S.C. 371.
37. Fox News/Opinion Dynamics poll of nine hundred registered voters, conducted July 12–13, 2005, with a margin of error of plus or minus 3 percent.
38. Through regular legislation, the Congress—both houses—may change the size of the Supreme Court. The president may either sign or veto the legislation.
39. For an excellent discussion of the size of the Supreme Court since 1789, see "The Numbers Game," *Supreme Court Historical Society 1977 Yearbook*, 1976 (available online at http://www.supremecourthistory.org/04_library/subs_volumes/04_c02_m.html). Additional information is available through the Web site of the Federal Judiciary Center, which serves as the educational and research arm of the judicial branch (http://www.fjc.gov/history/home.nsf). Throughout the nineteenth century, the size of the Supreme Court grew in proportion to the number of circuits added to the federal judiciary as a result of the expanding union. The First Judiciary Act of 1789 established a six member Court; an 1807 statute added a seventh justice; in 1837 the Court grew to nine justices; and with the addition of a tenth circuit in 1863 the Court grew to its largest membership of ten justices. In 1866 Congress reduced the Court to seven members and provided that no vacancies could be filled until that number was reached. The Court fell to eight members before an act of 1869 established a nine-justice Court, where the number has remained ever since.
40. Jane Butzner, ed, *Constitutional Chaff: Rejected Suggestions of the Constitutional Convention of 1787* (Port Washington, NY: Kennikat Press, 1970), pp. 116–17.
41. Chief Justice Roberts's 2006 annual end-of-year report is available online at the Supreme Court Web site, http://www.supremecourtus.gov/publicinfo/year-end/year-endreports.html. See also Robert Barnes, "Chief Justice Urges Pay Raise for Judges," *Washington Post*, January 1, 2007.
42. To be fair, as the chief justice noted, judges make about what first-year associates—just out of law school—are paid at top law firms, and less than many law professors are paid, too. Real judicial salaries, after inflation, have declined by 24 percent since 1969. Still, average Americans existing on a fraction of the current judicial salary might be excused for exhibiting a lack of sympathy.

4. Politics: American's Missing Constitutional Link

1. George Washington, "Farewell Address 1796," available online through the Yale Law School's Avalon Project at http://www.yale.edu/lawweb/avalon/.
2. Woodrow Wilson, *Constitutional Government in the United States* (New York: Columbia University Press, 1908), pp. 56, 206, 221–22, emphasis added.
3. See Rhodes Cook, *United States Presidential Primary Elections, 1968–1996: A Handbook of Election Statistics* (Washington, DC: CQ Press, 2000), p. 10. The District of Columbia also held a presidential primary in 1968.
4. Voters outside of the United States have also become involved in the nominating process thanks to the expansive reach of Internet voting. In 2004 Democrats living

abroad enjoyed an online vote in their parties' primaries and caucuses, sending twenty-two delegates to represent them at the Democratic National Convention. American Samoa held "territorial" caucuses to choose their delegates—nine for the Democratic convention and six for the Republican convention. Guam, Puerto Rico, and the Virgin Islands also hold territorial conventions or caucuses, though Puerto Rico's events were canceled in 2004. See Richard E. Berg-Andersson's *The Green Papers*, online at http://www.thegreenpapers.com.

5. *The Rhodes Cook Letter*, vol. 8, no. 2 (April 2007), pp. 3–4. For the presidential primary seasons from 1972 to 1984, the midpoint fell between May 5 and May 18. In 1988 a dramatic shift toward the early months of the election year began, and the midpoint became March 8. By 2004 the midpoint had edged back to March 2, and in 2007 the states joined a stampede to January and February 2008 for their primaries, shaving almost a full month off the midpoint date. Note that these midpoint calculations include only primary elections, not caucuses. However, the trend would be present even if caucuses were included.
6. The contest between President Ford and challenger Ronald Reagan for the 1976 GOP nomination went right down to the wire at the convention, and so did the 1984 Democratic battle between Walter Mondale and Gary Hart. Ford and Mondale edged Reagan and Hart, but the divisiveness at the conventions contributed to the defeat of both nominees in November.
7. For an overview of the major questions facing critics of the nominating process, see John Haskell, *Fundamentally Flawed: Understanding and Reforming Presidential Primaries* (London: Rowman and Littlefield, 1996), pp. 62–78. For an in-depth look at the nominating process, see Emmet H. Buell Jr. and William G. Mayer, eds., *Enduring Controversies in Presidential Nominating Politics* (Pittsburgh, PA: University of Pittsburgh Press, 2004).
8. This was the so-called Delaware plan, and it came up in 2000, failing at the convention. Some party officials hoped it might be implemented in time for the 2004 primaries, but it was not. Nothing similar appears to be on track for 2008, either. See "Nominating Process" in *Presidential Selection: A Guide to Reform* (University of Virginia Center for Governmental Studies, 2001).
9. A 2005 party commission headed by Congressman David Price of North Carolina and approved by the Democratic National Committee added a couple of states to the early process. Iowa still goes first, followed a few days later by caucuses in Nevada, then New Hampshire with the initial primary, followed by the South Carolina primary. The Granite State continued to fight the plan; moreover, four small states instead of two isn't a dramatic improvement. See Dan Balz, "Balancing Act: Iowa, N.H. vs. Critics: Democrats Weigh Plan to Stretch 2008 Calendar," *Washington Post*, December 28, 2005; David S. Broder, "The Democrats' Dysfunctional Calendar," *Washington Post*, August 31, 2006. For more information, visit the Web site of the Democratic Commission on Presidential Nomination Timing and Scheduling, located at http://www.democrats.org/page/s/nominating.
10. In early 1952 Senator Estes Kefauver of Tennessee defeated President Truman in the New Hampshire primary, after which Truman announced that he wouldn't run again. See Rhodes Cook, *Unites States Presidential Primary Elections*, p. 461. Meanwhile, General Dwight Eisenhower managed to defeat the early favorite for the Republican nomination, Senator Robert Taft of Ohio, in a foreshadowing of the convention result. For more on the 1952 New Hampshire primary, visit the New Hampshire Political Library, online at http://www.politicallibrary.org/.

11. LBJ won the primary with just a shade under 50 percent of the vote, with McCarthy at 41 percent. But McCarthy won the lion's share of the delegates at stake in the Granite State, and his psychological victory was huge.
12. In a large field of Democratic candidates, Carter received just 29 percent in Iowa and 28 percent in New Hampshire—remarkably small, but more than anyone else—and thus was a president made.
13. Keynote address, National Symposium on Presidential Selection, University of Virginia Center for Politics, April 5, 2001, Charlottesville, Virginia.
14. See Title LXIII of the New Hampshire code, NH ST, Sec. 653:9.
15. Congress does have the power to regulate party primary elections insomuch as the Fourteenth Amendment applies to protect the voting rights of citizens. "Where a primary election is an integral part of the procedure of choice, the right to vote in that primary election is subject to congressional protection." See Article I of the CRS Annotated Constitution, especially note 338, citing *United States v. Classic*, 313 U.S. 299, 315–21 (1941).
16. For example, "National Primary Day" would require all primaries to be held on the same day, likely increasing voter turnout in primaries, but the change would come at a cost to less-wealthy candidates, who cannot build the momentum they need to raise funds for national television advertising. Delaware GOP state chairman Basil Battaglia proposed the "Delaware Plan," which organizes the states into four groups in order of increasing population. See *Presidential Selection: A Guide to Reform*, supra at note 8. Another plan, the "Rotating Primary Plan" created by the National Association of Secretaries of State, would instead organize states by geography, dividing the nation into the Northeast, Midwest, West, and South, regions of roughly similar populations and electoral votes. The plan calls for rotating the starting order, that is, which region holds its primaries first. The order would be known years in advance. For more on these proposals, see the "Nominating Process" in *Presidential Selection: A Guide to Reform.*
17. These regions have about the same number of states: Northeast (twelve plus D.C.), South (thirteen), Midwest (twelve), West (thirteen).
18. In a few states, such as South Carolina and Virginia, the Democratic and Republican parties can separately choose their preferred method of nomination, without any interference by the state legislature. The legislature does have to pass enabling legislation to hold an election on the dates chosen, which is usually done as a matter of course. Should a party wish to pay for the election by itself, no legislation at all is needed. Given the cost of a statewide election, the parties almost always seek legislative approval. In most states, however, the parties must take their preferred methods and dates to the state legislature and seek its formal assent. On occasion, state legislatures have not given permission, and instead they have chosen another method and date for the nominating contest. Partisanship can come into play; obviously, it helps to be the party in the majority in the state legislature to obtain the most desirable electoral setup.
19. The twenty states with their number of congressional representatives in parentheses: Alaska (one), Arkansas (four), Delaware (one), Hawaii (two), Idaho (two), Kansas (four), Maine (two), Mississippi (four), Montana (one), Nebraska (three), Nevada (three), New Hampshire (two), New Mexico (three), North Dakota (one), Rhode Island (two), South Dakota (one), Utah (three), Vermont (one), West Virginia (three), and Wyoming (one).
20. Prior to 1804, the candidate for president with the second-highest number of electoral

votes was to become the vice president. In 1800 Jefferson and Burr attempted to run on a ticket, and the electors split their votes evenly among the two men, causing an unexpected tie. The House of Representatives was called upon to decide the winner, resulting in a week of deadlock that finally ended with a win for Jefferson. In 1804 the Twelfth Amendment established separate electoral ballots for president and vice president. For more on the 1800 election, see vol. 3, chap. 30 of Dumas Malone, *Jefferson and His Time* (Charlottesville, VA: University of Virginia Press, 1962), as well as John Ferling, *Adams vs. Jefferson: The Tumultuous Election of 1800* (New York: Oxford University Press, 2004).

21. In 1824 the college took center stage again, as four candidates received electoral votes, but none with a majority. The 1824 election was the only election since the passage of the Twelfth Amendment where a presidential election had to be resolved by a vote in the House of Representatives. After the Federalist Party dissolved, only the Democratic-Republican Party remained to field candidates, resulting in a four-way presidential election between Andrew Jackson (99 votes), John Quincy Adams (84 votes), William Harris Crawford (41 votes), and Henry Clay (37 votes). This led to the infamous backroom bargaining that sent John Quincy Adams, who had received fewer popular and electoral votes than Andrew Jackson, to the presidency. For more on the 1824 election, see Robert V. Remini, *John Quincy Adams* (New York: Times Books, 2002).
22. In 1876 neither New York governor Samuel Tilden nor Ohio governor Rutherford B. Hayes managed to secure the necessary number of electors, because the results in four states remained contested. Tilden's total stood at 184 undisputed votes, just one shy of the total needed at that time, and Hayes had 165. To resolve the dispute, the 15-member Electoral Commission (five members from the Republican Senate, five members from the Democratic House, and five from the Supreme Court) was convened. The Electoral Commission voted 8 to 7, along party lines, to give the electoral votes in each of the four disputed elections to the Republican Hayes, granting him the necessary 185 votes. See also William H. Rehnquist, *The Centennial Crisis: The Disputed Election of 1876* (New York: Knopf, 2004).
23. Only twelve years after the tumultuous 1876 election, a candidate for president would again win the popular vote and lose the electoral vote. Incumbent president Grover Cleveland earned 100,000 more votes than challenger Benjamin Harrison, but Harrison won the election by a landslide plurality of 65 electoral votes.
24. For more on the 1968 election, see Lewis L. Gould, *1968: The Election That Changed America* (Chicago: Ivan R. Dee, 1993).
25. Later in his career as governor of Alabama, Wallace recanted his segregationist past, and he even received the backing of a large share of African American Alabamans. Still, his role in the racial cauldron that was the 1960s was disgraceful, and he will always be remembered for "standing in the schoolhouse door" to try to prevent the admission of black students to his state's universities in 1963. See Lloyd Rohler, *George Wallace: Conservative Populist* (Westport, CT: Praeger, 2004) and Jody Carlson, *George C. Wallace and the Politics of Powerlessness: The Wallace Campaigns for the Presidency, 1964–1976* (New Brunswick, NJ: Transaction Books, 1981).
26. The first Deep South presidential candidate since 1848, Carter won all southern states except Virginia, most by wide margins, and this produced his popular vote lead, which was not matched in the state-by-state-based Electoral College. See also Patrick Anderson, *Electing Jimmy Carter: The Campaign of 1976* (Baton Rouge: Louisiana State University Press, 1994). In-depth statistics from the 1976 election

can be found on the Web site of the Office of the Clerk of the House of Representatives at http://clerk.house.gov/members/electionInfo/.

27. Due to a faithless elector in Minnesota, Kerry's official tally was 251 electoral votes.
28. Larry J. Sabato, ed., *Divided States of America* (New York: Pearson/Longman, 2005), pp. 58–59.
29. See George C. Edwards III, *Why the Electoral College Is Bad for America* (New Haven, CT: Yale University Press, 2004), as well as Lawrence D. Longley and Neal R. Pierce, *The Electoral College Primer, 2000* (New Haven, CT: Yale University Press, 1999).
30. Frederic D. Schwarz, "The Electoral College: How It Got That Way and Why We're Stuck With It," *American Heritage Magazine* 52.1 (Feb.–Mar. 2001), online at http://www.americanheritage.com/magazine/.
31. Two constitutional amendments (the Twelfth and Twenty-third) affect the Electoral College directly, and three amendments (the Fourteenth, Seventeenth, and Twenty-fourth) affect the qualifications and selection of electors. The Twelfth Amendment established two distinct ballots for president and vice president, a departure from the arrangement set forth in Article II whereby the runner-up in the electoral vote would be awarded the vice presidency. The Fourteenth Amendment dispensed with the three-fifths clause of Article I, declaring all persons regardless of color to be equally counted for the purposes of electoral apportionment. The Seventeenth Amendment mandated that electors in any given state must, at a minimum, meet the same qualifications as members of that state's largest house of legislature. The Twenty-third Amendment granted D.C. three electoral votes. The Twenty-fourth Amendment forbade poll taxes from being imposed on citizens when voting for electors.
32. The Federal Registrar provides instructions for state officials who oversee the selection of electors (http://www.archives.gov/federal-register/electoral-college/state_responsibilities.html). Those instructions state: "Under the Constitution, State legislatures have broad powers to direct the process for selecting electors, with one exception regarding the qualifications of electors. Article II, section 1, clause 2 provides that 'no Senator, Representative, or Person holding an Office of Trust or Profit under the United States' may be appointed as an elector. It is not settled as to whether this restriction extends to all Federal officials regardless of their level of authority or the capacity in which they serve, but we advise the States that the restriction could disqualify any person who holds a Federal government job from serving as an elector." While this remains an open question at the federal level, many states have had to determine the meaning of the phrase *office of trust or profit* with respect to their own, internal operations. For example, in April of 2005 the attorney general of Tennessee concluded that the phrase only encompassed those individuals required to take an oath of office in support of the Tennessee state constitution (Opp. Tenn. Attorney General 05-064, 27. April 2005).
33. Actually, an elector could vote for unqualified or even fictitious persons, but these votes could not elect a constitutionally qualified president or vice president in any event.
34. No constitutional provision or federal statute requires electors to vote for the popular vote winner in their states. In many states, electors are bound either by party pledges or by state law to vote for the popular vote winner. In *Ray v. Blair*, 343 U.S. 214 (1952), the Supreme Court ruled that such party pledges are constitutional—though the constitutionality of state laws binding electors has never been tested in the courts, nor has any potential enforcement mechanism for such provisions. At least one observer

concluded that "the preponderance of legal opinion seems to be that statutes binding electors, or pledges that they may give, are unenforceable." See Longley and Pierce, *The Electoral College Primer*, pp. 109–16. According to the Federal Registrar (http://www.archives.gov/federal-register/electoral-college/laws.html), the following states bind electors either through pledges or by statute: Alabama, Alaska, California, Colorado, Connecticut, the District of Columbia, Florida, Hawaii, Maine, Maryland, Massachusetts, Michigan, Mississippi, Montana, Nebraska, Nevada, New Mexico, North Carolina, Ohio, Oklahoma, Oregon, South Carolina, Vermont, Virginia, Washington, Wisconsin, and Wyoming.

35. A faithless Republican elector in the 1972 elector, Roger MacBride of Virginia, voted for John Hospers, the Libertarian nominee for president, instead of Republican Richard M. Nixon. Four years later, MacBride became the Libertarian nominee for president. Thus, faithlessness produced a political career, but it could not be termed successful. MacBride secured only 172,000 votes, or 0.21 percent of the 1976 national vote.

36. The Twelfth Amendment lays out the tie-breaking procedures in greater detail. In breaking an electoral tie for president, the House of Representatives shall only vote among the top three electoral vote recipients. A quorum will consist of "a member or members from two-thirds of the states," and a "majority of all the states shall be necessary to a choice" (meaning, in theory, a quorum of thirty-four representatives and a majority of twenty-six representatives could select a president—emphasizing even further the need for a Continuity of Government amendment as outlined in chapter 1). In breaking an electoral tie for vice president, the Senate selects between the two highest electoral vote recipients. A quorum consists of "two-thirds of the whole number of Senators, and a majority of the whole shall be necessary to a choice." It is unclear from the language of the Twelfth Amendment if the "whole number of Senators" means the whole number of Senate seats (100) or the whole number of Senators serving—something else a Continuity of Government could clarify. For more information, see *Provisions of the Constitution and United States Code Pertaining to Presidential Elections*, Office of the Federal Registrar, National Archives and Records Administration (July 20, 2000); *Electoral College and Presidential Elections*, ed. Alexandra Kura (Huntington, NY: Nova Science, 2001); Robert M. Hardaway, *The Electoral College and the Constitution: The Case for Preserving Federalism* (Westport, CT: Praeger, 1994).

37. Maine and Nebraska law provides for the allocation of one elector to the winner of each congressional district, and the two bonus senatorial electors go to the winner of the statewide vote. The Maine system was established in 1972 and the Nebraska version in 1996. See Richard E. Berg-Andersson's *The Green Papers*, online at http://www.thegreenpapers.com. Interestingly, every presidential winner in these two states has managed to capture all the state's electoral votes since the starting dates, preventing any split electoral tally.

38. The Republicans became the main opposition party, replacing the Whigs, in 1856, when the Democrat James Buchanan defeated the Republican John C. Fremont.

39. For more information on American political party development, see: Sidney M. Milkis, *Political Parties and Constitutional Government: Remaking American Democracy* (Baltimore: Johns Hopkins University Press, 1999); Wilfred E. Binkley, *American Political Parties: Their Natural History* (New York: Knopf, 1962); John Gerring, *Party Ideologies in America, 1828–1996* (Cambridge: Cambridge University Press, 1998); Joel H. Sibley, *The Partisan Imperative: The Dynamics of American*

Politics Before the Civil War (Oxford: Oxford University Press, 1987); Gerald M. Pomper, *Party Renewal in America: Theory and Practice* (New York: Praeger, 1980); William Nisbet Chambers and Walter Dean Burnham, *The American Party Systems: Stages of Political Development* (Oxford: Oxford University Press, 1967).

40. According to a Gallup Poll conducted October 11–14, 2004 (telephone interview with a random sample of 1,012 adults, error of plus or minus 3 percent), 61 percent of Americans favor abolishing the Electoral College in favor of electing the president on the basis of the popular vote. The poll asked: "Thinking for a moment about the way in which the president is elected in this country, which would you prefer—to amend the Constitution so the candidate who receives the most total votes nationwide wins the election, or to keep the current system, in which the candidate who wins the most votes in the Electoral College wins the election?" Sixty-one percent responded that they would favor an amendment, 35 percent said they would keep the current system, and 4 percent had no opinion. Poll results available online at http://www.fairvote.org/electoral_college/Gallup_Polls.pdf.

41. In all, nine faithless electors have defected since the inception of the Electoral College. For information on each incident, visit Richard E. Berg-Andersson's *The Green Papers*, specifically http://www.thegreenpapers.com/Hx/FaithlessElectors.html.

42. Bills proposing constitutional amendments to abolish the Electoral College in favor of direct election of the president and vice president have never been in short supply. Since 1999, sponsors of such bills have included Representative Barney Frank (D-MA), Senator Richard Durbin (D-IL), Senator Dianne Feinstein (D-CA), Representative Jesse Jackson Jr. (D-IL), Representative Ray LaHood (R-IL), Representative Jim Leach (R-IA), Representative Zoe Lofgren (D-CA), Representative Jim McDermott (D-WA), Representative Jose Serrano (D-NY), Representative Fortney Stark (D-CA), Representative Robert Wise Jr. (D-WV), and Representative Lynn Woolsey (D-CA). The direct-vote method is just one of many proposals that have been considered for ending the Electoral College. For more information, see *The Report of the National Symposium on Presidential Selection* (Charlottesville, VA: University of Virginia Center for Governmental Studies, 2001), pp. 43–46. A very recent proposal by the nonprofit group FairVote urges that each state legislature should require their electors to cast the state's electoral votes for the winner of the national presidential popular vote, regardless of how their state has actually voted. The program is supported by the findings published by FairVote titled "Presidential Election Inequality: The Electoral College in the 21st Century," available online. The plan would go into effect when states with at least 270 electoral votes pass such legislation. Note that this reform does not require a constitutional amendment. Of course, the odds of enough states doing this are quite small, and the plan suffers from the same drawbacks as all reforms that focus only on the popular vote. These flaws are discussed in the text of this chapter. For details of the proposal, visit http://www.nationalpopularvote.com/.

43. In "Gallup Poll Analyses" on January 5, 2001, Frank Newport discussed the public's view of the Electoral College. "One of the earliest times in which the public was asked about the Electoral College system was June 1944, just before Franklin Roosevelt's reelection to his fourth term. A Gallup Poll question asked, 'It has been suggested that the electoral vote system be discontinued and presidents of the U.S. be elected by total popular vote alone. Do you favor or oppose this proposal?' The answer: 65%

of Americans said they favored the proposal, with 23% saying they opposed it, and another 13% saying they had no opinion." For more information, see "American Support to Eliminate Electoral College System," January 5, 2001, http://gallup.com/poll/releases/pr010105.asp.

44. See Chris Mooney, "Why Does Louisiana Have Such an Odd Election System?" *Slate.com*, November 13, 2002, http://www.slate.com/?id=2073912.
45. See "Louisiana's Nonpartisan Primary: Model or Travesty of Reform?" published by *FairVote: The Center for Voting and Democracy*, February 2004, online at http://www.fairvote.org/?page=1495.
46. See Donald O. Dewey, "Madison's Views on Electoral Reform," *Western Political Quarterly* 15.1 (Mar. 1962): 140–45 (available online at http://links.jstor.org/sici?sici=0043-4078%28196203%2915%3A1%3C140%3AMVOER%3E2.0.CO%3B2-K). At the time of publication, Dewey was the assistant editor of the Papers of James Madison, University of Virginia. Madison's reforms included the abolition of the system of winner-take-all "bloc" electoral voting—with the candidate receiving a plurality of the vote in a state sweeping all the state's electors. Madison thought that one elector should be assigned to each congressional district, with the winner of that district receiving the elector. Actually, Madison insisted that the one-elector-per-district allocation was the intention of the framers, even though it had not been spelled out in the text of the Constitution. Bloc voting had come about in part because of partisan conflict in the 1800 presidential election. Supporters of President Adams sought to deny challenger Thomas Jefferson key electors in states where Adams's forces held sway, and the Jefferson backers did precisely the same thing in states they controlled. By the way, each state had and has the right to choose for itself either the winner-take-all system or the district allocation system. The Constitution does not mandate any method of elector allocation.
47. Ibid. Madison had much company in his preference for district allocation, by the way. Quite a number of the founders favored the reform by the 1820s, but the partisan maneuvering that accompanied the controversial election of 1824 between John Quincy Adams and Andrew Jackson, and Jackson's unrelenting comeback campaign for 1828, took center stage in the nation. Suspicions about who might gain or lose under a new system of electoral allocation may well have prevented the reform from progressing further.
48. Proponents of voting by electoral district began their campaign before the passage of the Twelfth Amendment and continued it for many years in the Senate. Chief Justice Melville Fuller summarized the history of this debate in *McPherson v. Blacker*, 146 U.S. 1, 33–34 (1892).
49. Rhodes Cook, "This Just In: Nixon Beats Kennedy," *The Rhodes Cook Letter*, May 2001.
50. Rhodes Cook discusses the results of historically close elections in "Electoral Reform: If the Electoral Vote was by Congressional District?" in the March 2001 issue of *The Rhodes Cook Letter*. He writes: "The election that would have been reversed was the razor-tight contest in 1960 between Democrat John F. Kennedy and Republican Richard M. Nixon. Kennedy's 118,574-vote edge in the popular vote was magnified into a comfortable 303–219 triumph in the Electoral College. But employing the district plan—which gives two electoral votes in each state to the statewide winner and one electoral vote for each congressional district carried—Nixon would have won 280 to 252."
51. Arthur Schlesinger Jr., "Fixing the Electoral College," *Washington Post*, December 19, 2000, p. A39.

52. See Larry J. Sabato and Glenn R. Simpson, *Dirty Little Secrets: The Persistence of Corruption in American Politics* (New York: Times Books, 1996), pp. 274–301. Also see Bruce K. Felknor, *Political Mischief: Smear, Sabotage, and Reform in U.S. Elections* (New York: Praeger, 1992) as well as Louise Overacker, *Money in Elections* (New York: Macmillan, 1932).
53. For more on the election of 1800, see note 20 above. For more on Burr, see Roger G. Kennedy, *Burr, Hamilton, and Jefferson: A Study in Character* (New York: Oxford University Press, 2000) and Joseph Wheelen, *Jefferson's Vendetta: The Pursuit of Aaron Burr and the Judiciary* (New York: Carroll and Graf, 2005).
54. See also note 20 above.
55. In other cases, an illness may take away the deciding vote, leaving a state delegation tied. Or some representatives may choose to cast a ballot for the winner of their district, or of their state, against their own party affiliation, taking untied delegations and tying them. One can easily conjure up other confusing scenarios that would utterly perplex the general public and fill the news media with critical speculation.
56. Since the District of Columbia has electoral votes, the delegate from D.C. should certainly be permitted to cast a ballot alongside the other 435 members. The delegates from territories without electoral votes would not have a presidential ballot.
57. By the way, if the Senate is expanded in the manner we have proposed in an earlier chapter, the possible selection of a vice president by the Senate would also be more democratic and representative of the broad body of the public, since the larger Senate would be more reflective of the heavily populated states. Of course, the vice president is only chosen by the Senate when no candidate receives a majority of the Electoral College vote.
58. Dewey, "Madison's Views on Electoral Reform," p. 144. See also James Madison's letter to George Hay, written from Madison's Virginia home, Montpelier, August 23, 1823, Library of Congress, Papers of James Madison (available online at http://presspubs.uchicago.edu/founders/documents/a2_1_2-3s10.html). My proposal here differs from Madison's 1823 suggestion only in that Madison wanted the whole House and Senate, voting together in a joint ballot, to choose the president whenever the Electoral College had deadlocked. Madison saw the inclusion of the Senate to be a useful concession to the smaller states—since their Senate representation was equal to that of the larger states. I would argue that this dilution of the democratic principle is unwarranted today, given the values of twenty-first-century America.
59. See chapter 1, "Toward a More Representative Senate," pp. 23–28.
60. See chapter 1, "Building a Bigger House," pp. 37–40.
61. Article V of the Constitution reads, in part that "no State, without its Consent, shall be deprived of its equal Suffrage in the Senate." In chapter 7, we will make an argument that a new Constitutional Convention can change this proviso as a part of its work. Thus, the constitutional bar to the expansion of the Senate could be removed.
62. Florida is still counted in Bush's column.
63. In our calculation, Gore would receive the blank ballot cast by one of D.C.'s Democratic electors; my plan abolishes faithless electors, after all. Finally, the total number of electors for the 2000 election (611) and for the 2004 election (612) differs by one because of rounding error in projecting state electoral totals based on population.
64. This author has written extensively about campaign finance reform in a series of

other books. See *PAC Power: Inside the World of Political Action Committees* (New York: Norton, 1985), *Paying for Elections: The Campaign Finance Thicket* (New York: Priority Press, 1989), and, with Glenn R. Simpson, *Dirty Little Secrets.* Other useful campaign reforms include instantaneous Internet-based disclosure of every dollar raised and spent in politics, as well as mandated, free television advertising time for candidates and political parties. Congress already has the authority to enact these reforms, and they are discussed in detail in the cited books.

65. See *Buckley v. Valeo*, 424 U.S. 1 (1976). For other writings on campaign finance reform, see Annelise Anderson, ed., *Political Money: Deregulating American Politics, Selected Writings on Campaign Finance Reform* (Stanford, CA: Hoover Institution Press, 2000).
66. Examples include Jon Corzine, the former chairman of Goldman Sachs, and current governor of New Jersey who sank more than $60 million of his own money to win the 2000 New Jersey U.S. Senate race, and John D. "Jay" Rockefeller IV, the West Virginia senator and great-grandson of oil tycoon John D. Rockefeller, who has spent a fortune on a long series of mostly successful elections in West Virginia for governor and the Senate, beginning in 1972. The rise of millionaire politics led to the so-called Millionaire's Amendment to the Bipartisan Campaign Reform Act of 2002 (BCRA), Public Law no. 107-155, which raises the ceiling on fund-raising for candidates who are challenged by very wealthy opponents. See Sean Loughlin and Robert Yoon, "Millionaires populate U.S. Senate," *CNN.com/Inside Politics*, June 13, 2003.
67. Providing some public money to candidates as a "floor" is superior to establishing a full taxpayer-financed system, with the public money provided as a "ceiling" allowing for no private money. Such ceilings are unrealistic and probably unenforceable. See Herbert E. Alexander, ed., *Campaign Money: Reform and Reality in the States* (New York: Free Press, 1976).
68. The Jack Abramoff lobbying scandal and the bribery conviction of former congressman Randy "Duke" Cunningham in 2005–06 are typical. For articles on Abramoff, see Susan Schmidt and James V. Grimaldi, "Abramoff Pleads Guilty to 3 Counts," *Washington Post*, January 4, 2004, as well as Philip Shenon, "U.S. Fraud Charge for Top Lobbyist," *New York Times*, August 12, 2005. For Cunningham, see Charles R. Babcock and Jonathan Weisman, "Congressman Admits Taking Bribes, Resigns," *Washington Post*, November 29, 2005, as well as John M. Broder, "Lawmaker Quits After He Pleads Guilty to Bribes," *New York Times*, November 29, 2005.
69. One reason for Congress's inaction is that public financing, full or partial, could disproportionately assist challengers in their battles with better-funded incumbents.
70. Most Western democracies register their citizens as voters automatically when a citizen becomes eligible. In New Zealand and Australia, voters register themselves, but unlike the United States, citizens are legally *required* to complete this process. Voting is compulsory in Australia, Belgium, Greece, and Italy. Only France joins the United States in leaving voter registration entirely to the prerogative of its citizens. See G. Bingham Powell Jr., "American Voter Turnout in Comparative Perspective," *American Political Science Review* 80.1 (Mar. 1986): 17–43.
71. A few places, such as North Dakota, have election-day registration, but these are rare exceptions.
72. See Sabato and Simpson, *Dirty Little Secrets*, pp. 274–301.

5. A Citizenship of Service: Asking What We Can Do for Our Country . . . and Ourselves

1. The Peace Corps periodically publishes first-person accounts from its volunteers. See *A Life Inspired: Tales of Peace Corps Service* (Washington, DC: Peace Corps, 2006) and *Peace Corps: The Great Adventure* (Washington, DC: Peace Corps, 1997). Another prominent anthology can be found in *From the Center of the Earth: Stories from the Peace Corps* (Santa Monica, CA: Clover Park Press, 1991). *Making a Difference: The Peace Corps at Twenty-Five* (New York: Weidenfeld and Nicolson, 1986) contains essays from numerous famous Peace Corps alumni, including Sargent Shriver, the agency's first director, and U.S. senator Christopher Dodd (D-CT). For a more academic look at the Peace Corps in historical context, see Elizabeth Hoffman Cobbs, *All You Need Is Love: The Spirit of the Peace Corps in the 1960s* (Cambridge: Harvard University Press, 2000).
2. See John Locke, *Political Writings*, ed. David Wootton (Indianapolis: Hackett, 1993).
3. E-mail to author, April 9, 2006.
4. "I must say that I have often seen Americans make great and real sacrifices to the public welfare; and I have noticed a hundred instances in which they hardly ever failed to lend faithful support to one another. The free institutions which the inhabitants of the United States possess, and the political rights of which they make so much use, remind every citizen, and in a thousand ways, that he lives in society. They at every instant impress upon his mind the notion that it is the duty as well as the interest of men to make themselves useful to their fellow creatures." From Alexis de Tocqueville's *Democracy in America* (book 2, chap. 4). Text available online at http://xroads.virginia.edu/~HYPER/DETOC/.
5. For an account of America's antibureaucratic political traditions, as well as the transition from privately sponsored welfare to government-sponsored welfare during the Great Depression, see Ellis W. Hawley, "Herbert Hoover, Associationalism, and the Great Depression Relief Crisis of 1930–1933," in *With Us Always: A History of Private Charity and Public Welfare* (Lanham, MD: Rowman and Littlefield, 1998): pp. 161–90. It is important to note that while federally sponsored welfare programs only became institutionalized during the New Deal, America inherited a strong tradition of social welfare from Britain, and both private and public welfare was prominent at the state and local level throughout the nineteenth century. See Merritt Ierley, *With Charity for All: Welfare and Society, Ancient Times to the Present* (New York: Praeger Special Studies, 1984). Hugh Heclo chronicles the ongoing tension in American politics between private individualism and public welfare in "General Welfare and Two American Political Traditions," *Political Science Quarterly* 101.2 (1986): 179–96.
6. Throughout most of the nineteenth century, American soldiers were overwhelmingly civilian volunteers or militiamen. Most served only for limited periods and quickly returned to civilian life. Americans fought the Revolutionary War without a regular army, relying on state militia, volunteers, and sheer "improvisation." During the nineteenth century, the peacetime army hovered around 7,000–10,000 men. In time of war, the army would expand rapidly as a result of volunteers who signed up for short terms, anywhere from six to twelve months. During the war of 1812 (1812–14), the army grew to 34,000 men, and during the Mexican War (1846–48), it expanded to around 31,000 men. The brief Spanish-American War was fought entirely with volunteers. See William G. Carleton, "Raising Armies Before the Civil War," *Current History* 54.322 (June 1968): pp. 327–32, 363–64. The military historian

Ricardo Herrera argues that early American military culture rested on a widespread belief in "the right and responsibility of the citizen to rule himself and his society." See Ricardo Herrera, "Self-Governance and the American Citizen as Soldier," *Journal of Military History* 65.1 (Jan. 2001): 21–52.

7. The Confederate Congress passed the first national draft law in American history on April 16, 1862, authorizing President Jefferson Davis to draft all men between the ages of eighteen and thirty-five into military service for three years. Would-be soldiers could not "buy" their way out of service, though substitution was permitted until December 1863. A number of additional acts relating to exemption were passed throughout the war, including one infamous clause that allowed owners of twenty slaves or more to stay home to look after their "property." In the North, four national drafts took place during the war, resulting in the calling up of 776,829 men. According to the Enrollment Act of 1863, individuals could be exempted from the draft for disability if they were able to find a substitute, or if they paid a three-hundred-dollar commutation fee. See William L. Shaw, "The Confederate Conscription and Exemption Acts," *Journal of American Legal History* 6.4 (Oct. 1962): 368–405; Peter Levine, "Draft Evasion in the North during the Civil War," *Journal of American History* 67.4 (Mar. 1981): 816–34.
8. There was a draft in World War I (the Selective Service Act of 1917), which supplemented volunteers for the armed services. Between September 1917 and November 1918, 2,810,296 men entered the armed forces as a result of conscription, eventually totaling more than one half of the active U.S. military force. The Selective Service System, "Induction Statistics," May 2003, http://www.sss.gov/induct.htm.
9. The first peacetime draft in history was the Selective Service and Training Act, which FDR signed into law September 16, 1940. The law authorized draftees to serve for a period of twelve months. In August of 1941 that service period was extended by an additional eighteen months. The extension passed the U.S. House of Representatives by a single vote, 203 to 202. It is important to note, however, that very few lawmakers were seriously considering eliminating the draft, and had the eighteen-month extension been voted down, another extension of at least six to twelve months almost certainly would have passed. See J. Garry Clifford and Samuel R. Spencer, *The First Peacetime Draft* (Lawrence: University Press of Kansas, 1986).
10. Most believed that it was both desirable and consonant with American military tradition to return to an all-volunteer force following World War II. The draft was extended a little over a year after the war to allow for an "orderly transition" to an all-volunteer military, and on March 3, 1947, President Truman stated his desire to place the military "on an entirely volunteer basis at the earliest possible moment." The draft lapsed briefly in 1947, but in 1948 the specter of communism and Soviet aggression changed the political landscape, and the draft was reinstituted for an additional twenty-one months. When the draft came up again in 1950, differing House and Senate bills went to conference with the expectation that only a skeletal Selective Service apparatus would remain in place, and the military would return to a primarily volunteer basis. Yet when conferees met on June 27 to discuss the bill, they were informed of President Truman's decision to intervene militarily in Korea. A new bill extended the draft for another year, after which it became generally (if sometimes grudgingly) accepted that a peacetime draft would be necessary for American security. See Richard Gillam, "The Peacetime Draft: Volunteerism to Coercion," in *The Military Draft* (Stanford: Hoover Institution Press, 1982).
11. Nixon first endorsed the idea of an all-volunteer military in a late November 1967 interview and continued to do so throughout the 1968 presidential campaign. Once

elected, he appointed a commission under former secretary of defense Thomas Gates, commonly known as the Gates Commission, to study the idea. The commission unanimously recommended the transition to an all-volunteer military, for which Nixon ordered the Defense Department to begin preparing in April of 1970. What followed was a somewhat rocky transition period, with the army instituting a number of VOLAR ("volunteer army") sites around the country to test how a volunteer army would function. The transition was put under the direction of a special assistant for the modern volunteer army (SAMVA), General George Forsythe. President Nixon made clear his determination to institute an all-volunteer force when he announced on June 28, 1972, that no draftees would be sent to Vietnam unless they volunteered to go. In June 1974 Nixon was officially informed that the transition to an all-volunteer force was "complete." For a comprehensive account, see Robert K. Giffith, *The U.S. Army's Transition to the All-Volunteer Force, 1968–1974* (Washington, DC: Center of Military History, United States Army, 1997).

12. The official name was the "**U**niting and **S**trengthening **A**merica by **P**roviding **A**ppropriate **T**ools **R**equired to **I**nterrupt and **O**bstruct **T**errorism Act," signed into law October 26, 2001 (P.L. 107-156). In the wake of 9/11, the USA PATRIOT Act passed Congress by margins of 98 to 1 in the Senate and 357 to 66 in the House. In a September 19, 2001, briefing, President Bush's then-press secretary, Ari Fleischer, said there was "no consideration of reinstating the draft," though at the time a *USA Today*/CNN Poll revealed that 80 percent of respondents favored military action in the War on Terror—even if it meant a renewed draft. See Bill Hendrick, "Selective Service's Rebirth Seems Faint Possibility," *Atlanta Journal-Constitution*, October 22, 2001; Kieran Nicholson and Stacie Oulton, "Military Service on Minds of Young in Wake of Attacks," *Denver Post*, September 24, 2001; and Jeffrey Robb, "War Threat Raises Talk About Reviving Draft," *Omaha World Herald*, September 22, 2001.
13. Nicholson and Oulton, "Military Service on Minds of Young."
14. E. J. Dionne and Kayla Meltzer Drogsz, "The Promise of National Service: A (Very) Brief History of an Idea," Brookings Institution, policy brief 120, June 2003, http://www.brookings.edu/comm/policybriefs/pb120.htm.
15. The controversy over troop levels first grabbed national headlines when the former army chief of staff Eric Shinseki testified before the Senate Armed Services Committee on February 25, 2003, that "hundreds of thousands of troops" might be required to secure Iraq. Only two days later, Deputy Secretary of Defense Paul Wolfowitz went out of his way to call that estimate "outlandish" before a congressional panel. Paul Bremer, the former director of the Coalition Provisional Authority in Iraq, revealed in his memoir that the Pentagon repeatedly rebuffed requests for additional troops to secure the country. Since then, at least seven retired generals have criticized the Bush administration's decision on troop levels and its failure to foresee the possibility of a sustained insurgency. Colin Powell has said explicitly that the United States "did not have enough force [in Iraq] to impose order," and that he warned President Bush as much before departing his post as secretary of state. See Eric Schmidt, "Pentagon Contradicts General on Iraq Occupational Force's Size," *New York Times*, February 28, 2003; James Fallows, "Blind into Baghdad," *Atlantic Monthly*, January 2004; pp. 52–74. "U.S. Military Opposed Bremer Call for More Iraq Troops," *Agence France Presse*, January 9, 2006; "Powell Questions U.S. Plans in Iraq War; Says He Urged Bush to Send More Troops," *News Service Reports*, May 1, 2006. Powell and the various generals were proven right, at least in part, when President Bush acknowledged that he failed to send enough troops to Iraq in a nationally televised address on January 10, 2007. During that address he announced that

he was sending an additional 21,500 troops to Iraq, bringing the overall American force there to more than 150,000.

16. According to published accounts, House and Senate information offices do not keep a comprehensive list of military parents, and not all legislators choose to openly discuss their children's military service. But during a key period of the Iraq War, for example (March 2005), the Associated Press reported that at least five congressmen had children serving in Iraq, including Representative Todd Akin (R-MO); Representative Duncan Hunter (R-CA); Representative Joe Wilson (R-SC); Senator Kit Bond (R-MO); and Senator Tim Johnson (D-SD). Other members of Congress at the time who confirmed that their children served elsewhere in the military included Representative John Kline (R-MN) and Representative Marilyn Musgrave (R-CO). See Laurie Kellman, "Half a Dozen Lawmakers Have Kids at War," *Associated Press Online*, March 14, 2005; Tom Ford, "Conflict with Iraq: Some Members of Congress Have Great Personal Interest in the War," *Minneapolis-St. Paul Star Tribune*, April 10, 2003. By January 2007 ABC News could report that only four U.S. senators and nine U.S. representatives—just 2.4 percent of the Congress—had had a child fight in Afghanistan or Iraq. *ABC World News Tonight*, January 12, 2007, segment with correspondent Jake Tapper.

17. The new 110th Congress elected in the 2006 midterm saw a continued decline in the number of legislators who have military experience. Just 24 percent of lawmakers in both houses have ever served in the military: 101 House members and 29 senators. This represented a decline from the 109th Congress, which included 140 veterans: 31 in the Senate, 8 of whom served in war zones; and 109 in the House, 27 of whom served in war zones. See Greg Giroux, "An Old Boys' Club with New Twists," *Congressional Quarterly Weekly*, February 26, 2007, pp. 604–8; and "Declining Military Experience in Congress," Military Officers Association of America, http://www.moaa.org/lac_declining_mil_exp_congress/index.htm; Tim Dyhouse, "Nine New Veterans Join Congress," *Veterans of Foreign Wars of the United States*, http://www.vfw.org/index.cfm?fa=news.magDtl&dtl=3&mid=2305. The current percentage of congressional veterans does not represent an all-time low. That distinction belongs to the Congresses of the early 1900s, where the percentage of veterans was consistently below 20 percent. See William T. Bianco and Jamie Markham, "Vanishing Veterans: The Decline of Military Experience in the U.S. Congress," in *Soldiers and Civilians: The Civil-Military Gap and American National Security* (Cambridge: MIT Press, 2001): pp. 275–88.

18. Phillip Marcus, "Some Aspects of Military Service," *Michigan Law Review* 39.6 (Apr. 1941): p. 927.

19. The Bill and Melinda Gates Foundation currently has an endowment of over $29 billion (Bill and Melinda Gates Foundation, "Foundation Fact Sheet," June 2006, http://www.gatesfoundation.org/MediaCenter/FactSheet/). Other prominent American nonprofits include the YMCA, the Special Olympics, the Rotary Foundation, and Big Brothers and Big Sisters of America.

20. Radio address, Franklin Delano Roosevelt, May 7, 1933. For more information on the Civilian Conservation Corps, see John A. Salmond, *The Civilian Conservation Corps, 1933–1942: A New Deal Case Study* (Durham, NC: Duke University Press, 1967); Olen Cole, *The African-American Experience in the Civilian Conservation Corps* (Gainesville: University Press of Florida, 1999).

21. A transcript of JFK's remarks is available on the Peace Corps Web site, http://www.peacecorps.gov/index.cfm?shell=learn.whatispc.history.speech. See

also "Founding Documents of the Peace Corps," National Archives and Records Administration, http://www.archives.gov/education/lessons/peace-corps/.

22. See "Founding Documents of the Peace Corps."
23. The original executive order simply created the Peace Corps as an organization "responsible for the training and service abroad of men and women of the United States in new programs of assistance to nations and areas of the world." The three goals for the Peace Corps listed in the text are specified in congressional legislation passed on September 22, 1961 (P.L. 87–293), and are available online at http://www.archives.gov/education/lessons/peace-corps/.
24. In 1971 President Richard Nixon undertook a massive reorganization of the federal bureaucracy. In his Reorganization Plan No. 1 of 1971, he created a new federal agency called ACTION, which combined programs involving 20,000 volunteers, 1,600 employees, and an annual budget of $140 million into a single agency. ACTION included programs such as the Peace Corps, VISTA, Foster Grandparents, and the Service Corps of Retired Executives (SCORE). Nixon's Reorganization Plan No. 1 is available online at http://www.access.gpo.gov/uscode/title5a/5a_4_95_2_.html. For additional information, see T. Zane Reeves, *The Politics of the Peace Corps and VISTA* (Tuscaloosa: University of Alabama Press, 1988).
25. Peace Corps volunteers are provided a cost-of-living stipend so they can live "in a manner similar to the local people they serve." Volunteers also receive complete medical and dental care, in addition to six thousand dollars for use in "transitioning" back to normal life after their stint in the corps. Statistics and information from the Peace Corps Web site, http://www.peacecorps.gov/index.cfm?shell=learn.whyvol.finben.
26. The idea of a domestic equivalent to the Peace Corps was first embodied in the National Volunteer Service Act, which was defeated by Congress in 1963 for fear of promoting integration and liberal political activities. Johnson revived the idea in VISTA, which was created under the supervision of the Office of Economic Opportunity through the Economic Opportunity Act of 1964. See Reeves, *The Politics of the Peace Corps and VISTA*.
27. Corporation for National and Community Service, *Vista . . . In Service to America* (Washington, DC, 2006); see also William H. Crook and Ross Thomas, *Warriors for the Poor: The Story of VISTA, Volunteers in Service to America* (New York: William Morrow, 1969).
28. Both the Peace Corps and VISTA continue to exist. In 1979 President Carter signed an executive order that gave the Peace Corps full autonomy. VISTA was folded into AmeriCorps as AmeriCorps*VISTA (under the aegis of the Corporation for National and Community Service) as a result of the National and Community Service Trust Act of 1993.
29. George H. W. Bush, Republican National Convention acceptance address, New Orleans, Louisiana, August 18, 1988.
30. George H. W. Bush, inaugural address, Washington, D.C., January 20, 1989.
31. The official White House statement on the "Points of Light" initiative is available online: *White House Fact Sheet on Points of Light Initiative*, June 22, 1989, George Bush Presidential Library and Museum, http://bushlibrary.tamu.edu/research/papers/1989/89062208.html.
32. Even though he used it extensively in his 1992 campaign, Clinton now plays down the event: "Much has been made of that brief encounter and its impact on my life . . . [It] was widely pointed to as the beginning of my presidential aspirations. I'm not sure about that." See William Jefferson Clinton, *My Life* (New York: Knopf, 2004), p. 62.

33. The National and Community Service Trust Act of 1993 (P.L. 103–82) was signed into law by President Clinton on September 21, 1993. It brought all domestic national service programs under a single roof, the newly created Corporation for National and Community Service (CNCS). In addition to consolidating existing national service programs, the act simultaneously created three new domestic service programs: Senior Corps, AmeriCorps, and Learn and Serve America. For more information, visit the CNCS Web site at http://www.nationalservice.gov/.
34. Will Marshall and Marc Porter Magee, eds., *The AmeriCorps Experiment and the Future of National Service* (Washington, DC: Progressive Policy Institute, 2005), p. 6.
35. Ibid, p. 10.
36. In 2005 full-time AmeriCorps participants received a subsistence stipend ranging from $10,197 to $20,934. By law, the federal government can only contribute 85 percent of the minimum payment, or about $8,700. The rest comes from members' programs. See Stephen A. Waldman, "National Service on a Community Scale," in *The AmeriCorps Experiment and the Future of National Service*, p. 90.
37. S. 1792, 107th Cong., 1st sess.
38. Critics in the White House claim the AmeriCorps*NCCC program is ineffective and too expensive. An OMB review found that it has a per-participant cost of $27,859, whereas other AmeriCorps programs have a per-participant cost of about $16,000. This is largely because other AmeriCorps programs use matching funds from state and local sources, whereas the NCCC program is funded entirely by the federal government. In the wake of Hurricane Katrina many have come out to vocally criticize the idea of cutting a program that allows young people to engage in natural disaster relief. In fact, Congress ignored George W. Bush's 2006 recommendation to cut AmeriCorps*NCCC drastically. See Christopher Lee, "AmeriCorps Civilian Program Faces $22 Million Budget Cut; Citing Cost, White House Aims to End Part of Clinton Creation," *Washington Post*, February 28, 2006; "Senator Mikulski Calls for Restoration of President's Massive AmeriCorps Cut," *US Fed News*, April 3, 2006; John Fales, "Congress Should Rethink Cutting Service Corps," *Washington Times*, June 5, 2006. Those interested in following the debate over AmeriCorps funding levels can visit Service-Learning United, which lobbies for increases in federal funding for service programs, at http://www.servicelearningunited.org/.
39. While the Peace Corps is almost universally accepted today, it, like AmeriCorps, began in the midst of partisan crossfire. President Eisenhower called the idea for the corps a "juvenile experiment," while Vice President Nixon compared it to "draft evasion." See Harris Wofford, "The Politics of Service," in *United We Serve: National Service and the Future of American Citizenship* (Washington, DC: Brookings Institution Press, 2003): pp. 45–51.
40. James L. Perry et al., "Inside a Swiss Army Knife: An Assessment of AmeriCorps," *Journal of Public Administration Research and Theory: J-PART* 9.2 (Apr. 1999): 232–33.
41. Ibid., p. 234.
42. See Leslie Lenkowski and James L. Perry, "Reinventing Government: The Case of National Service," *Public Administration Review* 60.4 (July–Aug. 2000): 298–307.
43. For a complete budget breakdown, see Corporation for National and Community Service, *Fiscal Year 2007, Congressional Budget Justification* (Washington, DC, 2006), p. 58. Available online at http://www.nationalservice.gov/pdf/2007_budget_justification.pdf.
44. A 1996 GAO study estimated the "total financial resources" available to every AmeriCorps*USA participant to be approximately $26,654, of which $17,600 came

directly from the Corporation for National and Community Service. The study emphasizes that its goal is not to estimate a cost for AmeriCorps programs but to determine what resources are available and how they are apportioned. Since the study was published, a number of legislative and procedural measures have been taken to decrease the per-participant cost of AmeriCorps programs. U.S. General Accounting Office (GAO). *AmeriCorps*USA: First-year Experience and Recent Program Initiatives* (Washington, DC, 1996).

45. Lenkowski and Perry, "Reinventing Government," p. 301.
46. See Jean Baldwin Grossman and Kathryn Furano, "Making the Most of Volunteers," *Law and Contemporary Problems* 62.4 (Autumn 1999): 199–218; James Clotfelter, "Comment: Enabling Public Service," ibid., pp. 257–63.
47. According to the National Center for Education Statistics, 67 percent of high school graduates enrolled in either a two- or a four-year college program in the fall immediately after graduation. Information available online at http://nces.ed.gov/fastfacts/display.asp?id=51.
48. Draft boards continue to be an integral component of the Selective Service system. There are currently over 2,030 draft boards around the country, each composed of five citizen volunteers appointed by the director of Selective Service on recommendation from state governors or other designated public officials. Draft board members receive an initial eight hours of training on Selective Service regulations with additional training sessions annually. In the instance of a renewed draft, these boards would be responsible for deciding who in their communities would receive deferments, postponements, or exemptions from military service. See the Selective Service System, "Local Boards," June 2004, http://www.sss.gov/fslocal.htm. See also Pauline Jelinek, "U.S. Does Not Have a Military Draft, but Thousands Sit on Draft Boards Just in Case," *Associated Press Worldstream*, April 20, 2006.
49. This number is the sum of individuals ages four through twelve reported in the 2000 census, since those individuals will be turning eighteen over the eight-year period between 2006 and 2014. Data from the U.S. Census Bureau, Census 2000 Summary File 1, Matrix PCT12 ("Single Years of Age Under 30, Years and Sex"). Available online at http://factfinder.census.gov/servlet/SAFFPeople?_submenuId=people_2&_sse=on.
50. According to the Department of Defense, as of April 30, 2006, there were 1,376,545 men and women in the military, in addition to 40,626 in the Coast Guard (who are under the control of the Department of Homeland Security in peacetime). Statistics from Department of Defense Personnel and Procurement Statistics, *Service Totals: Current Month*, April 30, 2006, http://siadapp.dior.whs.mil/personnel/MILITARY/mso.pdf.
51. Legislation governing the Corporation for National and Community Service has a similar prohibition barring it from providing money to organizations whose purpose is primarily political. Especially during the contentious Clinton years, the debate about which organizations should receive funding through CNCS became intense, with accusations from Republicans that the CNCS was funding overtly liberal programs. The CNCS employs an inspector-general to investigate any claims of improper apportionment of funds, and the CNCS monitors grant recipients to ensure they are using their grant money in cooperation with CNCS rules and regulations. See Lenkowski and Perry, "Reinventing Government," p. 301.
52. For a comprehensive discussion of issues surrounding compulsory service and religious organizations, see Rodney A. Smolla, "The Constitutionality of Mandatory Public School Community Service Programs," *Law and Contemporary Problems*

62.4 (Autumn 1999): 138. Smolla concludes that, in general, it is constitutionally safer to include religious organizations in service programs rather than exclude them. He cites: *Rosenberger v. University of Virginia* 515 U.S. 819 (1995) at 845–46; *Lamb's Chapel v. Center Moriches Union Free Sch. Dist.*, 508 U.S. 384 (1993); *Widmar v. Vincent*, 454 U.S. 263 (1981); see also *Board of Educ. of Kiryas Joel Village Sch. Dist. v. Grumet*, 512 U.S. 687,714 (1994) (Justice O'Connor, concurring in part and concurring in judgment) ("We have time and again held that the government generally may not treat people differently based on the God or gods they worship, or do not worship").

53. Certain UNS jobs, such as the Peace Corps in some countries and the Disaster Strike Force, inevitably carry risk of injury and permanent disability. Incidents will occur, and though they will be rare, the program must be prepared to deal with the consequences through a good insurance system.

54. Will Marshall and Marc Porter Magee, "The Voluntary Path to Universal Service," in *The AmeriCorps Experiment and the Future of National Service*, pp. 114–15; see also Marc Magee and Steven J. Nider, *Citizen Soldiers and the War on Terror* (Washington, DC: Progressive Policy Institute, 2002); Marc Magee and Steven J. Nider, *Uncle Sam Wants You! . . . For 18 Months: Benchmarks for a Successful Citizen Soldier Program* (Washington, DC: Progressive Policy Institute, 2003); Charles Moskos, "Patriotism-Lite Meets the Citizen Soldier," in *United We Serve: National Service and the Future of Citizenship* (Washington, DC: Brookings Institution Press, 2003): pp. 33–44.

55. According to the Peace Corps Web site, 6 percent of its volunteers are over the age of fifty—with the oldest being seventy-nine. See "Fast Facts," http://www.peacecorps.gov/index.cfm?shell=learn.whatispc.fastfacts.

56. This cost-benefit ratio is the average taken across seven separate studies of AmeriCorps. See Marshall and Magee, *The AmeriCorps Experiment*, pp. 16–19. By the way, the benefits cited for society include such items as the dollar value of the services performed by AmeriCorps participants and future earnings for the participants based on the new training they receive in the program. Another noteworthy finding is that AmeriCorps outshone many other service-oriented programs, which often had a cost-benefit ratio of barely more than a dollar spent for a dollar of benefits gained.

57. Donald J. Eberly and Michael W. Sheridan, "A Proposal for National Service for the 1980s," in *National Service: Social, Economic, and Military Impacts* (Elmsford, NY: Pergamon Press, 1982), p. 106.

58. William A. Galston, "The Case for Universal Service," in *The AmeriCorps Experiment and the Future of National Service*, p. 1.

59. Office of Management and Budget, "Program Assessment: AmeriCorps National Civilian Conservation Corps," January 13, 2006, http://www.whitehouse.gov/omb/expectmore/summary.10004457.2005.html.

60. "Blood and Treasure; Paying for Iraq," *Economist*, U.S. edition, April 8, 2006: p. 34 (U.S. edition).

61. These are admittedly rough calculations, derived by multiplying the average number of individuals who will turn eighteen each year between 2006 and 2014 by the estimated unit cost per participant of a UNS program. However, not all 4 million individuals who become eligible for national service each year will immediately join a UNS program, since I propose that individuals give two years of service between the ages of eighteen and twenty-six and not two consecutive years immediately upon their eighteenth birthday. Moreover, not all participants in UNS would

receive full funding from the federal government. Teach for America participants, for example, are members of AmeriCorps but receive a salary through their individual schools. The precise cost of a UNS program therefore rests on the sorts of legislative details to be determined by Congress. The numbers here are meant to serve as a benchmark in order to clarify the approximate budgetary needs of such a program.

62. Marshall and Magee, "The Voluntary Path to Universal Service," p. 36; David Eisner, "A Frontline View," in *The AmeriCorps Experiment and the Future of National Service*, p. 59.
63. Marshall and Magee, "The Voluntary Path to Universal Service," p. 33.
64. See Helmut K. Anheier and Lester M. Salamon, "Volunteering in Cross-National Perspective: Initial Comparisons," *Law and Contemporary Problems* 62.4 (Autumn 1999): 43–65. Anheier and Salamon conclude that norms surrounding volunteerism can very drastically across countries and cultures: "In some European countries, such as Sweden and Germany, volunteers were, until recently, regarded as amateurish 'do-gooders,' as relics of the past to be replaced by paid professional staff capable of performing tasks more effectively and efficiently . . . The Japanese government, for example, drew up contingency plans for responding to natural disasters in which volunteers had no role. . . . When the Kobe earthquake hit in 1995, conflicts soon erupted between a government too slow to respond, and the thousands of Japanese citizens who had spontaneously decided to volunteer their services to help ease the critical situation" (43–44). Compare this with the United States, where young people contribute more than 1.3 billion hours of community service annually, and 38 percent of young people report having participated in community service as a component of a school activity or requirement. See the Corporation for National and Community Service (CNCS), "Youth Helping America: Service-Learning Related Activities and Civic Engagement." http://www.nationalservice.gov/pdf/05_1130_LSA_YHA_SL_factsheet.pdf; CNCS, "Youth Helping America: The Role of Social Institutions in Teen Volunteering," http://www.nationalservice.gov/pdf/05_1130_LSA_YHA_SI_factsheet.pdf.
65. There have been several high-profile calls for national service in recent years, though none has passed. Representative Charles Rangel (D-NY) and Representative John Conyers (D-MI) grabbed headlines with the Universal National Service Act of 2006, which would reinstate the military draft and create a more socioeconomically diverse armed forces (H.R. 4752, 109th Cong., 2nd sess.); then-Senator Fritz Hollings (D-SC) proposed the National Service Act of 2003 to reinstate the draft for men *and* women, with the option of nonmilitary civic service that, "as determined by the President, promotes the national defense" (S. 89, 198th Cong., 1st sess.); Senator John McCain (R-AZ) and Senator Evan Bayh (D-IA) proposed the Call to Service Act of 2001, which would have dramatically expanded AmeriCorps to a force of 250,000 volunteers, increased incentives for military service, and required universities to promote student involvement in the community (S. 1792, 107th Cong., 1st sess.). Other national service proposals have been suggested by Senator Edward Kennedy (D-MA), Senator John Kerry (D-MA), and Representative Harold Ford Jr. (D-TN), among others. Incidentally, former secretary of defense Melvin Laird, who ended the military draft under President Nixon, now backs a UNS program like the one proposed in this chapter. See Melvin R. Laird, "Turning Apathy into Good Deeds," *Washington Post*, May 28, 2007.
66. See John M. Bridgeland, Stephen Goldsmith, and Leslie Lenkowsky, "Service and the Bush Administration's Civic Agenda," in *United We Serve*, p. 54.

67. See Kathy Roth-Douquet and Frank Schaeffer, *AWOL: The Unexcused Absence of America's Upper Classes from the Military—and How It Hurts Our Country* (New York: Smithsonian Books, 2006); see also Terrence Cullinan, "The Courage to Compel," in *The Military Draft* (Stanford: Hoover Institution Press, 1982): pp. 446–59.
68. Galston, "The Case for Universal Service," p. 104.
69. See Theda Skocpol, "Will September 11 Revitalize American Democracy?" in *United We Serve*, pp. 20–32. Skocpol convincingly argues that in the absence of leadership on the issue of national service, "the legacy of 9/11 will be little more than to leave ripples on the managerial routines of contemporary U.S. civic life."
70. Quoted in Galston, "The Case for Universal Service," p. 103. Galston quite effectively uses "libertarian" arguments to make the case that individuals have a duty to contribute to the common good in a democracy, and hence uses Mill's own logic in support of UNS.
71. In the initial fight over AmeriCorps, then-Representative Dick Armey (R-TX) called national service programs "welfare for aspiring yuppies." Quoted in Will Marshall and Marc Magee, "Thinking Bigger about Citizenship," in *United We Serve*, p. 75.
72. http://www.quotationspage.com/quote/2236.html. I am grateful to my student Grayson Lambert for this citation.
73. My father was a justifiably proud vet of World War II, a life-changing time for him. He shared what he had learned from military service with me, demonstrating civic commitment throughout his life, and persuading me to dedicate part of my life to the same goal. Hundreds of thousands of baby-boom children could no doubt report similar experiences.

6. Vox Populi: What Do the People Think of Constitutional Change?

1. In election campaigns, many observers have learned to look for the Rasmussen results. In my experience, they are right on the money. There is no question Rasmussen produces some of the most accurate and reliable polls in the country today. For an analysis of Rasmussen's accuracy in the 2006 midterm elections, see Carl Bialik, "Grading the Pollsters," *Wall Street-Journal Online*, November 16, 2006. For a 2004 report from the National Council on Public Polls, visit http://www.ncpp.org/files/2004%20Election%20Polls%20Review.pdf.
2. I do not favor a tax on nonvoting either, but once during a boring public forum on "reform," I decided to enliven the discussion and play devil's advocate with this very idea. The audience erupted in protest—by a margin of about 80 percent to 20 percent—very close to our poll's result.

7. Calling the Twenty-first-Century Constitutional Convention

1. "The Debates in the Federal Convention of 1787 reported by James Madison: September 15," the Avalon Project at Yale Law School (updated Aug. 14, 2006), http://www.yale.edu/lawweb/avalon/debates/915.htm. Pinckney was responding to a motion by Edmund Randolph that after ratification of the Constitution, a second convention be called to rectify its defects.
2. Laurence S. Tribe, "Issues Raised by Requesting Congress to Call a Constitutional Convention to Propose a Balanced Budget Amendment," *Pacific Law Journal* 10 (1979): 628. Professor Tribe was speaking before the Committee on Ways and Means of the California State Assembly, advising against applying for an Article V convention to propose a Balanced Budget Amendment. Another commentator on the possibility of a second convention, Ralph Carson, put it this way: "[A general

convention], some have intimated, will serve as a useful school in the democratic process, educate the voters on a continental scale, and give the people new opportunity to revise their organic law. Nothing in my view could be more wrong . . . A general and unlimited federal constitutional convention would be at least a futility and might be a disaster." See Ralph M. Carson, "Disadvantages of a Federal Constitutional Convention," *Michigan Law Review* 66.5 (Mar. 1968): 921–30.

3. See Rexford Tugwell, *The Compromising of the Constitution (Early Departures)* (South Bend, IN: University of Notre Dame Press, 1976). Tugwell (1891–1979) began his career as an agricultural economist and was a member of Franklin Roosevelt's "Brain Trust" during the 1930s. After serving as governor of Puerto Rico and a professor at the University of Chicago, Tugwell continued to write and publish until his death. A biography of Tugwell is available on the National Park Service Web site (http://www.nps.gov/archive/elro/glossary/tugwell-rexford.htm).
4. The formation of the Article V Amendment process rarely comes up in Madison's convention notes, but two passages are particularly instructive on this point. When the question of adding an amendment process to the new Constitution first came before the convention, Elbridge Gerry noted that "the novelty & difficulty of the experiment requires periodical revision. The prospect of such a revision would also give intermediate stability to the Govt." Later in the convention, George Mason backed a proposition that would have denied the Congress any role in the amendment process for fear that Congress would be too slow in proposing change. Said Mason: "The plan now to be formed will certainly be defective, as the Confederation has been found on trial to be. Amendments therefore will be necessary, and it will be better to provide for them, in an easy, regular, and Constitutional way than to trust to chance and violence." See *The Records of the Federal Convention of 1787*, ed. Max Ferrand, vol. 1 (New Haven, CT: Yale University Press, 1966), pp. 121–22 and p. 202. For a good discussion of these passages, see Anne Stuart Diamond, "A Convention for Proposing Amendments: The Constitution's Other Method," *Publius* 11.3/4 (Summer 1981): 113–46.
5. Donald S. Lutz, "Toward a Theory of Constitutional Amendment," *American Political Science Review* 88.2 (Jun. 1994): 355–70.
6. See the Preamble, where we already discussed these two alternate methods of constitutional change. See also Daniel T. Young, "Disarming the Constitutional Time Bomb: Making Sense of Article V," Politics Honors Undergraduate Thesis, University of Virginia, April 2007.
7. C-SPAN, *Capital Questions*, June 9, 2000, online at http://www.c-span.org/questions/weekly54.asp. C-SPAN calculated how many amendments had been proposed and defeated in Congress over the 1990s.

Congress	*Number of Proposed Amendments*
106th (1999)	60
105th (1997–98)	103
104th (1995–96)	158
103rd (1993–94)	156
102nd (1991–92)	165
101st (1989–90)	214

8. *A Constitutional Convention: How Well Would It Work?* American Enterprise Institute (AEI) Forum, Washington, D.C., May 23, 1979. Moderator John Charles Daly. Transcript copyright 1979 by AEI.

9. Henry St. George Tucker (1780–1848) was a congressman from Virginia, in addition to practicing as an attorney, serving as a state senator, and teaching as a law professor at the University of Virginia (1841–45). His commentaries on the U.S. Constitution were some of the most influential of the nineteenth century. See "Tucker, Henry St. George (1780–1848)," *Biographical Directory of the United States Congress*, online at http://bioguide.congress.gov/scripts/biodisplay.pl?index=T000398.
10. See St. George Tucker, *Blackstone's Commentaries: With Notes of Reference to the Constitution and Laws of the Federal Government of the United States and of the Commonwealth of Virginia*, 5 vols. (Philadelphia, 1803; reprint, South Hackensack, NJ: Rothman Reprints, 1969), specifically 1:app. 371–72.
11. There is some debate in the scholarly community as to whether or not a second Constitutional Convention would have to be "general" (that is, it could propose any amendments it chose for ratification) or if it could be "limited" (meaning it could only propose amendments germane to its mandate). To offer an example: If the required thirty-four states had submitted applications asking that a convention be called for the purpose of proposing a Balanced Budget Amendment in the early 1990s, could that convention have proposed amendments other than a Balanced Budget Amendment once convened? Scholars are divided on this question. If the answer is no, Congress would have some supervisory power to "filter" which potential amendments were forwarded to the states for ratification—though there is a strong historical argument for setting up the convention to be as free from congressional interference as possible. See below, note 22, as well as "What Will Be the Convention's Scope?" in chapter 7.
12. While there is some controversy about the president's role in the amendment process, the question is generally considered settled. See Tribe, "Issues Raised," p. 634.
13. In the political calculus surrounding the passage of the Eighteenth Amendment instituting Prohibition, there was a great deal of controversy about the proper role of the legislature vis-à-vis the electorate. Ohio is the quintessential example. Substantial majorities in both the Ohio House and Senate voted in 1919 to ratify the amendment. Ohio law, however, allowed citizens to petition for a referendum on legislative decisions, and Prohibition opponents filed such a petition shortly after the legislature approved the amendment. The Ohio secretary of state allowed the referendum to go forward, and the Prohibition amendment failed by a narrow majority. That raised a tricky question: Had Ohio ratified the amendment by legislative action, or had the referendum overturned Ohio's ratification? The Supreme Court in *Hawke v. Smith* (253 U.S. 221, 1920) overturned the Ohio referendum and, in the process, created some antipathy between citizens and their legislatures on questions of ratification. This was one of the reasons that the Twenty-first Amendment was sent to state conventions rather than the legislatures for ratifications—essentially, to appease state electorates for the browbeating they believed they had received in the Eighteenth Amendment debate. In another sense, however, the decision was tactical. By 1933 most everyone recognized that Prohibition was unenforceable and a fiasco, but there was a fear that voting for ratification of the repeal amendment in a temperance-minded district would be suicidal for many state legislators. Sending the amendment to conventions gave individual legislators political cover. For more information, see Thomas Schaller, "Democracy at Rest: Strategic Ratification of the Twenty-first Amendment," *Publius* 28.2 (Spring 1998): 81–97.
14. The exact number of petitions filed by the states for a convention is difficult to ascertain. There is no central clearinghouse for convention petitions, and the *Congressional Record* from the early 1900s isn't digitized. Moreover, the exact motivation for

Congress in approving the Seventeenth Amendment is a matter of scholarly controversy. The explanation mentioned here—that Congress was circumventing a second Constitutional Convention—appears multiple times, most notably in an article from the Article V scholar William Van Alstyne. However, another scholar, Kris Kobach, criticizes Van Alstyne for not producing any concrete historical evidence or numbers to back up that claim. Instead, Kobach argues that many states had instituted systems whereby U.S. senators were de facto popularly elected through primaries and then sent to Washington by legislatures under electoral pressure. By 1911, Kobach argues, twenty-eight states had "popularly elected" senators, and those senators didn't dare vote against an amendment that would "constitutionalize" the arrangement under which they were elected. See William Van Alstyne, "Notes on a Bicentennial Constitution," *University of Illinois Law Review* Rev. 933 (1984), pp. 933–58; Kris W. Kobach, "Rethinking Article V: Term Limits and the Seventeenth and Nineteenth Amendment," *Yale Law Journal* 103.7 (May 1994): 1971–2007.

15. *Baker v. Carr* (1962), which determined state legislative apportionment was subject to judicial review, 369 U.S. 186; *Reynolds v. Simms* (1964), which required both houses of bicameral state legislatures to be apportioned on the basis of population, 377 U.S. 533.
16. "Balanced Budget Amendment Picking Up Steam," *St. Louis Post-Dispatch*, April 26, 1992. The exact number of states that had passed petitions for a convention is in question, given that there is no consensus on counting rules. See Michael Stokes Paulsen, "A General Theory of Article V: The Constitutional Lessons of the Twenty-seventh Amendment," *Yale Law Journal* 103.3 (Dec. 1993): 736.
17. Tribe, "Issues Raised," pp. 634–35.
18. Special Constitutional Convention Study Committee, *Amendment of the Constitution by the Convention Method under Article V* (Chicago: American Bar Association, 1974). Hereafter referred to as *ABA Study*.
19. See Paulsen, "A General Theory of Article V."
20. Charles L. Black Jr., "Amending the Constitution: Letter to a Congressman," *Yale Law Journal* 82.2 (Dec. 1972): 189–215.
21. Ibid., p. 199.
22. Walter E. Dellinger, "The Recurring Question of the 'Limited' Constitutional Convention," *Yale Law Journal* 88.8 (July 1979): 1623–40.
23. Professor Dellinger argues that the method of proposing amendments by a state-called convention emerged from Philadelphia precisely because the founders wanted a mechanism to alter the Constitution that would circumvent Congress as much as possible. The logical fear was that, were the national legislature left in sole control of the amendment process, it could simply refuse to act on amendments, demanded by the states, that would erode its own power. Indeed, were Congress to decide to call a limited convention, it would necessarily interject itself into the very substance of the convention's deliberative process. Not only would Congress face the difficult, if not intractable, problem of "subject matching"—that is, determining whether or not thirty-four applications sufficiently overlap to mandate a convention call—but Congress would also be free to refuse to submit any amendment proposed by the convention for ratification if it felt that amendment was outside of the convention's original purview. At either stage, Congress would have enormous power either to refuse to call a convention (citing an insufficient "consensus" among applications to merit the convocation) or to refuse to submit its work to the states.
24. For a supporting view, see C. Herman Pritchett, "Congress and Article V Conventions," *Western Political Quarterly* 32.2 (June 1982): 222–27.

25. U.S. Cong., Senate, 90th Cong., 1st sess., *S. 2307* (introduced in the U.S. Senate Aug. 17, 1967). Hereafter referred to as "Ervin bill." See also U.S. Cong., Senate, 102nd Cong., 1st sess., *S. 214, Constitutional Convention Implementation Act of 1991* (introduced in the U.S. Senate Jan. 15 1991). Hereafter referred to as "Hatch bill."
26. Sam J. Ervin Jr., "Proposed Legislation to Implement the Convention Method of Amending the Constitution," *Michigan Law Review* 66.5 (Mar. 1968): 880–85.
27. *ABA Study*, p. 18.
28. William W. Van Alstyne, "Does Article V Restrict the States to Calling Unlimited Conventions Only?" *Duke Law Journal* 6 (Jan. 1979): 1303.
29. From Louisiana: "When the people, acting under a proper resolution of the legislature, vote in favor of calling a constitutional convention, they are presumed to ratify the terms of the legislative call, which thereby becomes the basis of the authority delegated to the convention" (*State v. American Sugar Refining Company*, 137 La. 407, 415, 68 So. 742, 745 [1915]). And from South Carolina: "Certainly, the people may, if they will, elect delegates for a particular purpose without conferring on them all their authority" (*State ex rel. McCready v. Hunt*, 20 S.C. [2 Hill's Law] 1,271 [1834]).
30. Consider Senator Hatch's bill, which states explicitly that "any determination or decision made under this Act" is reviewable by the Supreme Court" (Sec. 15). This approach is in opposition to the more traditional "political question" doctrine codified in *Coleman v. Miller* (307 U.S. 433). According to this view, Congress is the sole arbiter of the amendment process under the federal Constitution; the Supreme Court has no role to play in answering many of the seemingly intractable questions posed by the amendment process under Article V; and as such, the Court will defer to Congress in all but the most egregious cases. Many prominent scholars have since argued that the *Coleman* case was improperly decided. See Van Alstyne, "Does Article V Restrict the States," pp. 1301–02; see also Dellinger, Walter, "The Legitimacy of Constitutional Change: Rethinking the Amendment Process," *Harvard Law Review* 97.2 (Dec. 1983): 418. For a good discussion of previous Supreme Court decisions regarding Article V, see David Castro, "A Constitutional Convention: Scouting Article Five's Undiscovered Country," *University of Pennsylvania Law Review* 134.4 (Apr. 1986): 964–65.
31. Akhil Amar, "The Consent of the Governed: Constitutional Amendment Outside Article V," *Columbia Law Review* 94.2 (Mar. 1994): 457–508; also Amar, "Philadelphia Revisited: Amending the Constitution Outside Article V," *University of Chicago Law Review* 55.4 (Autumn 1988): 1043–1104.
32. Jonathan Elliot, *The Debates in the Several State Conventions on the Adoption of the Federal Constitution* (Philadelphia: Lippincott, 1881), p. 432 and quoted in Amar, "Consent of the Governed," p. 464.
33. Paulsen, "A General Theory of Article V," p. 738.
34. For a complete account, see Ruth Ann Strickland, "The Twenty-seventh Amendment and Constitutional Change by Stealth," *PS: Political Science and Politics* 26.4 (Dec. 1993): 716–22.
35. Wyoming took the amendment off the shelf to ratify it in 1978—the only state to ratify the amendment since 1873.
36. 256 U.S. 368 (1921).
37. Ibid. at 373–74.
38. 307 U.S. 433.
39. Chief Justice Hughes, writing for the majority.
40. Term coined by Michael Paulsen. See Paulsen, "A General Theory of Article V," p. 724.

41. Paulsen refers to his model as the *concurrent legislation model.* Paulsen proposes that we consider the necessary legislative enactments that accompany the amendment process, at both the congressional and state level, as analogous to normal pieces of statutory legislation. Like all laws, these enactments remain in effect unless they contain a textual "sunset provision." Moreover, like normal laws, these provisions can be made conditional and can be altered or rescinded at any time. See Paulsen, "A General Theory of Article V," p. 722–23.
42. Ibid.
43. We should clarify one of Paulsen's key counting rules. If we accept that a limited convention is a legitimate possibility under Article V (an assertion with which Paulsen himself disagrees), we have to decide what to do when a state submits a petition for a general convention and then, at a later date, submits a petition for a limited convention (say, for a Balanced Budget Amendment). As Paulsen outlines, there are two possibilities: Either a state's light is on for both a general and a limited convention, or the state's petition for a limited convention turns off its light for a general one. The concurrent legislation model, however, holds that we should think of convention applications like statutes insofar as possible—that is, they do not expire unless explicitly rescinded. Thus, Paulsen begins with a state's most recent convention application. If it is for a limited convention (i.e., explicitly says that the convention should deal solely and exclusively with a particular topic), he looks to the next most recent application to determine if the state's light is on or off for a general convention. It is through this procedure that he arrives at his surprising conclusion. Paulsen's method, of course, has the effect of setting aside applications for a limited convention, so the problem of "subject matching" applications never comes up. No one, it seems, has attempted to reach an application total for each and every particular subject for which states have requested limited conventions. Given the status of the available information, that would be a massive and likely fruitless undertaking. See note 46 below.
44. Virginia passed its application for a second Constitutional Convention on October 30, 1788. New York and North Carolina soon followed suit. See Kurt T. Lash, "Rejecting Conventional Wisdom: Federalist Ambivalence in the Framing and Implementation of Article V," *American Journal of Legal History* 38.2 (Apr. 1994): 220.
45. AZ: 149 *Congressional Record* S. 6976 (May 22, 2003); UT: 147 *Congressional Record* S. 10384 (Oct. 9, 2001); ID: 146 *Congressional Record* S. 739 (Feb. 23, 2000).
46. Consider the following petition from Alabama, 144 *Congressional Record* S. 4902 (May 14, 1998):

> Be It Resolved by the Legislature of Alabama, both Houses thereof concurring, as follows:
>
> 1. That we hereby urge the Congress of the United States to prepare and submit to the several states an amendment to the Constitution of the United States to add a new article providing as follows:
>
> *"Neither the Supreme Court nor any inferior court of the United States shall have the power to instruct or order a state or a political subdivision thereof, or an official of such a state or political subdivision, to levy or increase taxes."*
>
> 2. That this resolution constitutes a continuing application in accordance with Article V of the Constitution of the United States.

3. That we urge the legislatures of each of the several states comprising the United States that have not yet made a similar request to apply to the United States Congress requesting enactment of an appropriate amendment to the United States Constitution, and apply to the United States Congress to propose such an amendment in the United States Constitution.

It should go without saying, contrary to item 3, that the several states *have no power under the Constitution* to force Congress to propose an amendment. States, of course, may send resolutions to Congress politely asking it to propose an amendment, but such resolutions have no legal or constitutional power. How, then, is Congress to interpret item 2, in which Alabama declares its request a "continuing application" under Article V? The only thing the states can "apply" for under Article V is, of course, a Constitutional Convention—yet, clearly (or perhaps not so clearly?) that was not the intent of the Alabama legislature.

47. This situation has resulted in a historical and legal morass regarding the status of state petitions. Paulsen describes his attempt to catalog all known applications this way: "It should be noted that many of the citations provided in other secondary sources are inaccurate, referencing page numbers in the *Congressional Record* where the applications are not in fact present, omitting numerous applications, and counting as applications resolutions that do not in fact purport to apply for a constitutional convention. Many of these secondary sources appear uncritically to repeat lists provided by other (inaccurate) secondary sources." See Paulsen, "A General Theory of Article V," p. 764.
48. Paul G. Kauper, "The Alternative Amendment Process: Some Observations," *Michigan Law Review* 66.5 (Mar. 1968): 906.
49. *ABA Study*, pp. 19–20.
50. On February 21, 1787, the Continental Congress resolved that "it is expedient that on the second Monday in May next a Convention of delegates who shall have been appointed by the several States be held at Philadelphia for the sole purpose of revising the articles of Confederation and reporting to Congress and the several legislatures such alterations and provisions therein as shall, when agreed to in Congress and confirmed by the States, render the federal Constitution adequate to the exigencies of government and the preservation of the Union."
51. *ABA Study*, p. 34.
52. *Baker v. Carr* (1962) and *Reynolds v. Simms* (1964). See supra at note 15. For a good discussion of the "one man, one vote" principle in practice, see Richard L. Hansen, *The Supreme Court and Election Law: Judging Equality from* Baker v. Carr *to* Bush v. Gore (New York: New York University Press, 2003).
53. 397 U.S. 50 (1970).
54. §7(a) of both the Ervin and Hatch bills grants each state a number of delegates equal to its representatives and senators. It seems likely, however, that the Supreme Court's application of the "one man, one vote" rule to state legislatures and government functionaries would render this arrangement open to serious court challenge.
55. At the 2004 Democratic Presidential Convention in Boston there were 4,322 voting delegates. The Republican Convention in New York boasted its own 2,509 delegates. This is, of course, in addition to thousands of additional alternates, members of the media, et cetera. Numbers available online at http://www.thegreenpapers.com/P04/D.phtml and http://www.thegreenpapers.com/P04/R.phtml.

56. In chapter 1 of this volume, we criticized the current House districts as partisan gerrymandering, and alas, the delegates would reflect that current arrangement. However, most of the convention delegates would have no lasting stake in perpetuating the gerrymanders and thus ought to be willing to consider redistricting reforms such as those proposed in chapter 2.
57. According the U.S. Census Bureau, the average congressional district contains 646,952 citizens. Four states have populations below that average: North Dakota (643,756), Alaska (628,933), Vermont (609,890), and Wyoming (495,304). Complete apportionment numbers are available at http://www.census.gov/population/cen2000/tab01.xls.
58. *ABA Study*, pp. 35–36.
59. Ibid., pp. 36–37.
60. A conflict-of-interest argument could be made that state legislators, for instance, could seek to strengthen states and weaken the federal government, yet many of those legislators eventually hope to become members of Congress. Thus, this argument is less than compelling.
61. Senator Hatch's bill includes this kind of prohibition on sitting congressmen serving as convention delegates. See Hatch bill, Sec. 7(a).
62. See *Buckley v. Valeo*, 424 U.S. 1 (1976). See also Annelise Anderson, ed., *Political Money: Deregulating American Politics, Selected Writings on Campaign Finance Reform* (Stanford, CA: Hoover Institution Press, 2000).
63. The constitutional relationship between free speech and financial contributions was definitively established by the Supreme Court in *Buckley v. Valeo*, 424 U.S. 1 (1976). The 15 percent criterion for determining electoral support comes from the Commission on Presidential Debates, which utilizes a similar measure. For more information, see the commission's "Candidate Selection Process" Web site, http://www.debates.org/pages/candsel2004.html.
64. Cf. Ervin bill, Sec. 7(a).
65. Cf. ibid., Sec. 7(d) and Hatch bill, Sec. 8(b).
66. Cf. Ervin bill, Sec. 7(c).
67. Hatch bill, Sec. 8(a).
68. Ervin bill, Sec. 8(a).
69. See Kauper, "The Alternative Amendment Process," pp. 909–10 for a good outline of the available voting options.
70. There is an additional, theoretical argument for doing away with unit voting. As Professor Amar analogizes, the states that convened in Philadelphia were not part of a single nation but rather a federation of separate republics, akin to the confederate leagues of eighteenth-century Europe. The Constitution, however, created a single "we the People" out of the thirteen separate sovereignties which had existed before its adoption. Amar makes the comparison to corporate law: If two companies, A and B, are contemplating a potential merger, that merger must be approved by a majority of shareholders in both company A and company B (as was the ratification of the Constitution). However, once the merger is complete, corporate decisions are subject to the single, unified majority of shareholders under United A&B. Similarly, individual voting, rather than voting by unit rule, would recognize that the Constitution had created a single, unified polity from the independent sovereignties of the several states, and it is that polity, and not the states themselves, that is charged with formulating proposals under Article V. See Amar, "Consent of the Governed," p. 489.

71. The ABA argues that the old system of unit rule voting is "undemocratic and archaic," and while it may have been justifiable when "the states were essentially independent, there can be no justification for such a system today." *ABA Study*, p. 35.
72. *Hawke v. Smith*, 253 U.S. 221 (1920), in which the Court held that a provision in the Ohio state constitution requiring amendments ratified by the state legislature to be further approved by statewide referendum was unconstitutional. Justice Day, writing for the majority, held that "the power to ratify a proposed amendment to the federal Constitution has its source in the federal Constitution. The act of ratification by the state derives its authority from the federal Constitution to which the state and its people have alike assented."
73. Cf. Hatch bill, Sec. 8(b.)
74. Cf. ibid., Sec. 8(c).
75. See Walter Dellinger, "The Legitimacy of Constitutional Change: Rethinking the Amendment Process," *Harvard Law Review*, vol. 97, no. 2 (December 1983): pp. 386–432.
76. See Larry J. Sabato, Howard R. Ernst, and Bruce A. Larson, *Dangerous Democracy? The Battle over Ballot Initiatives in America* (Lanham, MD: Rowman and Littlefield, 2001). See also David S. Broder, *Democracy Derailed: Initiative Campaigns and the Power of Money* (New York: Harcourt, 2000); Richard J. Ellis, *Democratic Delusions: The Initiative Process in America* (Lawrence: University Press of Kansas, 2002); Elizabeth R. Gerber et. al., *Stealing the Initiative: How State Government Responds to Direct Democracy* (Upper Saddle River, NJ: Prentice Hall, 2001).
77. There are a number of precedents for using "advisory" referenda to influence constitutional processes. While ratification cannot be bound explicitly to a referendum (*Hawke v. Smith*), there is nothing preventing legislatures from using a referendum to gauge public opinion before casting their own vote. This was the essence of the "Oregon system" that developed in the early 1900s, when as many as twenty-eight states adopted measures to approximate the popular election of senators without the benefit of the Seventeenth Amendment. See Kovach, "Rethinking Article V," pp. 1971–72.
78. Supra at note 40.
79. As cited in the AEI transcript for *A Constitutional Convention: How Well Would It Work?* May 23, 1979.
80. Supra at note 30.
81. Senator Ervin apparently agreed with this generous interpretation of congressional power vis-à-vis an Article V convention. Cf. Ervin bill, Sec. 13(c), which declares all questions "concerning state ratification or rejection of amendments" to be answerable only by the Congress, whose decisions shall be binding on all state and federal courts. There is substantial question whether this kind of supererogatory congressional authority is even constitutional under the tenets of judicial review.
82. See Castro, "A Constitutional Convention," supra at note 30. The ABA, after extensively examining the issue of judicial review, concludes that judicial oversight of the amendment process, in opposition to a plenary view of congressional power in this arena, is both "desirable and feasible" (*ABA Study*, pp. 20–25). The ABA points out that a number of landmark Supreme Court cases, including *Baker v. Carr*, 369 U.S. 186 (1962), and *Powell v. McCormack*, 395 U.S. 486 (1969), indicate an increased willingness on the part of the Court to interject itself into the "political process" in areas where it might have once been more tepid. In *Baker*, the Court defined a true "political question" as one in which there was a "textually demonstrable con-

stitutional commitment of the issue to a coordinate political department; or a lack of judicially discoverable and manageable standards . . . or an impossibility of a court's undertaking independent resolution without expressing a lack of respect due coordinate branches of government." Many of the questions surrounding the amendment process do not meet these criteria, and hence are likely justiciable before the federal courts.

83. *ABA Study*, p. 25.
84. Hatch bill, Sec.15. In fact, Hatch's bill goes so far as to allow any state "aggrieved by any determination or finding" under the legislation authorizing the convention, or by a failure of Congress to act appropriately, to file a suit with the Supreme Court which will be granted "priority" on the Court's docket.
85. There is very little discussion of the Senate proviso in the literature. One very fanciful article from 1930 proposes a constitutional amendment that would eliminate the Senate altogether. Without a Senate, so the argument goes, the Senate proviso no longer applies. See Blewitt Lee, "Abolishing the Senate by Amendment," *Virginia Law Review* 16.4 (Feb. 1930): 364–69.
86. This brief foray into the world of Article V offers only a glimpse into the fascinating, if at times confounding, array of legal and theoretical issues surrounding the process of constitutional amendment. For a discussion of constitutional amendment more generally, see Donald S. Lutz, "Toward a Theory of Constitutional Amendment," *American Political Science Review* 88.2 (June 1994): 355–70. For a more pessimistic view of constitutional amendment by convention, see Ralph M. Carson, "Disadvantages of a Federal Constitutional Convention," *Michigan Law Review* 66.5 (Mar. 1968): 921–30. For a good discussion of the various methods of constitutional change, see John R. Vile, "Three Kinds of Constitutional Founding and Change: The Convention Model and Its Alternatives," *Political Research Quarterly* 46.4 (Dec. 1993): 881–95.

Conclusion: Getting There from Here

1. George Washington to Bushrod Washington, November 10, 1797, appearing in Michael Kammen, ed., *The Origins of the American Constitution: A Documentary History* (New York: Penguin, 1986), p. 83, and cited in Sanford Levinson, *Our Undemocratic Constitution: Where the Constitution Goes Wrong (And How We the People Can Correct It)* (Oxford: Oxford University Press, 2006), p. 21. Emphasis added. Washington left the presidency in March 1797.
2. See Robert H. Bork, *The Tempting of America: The Political Seduction of the Law* (New York: Simon and Schuster, 1991) and Antonin Scalia, *A Matter of Interpretation: Federal Courts and the Law*, ed. Amy Gutmann (Princeton: Princeton University Press, 1998). For a more academic look at the originalist position, see Jonathan O'Neil, *Originalism in American Law and Politics: A Constitutional History* (Baltimore: Johns Hopkins University Press, 2005) and Keith E. Whittington, *Constitutional Interpretation: Textual Meaning, Original Intent, and Judicial Review* (Lawrence: University Press of Kansas, 1999). There are other scholars who are either suspicious of originalism as a viable theory of constitutional interpretation or who reject the marriage between originalism and conservative ideology currently ascendant in American politics. See Akhil Amar, *America's Constitution: A Biography* (New York: Random House, 2005) and Jack N. Rakove, *Original Meanings: Politics and Ideas in the Making of the Constitution* (New York: Knopf, 1996).

3. All of these findings are from a telephone survey of 1,004 Americans conducted by the Hearst Corporation to mark the Constitution's bicentennial, October 20 to November 2, 1986. The margin of error was plus or minus 3.2 percent. See Hearst Report, *The American Public's Knowledge of the U.S. Constitution: A National Survey of Public Awareness and Personal Opinion* (New York: Hearst Corporation, 1987), ED 289 812. See also Ruth Marcus, "Constitution Confuses Most Americans: Public Ill-Informed on U.S. Blueprint," *Washington Post*, February 15, 1987.
4. http://www.constitutioncenter.org/PressRoom/PressReleases/1998_09_02_1265.shtml. Survey conducted by the National Constitution Center and released at a September 2, 1998 Senate hearing.
5. A telephone survey of 1,213 Americans conducted July 21–29, 2006, with a margin of error of 2.9 percent. See http://www.zogby.com/wf-AOL%20National.pdf.
6. From a telephone survey of 509 adults conducted by Talmey Associates for the *Denver Post,* June 14–19, 1988. The margin of error was plus or minus 4.5 percent.
7. Survey of 1,002 adults polled between August 3 and 16, 2006, with a sampling error of plus or minus 3 percent, conducted for the Annenberg Public Policy Center by Princeton Survey Research Associates International.
8. Telephone survey of 1,000 adults nationwide. More information is available at the National Constitution Center Web site: http://www.constitutioncenter.org/CitizenAction/CivicResearchResults/NCCNationalPoll.
9. Long was the longtime boss of Louisiana who achieved the governorship, a Senate seat, and near dictatorial powers in the Bayou State in the 1920s and 1930s. See Richard D. White, *Kingfish: The Reign of Huey P. Long* (New York: Random House, 2006); T. Harry Williams, *Huey Long* (New York: Knopf, 1969); Huey P. Long, *Every Man a King: The Autobiography of Huey P. Long* (New Orleans: National Book, 1933); and of course, the fictionalized account by Robert Penn Warren, *All the King's Men* (New York: Harcourt, Brace, 1946). McCarthy was the Wisconsin U.S. senator who led a witch hunt for nonexistent, or rare, Communists in the State Department, Hollywood, and elsewhere during the 1950s, ruining many careers before he was censured by the U.S. Senate. See Robert Griffith, *The Politics of Fear: Joseph R. McCarthy and the Senate* (Lexington: University Press of Kentucky, 1970); Richard Halworth Rovere, *Senator Joe McCarthy* (New York: Harcourt, Brace, 1959); David M. Oshinsky, *A Conspiracy So Immense: The World of Joe McCarthy* (Oxford: Oxford University Press, 2005).
10. Other examples include Presidential Classroom, the League of Women Voters, YMCA Civic Engagement, the Close Up Foundation, the Institute of Politics at the John F. Kennedy School of Government of Harvard University, We The People—a program of the Center for Civic Education, the University of Maryland's Center for Innovation and Research in Civic Learning and Engagement (CIRCLE), the National Council of Secretaries of State, and Kids Voting.
11. The Eighteenth Amendment (instituting Prohibition) was also passed during this period. While that amendment had some Progressive support, it was also advocated strenuously by a broad-based coalition of religious groups, not just Progressives. For a general overview of Prohibition and the Progressive era, see Edward Behr, *Prohibition: Thirteen Years that Changed America* (New York: Arcade, 1996) and Michael E. McGerr, *A Fierce Discontent: The Rise and Fall of the Progressive Movement in America* (New York: Free Press, 2003). For a sociological interpretation of the Prohibition movement, see Anne-Marie E. Szymanski, *Pathways to Prohibition:*

Radicals, Moderates, and Social Movement Outcomes (Durham, NC: Duke University Press, 2003).

12. As outlined in our discussion of a second Constitutional Convention, the precise reasons motivating congressmen to finally approve the Seventeenth Amendment are a matter of some historical controversy, though the reason cited here—that congressmen feared a likely convention under Article V—appears repeatedly in the literature. See chapter 7, "Calling the Twenty-first-Century Constitutional Convention," at note 13.
13. http://dailykos.com/.
14. Just to mention a handful of the hundreds of major blogs that have sprouted on the Internet in the past few years: From the left—DailyKos, MyDD, TPM Café, the Huffington Post, the Plank, Talk Left, Atrios, AMERICAblog, Raw Story, Crooks and Liars, Common Dreams, Firedoglake, and Talking Points Memo. From the right—Townhall, the Corner, Powerline, RedState, Right Wing News, Instapundit, Captain's Quarters, Extreme Mortman, RCP Blog, the Right Angle, Little Green Footballs, Michelle Malkin, the Volokh Conspiracy, and RealClearPolitics. A full listing of political blogs appears at http://directory.etalkinghead.com/.
15. See also the innovative ideas for combining the Internet and the town hall concept in Kevin O'Leary, *Saving Democracy: A Plan for Real Representation in America* (Palo Alto, CA: Stanford University Press, 2006).
16. "A More Perfect Union," Political Campaign Adventure CD-ROM. Teachers can request a free copy by visiting http://www.youthleadership.net/whysignup/perfectunion.jsp.
17. Presidential Classroom (www.presidentialclassroom.org) provides the next generation of civic leaders with an extraordinary academic and leadership development experience in Washington, D.C. High School sophomores, juniors, and seniors travel to the nation's capital, to observe the federal government at work, witness the development of public policy, and explore the roles of citizens, lawmakers, experts, and businesses in the world's most successful democracy. Close Up Foundation (www.closeup.org) is the nation's largest nonprofit (501[c][3]), nonpartisan citizenship education organization. Since its founding in 1970, Close Up has worked to promote responsible and informed participation in the democratic process through a variety of educational programs. Each year, more than twenty thousand students, teachers, and other adults take part in Close Up's programs in Washington, D.C. Since the inception of its Washington-based programs in 1971, the Close Up Foundation has welcomed nearly 650,000 students, educators, and other adults to the nation's capital. KidsVoting (www.kidsvotingusa.org) gets students involved and ready to be educated, engaged citizens. Students learn about democracy through a combination of classroom activities, an authentic voting experience, and family dialogue. CIRCLE (www.civicyouth.org) has conducted, collected, and funded research on the civic engagement, political participation, and civic education of young Americans. CIRCLE is based in the University of Maryland's School of Public Policy and is funded by the Pew Charitable Trusts and Carnegie Corporation of New York.
18. Many colleges have literary and debating societies which thrive on these kinds of fascinating hypothetical scenarios. The prestigious Thomas Jefferson Literary and Debating Society at my own University of Virginia is an emblematic example. There are countless other forums nationwide, such as Harvard and Yale's Model

Congress programs, which would provide similar opportunities for high school and college students.

19. One author, Professor Richard Labunski, offers a detailed plan of action for his constitutional reform proposals, which are admittedly mostly different from mine. Still, the follow-through has similarities. See Richard E. Labunski, *The Second Constitutional Convention: How the American People Can Take Back Their Government* (Versailles, KY: Marley and Beck Press, 2000).

SELECTED BIBLIOGRAPHY

A comprehensive bibliography on the U.S. Constitution would be a book unto itself. In the selected bibliography that follows, only sources that were especially useful and influential to the writing of this volume are cited. The notes section contains references to many more books and articles on constitutional history, development, and practice.

Abney, Glenn, and Thomas P. Lauth. "The Line-Item Veto in the States: An Instrument for Fiscal Restraint or an Instrument for Partisanship?" *Public Administration Review* 45.3 (May–June 1989), pp. 372–77.

Abraham, Henry J. *Justices, Presidents, and Senators: A History of the U.S. Supreme Court Appointments from Washington to Clinton.* Lanham, MD: Rowman and Littlefield, 1999.

Adams, Willi Paul. *The First American Constitutions: Republican Ideology and the Making of the State Constitutions in the Revolutionary Era.* Translated by Rita Kimber and Robert Kimber. Expanded ed. Lanham, MD: Rowman and Littlefield, 2001.

Adler, David Gray. "The Constitution and Presidential Warmaking: The Enduring Debate." *Political Science Quarterly* 103.1 (Spring 1988), pp. 1–36.

Ahneier, Helmut K., and Lester M. Salamon. "Volunteering in Cross-National Perspective: Initial Comparisons." *Law and Contemporary Problems* 62.4 (Autumn 1999), pp. 43–65.

Amar, Akhil. *America's Constitution: A Biography.* New York: Random House, 2005.

———. "The Consent of the Governed: Constitutional Amendment Outside Article V." *Columbia Law Review* 94.2 (Mar. 1994), pp. 457–508.

———. "Philadelphia Revisited: Amending the Constitution Outside Article V." *University of Chicago Law Review* 55.4 (Autumn 1998), pp. 1043–1104.

"Amendments: Thousands Proposed, Few Ratified." *Congressional Quarterly Weekly*, February 28, 2004, p. 533.

Anderson, Thornton. *Creating the Constitution: The Convention of 1787 and the First Congress.* University Park, PA: Pennsylvania State University Press, 1993.

Baker, Lynn A., and Samuel H. Dinkin. "The Senate: An Institution Whose Time Has Gone?" *Journal of Law and Politics* 21.13 (Winter 1997), pp. 21–102.

Barron, Jerome A., C. Thomas Dienes, Wayne McCormack, and Martin H. Redish, eds. *Constitutional Law, Principles and Policy: Cases and Materials.* 6th ed. Newark, NJ: LexisNexis, 2002.

Bickel, Alexander. *The Least Dangerous Branch: The Supreme Court at the Bar of Politics.* New York: Bobbs-Merrill, 1962.

Black Jr., Charles L. "Amending the Constitution: Letter to a Congressman." *Yale Law Journal* 82.2 (December 1972), pp. 189–215.

Boyd, Julian P., John Catanzariti, Charles T. Cullen, and Barbara Oberg, eds. *The Papers of Thomas Jefferson.* 33 vols. Princeton, NJ: Princeton University Press, 1950– .

Buell Jr., Emmet H., and William G. Mayer, eds. *Enduring Controversies in Presidential Nominating Politics.* Pittsburgh, PA: University of Pittsburgh Press, 2004.

Butzner, Jane, ed. *Constitutional Chaff: Rejected Suggestions of the Constitutional Convention of 1787.* Port Washington, NY: Kennikat Press, 1970.

Cain, Bruce E., and Thad Kousser. "Adapting to Term Limits in California: Recent Experiences and New Directions." National Conference on State Legislatures, *Joint Project on Term Limits, 2004.* http://www.ncsl.org/jptl/casestudies/CaseContents.htm.

Carey, John M., Richard G. Niemi, and Lynda W. Powell. *Term Limits in the State Legislatures.* Ann Arbor: University of Michigan Press, 2000.

Carrington, Paul D., and Roger C. Cramton. "The Supreme Court Renewal Act: A Return to Basic Principles." January 2, 2005. http://zfacts.com/metaPage/lib/2005-SUPREME-COURT.pdf.

Carson, Ralph M. "Disadvantages of a Federal Constitutional Convention." *Michigan Law Review* 66.5 (March 1968), pp. 921–30.

Castro, David. "A Constitutional Convention: Scouting Article Five's Undiscovered Country." *University of Pennsylvania Law Review* 134.4 (April 1986), pp. 939–66.

Chambers, William Nisbet, and Walter Dean Burnham. *The American Party Systems: Stages of Political Development.* Oxford: Oxford University Press, 1967.

Cole, Olen. *The African-American Experience in the Civilian Conservation Corps.* Gainesville, FL: University Press of Florida, 1999.

Continuity of Government Commission. *Preserving Our Institutions: The Continuity of Congress.* Washington, DC: American Enterprise Institute/Brookings Institution, 2003. http://www.continuityofgovernment.org/pdfs/FirstReport.htm.

Crosthwait, Gay Aynesworth. "Article III Problems in Enforcing the Balanced Budget Amendment." *Columbia Law Review* 83.4 (May 1983), pp. 1065–1107.

Cullinan, Terrence. "The Courage to Compel." In *The Military Draft.* Stanford: Hoover Institution Press, 1982.

Dellinger, Walter E. "The Recurring Question of the 'Limited' Constitutional Convention." *Yale Law Journal* 88.8 (July 1979), pp. 1623–40.

Dewey, Donald O. "Madison's Views on Electoral Reform." *Western Political Quarterly* 15. 1 (Mar. 1962), pp. 140–45. http://links.jstor.org/sici?sici=00434078%28196203%2915%3A1%3C140%3AMVOER%3E2.0.CO%3B2-K.

Diamond, Anne Stuart. "A Convention for Proposing Amendments: The Constitution's Other Method." *Publius* 11.3/4 (Summer 1981), pp. 113–46.

Dionne, E. J., and Kayla Meltzer Drogsz. "The Promise of National Service: A (Very) Brief History of an Idea." Brookings Institution, policy brief 120 (June 2003). http://www.brookings.edu/comm/policybriefs/pb120.htm.

Dugene, Sarah Helene, and Mary Beth Collins. "Natural Born in the USA: The Striking Unfairness and Dangerous Ambiguity of the Constitution's Presidential Qualifications Clause and Why We Need to Fix It." *Boston University Law Review* 53.85 (Feb. 2005), pp. 53–154.

Eberly, Donald J., and Michael W. Sherraden. "A Proposal for National Service for the 1980s." In *National Service: Social, Economic, and Military Impacts*, edited by Donald J. Eberly and Michael W. Sherraden. Elmsford, NY: Pergamon Press, 1982, pp. 99–114.

Edwards III, George C. *Why the Electoral College Is Bad for America*. New Haven, CT: Yale University Press, 2004.

Elhauge, Einer. "Are Term Limits Undemocratic?" *University of Chicago Law Review* 64.1 (Winter 1997), pp. 83–201.

Elliott, E. Donald. "Constitutional Conventions and the Deficit." *Duke Law Journal* 1985.6 (Dec. 1985), pp. 1077–1110.

Ely, John Hart. *War and Responsibility: Constitutional Lessons of Vietnam and Its Aftermath*. Princeton, NJ: Princeton University Press, 1993.

Epps, Garrett. *Democracy Reborn: The Fourteenth Amendment and the Fight for Equal Rights in Post–Civil War America*. New York: Holt, 2006.

Ervin Jr., Sam J. "Proposed Legislation to Implement the Convention Method of Amending the Constitution." *Michigan Law Review* 66.5 (Mar. 1968), pp. 880–85.

Farmer, Rick, John David Rausch Jr., and John C. Green, eds. *The Test of Time: Coping with Legislative Term Limits*. Lanham, MD: Lexington Books, 2003.

Farrand, Max, ed. *The Records of the Federal Convention of 1787*. Rev. ed. 4 vols. New Haven, CT: Yale University Press, 1966.

Fiorina, Morris. *Congress: Keystone of the Washington Establishment*. New Haven, CT: Yale University Press, 1989.

Fisher, Louis. *American Constitutional Law*. 6th ed. Durham, NC: Carolina Academic Press, 2005.

———. *Presidential War Power*. 2nd ed. Lawrence: University Press of Kansas, 2004.

Fitzpatrick, John C., ed. *The Writings of George Washington, from the Original Manuscript Sources*. 39 vols. Washington, DC: U.S. Government Printing Office, 1931–44.

Ford, Henry Jones. *The Rise and Growth of American Politics: A Sketch of Constitutional Development.* New York: Macmillan, 1898.

Ford, Paul Leicester, ed. *Essays on the Constitution of the United States: Published During Its Discussion by the People, 1787–1788.* Brooklyn, NY: Historical Printing Club, 1892.

———. *The Writings of Thomas Jefferson.* 10 vols. New York: Putnam's, 1892–1899.

Fulbright, J. William. *The Arrogance of Power.* New York: Random House, 1967.

Gillam, Richard. "The Peacetime Draft: Volunteerism to Coercion." In *The Military Draft.* Stanford: Hoover Institution Press, 1982.

Gillman, Howard. *The Constitution Besieged: The Rise and Fall of Lochner Era Police Powers Jurisprudence.* Durham, NC: Duke University Press, 1993.

Goldstein, Yonkel. "The Failure of Constitutional Controls over War Powers in the Nuclear Age: The Argument for a Constitutional Amendment." *Stanford Law Review* 40.6 (July 1988): pp. 1543–92.

Goldstone, Lawrence. *Dark Bargain: Slavery, Profits, and the Struggle for the Constitution.* New York: Walker, 2005.

Goldwin, Robert A., and William A. Schambra, eds. *The Constitution, the Courts, and the Quest for Justice.* Washington, DC: American Enterprise Institute for Public Policy Research, 1989.

Hamilton, Alexander, John Jay, and James Madison. *The Federalist Papers.* Edited by Clinton Rossiter. New York: Penguin, 1961.

Hansen, Richard L. *The Supreme Court and Election Law: Judging Equality from* Baker v. Carr *to* Bush v. Gore. New York: New York University Press, 2003.

Hardaway, Robert M. *The Electoral College and the Constitution: The Case for Preserving Federalism.* Westport, CT: Praeger, 1994.

Haskell, John. *Fundamentally Flawed: Understanding and Reforming Presidential Primaries.* London: Rowman and Littlefield, 1996.

Heclo, Hugh. "General Welfare and Two American political Traditions." *Political Science Quarterly* 101.2 (1986), pp. 179–96.

Holton, Woody. *Unruly Americans and the Origins of the Constitution.* New York: Hill and Wang, 2007.

Hood III, M. V., Irwin L. Morris, and Grant W. Neeley. "Penny Pinching or Politics? The Line Item Veto and Military Construction Appropriations." *Political Research Quarterly* 52.4 (Dec. 1999), pp. 753–66.

Hunt, Gaillard, ed. *The Writings of James Madison.* 9 vols. New York: Putnam's, 1900–1910.

Hutchinson, William T., William M. E. Rachal, et al., eds. *The Papers of James Madison.* 17 vols. Chicago: University of Chicago Press, 1962–83.

Irons, Peter. *War Powers: How the Imperial Presidency Hijacked the Constitution.* New York: Metropolitan, 2005.

Jensen, Merrill, John P. Kaminski, and Gaspare J. Saladino, eds. *The Documentary History of the Ratification of the Constitution.* 21 vols. Madison: State Historical Society of Wisconsin, 1976– .

Jillson, Calvin C. *Constitution Making: Conflict and Consensus in the Federal Convention of 1787*. New York: Agathon Press, 1988.

Joyce, Philip G., and Robert D. Reischauer. "The Federal Line-Item Veto: What Is It and What Will It Do?" *Public Administration Review* 57.2 (Mar.–Apr. 1997), pp. 95–104.

Kammen, Michael, ed. *The Origins of the American Constitution: A Documentary History*. New York: Penguin, 1986.

Karp, Jeffery A. "Explaining Public Support for Legislative Term Limits." *Public Opinion Quarterly* 59.3 (Autumn 1995), pp. 373–91.

Key, V. O. *The Responsible Electorate: Rationality in Presidential Voting, 1936–1960*. Cambridge: Harvard University Press, 1966.

Kobach, Kris W. "Rethinking Article V: Term Limits and the Seventeenth and Nineteenth Amendments." *Yale Law Journal* 103.7 (May 1994), pp. 1971–2007.

Koch, Adrienne. *Jefferson and Madison, the Great Collaboration*. Gloucester, MA: Peter Smith, 1970.

Kousser, J. Morgan. "Colorblind Injustice: Minority Voting Rights and the Undoing of the Second Reconstruction." *Public Affairs Report* 40.3 (May 1999). http://www.igs.berkeley.edu/publications/par/2/kousser.html.

Kousser, Thad. *Term Limits and the Dismantling of State Legislative Professionalism*. Cambridge: Cambridge University Press, 2005.

Labunski, Richard E. *The Second Constitutional Convention: How the American People Can Take Back Their Government*. Versailles, KY: Marley and Beck Press, 2000.

Lazare, Daniel. *The Frozen Republic: How the Constitution Is Paralyzing Democracy*. New York: Harcourt Brace, 1996.

Lee, Blewitt. "Abolishing the Senate by Amendment." *Virginia Law Review* 16.4 (Feb. 1930), pp. 364–69.

Lee, Frances E., and Bruce I. Oppenheimer. *Sizing Up the Senate: The Unequal Consequences of Equal Representation*. Chicago: University of Chicago Press, 1999.

Lenkowski, Leslie, and James L. Perry. "Reinventing Government: The Case of National Service." *Public Administration Review* 60.4 (July–Aug. 2000), pp. 298–307.

Levinson, Sanford. *Our Undemocratic Constitution: Where the Constitution Goes Wrong (And How We the People Can Correct It)*. Oxford: Oxford University Press, 2006.

Lobel, Jules. "Emergency Power and the Decline of Liberalism." *Yale Law Journal* 98.7 (May 1989), pp. 1385–1433.

Lofgren, Charles A. "War-Making under the Constitution: The Original Understanding." *Yale Law Journal* 81.4 (March 1972), pp. 672–702.

Longley, Lawrence D., and Neal R. Pierce. *The Electoral College Primer, 2000*. New Haven, CT: Yale University Press, 1999.

Lutz, Donald S. "Toward a Theory of Constitutional Amendment." *American Political Science Review* 88.2 (June 1994), pp. 355–70.

Mann, Thomas E., and Norman Ornstein. *The Broken Branch: How Congress Is Failing America and How to Get It Back on Track.* New York: Oxford University Press, 2006.

Marshall, Will, and Marc Porter Magee, eds. *The AmeriCorps Experiment and the Future of National Service.* Washington, DC: Progressive Policy Institute, 2005.

Mason, Alpheus, and Donald Grier Stephenson Jr. *American Constitutional Law: Introductory Essays and Selected Cases.* 14th ed. Upper Saddle River, NJ: Pearson Education, 2005.

Mayhew, David. *Congress: The Electoral Connection.* New Haven, CT: Yale University Press, 2004.

Milkis, Sidney M. *Political Parties and Constitutional Government: Remaking American Democracy.* Baltimore: Johns Hopkins University Press, 1999.

Morgan, Robert J. *James Madison on the Constitution and the Bill of Rights.* New York: Greenwood Press, 1988.

National Conference of State Legislatures. "Redistricting Commissions and Alternatives to the Legislature Conducting Redistricting." http://www.ncsl.org/programs/legismgt/redistrict/com&alter.htm.

Nice, David C. "Party Realignment and Presidential Tenure: Some Implications for the Six-Year Term Proposal." *Policies Studies Journal* 13.2 (Dec. 1984), pp. 295–302.

———. "State Support for Constitutional Balanced Budget Requirements." *Journal of Politics* 48.1 (Feb. 1986), pp. 134–42.

O'Brien, David M. *Constitutional Law and Politics.* 5th ed. 2 vols. New York: Norton, 2003.

———. *Storm Center: The Supreme Court in American Politics.* New York: Norton, 2005.

O'Connor, Alice. *So Great a Power to Any Single Person: The Presidential Term and Executive Power.* Washington, DC: Jefferson Foundation, 1984.

O'Leary, Kevin. *Saving Democracy: A Plan for Real Representation in America.* Palo Alto, CA: Stanford University Press, 2006.

Olson, Mancu. *The Logic of Collective Action: Public Goods and the Theory of Groups.* Cambridge, MA: Harvard University Press, 1971.

O'Neil, Jonathan. *Originalism in American Law and Politics: A Constitutional History.* Baltimore: Johns Hopkins University Press, 2005.

Palmer, Niall A. *The New Hampshire Primary and the American Electoral Process.* Westport, CT: Praeger, 1997.

Paulsen, Michael Stokes. "A General Theory of Article V: The Constitutional Lessons of the Twenty-seventh Amendment." *Yale Law Journal* 103.3 (Dec. 1993), pp. 677–789.

Pomper, Gerald M. *Party Renewal in America: Theory and Practice.* New York: Praeger, 1980.

Pritchett, C. Herman. "Congress and Article V Conventions." *Western Political Quarterly* 32.2 (June 1982), pp. 222–27.

Pryor, Jill A. "The Natural-Born Citizen Clause and Presidential Eligibility: An Approach for Resolving Two Hundred Years of Uncertainty." *Yale Law Journal* 97.5 (Apr. 1988), pp. 881–99.

Rakove, Jack N. *James Madison and the Creation of the American Republic.* New York: HarperCollins, 1990.

———. *Original Meanings: Politics and Ideas in the Making of the Constitution.* New York: Knopf, 1996.

Randall, Richard S. *American Constitutional Development.* 2 vols. New York: Addison Wesley Longman, 2002.

Reese, Catherine C. "The Line-Item Veto in Practice in Ten Southern States." *Public Administration Review* 57.6 (Nov.–Dec. 1997), pp. 510–16.

Reeves, Zane T. *The Politics of the Peace Corps and VISTA.* Tuscaloosa: University of Alabama Press, 1988.

Report of the National Symposium on Presidential Selection, The. Charlottesville: University of Virginia Center for Government Studies, 2001.

Robinson, Donald L., ed. *Reforming American Government: The Bicentennial Papers of the Committee on the Constitutional System.* Boulder, CO: Westview Press, 1985.

Roth-Douquet, Kathy, and Frank Schaeffer. *AWOL: The Unexcused Absence of America's Upper Classes from the Military—and How It Hurts Our Country.* New York: Smithsonian Books, 2006.

Rutland, Robert A., ed., et al. *The Papers of James Madison.* Vol. 11. Charlottesville, VA: University Press of Virginia, 1977.

Sabato, Larry J., and Glenn R. Simpson. *Dirty Little Secrets: The Persistence of Corruption in American Politics.* New York: Times Books, 1996.

Salmond, John A. *The Civilian Conservation Corps, 1933–1942: A New Deal Case Study.* Durham, NC: Duke University Press, 1967.

Scala, Dante J. *Stormy Weather: The New Hampshire Primary and Presidential Politics.* New York: Palgrave Macmillan, 2003.

Schaller, Thomas. "Democracy at Rest: Strategic Ratification of the Twenty-first Amendment." *Publius* 28.2 (Spring 1998), pp. 81–97.

Schlesinger Jr., Arthur M. *The Imperial Presidency.* New York: Popular Library, 1974.

Schwarz, Frederic D. "The Electoral College: How It Got That Way and Why We're Stuck with It." *American Heritage Magazine* 52.1 (February–March 2001). http://www.americanheritage.com/magazine/.

Special Constitutional Convention Study Committee. *Amendment of the Constitution by the Convention Method under Article V.* Chicago: American Bar Association, 1974.

Spitzer, Robert J. "The Constitutionality of the Line-Item Veto." *Political Science Quarterly* 112.2 (Summer 1997), pp. 261–83.

Storing, Herbert J., ed. *The Complete Anti-Federalist.* 7 vols. Chicago: University of Chicago Press, 1981.

Story, Joseph, ed. *Commentaries on the Constitution of the United States: With a Preliminary Review of the Constitutional History of the Colonies and States,*

Before the Adoption of the Constitution. 2 vols. Clark, NJ: Lawbook Exchange, 2005.

Strickland, Ruth Ann. "The Twenty-seventh Amendment and Constitutional Change by Stealth." *PS: Political Science and Politics* 26.4 (Dec. 1993), pp. 716–22.

Sundquist, James L. *Constitutional Reform and Effective Government.* Washington, DC: Brookings Institution, 1986.

Tocqueville, Alexis de. *Democracy in America.* Edited by J. P. Mayer. Translated by George Lawrence. New York: Harper and Row, 1966.

Tribe, Laurence H. "Issues Raised by Requesting Congress to Call a Constitutional Convention to Propose a Balanced Budget Amendment." *Pacific Law Journal* 10 (1979), pp. 627–40.

Tugwell, Rexford. *The Compromising of the Constitution (Early Departures).* South Bend, IN: University of Notre Dame Press, 1976.

Van Alstyne, William W. "Does Article V Restrict the States to Calling Unlimited Conventions Only?" *Duke Law Journal* 6 (Jan. 1979), pp. 1295–1306.

———. "Notes on a Bicentennial Constitution." *University of Illinois Law Review* 933 (1984), pp. 933–58.

Vile, John R. "Three Kinds of Constitutional Founding and Change: The Convention Model and its Alternatives." *Political Research Quarterly* 46.4 (Dec. 1993), pp. 881–95.

Ward, Artemus. *Deciding to Leave: The Politics of Retirement from the United States Supreme Court.* Albany: State University of New York Press, 2003.

Whittington, Keith E. *Constitutional Interpretation: Textual Meaning, Original Intent, and Judicial Review.* Lawrence: University Press of Kansas, 1999.

Will, George. *Restoration: Congress, Term Limits and the Recovery of Deliberative Democracy.* New York: Free Press, 1993.

Wilson, Woodrow. *Constitutional Government in the United States.* New York: Columbia University Press, 1908.

INDEX

A NOTE ON THE AUTHOR

The founder and director of the renowned Center for Politics at the University of Virginia, **Larry J. Sabato** has been called "the Dr. Phil of American politics." He has appeared on national television and radio programs including *60 Minutes*, *Today*, *Hardball*, *The O'Reilly Factor*, and *Nightline*. A Rhodes scholar, he received his doctorate in politics from Oxford and has been on the faculty of UVA since 1978. He is the author of countless articles and some twenty books, including *Feeding Frenzy: Attack Journalism & American Politics*, *The Rise of Political Consultants: New Ways of Winning Elections*, and most recently *The Sixth Year Itch: The Rise and Fall of the George W. Bush Presidency*, and he coanchored the BBC's coverage of the 2006 election. In 2002 the University of Virginia gave him its highest honor, the Thomas Jefferson Award, given annually to one person since 1955.